THE EVOLUTION OF THE BRITISH FUNERAL INDUSTRY IN THE 20TH CENTURY: FROM UNDERTAKER TO FUNERAL DIRECTOR

EMERALD STUDIES IN DEATH AND CULTURE

Series Editors: Ruth Penfold-Mounce, University of York, UK; Julie Rugg, University of York, UK; Jack Denham, University of York St John, UK

Editorial Advisory Board: Jacque Lynn Foltyn, National University, USA; Lisa McCormick, University of Edinburgh, UK; Ben Poore, University of York, UK, Melissa Schrift, East Tennessee State University, USA; Kate Woodthorpe, University of Bath, UK

Emerald Studies in Death and Culture provides an outlet for cross-disciplinary exploration of aspects of mortality. The series creates a new forum for the publication of interdisciplinary research that approaches death from a cultural perspective. Published texts will be at the forefront of new ideas, new subjects, new theoretical applications and new explorations of less conventional cultural engagements with death and the dead.

Forthcoming titles
Tim Bullamore, *The Art of Obituary Writing*
Ruth Penfold-Mounce, *Death, the Dead and Popular Culture*
Matthew Spokes, Jack Denham and Benedikt Lehmann, *Death, Memorialization and Deviant Spaces*

THE EVOLUTION OF THE BRITISH FUNERAL INDUSTRY IN THE 20TH CENTURY

FROM UNDERTAKER TO FUNERAL DIRECTOR

BRIAN PARSONS

United Kingdom – North America – Japan India – Malaysia – China

Emerald Publishing Limited
Howard House, Wagon Lane, Bingley BD16 1WA, UK

First edition 2018

Copyright © Brian Parsons, 2018
Published under exclusive licence by Emerald Publishing Limited

Reprints and permissions service
Contact: permissions@emeraldinsight.com

No part of this book may be reproduced, stored in a retrieval system, transmitted in any form or by any means electronic, mechanical, photocopying, recording or otherwise without either the prior written permission of the publisher or a licence permitting restricted copying issued in the UK by The Copyright Licensing Agency and in the USA by The Copyright Clearance Center. Any opinions expressed in the chapters are those of the authors. Whilst Emerald makes every effort to ensure the quality and accuracy of its content, Emerald makes no representation implied or otherwise, as to the chapters' suitability and application and disclaims any warranties, express or implied, to their use.

British Library Cataloguing in Publication Data
A catalogue record for this book is available from the British Library

ISBN: 978-1-78743-630-5 (Print)
ISBN: 978-1-78743-629-9 (Online)
ISBN: 978-1-78743-672-5 (Epub)

Printed and bound by CPI Group (UK) Ltd, Croydon, CR0 4YY

ISOQAR certified Management System, awarded to Emerald for adherence to Environmental standard ISO 14001:2004.

Certificate Number 1985
ISO 14001

INVESTOR IN PEOPLE

Contents

List of Illustrations — *vii*

List of Tables — *ix*

Abbreviations — *xi*

Acknowledgments — *xiii*

Preface — *xv*

Introduction — *1*

Chapter 1 Death, the Funeral and the Funeral Director in the Twentieth Century — *3*

Chapter 2 From Front Parlour to Funeral Parlour: The Development of the Chapel of Rest and Funeral Home — *23*

Chapter 3 Caretaker of the Dead — *49*

Chapter 4 Furnishing the Funeral — *77*

Chapter 5 Transport to Paradise — *99*

Chapter 6 Organisational Change — *125*

Chapter 7	**Funerals and Finance**	*167*
Chapter 8	**The Newest Profession?**	*199*

Bibliography	*237*
Index	*269*

List of Illustrations

1.	A busker's funeral	*16*
2.	An Asian funeral	*19*
3.	A woodland burial ground	*20*
4.	A display of contemporary coffins	*22*
5.	A chapel of rest	*32*
6.	A funeral home	*41*
7.	Embalming equipment	*61*
8.	Coffins being constructed	*81*
9.	Caskets being constructed	*85*
10.	An eco coffin	*96*
11.	A funeral director at work	*101*
12.	A horse-drawn hearse	*107*
13.	A motorcycle funeral	*115*

List of Tables

Table 1 F. W. Paine and Cremations: 1918–1968　　　　　　*120*

Abbreviations

Publications:

BMJ	*British Medical Journal*
FSJ	*Funeral Service Journal*
TUJ	*The Undertakers' Journal*
TUFDJ	*The Undertakers' and Funeral Directors' Journal*
BUA Monthly	*British Undertakers' Association Monthly*
TNFD	*The National Funeral Director*
TFD	*The Funeral Director (Monthly)*

Trade Associations:

BES	British Embalmers' Society
BFWA	British Funeral Workers' Association
BIFD	British Institute of Funeral Directors
BIE	British Institute of Embalmers
BIU	British Institute of Undertakers
BUA	British Undertakers' Association
IBCA	Institute of Burial and Cremation Administration
FBCA	Federation of British Cremation Authorities/Federation of Burial & Cremation Authorities
ICCM	Institute of Cemetery and Crematorium Management
LAFD	London Association of Funeral Directors
NACCS	National Association of Cemetery (and Crematorium) Superintendents

NAFD	National Association of Funeral Directors
NCDD	National Council for the Disposition of the Dead
SAIF	National Society of Allied and Independent Funeral Directors

Others:

MMC	Monopolies and Mergers Commission
OFT	Office of Fair Trading
SCI	Service Corporation International

Acknowledgments

I acknowledge the help of the following in the writing of this book:

Wellcome Library; London Library; British Library Newspaper Library; National Archive; New England Institute at Mount Ida College; David Kaye; Jacqui Lewis; Julie Callender and Tim Morris at the ICCM; the Revd. Dr. Peter Jupp; Dr. Julie Rugg; Stephen White; staff at J.H. Kenyon (the late Simon Constable and Dr. Philip Smyth); the late Barry Albin; Bunny and Michael France; Andrew and Peter Miller; Professor Robin Theobald; Jeremy and Charlie Field; colleagues at the University of Bath, particularly Dr. Kate Woodthorpe and Dr. John Troyer; Dr. Pam Fisher; Christopher Henley for access to material from his late father Des Henley; Jason Downing; Robert Lodge; Adrian Haler; the Revd Paul Sinclair; Sam Kershaw; Drawn Trigg and Sue Harvey at the F.W. Paine Museum in Kingston; Dean Reader and Sandra Mitchell of the Classic Hearse Register.

Preface

In 1963, Robert Habenstein and William Lamers published *The History of American Funeral Directing*. Now in its sixth edition, the volume traces the origins of funeral service in the United States from the Egyptians to contemporary times. The subject has since been brought even further up-to-date by Gary Laderman's *Rest in Peace: A Cultural History of Death and the Funeral Home in Twentieth-Century America*. This side of the Atlantic, those wishing to investigate a similar period of history need only refer to Julian Litten's authoritative work *The English Way of Death: The Common Funeral Since 1450*. His survey, however, concludes towards the end of the nineteenth century. The intention of this book is to start at this point by providing a comprehensive account of how funeral service developed in Britain during the following 110 years. In a period that has seen a shift from burial to cremation, the replacement of the horse-drawn hearse by motor vehicles, the introduction of embalming and the growth of large funeral firms operating on a centralised basis, there has also been an increasing preference by the industry for the description 'undertaker' to be replaced with 'funeral director'. Endorsing the desire to be perceived as a professional, this new term reflects the increase in responsibility and complexity of funerals acquired during the twentieth century.

This book draws together research I have carried out over the last 20 years. Some material was presented in 1997 to the University of Westminster as a thesis entitled 'Change and Development in the British Funeral Industry, with Special Reference to the Period 1960–1990'. Teaching on the foundation degree in Funeral Service at the University of Bath prompted the revision of the original along with new material, a move greatly assisted by unlimited access to the *Undertakers' Journal/Funeral Service Journal* and the *BUA Monthly/National Funeral Director/Funeral Director Monthly*.

The development of the British funeral industry is a vast subject. It is hoped that this first text on the subject will provide a good starting point for anyone wishing to become acquainted with a fascinating but largely unexplored part of our social and industrial history.

Brian Parsons

Introduction

The occupation of the undertaker first emerged in the seventeenth century as a supplier of coffins, funerary paraphernalia and the means of transport to the place of burial. However, as the disposal of the dead has gradually increased in complexity, the work and role of the undertaker has mirrored this change by beginning to include care for the body and provision of the place of repose in the interval between death and the funeral. This responsibility for the custody of and access to the dead has also presented the opportunity to carry out embalming. Other developments have also impacted on the role, such as changes to the production of coffins and the shift to motorised transport. These factors, together with the issue of succession for family funeral businesses, have coincided with the growth through acquisition of the large organisation. Managing funerals on a centralised basis where all capital-intensive resources are organised in a single location enables operational efficiencies to be achieved through the control of high fixed overheads. Despite this structural change, the independent/family owned business continues to dominate funeral service in the UK in terms of market share.

It is against this background of organisational change that the occupation has sought to reposition itself from 'undertaker' to 'funeral director' in an attempt to gain recognition as a professional service provider. The formation of a trade association, the launch of a code of practice, the education of funeral directors and attempts at registration have been components of this process. In striving for this status, however, the funeral director has been hindered by two key issues of stigmatisation: handling the dead and making a profit from loss.

Predominantly historical in approach, the first six chapters explore how care towards the body, coffins, transport and the structure of the industry have changed over the twentieth century. Chapter 1 examines the emergence of the first undertakers, followed by an appraisal of change during the nineteenth century. The concluding section identifies the three key factors that have impacted upon funeral directors during the twentieth century: custody of the dead body, cremation and the funeral reform movement. Chapters 2–6 explore the effects of these changes. Possession of the body and the provision of chapels of rest and embalming are covered in Chapters 2 and 3, while Chapter 4 examines how coffins have changed through increased use of technology and the impact of cremation. The shift from animate power to motor hearse together with the use of alternative funerary transport is considered in Chapter 5. The combined effects of these changes and the challenges facing small firms have enabled the growth of the large firms. This period of expansion is appraised in Chapter 6. The penultimate chapter assesses attempts by external organisations to regulate the industry in an attempt to control funeral costs, while the final chapter identifies seven key areas in the process of professionalisation as the undertaker has sought to become the funeral director.

Chapter 1

Death, the Funeral and the Funeral Director in the Twentieth Century

The Funeral Director

The funeral is the ultimate rite of passage.[1] It is a complex social drama in which performance and rituals are prescribed by social, religious and economic criteria together with personal preference.[2] As a leave-taking ceremony, the funeral has been defined as 'an organized, purposeful, time-limited flexible group-centred response to death.'[3] It has a number of functions: the primary ones being for the disposal of the dead, release of the soul and social interaction.[4] The body is the principal,

---

[1] Van Gennep A. (1960) *The Rites of Passage*, trans M.B. Vizedom and G.L. Caffee, London: Routledge and Kegan Paul, p. 146.
[2] Prior L. (1989) *The Social Organization of Death: Medical Discourse and Social Practices in Belfast*, Hampshire: The Macmillan Press, p. 155.
[3] Kastenbaum R.J. (1981) *Death, Society and Human Experience,* second edition, St Louis: Mosby, p. 221 and Lamers W.M. Jr (1975) quoted in Raether H.C. and Slater R.C. *The Funeral Director and His Role as Counselor*, Milwaukee: National Funeral Directors Association.
[4] Pine V.R. (1969) 'Comparative Funeral Practices', *Practical Anthropology*, No. 16, pp. 49–62. See also Raether H.C. (1990) *Funeral Service: A Historical Perspective,* Milwaukee: National Funeral Directors Association, p. 39 and Warwick T. (1994) 'The Funeral: Meaning, Value and Function', *Australian Funeral Director*, March, pp. 25–28.

non-participatory guest at the obsequies; without it no funeral can take place.[5] It is the presence of the body that necessitates the existence of a specialist responsible in an agency capacity for arranging the disposal: the funeral director. While the funeral director does not literally effect burial or cremation of the dead, he/she acts as the intermediary between the bereaved and the organisations that control the mode of disposal.

Funeral directors provide services within the context of a ritual. The latter, such as walking in front of the hearse, have been handed down through tradition, while other services including care of the body have emerged according to changing needs. One industry-generated definition summarises this role: 'technical adviser, agent, contractor, master of ceremonies and custodian of the dead'.[6] The occupation is no longer about carrying out or simply 'undertaking' the disposal of the dead; it is, in the words of Rabbi Earl Grollman, 'Caretaker, caregiver and gatekeeper; that is caretaker of the dead, caregiver to the bereaved... [and]... from the perspective of the community... the secular gatekeeper between the living and the dead'.[7]

The origins of undertaking can be traced to the end of the seventeenth century when William Boyce opened his business in London, around 1675. It was William Russell's undertaking business, however, that received approval from the College of Arms to undertake certain funerals that ended the involvement of the College and usurped Herald's function. Following the death of Queen Mary in 1694 and her funeral a year later, the College realised that private enterprise had become a significant competitor. Coupled with the fact that the nobility had reviewed its obsequial requirements, it is surprising that the College's involvement in funerals lasted until 1751. These early years of the undertaking business have been well covered by a number of writers.[8]

---

[5]Hertz R. (1960) *Death and the Right Hand: A Contribution to the Study of the Collective Representations of Death*, trans R. Needham & C. Needham, London: Cohen and West.
[6]*Manual of Funeral Directing* (2009) Solihull: National Association of Funeral Directors, Ch.18, pp. 2–3.
[7]Quoted in Leming M.R. and Dickinson G.E. (1994) *Understanding Dying, Death and Bereavement,* third edition, Fort Worth: Harcourt Brace, p. 467. Pine quotes Earl Grollman, who emphasises the caring role: 'The funeral director is someone who cares about, who takes care, and who takes care of. He is called upon to cure, to encourage as well as to console, to overcome soul-wounds. He is part of a meaningful, caretaking profession'. Pine V.R. (1975) *Caretaker of the Dead: The American Funeral Director*, New York: Irvington, p. 154.
[8]Fritz P.S. (1994) 'The Undertaking Trade in England: Its Origins and Early Development, 1660–1830', *Eighteenth-Century Studies,* Vol. 28, No. 2, pp. 241–253 and

With the population of urban areas expanding during the nineteenth century, the undertaking trade reflected this greater need; the large number of firms listed in the London Post Office Directories underpins this trend. Many were owner–operator businesses that made coffins and hired hearses and carriages from specialist carriage masters who supplied firms in a locality. However, while the provision of a coffin and transport to the place of burial continued to be the two key functions of the occupation, a further dimension became apparent. It was items such as mourning wear and jewellery and the need to create a display at funerals that have retrospectively been described as the 'Victorian Celebration of Death'.[9] The nineteenth century also fostered the need for the poor to avoid the disgrace of a pauper's funeral, as the stigma lasted well beyond the grave.[10] As the conduct of funerals of the period was governed by money and custom, commentators accused the undertaking (or 'dismal') trade of exploitation.[11] After observing the displays at funerals, Charles Dickens quoted in *Household Words* the supposed sales techniques employed by an unscrupulous undertaker.[12] His most robust tirade was published in

---

Litten J.W.S. (2002) *The English Way of Death: The Common Funeral Since 1450*, London: Robert Hale, p. 17. See also Hitchcock B. (1924) 'The Upholders' Company', *BUA Monthly*, December, pp. 161–162 and Doyle C.G. (1974b) 'Undertakers and Undertaking', *TFD*, May, pp. 239–242 and July, pp. 335–343.

[9] For death during the nineteenth century see Cannadine D. (1981) 'War and Death, Grief and Mourning in Modern Britain', in J. Whaley ed., *Mirrors of Mortality*, London: Europa; Curl J.S. (2002) *Death and Architecture*, Stroud: Sutton Publishing; Morley J. (1971) *Death, Heaven and the Victorians*, London: Studio Vista; Richardson R. (1989) 'Why Was Death So Big in Victorian Britain?' in R. Houlbrook ed., *Death, Ritual and Bereavement*, London: Routledge; Jalland P. (1996) *Death in the Victorian Family*, Oxford: Oxford University Press; and Jalland P. (1999) 'Victorian Death and Its Decline 1850–1918', in P. C. Jupp and C. Gittings, *Death in England*, Manchester: Manchester University Press.

[10] Strange J-M. (2005) *Death, Grief and Poverty in Britain, 1870–1914*, Cambridge: Cambridge University Press. See also Laqueur T.W. (1983) 'Bodies, Death, and Pauper Funerals', *Representations*, Vol. 1, No. 1, February, p. 109. There is little wonder that an editorial in *TUJ* was prefaced by 'Rattle his bone over the stones/ He's only a pauper whom nobody owns.' 'Editorial: Pauper Funerals' (1905) *TUJ*, March, pp. 63–64.

[11] Puckle B.S. (1926) *Funeral Customs: Their Origin and Development*, London: Werner Laurie, pp. 97–98.

[12] Dickens C. (1850) 'From the Raven in the Happy Family', *Household Words*, 8 June, pp. 241–242. See also Leigh P. (1850) 'Address from an Undertaker to the Trade', *Household Words*, No. 13, 22 June, pp. 301–304. For other references to funerals in Dickens' writings see Parsons B. (2012b) 'Dickens, the Undertakers and Burial', *ICCM Journal*, Vol. 80, No. 4, pp. 22–44; Tylee F. (1929) 'Black Bands and Orange

1852 as 'Trading in Death'; in it, he lambasted the competition between the classes for gentility, this being 'estimated by the amount of ghastly folly in which the undertaker was permitted to run riot'.[13] It is largely from this social convention to emulate wealthier classes that undertakers can be seen to have seized the opportunity to capitalise upon the prevailing attitude. However, lack of evidence means that the scale of this alleged corruption is in question. Indeed, the undertaking business during the nineteenth century awaits a thorough analysis and critique.

By the end of the nineteenth century undertakers in Britain were dealing with around 670,000 funerals a year. Over the next 110 years or so the practice of the undertaker supplying little more than the coffin and transportation would change significantly as the occupation gradually became the 'funeral director'. To fully contextualise this transition a brief examination of the changing environment of death and funerals during this period is required.

Death and Funerals in the Twentieth Century

Although the last 30 years have seen a flurry of publications examining various aspects of mortality, literature specifically concerning funerals is in short supply. With the exception of the research carried out by Jupp exploring the shift towards cremation, a comprehensive study focusing on post-death rituals in the United Kingdom is still awaited. There are, however, a few texts that survey the century in more general terms. In *Death in War and Peace: A History of Loss & Grief in England, 1914–1970*, Pat Jalland assesses the reaction to large-scale mortality during and following both world wars along with the impact of the increasing medicalisation of death, a development that has not only brought about an improvement in life expectancy and a reduction in deaths from infectious disease, but has also led to a culture of death avoidance.[14] The declining influence of religion and particularly that of the established church is also considered, particularly at the deathbed. Jalland critiques Gorer's

---

Blossom', *The Dickensian*, Vol. 25, pp. 277–280; and Irwin M. (2008) 'The Bright Side of Death: Dickens and Black Humour', *The Dickensian*, Spring, No. 272, Part 1, pp. 17–31.
[13]Dickens C. (1852) 'Trading in Death', *Household Words*, 27 November, pp. 140–245.
[14]Jalland P. (2010) *Death in War and Peace: A History of Loss & Grief in England, 1914–1970*, Oxford: Oxford University Press.

well-known 1965 publication *Death, Grief and Mourning in Contemporary Britain*, in which he concluded that discussions about death had become suppressed.[15] This followed his essay 'The Pornography of Death' from a decade earlier arguing that whereas in the nineteenth century sex was a forbidden or an 'unmentionable' subject, it has been replaced by death in the twentieth century: 'The natural processes of corruption and decay have become disgusting as the natural processes of birth and copulation were a century ago...'.[16]

Although Jalland's study embraces funeral rituals among the northern working classes during the interwar years, and the preference for cremation by one aristocratic figure, her research terminates in the 1970s. With the exception of one paragraph, there is no coverage of contemporary developments, although in the epilogue she does identify the recent innovation of the 'natural woodland burial movement'. Improvements in health, longevity and welfare, along with the shift from burial to cremation and changes regarding the afterlife and approaches to loss, are succinctly summarised in the concluding chapter by Peter Jupp and Tony Walter in *Death in England. An Illustrated History*.[17]

The anthropologist Douglas Davies in his *Mors Britannica: Lifestyle and Death-Style in Britain Today* regards the Church of England and the National Health Service as the two institutions that have come to dominate death in the first and second halves of the twentieth century, respectively. He too acknowledges woodland burial as an important departure from cremation, although figures indicating the extent of its usage are not given.

These texts, along with more theoretical perspectives concerning mortality in the twentieth century by Walter, particularly in *The Revival of Death* with his exploration of individualism and examples of postmodern funeral rituals, contribute towards our understanding of change. It is from reviewing these texts that three external factors impacting upon

---

[15] Gorer G. (1955) 'The Pornography of Death', *Encounter*, October, pp. 49–52. For a reassessment of Gorer's essay see Jalland P. (2010) *Death in War and Peace: A History of Loss & Grief in England, 1914–1970*, Oxford: Oxford University Press, pp. 215–228; Walter T. (1987) 'Emotional Reserve and the English Way of Death', in K. Charmaz, G. Howarth and A. Kellehear eds, *The Unknown Country: Death in Australia, Britain and the USA*, Basingstoke: Macmillan; Walter T. (1998) 'A Sociology of Grief?' *Mortality*, Vol. 3, No. 1, pp. 83–87; and Naylor M. (2004) 'Opening Geoffrey Gorer's Door: A Personal Overview of Funerals 1983–2003', *Pharos International*, Vol. 70, No. 3, pp. 17–23.

[16] Gorer G. (1955) 'The Pornography of Death', *Encounter*, October, p. 51.

[17] Jupp P.C. and Walter T. (1999) 'The Healthy Society: 1918–98', in P.C. Jupp and C. Gittings eds, *Death in England*, Manchester: Manchester University Press.

the work of the undertaker/funeral director can be discerned: the changing place of death, the preference towards cremation and the reform of funerals.[18] These are outlined below and then examined more thoroughly in this study in the context of organisational change and professionalisation.

The Changing Place of Death

The transition of the place of death from the home to the institution has been a gradual development in the twentieth century. While the Great War separated the living from the physical presence of death by distance on an unprecedented scale, over time it was improvements in medical science that can be identified as the fundamental reason behind this shift. The hospital has become not only the formal place for treatment of the living but also the established place for death, which tends to occur hidden from sight.[19] It is in such institutions that death has become 'transposed, insulated, technologised and decontextualised'.[20] This has led to hospital death being an isolating experience, and either partially or totally from the perspective of the dying; deaths frequently occur with no one else present.[21] As soon as a death occurs, standardised procedures regarding medical certification, registration and possibly investigation by the coroner commence.[22]

The institutionalisation and medicalisation of death has had a considerable effect on twentieth-century attitudes and a number of interrelated

---

[18]These changes are not dissimilar to those identified in the US by Harrington D.L. (2007) 'Markets. Preserving Funeral Market with Read-to-Embalm Laws', *Journal of Economic Perspectives,* Vol. 21 No. 4, pp. 201–216.
[19]Blauner R. (1966) 'Death and Social Structure', *Psychiatry,* Vol. 29, pp. 378–394.
[20]Kastenbaum R.J. and Aisenberg R. (1976) *The Psychology of Death,* New York: Springer, p. 208. See also Rando T.A. (1989) 'The Funeral Director as a Grief Facilitator', in H.C. Raether ed., *The Funeral Director's Practice Management Handbook,* Englewood Cliffs: Prentice Hall, p. 23. See also Mauksch H.O. (1975) 'The Organizational Context of Dying', in E. Kübler-Ross ed., *Death: The Final Stage of Growth,* New York: Touchstone/Simon & Schuster.
[21]Ariès P. (1974) *Western Attitudes Towards Death from the Middle Ages to the Present,* London: Marion Boyars.
[22]See Glasser B. and Strauss A. (1968) *Time for Dying,* Chicago: Aldine; Sudnow D. (1967) *Passing On: The Social Organization of Dying,* Englewood Cliffs: Prentice-Hall; Mulkay M. (1993) 'Social Death in Britain', in D. Clark ed., *The Sociology of Death: Theory, Culture, Practice,* Oxford: Blackwell; and Prior L. (1989) *The Social Organization of Death: Medical Discourse and Social Practices in Belfast,* Hampshire: The Macmillan Press.

points can be made. First, through the increase in life expectancy that has occurred since the last quarter of the previous century, the tendency is to associate death with the elderly. Illich et al. indicate that past generations accepted death as an inevitable consequence of mortal existence.[23] They believe that contemporary society sees death as something over which we will gradually triumph. Its occurrence in the young is therefore more often than not deemed to be negligence on the part of the medical profession, who regard those who die young as 'deviants'.[24]

Furthermore, body handling is assigned to lowly workers: the hospital porters and ultimately funeral directors. Mortuaries are usually in an unsignposted and marginally accessible location, thus confirming the 'invisible' nature of death. Secondly, as death increasingly occurs in the highly regulated, formal and sanitised environment of the hospital, society has consequently become less knowledgeable and therefore less experienced about the practical processes of dying and death as well as supportive mourning rituals. Although Parkes sees no reason to suggest that this society actually denies death any more than previous ones, it is simply 'dead ignorant about death.'[25]

The hospice movement that emerged in the 1960s has contributed towards the improved experience of both the dying and their carers.[26] As a place specifically for the terminally ill, as opposed to the hospital where the emphasis is on survival, the hospice encourages those within to face death. It was a reversal of prevailing medical philosophy, as Littlewood expresses: '[the] hospice involves a change in perspective from "nothing more can be done" to "we must provide the best kind of human care possible for this person"'.[27]

Figures charting the shift in the place of dying are difficult to trace and validate. Research cited by Jalland states that up to 1957, 40 per cent of deaths occurred in hospital and by 1973 this had increased to

---

[23]Illich I., Zola I.K., McKnight J., Caplan J. and Shaiken H. (1977) *Disabling Professions,* London: Marion Boyars.
[24]See Littlewood J. (1992) *Aspects of Grief: Bereavement in Adult Life,* London: Routledge, p. 7.
[25]Parkes C.M. (1996) *Bereavement: Studies of Grief in Adult Life,* third edition, London: Routledge.
[26]Saunders C.M. ed. (1990) *Hospice and Palliative Care: An Interdisciplinary Approach,* London: Edward Arnold. See also Worpole K. (2006) *Modern Hospice Design,* London: Routledge.
[27]Littlewood J. (1992) *Aspects of Grief: Bereavement in Adult Life,* London: Routledge, p. 16. See also Palgi P. and Abramovitch H. (1984) 'Death: A Cross-Cultural Perspective', *American Review of Anthropology,* Vol. 13, p. 404.

60 per cent.[28] Funeral directors' records provide a reliable source of data. For example, an assessment of information from the Croydon firm of Thomas Ebbutt reveals that in 1937 two-thirds of deaths occurred at home. Correspondingly, of the 2,552 funerals arranged in 1958 by the south-west London firm of Frederick W. Paine, 56 per cent occurred in hospitals and nursing homes. In 1977, it was just over 63 per cent.[29] A survey conducted in Sussex during 2010 shows that 22.2 per cent occurred at home while 55.9 per cent were in hospital and 21.9 per cent in a nursing home.[30] It is possible that regional in addition to rural/urban variations influence these figures.

In the first two chapters, we will discuss that during the twentieth century the funeral director has gradually become the 'caretaker of the dead'.[31] Transportation, storage, preparation and access to the body have expanded the remit of responsibility and resulted not only in a change in the occupational role, along but also with the development of premises to provide mortuary accommodation and viewing space along with facilities for embalming. In the final chapter, however, it is argued that increased contact with the dead has hindered the progression towards professionalisation of the funeral director.

Cremation

Despite cremation having its origins in the late nineteenth century, it would be 1967 before it replaced burial as the preferred mode of disposal in the United Kingdom. In 1900, 0.07 per cent of the number of deaths were followed by cremation; by 1939 this still represented only 3.5 per cent. It was, however, only in the post-World War II years that a considerable increase was recorded and particularly in the two decades following 1945 when cremations rose from 7.8 to 44.28 per cent. Over the same period, the number of crematoria increased from 58 to 184. In 2016, 76.54 per cent of deaths were followed by cremation at the 277 crematoria in operation.

---

[28]Jalland P. (2010) *Death in War and Peace: A History of Loss & Grief in England, 1914–1970*, Oxford: Oxford University Press, p. 185.
[29]Parsons B. (Forthcoming-b) 'Portrait of Mortality: Croydon 1937. Death and Disposal in a London Suburb'.
[30]Hilton D.D. and Okubadejo O.A. (2010) 'Where Do People Die?' *Resurgam*, Vol. 53, No. 3, pp.148–149.
[31]*The Manual of Funeral Directing* (2009) Solihull Ch.18, p. 2.

The social and religious reasons why cremation has increased during the twentieth century have been thoroughly examined by Peter Jupp, and it unnecessary to repeat these here.[32] Undertakers were instrumental in providing the coffin, transport and organisational elements of the first cremations, but in reflection of the modest preference these were only occasional activities. They were also expensive due to transportation costs.[33] Rather than perceiving cremation as a threat to revenue through the potential use of less-expensive coffins than would be used for burial, there is evidence to indicate that the funeral directors promoted cremation at a local level through sustained advertising of their willingness to receive instructions for 'funerals and cremations'. Even where funeral directors did not specifically advertise cremations, ultimately they accepted the instructions for a funeral irrespective of the mode of disposition.

Cremation not only impacted upon coffin design and construction; but also changed the 'pace' of funerals, particularly following the introduction of motor transport and also as the preference for it increased. These factors are discussed in Chapters 4 and 5.

The 'Funeral Reform Movement'

The final area that has impacted upon the work of the funeral director is changing funerary practices. Although, as noted above, the twentieth century can be characterised by the shift in preference towards cremation, it is both the ritual preceding and that conducted at the time of disposal that has been the subject of considerable change. Nowhere is this more apparent than in the last two decades of the twentieth century. In many respects, funerals have been continually reforming through a process of evolution to meet changing needs and demands. However, whereas the reforming movement of the late nineteenth century focused on reducing expenditure by eliminating ostentation, and then in the early part of the twentieth century through the shift from burial to cremation, more recently the emphasis has been on creating meaningful and personal funeral ceremonies.

---

[32] Jupp P.C. (2006) *From Dust to Ashes: Cremation and the British Way of Death,* Basingstoke: Palgrave Macmillan and Jupp P.C. et al. (2017) *Cremation in Modern Scotland: History, Architecture and the Law,* Edinburgh: Birlinn.
[33] Parsons B. (2005a) *Committed to the Cleansing Flame: The Development of Cremation in Nineteenth Century England,* Reading: Spire Books.

Although Britain has escaped the criticism levelled at the industry in the United States during the 1960s by writers such as Harmer and Mitford concerning funeral costs and embalming, two decades on it became apparent that a degree of dissatisfaction was being expressed at funeral performance and, in particular, services at crematoria.[34] With this mode of disposal overtaking the preference for burial, the 20-minute service in the crematorium chapel conducted by a duty clergyman created a 'conveyor-belt' means of disposal.[35] By the 1970s, funerals in England were said to take place 'simply, speedily and sincerely'.[36] Although an element of ostentation undoubtedly continued at some funerals, many could be described as 'traditional', being a religious service with sacred music but including little recognition of the deceased person's life. In addition, arrangements such as the 'public reading time' where a communal burial service was conducted with multiple unrelated families present still took place in the 1960s.[37] When the pioneer of green burial, Ken West, started working in a cemetery in the 1960s he described funerals as being 'Churchillian'.[38] In

---

[34] Harmer R.M. (1963) *The High Cost of Dying,* New York: Collier Books; Mitford J. (1963) *The American Way of Death,* London: Quartet; Mitford J. (1997) 'Death, Incorporated', *Vanity Fair*, March, pp. 54–61; and Mitford J. (1998) *The American Way of Death Revisited,* London: Virago. For a critique of Mitford's writings see Canine J.D. (1996) *The Psychosocial Aspects of Death and Dying,* Stamford: Appleton & Lange; Lynch T. (1998) A Deathly Silence', *The Sunday Telegraph Magazine,* 11 October, pp. 28–31; and Laderman G. (2003) *Rest in Peace: A Cultural History of Death and the Funeral Home in Twentieth-Century America,* Oxford: Oxford University Press. For a survey of the personalisation of funerals in the US see Garces-Foley K. and Holcomb J.S. (2006) 'Contemporary American Funerals: Personalizing Tradition', in K. Garces-Foley ed., *Death and Religion in a Changing World,* New York: ME Sharpe.
[35] Davies D. (1995) *British Crematoria in Public Profile,* Maidstone: The Cremation Society of Great Britain, p. 22. See also Davies D. (2012) 'Revisiting British Crematoria in Public Profile', *Pharos International,* Vol. 78, No. 3, pp. 4–7. For critiques of British funerals see Ironside V. (1996) *You'll Get Over It: The Rage of Bereavement,* London: Hamish Hamilton, pp. 14–29; Callender R. (2012a) 'Dancing Around the Bonfire', in R. Callender ed., *Writing on Death,* Winchester: Natural Death Centre/Strange Attractor Press; and Plimmer M. (1997) 'How I Let My Father Leave by the Backdoor', *The Daily Telegraph,* 24 May.
[36] Nicholson P. (1974) 'The British Way of Death', *The Illustrated London News,* Vol. 262, No. 6912, July, pp. 64–66. For a brief observation of funerals in the 1970s see Turner E. (1977) 'The British Way of Death', *Resurgam,* Vol. 20, No. 1, pp. 4–5.
[37] See McHale B. in Fox J. (1994) 'The Future of Funerals: Options for Change' 'Dead Citizens Charter', *FSJ,* August, pp. 61–63. For a description of this practice see 'Mass Burials' (1933) *TUJ,* April, p. 114.
[38] West K. (2010) *A Guide to Natural Burial,* London: Shaw & Sons, p. 153.

other words, the service read at Sir Winston Churchill's funeral, being the 'Order for the Burial of the Dead' from the *Book of Common Prayer*, was used at all services conducted by a Church of England clergyman. As this did not include even the name of the deceased, the impersonal and dispassionate nature of the ceremony can be identified as a low point in funeral performance. However, it soon became a turning point.

One of the first texts to highlight the inadequacies of funerals taking place in the late 1980s was by Tony Walter, who noted that 'Funerals today are far too impersonal, hypocritical, and bureaucratic, replacing mystery with mistrust.'[39] And in the foreword to the *Dead Citizens Charter*, published six years later, the chairman of the National Funerals College, Malcolm Johnson, recognised this when he wrote:

> The average British funeral is a miserable and disappointing affair. For those who are not well known figures or members of churches – most of us – the contemporary funeral lacks meaningful symbolism, dignity, adequate time and comfort for those who mourn.[40]

While these statements were unsupported by data, their appearance coincided with a number of factors marking a rediscovery of interest in the broad environment of death along with a significant change in the performance of funerals. The sections below identify three factors that have stimulated change, followed by an overview of the range of options now encountered at funerals.

First, the ceremonies for those dying from HIV and AIDS in the early 1990s often took place without recourse to organised religion.[41] Frequently comprising secular readings and music, they were often constructed by partners and friends and occasionally held in non-religious venues including hospices. However, such funerals must be seen in perspective as, although radical and predominantly attended by a younger generation, they only concerned a modest number of ceremonies. Nevertheless, the

---

[39] Walter T. (1990) *Funerals And How To Improve Them*, London: Hodder and Stoughton, p. 9. See also Walter T. (1996) 'Ritualising Death in a Consumer Society', *Royal Society of Arts Journal*, April, pp. 32–40.

[40] Foreword to the *Dead Citizens Charter: A Citizens Charter for the Dead* (1996) Stamford: The National Funerals College. See also Jupp P.C. (1997a) 'Unsatisfactory Services for the Dead', *Church Times*, 23 May.

[41] Working in west London at the time, the author recalls many highly elaborate and participative funerals taking place at the London Lighthouse (a hospice for those dying from HIV-related diseases).

funeral service for Terry Madeley, who died from an HIV-related illness in 1987, was broadcast by the BBC and highlighted to a wide audience the potential for a ceremony at variance to the 'traditional'.[42] Rediscovering and formulating new rituals also became evident as communities sought to deal with loss from the series of mass fatalities that occurred in the 1980s and 1990s. Those after the tragedy at Hillsborough Stadium in 1989 have been well documented.[43] Others include the prevalence of roadside memorials and the community-led act of witness when military funerals passed through Royal Wootton Bassett.[44]

Secondly, as part of a consumer-driven culture there has been increasing willingness to challenge convention and 'do something different'. This coincides with the prevailing trend towards individualism; as Tony Walter has identified, it is stimulated by 'a fear we will lose our "I", our "me-ness"'.[45] He sees the decline of 'settled communities' as a measure of the familiarity with death and communal funeral rituals. Where this is not the case, Walter believes people turn to others for advice; those gravitating to urban areas during the nineteenth century utilised the services of an undertaker. In the late twentieth century, families continue to turn to the funeral director to organise a wide range of ceremonies, from direct cremation to elaborate funerals taking place over several days.

It is also possible that the so-called 'Diana effect' has been instrumental in indicating that a funeral need not conform to an established format.[46] It should be noted, however, that this process had started before 1997 and that her funeral service was not at significant variance from many other

---

[42] *Remember Terry* was broadcast by the BBC on 17 December 1987. See Walter T. (1990) *Funerals And How To Improve Them,* London: Hodder and Stoughton, pp. 146–147. See also Cave D. (2002) 'Gay and Lesbian Bereavement', in D. Dickenson, M. Johnson and J. S. Katz eds, *Death, Dying and Bereavement,* second edition, London: Sage, pp. 363–366.

[43] Walter T. (1991) 'The Mourning after Hillsborough', *Sociological Review,* Vol. 39, No. 3, August, pp. 599–625 and Brennan M. (2008) 'Mourning and Loss: Finding Means in the Mourning for Hillsborough', *Mortality,* Vol. 13, No. 1, pp. 1–23. See also Searle C. and Chew S. eds (1990) *Remember Hillsborough,* Runcorn: Archive/Sheffield City Council/Sheffield Star.

[44] 'Grief, and its Consequences', *The Economist,* 10 September 2011, p. 36.

[45] Walter T. (1994) *The Revival of Death,* London: Routledge, p. 3.

[46] See Kear A. and Steinberg D.L. eds (1999) *Mourning Diana: Nation, Culture and the Performance of Grief,* London: Routledge; Walter T. (1999) *The Mourning for Diana,* Oxford: Berg; Denison K.M. (2000) 'The Implications of Events Surrounding the Death and Funeral of Diana, Princess of Wales', *Pharos International,* Vol. 66, No. 2, pp. 5–8; and Berridge K. (2001) *Vigor Mortis,* London: Profile, pp. 71–104. The events following 11 September 2001 also await analysis.

high-profile ceremonies that were predominantly religious in character, but inclusive of secular elements.

Thirdly, those involved in funeral provision, such as cemetery and crematorium managers, officiants, funeral directors and suppliers, started to review their services in an attempt to become more consumer-focused.[47] Driven by documents such as the National Funeral College's *Dead Citizens Charter* (along with their conferences), the Institute of Cemetery and Crematorium Management's *Charter for the Bereaved* and the Natural Death Centre's *The Natural Death Handbook,* facilities improved and the range of services widened.[48] Change has also been instigated by greater accommodation of the needs of ethnic-minority communities (Fig. 2).[49]

---

[47] See Rickman C. (2007) 'Improving the Crematorium Experience for…Mourners: A Funeral Director's View 1', *Pharos International,* Vol. 73, No. 1, pp. 3–5; Yardley J. (2007) 'Improving the Crematorium Experience for…Mourners: The Private Company Crematorium Manager's Perspective', *Pharos International,* Vol. 73, No. 3, pp. 3–5; and Squires D. (2007) 'Improving the Crematorium Experience for…Mourners: The Local Authority Perspective', *Pharos International,* Vol. 73, No. 3, pp. 6–9.

[48] Jupp P.C. (1995) 'The Work of Funerals and the National Funerals College', *Pharos International,* Vol. 61, No. 2, pp. 48–54 and Jupp P.C. (1997b) 'The Dead Citizens Charter', *Pharos International,* Vol. 63, No. 4, pp. 18–28. See also Cromer M. (2006) *Exit Strategy: Thinking Outside the Box,* New York: Jeremy P. Tarcher/Penguin; Francis J. (2004) *Time to Go: Alternative Funerals. The Importance of Saying Goodbye,* Lincoln: IUniverse; Morrell J. and Smith S. (2006) *We Need to Talk About the Funeral,* Totnes: Alphabet and Image Publishers; Gill S. and Fox J. (2004) *The Dead Good Funerals Book,* Ulverston: Engineers of the Imagination; Wadey A. (2010) *What To Do When Someone Dies,* London: Which? Books; and Dunn M. (2000) *The Good Death Guide,* Oxford: Pathways Books. See also Johnson M., Cullen L., Heatley R. and Hockey J. (2001) *The Psychology of Death: An Exploration of the Impact of Bereavement on the Purchasers of 'At Need' Funerals,* Bristol: International Institute on Health and Ageing, p. 20 and Hockey J. (2003) 'Purchasing At Need Funerals: The Changing Context', *Pharos International,* Vol. 69, No. 2, pp. 8–11. For the work of the Natural Death Centre see Inman-Cook R. (2011) 'The Funeral Industry Interview', *TFD,* May, pp. 34–36 and Callender R. et al. (2012b) *The Natural Death Handbook,* fifth edition, London: Natural Death Centre/Strange Attractor Press.

[49] Laungani P. (1998) 'The Changing Patterns of Hindu Funerals in Britain', *Pharos International,* Vol. 64, No. 4, pp. 4–10; Firth S. (2002) 'Changing Hindu Attitudes to Cremation in the UK', *Pharos International,* Vol. 68, No. 1, pp. 35–40; Firth S. (1996) 'The Good Death: Attitudes of British Hindus', in G. Howarth and P.C. Jupp eds, *Contemporary Issues in the Sociology of Death, Dying and Disposal,* Basingstoke: Macmillan Press; and Cribb P.W. (1980) 'Some Observations on the Funeral Customs of Immigrant Communities at the Crematorium', *Resurgam,* Vol. 23, No. 1, pp. 5–7.

Fig. 1. A busker's funeral. *Note:* Although the 'personalisation' of funerals is often considered to be a recent initiative, many examples can be found from the past. In August 1954 Pearly Kings and Queens accompanied the hearse containing Jack Marriott on his final journey. Those attending funerals today will wear clothing ranging from 'bright colours' to uniforms, or dress associated with an occupation, hobby or membership of an organisation (Author's collection).

The impact on funeral performance has been considerable, as this summary indicates. Coffins, considered to be the main component at a funeral, are produced not only in solid wood and MDF (medium-density fibreboard), but also in a range of alternative colours and materials including wicker, cardboard and bamboo. The vehicle used to convey the coffin is not restricted to a traditional motor hearse, but now embraces horse-drawn vehicles, motorcycle hearses, VW camper vans and vintage lorries. Although the preference for cremation has been fairly static in the last decade, the expansion in the number of new crematoria has given the opportunity for facilities to increase service duration time from 30 to 45 minutes or even one hour. The availability of sound-reproducing equipment, mainly at crematoria, along with the facility to download recordings from the internet has coincided with the replacement of congregational singing by listening to recorded secular music.[50] Some crematoria have

---

[50]See Parsons B. (2012d) 'Identifying Key Changes. The Progress of Cremation and Its Influence of Music at Funerals in England, 1874–2010, *Mortality,* Vol. 17,

screens where a visual presentation of the deceased's life can be displayed during the funeral along with equipment to stream the funeral via the internet. A broad range of funeral officiants or celebrants, including those who will conduct services that are part-religious and part-secular, have also emerged.[51] In many cases, the eulogy (and sometimes more than one) will be given by a family member or friend rather than an officiant not known to the deceased or family. The production of printed orders of service is more widespread now than at any time in the past. Flowers continue to be given at funerals, although the level of donations in lieu is significant, with the latter often being collected online.

The releasing of doves, 'themed' funerals such as a pirate funeral or 'Batman and Robin' for a child, along with those linked with a football club, such as Midland's Co-operative with Birmingham City, are not unusual.

Since the 1980s, the deceased have increasingly been dressed in their own clothing, while a range of personal and novel items are often placed in coffins.[52]

Other aspects of reappraisal are evident, such as the disposal of ashes.[53] Figures indicate a sharp increase in those removed from a crematorium (74.06 per cent in 2015) in contrast to scattering in the Gardens of

---

No. 2, pp. 2–15 and Adamson S. Holloway M. (2012) "A Sound-Track of Your Life' – Music in Contemporary UK Funerals', *Omega,* Vol. 65, No. 1, pp. 33–54. See also Parsons B. (2008a) 'Music at Funerals: The Challenge of Keeping in Tune with the Needs of the Bereaved', in P.C. Jupp ed., *Death Our Future: Christian Theology and Funeral Practice,* London: Epworth and Denyer P. (1997) 'Singing the Lord's Song in a Strange Land', in P.C. Jupp and T. Rogers eds, *Interpreting Death: Christian Theology and Pastoral Practice*, London: Cassell, pp. 200–201. See also 'UK Crematoria Survey 2016' (2016) *Pharos International,* Vol. 82, No. 4, pp. 36–37.
[51]See Pearce J. (1996) 'Non-religious Funerals in the 90's', *FSJ,* April, pp. 48–55; and Cowling C. (2010a) *The Good Funeral Guide*, London: Continuum, pp. 81–91; Cowling C. (2012) 'The New Priests: Secular Celebrants and Ceremonies', in R. Callender (2012a) *Writing on Death*, Winchester: Natural Death Centre/Strange Attractor Press; Holloway M. et al. (2010) *Spirituality in Contemporary Funerals: Final Report,* Arts and Humanities Research Council/University of Hull; and Holloway M. et al. (2013) "Funerals Aren't Nice But it Couldn't Have Been Nicer'. The Makings of a Good Funeral', *Mortality,* Vol. 18, No. 1, pp. 30–53.
[52]For examples of items see 'Legislation Report' (1993) *TFD,* February, pp. 8–9.
[53]Parsons B. (2005b) 'Where Did the Ashes Go? The Development of Cremation and Disposal of Ashes 1885–1950. Part 1: Burying the Cremated', *ICCM Journal,* Vol. 73, No. 1, pp. 6–12; Parsons B. (2005c) 'Where Did the Ashes Go? The Development of Cremation and Disposal of Ashes 1885–1950. Part 2 – From Grave to Gardens: Scattering and Gardens of Remembrance', *ICCM Journal,* Vol. 73, No. 2, pp. 28–42.

Remembrance.[54] The range of alternative places for disposal includes retention at home, scattering at sea or in a location favoured by the deceased, placed into a firework and also manipulated into a man-made diamond.[55] Although some of these rituals are not new, merely rediscovered, they have given contemporary funerals a personal and more expressive dimension as the format of traditional funerals becomes increasingly challenged (Fig. 1).[56]

These reforms need to be assessed from a broader context as other factors have brought disposal-related matters under the spotlight. Cemeteries have faced issues of memorial safety and shortage of burial space,[57] but in some cases have widened their range of memorial options.[58] Environmental concerns have also impacted on funerals.[59] Emissions from crematoria were first addressed by legislation in 1990, while more

---

[54] 83.2 per cent of ashes were strewn in the Garden of Remembrance. See 'The Disposal of Cremation Ashes' (1977) *Resurgam,* Vol. 20, No. 1, p. 11 and 'Disposition of Cremated Remains in Great Britain' (2016) *Pharos International,* Vol. 82, No. 4, p. 12.

[55] See Kellaher L.A. (2000) 'Ashes as a Focus for Memorialisation?' *Pharos International,* Vol. 66, No. 2, pp. 9–16. See Kellaher L.A. and Hockey J.L. (2002) 'Where Have All the Ashes Gone?' *Pharos International,* Vol. 68, No. 4, pp. 14–19 and Kellaher L.A. and Prendergast D. (2004) 'Resistance, Renewal or Reinvention: The Removal of Ashes from Crematoria', *Pharos International,* Vol. 70, No. 4, pp. 13–20.

[56] Parsons B. (2010) 'New or Rediscovered', *ICCM Journal,* Vol. 78, No. 3, pp. 47–53. See also Gittings C. (2007) 'Eccentric or Enlightened? Unusual Burial and Commemoration in England, 1689–1823', *Mortality,* Vol. 12, No. 4, pp. 321–349.

[57] See *Cemeteries Report and Proceedings of the Committee together with the Minutes of Evidence taken before the Environment Sub-Committee* (2000) London: The Stationery Office. See also 'Child's Death in Cemetery Raises Questions on Safety and Sensitivity' (2000) *FSJ,* October, pp. 66–72 and Rugg J. and Hussein I. (2003) 'Burying London's Dead: A Strategic Failure', *Mortality,* Vol. 8, No. 2, pp. 209–221.

[58] *Cemeteries.* (2001) Environment, Transport and Regional Affairs Committee HC91-1; *Burial Law and Policy in the 21st Century: The Need for a Sensitive and Sustainable Approach* (2004) London: HMSO; Davies D. and Shaw A. (1995) *Reusing Old Graves: A Report on Popular British Attitudes,* Crayford: Shaw and Sons; Dunk J. and Rugg J. (1994) *The Management of Old Cemetery Land,* Crayford: Shaw and Sons; and 'Lift & Deepen: London Leads the Way', (2007) *ICCM Journal,* Vol. 75, No. 3, p. 10. For grave visiting see Francis D., Kellaher L. and Neophytou G. (2005) *The Secret Cemetery,* Oxford: Berg.

[59] West K. (2007) 'How Green is My Funeral?' *ICCM Journal,* Vol. 75, No. 4, pp. 13–15 and West K. (2010) *A Guide to Natural Burial,* London: Shaw & Sons, p. 153.

Fig. 2. An Asian funeral. *Note:* The scene captured in West London the day after the great storm of 15–16 October 1987. Here an Asian family carries a coffin from their home over a tree to the waiting hearse for the final journey to the crematorium (Author's collection).

recently the effects of mercury and harmful substances released from combustion have made necessary the installation of costly filtration equipment.[60] Although not indicating a shift from cremation, the growth in the number of woodland burial grounds since the first opened in 1995 at Carlisle has been significant. With over 270 sites in Great Britain, they are perceived more as a 'green' mode of burial (Fig. 3).[61] Figures

---

[60]See Hay A. (1985) 'Cremation and the Environment', *Pharos International,* Vol. 52, No. 1, pp. 16–25 and Mallalieu A. (2009) 'Up in Smoke or Six Feet Under', *Pharos International,* Vol. 75, No. 2, pp. 4–9.

[61]'Carlisle's New 'Return to Nature' Cemetery' (1991) *FSJ,* October, p. 9. See also Speyer J. (2006) 'An Argument for Environmentally Friendly Natural Burial', *Pharos International,* Vol. 72, No. 2, pp. 6–8; Woodthorpe K. (2010) 'Private Grief in Public Spaces: Interpreting Memorialisation in the Contemporary Cemetery', in J. Hockey, C. Komaromy and K. Woodthorpe eds, *The Matter of Death: Space, Place and Materiality,* Basingstoke: Palgrave Macmillan. See also Stewart M. (2010) 'Are There Regional Variations in Woodland Burials? Does It Appeal to a Specifically English, rather than British, Culture of Tree and Countryside?' Paper given at the University of Bath's Conference 'A Good Send Off', 19 June 2010. See also Davies D. and Rumble H. (2012) *Natural Burial: Traditional – Secular Spiritualties and Funeral Innovation,* London: Continuum and Clayden A.,

Fig. 3. A woodland burial ground. *Note:* The first woodland burial ground opened in Carlisle in 1995. There are now over 270 sites in the UK ranging the from purpose-designed to former agricultural land now assigned to single-depth interments marked by a tree or shrub (Author's collection).

indicating usage, however, are elusive. Most such grounds encourage the burial of an unembalmed body in a biodegradable coffin with only minimal marking of the grave permitted.[62] Although in theory funeral pyres are a possibility in England and Wales following legal challenges after an open-air cremation in July 2006, obstacles such as planning and emission controls need to be considered.[63] Other disposal methods

---

Green T., Hockey J. and Powell M. (2014) *Natural Burial. Landscape, Practice and Experience*, London: Routledge.
[62] See Moar D. (2000) 'How Green is Green? The Argument for Deep Research', *FSJ*, April, pp. 60–63 and Bradfield J. (1997) 'DIY and Green Funerals – ABN Welfare & Wildlife Trust', *TFD*, August, pp. 7–12.
[63] White S. (2006) 'Funeral Pyres and the Law in England and Wales', *Pharos International*, Vol. 72, No. 1, pp. 19–23; 'Funeral Pyres' (2006) *Resurgam*, Vol. 49, No. 3, pp. 142–151; 'Hindu Pyre Law Probe is Needed' (2007) *Resurgam*, Vol. 50, No. 2, pp. 81–83; Singh G. (2007) 'Sikhs Say 'No' to Funeral Pyres', *Pharos International*, Vol. 73, No. 3, pp. 32–36; Singh H. (2008) 'Sikhs Say 'No' to Funeral Pyres', *Pharos International*, Vol. 74, No. 1, pp. 44–55; White S. (2009a) 'Open Air Funeral Pyres', *Pharos International*, Vol. 76, No. 2, pp. 4–5; White S. (2009b) 'Religion – Human Rights – Open Air Funerals' (2009) *Pharos International*,

have been promoted, but as yet not practised, such as resomation and promession.[64] A further disposal issue responsible for generating much media attention has been the Shipman Inquiry, which highlighted deficiencies in the death certification system.[65] Changes have already been introduced in Scotland, but are awaited by the remainder of the United Kingdom (Fig. 3).[66]

This increasing interest in funerals and their costs has also prompted greater scrutiny of the funeral director's role and the funeral 'industry'.[67] At the extreme, this has led to self-managed funerals where the services of a funeral director have been completely dispensed with or are used solely for specific items such as providing body storage.[68] This issue, together with aspects such as music, alternative rituals and participation, are subjects discussed at publicity-generating events like the Joy of Death Conference in September 2012 and the annual Good Funeral Awards. The need to think about end-of-life issues in general has been stimulated by the annual Dying Matters Awareness Week and also the Death Café movement (Fig. 4).

For the funeral director, contemporary ceremonies necessitate offering the client a broad range of services, products, options and facilities. Unlike care of the deceased and cremation, which are now firmly embedded into the funeral director's work, innovation propelled by stakeholders

---

Vol. 75, No. 4, pp. 10–11; and White S. (2010) 'Funeral Pyres in a Legal Limbo', *Pharos International,* Vol. 76, No. 3, pp. 30–35.

[64]Sullivan S. (2006) 'Water Resolution', *Pharos International,* Vol. 72, No. 4, pp. 14–18; Sullivan S. (2007) 'Water Resomation – A Mercury Free Alternative to Cremation', *Resurgam,* Vol. 50, No. 1, pp. 14–18; and Sullivan S. and Fisher D. (2008) 'Resomation User', *Pharos International,* Vol. 74, No. 1, pp. 3–18. See also Sullivan S. (2009) 'Resomation Update', *Pharos International,* Vol. 75, No. 3, pp. 4–8. See also Pearson F. (2007) 'Flameless Combustion', *Pharos International,* Vol. 73, No. 3, pp. 26–29 and Wiigh-Mäsak S. (2006) 'Promession', *Pharos International,* Vol. 72, No. 1, pp. 3–4.

[65]Smith J. (2003a) *The Shipman Inquiry: Death Certification and the Investigation of Deaths by Coroners,* Second Report, Cm 5853 and Smith J. (2003b) *The Shipman Inquiry: Death Certification and the Investigation of Deaths by Coroners,* Third Report, Cm 5854.

[66]See Burial and Cremation (Scotland) Act 2016.

[67]West K. (1994) 'Seeing Ourselves as Others See Us', *FSJ,* November, pp. 56–63 and '1999 Conference Debate: "This House Believes that DIY Funerals are an Irresistible Trend in the 21st Century"', *Pharos International,* Vol. 66, No. 3, pp. 43–48. Chapters 6 and 8 refers to television documentaries about funeral directors.

[68]Spottiswood J. (1991) *Undertaken With Love,* London: Robert Hale. See also Spottiswood J. (1987) 'A Matter of Love and Death', *Evening Standard,* 30 November, pp. 26–27.

Fig. 4. A display of contemporary coffins. *Note:* A skip and a guitar case form part of the Crazy Coffins range displayed at the London Southbank Centre's Death: Festival for the Living held in January 2012 (Author's collection).

in funeral provision along with clients striving for a unique funeral will continue to drive forward the funeral reform movement and shape the direction of the work.

Chapter 2

From Front Parlour to Funeral Parlour: The Development of the Chapel of Rest and Funeral Home

Retention of the body at home in the interval between death and the funeral has been a long tradition. By the end of the nineteenth century, however, the need for an alternative to the familial environment was all too apparent, with the solution being chapels of rest provided by the funeral director. But the transition to utilising this commercial space was slow and it was not until the 1950s that this finally became routine.

Provision of the chapel of rest along with embalming facilities often necessitated reconfiguration of the funeral director's premises. In time, other aspects would also change, such as stables being converted into garages and mechanisation of the coffin workshop. A further influence was the creation of the branch office structure served from a central location. Increased responsibility created a 'behind the scenes' area dividing operational functions from public visibility.

Death at Home and the First Mortuaries

Throughout history the familial environment has occupied the dual role of being the place where death occurred as well as the place where the body was retained. Deathbed scenes have been a popular subject for artists, the coffin resting at home less so, although William Hogarth's sixth and final engraving of *A Harlot's Progress* (1731) is an exception. The comical perspective of the engraving belies a more unpalatable reality; that decomposition commenced immediately after death and that the only place for the body to be accommodated until the funeral was where the family lived. The situation came to crisis point in the nineteenth century through the expansion of urban areas. In his 1843 review, *A Supplementary Report on the Results of a Special Inquiry into the Practice of Interment in Towns,* Sir Edwin Chadwick's research revealed many accounts of the living conditions where the bodies were kept until the funeral.[1] These confirmed that custody of the body until the funeral was not within the remit of the undertaker; their contact was limited to visiting the house to obtain a body measurement, constructing the coffin and then returning with it so that the deceased could be placed in it. Preparation of the body was a community-centred task, with the midwife performing the washing and dressing.[2] Undertakers could not offer facilities for storing the coffin and public mortuary provision was grossly inadequate even for cases requiring investigation by the coroner. In June 1867, the *BMJ* noted that 'Mortuaries are among the pressing necessities of London', and recounted the stench arising from the non-interment of a body in Wandsworth along with the grotesque spectacle in Hornsey where a 'public post mortem in a churchyard took place in the presence of a gaping crowd'.[3] A large part of the problem arose from the fact that the law requiring provision was discretionary and authorities took advantage of this not to burden themselves with the expense of opening facilities. The Sanitary Act 1866 merely *permitted* boards of health to provide mortuaries.

From the 1870s, the medical press published numerous accounts of insanitary conditions in which bodies were retained along with the continued prevarication by parishes, districts, the Metropolitan Board of Works and the Home Office over the provision of mortuaries.[4] After the Board of Works for the Strand District's petition to the Metropolitan Board of Works to construct mortuary buildings was rejected in 1875, the matter was taken up by *The Times*, which usefully explained the legal position and suggested that they be built in local graveyards.[5] The situation was not

---

[1] Chadwick E. (1843) *A Supplementary Report on the Results of a Special Inquiry into the Practice of Interment in Towns,* London: W Clowes, pp. 31–33, 38 & 47.
[2] Chamberlain M. and Richardson R. (1983) 'Life and Death', *Oral History,* Vol. 11, No. 1, pp. 31–43.
[3] 'Houses for the Dead', *BMJ,* 29 June 1867, p. 777.
[4] See Fisher P. (2009a) 'Houses for the Dead: The Provision of Mortuaries in London 1866–1889', *The London Journal,* Vol. 34, No. 1, March, pp. 1–15 and Fisher P. (2009b) 'Death, Decomposition and the Dead-House: The English Public Mortuary', *FSJ,* May, pp. 90–95. See also Chambers D. (1985) 'The St Pancras Coroner's Court', *Camden History Review,* Vol.13, pp. 22–25.
[5] *The Times,* 1 November 1875.

improved by the Public Health Act 1875, which enabled the Local Government Board 'to compel sanitary authorities in the provinces to provide mortuary accommodation, but in London this power does not exist'.[6]

In 1875, the *BMJ* surveyed facilities in the metropolis and found that out of the 20 districts that replied, just under half had no mortuary accommodation while 13 had no post-mortem room. The largest district was St Pancras, with a population of 230,000, and it could only offer the workhouse to store bodies. With 112,001 inhabitants and accommodation for 40, Poplar had the greatest provision.[7] A small number of cemetery chapels also had mortuaries for reception of the coffin in advance of the funeral, such as the Westminster Cemetery in West London, but these were exceptional. The few mortuaries that had been opened, such as Clerkenwell, Marylebone and Bow, were poorly appointed, leading to a degree of reticence by those who most needed to use them. A report on the health of Marylebone published in 1875 revealed how the storing coffins in the public mortuary had declined over a one-year period. *The Lancet* remarked, 'The duty of educating the poor to overcome their prejudice against using mortuaries is as clear as is the duty of the urban sanitary authorities to provide them.'[8] This was confirmed in 1926 by Bertram Puckle when he noted,

> The thought that the bodies of friends and relations should be taken to a mortuary suggests to the average mind an indignity, a social degradation. The mortuary is regarded as especially provided by the State for the bodies of unfortunate outcasts picked up from the gutter, or dragged from the river, or at the best, as a place where the suicide or a person meeting with some dreadful accident is impounded till a jury can be called together for an inquest. We associate it mentally with the prison and the workhouse.[9]

The Public Health (London) Act 1891 finally made it mandatory for every sanitary authority in the capital to provide a mortuary.[10] Mortuaries

---

[6] See 'Mortuaries in London', *The Lancet,* 9 August 1890, p. 290 and 'Mortuaries', 14 July 1894, p. 94.
[7] 'Mortuaries for the Metropolis', *BMJ*, 25 December 1875, pp. 802–803.
[8] 'Prejudice Against Mortuaries', *The Lancet,* 28 August 1875, p. 331.
[9] Puckle B.S. (1926) *Funeral Customs: Their Origin and Development,* London: Werner Laurie, p. 28.
[10] 'A Public Mortuary and Post-Mortem Room', *The Lancet,* 27 August 1870, p. 318. See Freeman, A.C. (1906a) *The Planning of Poor Law Buildings and Mortuaries,* London: St Bride's Press for Plans of Mortuaries.

took different forms; in 1904 the Borough of Kensington constructed a 'chapel of rest', as it was termed, in Avondale Park, Notting Hill.[11] Despite being located in an area of dense housing, its use was only modest, as the local authority reported in 1927:

> We fear, however, that there is a still a tendency on the part of persons living in tenements of one, two or three rooms to retain in their tenements the bodies of deceased relatives awaiting burials, and that the accommodation afforded by the chapel was greatly overlooked.[12]

Undertaking Premises and the First Chapels of Rest

Descriptions or images of undertakers' premises from the late nineteenth to early twentieth century are relatively scarce. From the few that can be traced, however, a number of observations can be made. Elaborate signage was often a feature, such as at Beckett & Sons and Francis & C. Walters Ltd, in north and east London, respectively. Windows either had a display or gave a view of the interior. A photo dating from around 1912 of Beckett & Sons' premises in Kentish Town Road depicts small marble angels and French wreathes or 'Immortelles' (ceramic flowers under a glass dome for placing on graves). It also includes some hatchments, being diamond-shaped shields bearing coats of arms.[13] Many undertakers featured them, such as S.E. Gregory in Chiswick and branches of Frederick W. Paine. Although the heraldry was likely to be spurious, these devices were popular with undertakers as they linked contemporary funeral service to the work of the historic College of Arms (*TUJ* even ran an eight-part series about their significance).[14] In contrast the windows sometimes revealed 'behind the scenes' activities. An advertisement in 1916 for Wathall & Sons in Derby shows a large window frontage with horse-drawn carriages parked behind.[15] Coffin-making is clearly visible through the six

---

[11]Borough of Kensington Council minutes, 29 March 1904, p. 236 and 5 July 1904, p. 346.
[12]Borough of Kensington Council minutes, 18 January 1927, p. 111.
[13]Parsons B. (2001) *The London Way of Death,* Stroud: Sutton Publishing, p. 90. See also the premises of W.S. Bond at Shepherd's Bush, 'W.S. Bond. Funeral Directors & General Carriage Proprietor' (1907) *TUJ,* March, pp. 65–68.
[14]'Symbolism and Heraldry Relating to the Funeral Trade', *TUJ,* pp. 1902–1903. Examples of hatchments can be seen in the F.W. Paine museum.
[15]Advertisement (1916) *TUJ,* March, p. xxiv. The vehicles in the garage at Co-operative Funeralcare in Woolwich Arsenal remain on view today.

windows looking into Henry Smith's premises on Battersea Park Road in 1907 and also at F.A. Albin in Bermondsey.[16] Funeral arrangements were probably conducted in a small office, although in firms carrying out only a modest number of funerals it is possible that the proprietor's front parlour would be used for such transactions. Some undertakers would have a display of miniature coffins and also handles.

When in 1916 Henry Sherry opened new premises in Marylebone, *TUJ* published a photo of the interior immediately behind the window display. It showed a wooden-panelled room containing a simple desk and chairs. The accompanying text noted that

> There is nothing at all suggestive of the lugubriousness of the final ends of mortality. Of course one can imagine that when a client calls the needful articles of sepulture are not far to seek, but they are not thrown obtrusively at you. There is not even a shaving on view or patent to the olfactory sense.[17]

Evidence exists to indicate that in the last two decades of the nineteenth century undertakers had begun to address the issue of accommodation for the body. At the end of 1880, the Battersea Vestry inspected 23 undertakers' premises to ascertain whether occasional use could be made for this purpose. They reported that three already had private mortuaries and that nineteen 'take charge of corpses… in their shops, or in stables, or sheds'.[18] It is perhaps pertinent to note, however, that 20 years later the coroner for south London ruled that undertakers' premises were unsuitable for the retention of bodies.[19] Nevertheless, from around 1900 a number of examples of undertakers providing mortuary accommodation can be traced. In 1902, the London Necropolis Company, proprietors of Brookwood Cemetery, opened a new station with a private siding for their funeral train

---

[16]'Henry Smith' Advertisement (1907) *TUJ*, May, p. v. Images taken a few years later show the windows to be blacked out. See 'Henry Smith' Advertisement (1910) *TUJ*, February, p. ii; 'Our Visit to Mr Henry Smith's Establishment at Battersea' (1922) *BUA Monthly*, May, pp. 254–255; and 'Two Undertakers' Chapels. How Undertakers are Giving the Public Service' (1930) *BUA Monthly*, September, p. 71. See also Albin-Dyer B. (2002) *Don't Drop the Coffin*, London: Hodder & Stoughton.

[17]'Mr Henry A Sherry's New Business Premises. His Faith in the Renewed Association Life' (1916) *TUJ*, April, pp. 100–101.

[18]'Private Mortuaries', *The Lancet*, 13 November 1880, p. 789.

[19]*South London Press*, 15 February 1902.

in premises on Westminster Bridge Road, adjacent to Waterloo station. Their building included a number of chapels of rest where undertakers could bring the body to await the train journey to the cemetery. Frederick Smith, chief superintendent of the funeral department, commented:

> But the feature of the Necropolis premises is the beautiful mortuary chapels, used, of course, for the reception of bodies en route, or where delay in burial is unavoidable. Any country undertaker who has a funeral in or near London can send his coffin here to remain over-night or until such time as is needful, and the mourners can assemble in the chapel and thence depart to the burial place.[20]

A photograph of the interior of one of their rooms shows the walls with glazed tiling, but devoid of any religious decoration. In contrast, the 'Chappell Ardente' on the top floor of the building had ecclesiastical furnishings including an altar.

An increasing number of firms provided accommodation for the body and advertised their availability in newspapers and on letter headings. The term 'Private Mortuaries' was used at first, but chapel of rest was eventually adopted as the former was linked with the invasive post-mortem examination and the cold communal space for unclaimed and/or infectious bodies. In contrast, a chapel of rest fostered an image of a private, sacred and dedicated environment in which the body could remain undisturbed until the funeral.

In November 1919, *TUJ* published a photograph and description of the chapel opened by Thomas Porter & Sons in Liverpool.[21] It was noted how the chapel had been in much demand. In the same year, Dottridge Bros publicised their 'Mortuary Chamber for the use of trade customers' on the cover of *TUJ*.[22] A photograph and premises plan of an unidentified undertaking premises in Liverpool from around this date shows the mortuary, which was accessed through the men's dining room. The remaining premises comprised stables, a harness room and a covered shed.[23]

---

[20]'Interview with Mr F.E. Smith of the London Necropolis Company' (1909) *TUJ*, April, p. 89. See also Clarke J.M. (2006) *The Brookwood Necropolis Railway*, fourth edition, Usk: Oakwood Press, pp. 35–37.
[21]'A Superb Private Mortuary Chapel' (1919) *TUJ*, August, p. 230. See also 'Private Chapels and Mortuaries' (1934) *BUA Monthly*, January, p. 133.
[22]*TUJ (1919) November cover image.*
[23]Photos in author's collection.

Over the next 20 years many chapels were featured in the pages of *TUJ* and also the *BUA Monthly*.[24] They were often a converted room, for example at Attree & Kent in Brighton.[25] Where this was not possible a chapel was constructed adjacent to the building. Not all premises were suitable and encouragement was still given to the use of the public mortuary, as this note from 1908 reveals:

> The Medical Officer of Islington directed attention to the objectionable practice on the part of undertakers of keeping on their premises before interment dead bodies that are removed, for sanitary or other reasons, from the residences of the deceased. The undertakers have been urged to utilize the mortuary for the purpose, but it seems that not one has taken advantage of the offer. The advisability of instituting legislation to compel undertakers to make use of mortuaries in this way is pointed out by the doctor.[26]

In 1921, Hammersmith funeral director J.F. Fletcher was prosecuted for removing an infectious body to his premises after a sanitary inspector visited and reported that 'the room was said to be used as a polishing shop in winter, but was not actually in use as a workroom'. Fletcher said that 'it had not been used as a living, sleeping room, or workroom, but solely as a mortuary chamber. That on every occasion after such use the room was sprayed with disinfectant'.[27] Two years earlier, the London County Council wrote to local authorities about the practice of undertakers keeping bodies in their premises for 'considerable time awaiting interment'.[28] The embalming pioneer Albert Cottridge described the arrangements:

---

[24] Griffiths J. (1924) 'A Model Funeral Directing Establishment: The Derby & District Funeral Company Limited's Efficient Organisation', *BUA Monthly*, January, pp. 546–549.
[25] 'Interview with Mr A.E. Cockburn of Messrs Attree & Kent Ltd Brighton' (1922) *TUJ*, January, pp. 23–24.
[26] 'Notes' (1908) *TUJ*, October, pp. 213–214.
[27] 'Legal Intelligence: Hammersmith Borough Council v Fletcher' (1921) *BUA Monthly*, August, p. 47 and 'Charges Against an Undertaker' (1921) *TUJ*, August, pp. 271–272.
[28] Metropolitan Borough of Paddington, *Report of the Public Health Committee*, 24 July 1919, p. 275. See also 18 September 1919, p. 386 and 5 September 1919, p. 386, and 'Notes of the Week: Undertakers' Responsibility for Delayed Burials' (1919) *The Medical Officer*, 18 October, p. 149. See also Borough of Kensington

Undertakers are being obliged, increasingly, to make provision on their own premises for the custody of the bodies awaiting burial. Some of them with no special accommodation available actually receive bodies for a day or two in their offices and workshops. In other cases special buildings or apartments have been equipped as mortuary chapels or solely as "utility" reception rooms.[29]

Despite these comments, a number of firms sought to improve their premises. A feature of the Derby and District Funeral Company in *TUJ* during 1924 emphasised its 'modern' facilities and the division between client-facing and backstage functions. A waiting room with coal and electric fires, toilets, a coffin showroom and a chapel of rest were separated from the backstage, where the well-equipped workshop, store of shrouds and coffin fittings, stables and adjacent harness room could be found.[30]

The Co-operative societies that entered the market during the 1920s were often anxious to promote a modern image. In 1933, the Royal Arsenal Co-operative Society opened a branch at Earlsfield in south-west London and included a chapel at the rear of their premises.[31] A similar scheme was adopted by Frederick W. Paine, also in south-west London. While most were located on the premises, where this was not possible an external chapel was constructed at the rear, such as at Sutton and Worcester Park.[32]

In supporting its description, the chapel of rest exhibited an overtly Christian identity. Although the focus was the coffin resting on trestles, a key feature was an altar upon which was placed a brass cross or crucifix with matching candlesticks and vases. These accessories could be purchased from the funeral supply firms. In confirming the ecclesiastical identity, a prie-dieu (prayer desk) could sometimes be found; occasionally a sanctuary lamp was included. The Marylebone firm of William Garstin

---

council minutes, 29 July 1919, pp. 298–299. The accommodation of bodies on undertakers' premises had also been criticised in 1909. See 'Undertakers and Public Mortuaries' (1909) *The Medical Officer*, 20 January, p. 595 and 'Conference of London Sanitary Authorities' (1911) *The Medical Officer*, 15 April, p. 189.

[29]Cottridge A.J.E. (1933a) 'The Professional Undertaker and the Public Health', *Public Health*, January, p. 133.

[30]Griffiths J. (1924) 'A Model Funeral Directing Establishment: The Derby & District Funeral Company Limited's Efficient Organisation', *BUA Monthly*, January, pp. 546–549.

[31]'A Chapel of Repose' (1933) *TUJ*, November, pp. 353–354.

[32]See 'Dedication of a Mortuary' (1929) *BUA Monthly*, December, p. 132. This mortuary in the rear of G. Moss at Clapton, in east London, was demolished c2000.

included stained-glass windows depicting saintly figures behind the altar in their chapel of rest at Wigmore Street in central London, as did C.R. Windley in Sheffield.[33] Overall, these spaces replicated a side chapel of a church or private oratory. That of Thomas Porter mentioned above exemplifies the style. The walls were invariably panelled with wood, the floors carpeted and a few chairs provided. The emphasis on privacy was achieved through only having one coffin in the chapel, to be visited by the bereaved (Fig. 5).

As a new facility for the local community, funeral directors took enormous pride in announcing the opening of their chapel; guests usually included civic dignitaries, such as the mayor and the Medical Officer of Health along with clergy. In October 1933, the Lord Bishop of Willesden dedicated the chapel of rest at Buckley Corner in Kilburn for the firm of James Crook. A religious service comprising a scriptural reading, hymns, prayers and an address became the feature of such events.[34]

The shift, however, by the public to utilise the chapel was slow. In *The Classic Slum*, about life in Salford in the first quarter of the twentieth century, Roberts found that children:

> made a common habit of visiting a house where someone had just passed away to ask reverently to view the body, a request that was never refused. One friend of my youth boasted of having seen thirty-seven corpses over a wide area.[35]

This experience is supported by evidence from a clergyman working in Leeds during the 1930s when he recounted a situation that echoed the findings of Edwin Chadwick 80 years prior:

> In many houses in this city, the birth of a child takes place in the living room downstairs, for there is no spare bedroom where the mother may lie for her confinement. When death enters the house, the body is frequently laid out in the same room. The clergy who have to visit such houses are accustomed to the sight of the family sitting down to meals... in the same room where the corpse is laid out.[36]

---

[33] 'A Famous London Firm: Messrs W. Garstin and Sons Ltd' (1936) *TUFDJ*, December, pp. 392–395 (the windows are now at J.H. Kenyon, 83 Westbourne Grove, London, W2) and 'Funeral Chapel Dedicated' (1936) *TUFDJ*, April, p. 125.
[34] 'A Chapel of Rest' (1933) *TUJ*, November, pp. 351–352.
[35] Roberts R. (1971) *The Classic Slum: Salford Life in the First Quarter of the Century*, Harmondsworth: Penguin Books, p. 124.
[36] Hammerton H.J. (1952) *This Turbulent Priest: The Story of Charles Jenkinson, Parish Priest and Housing Reformer*, London: Lutterworth Press, p. 73. For a film

Fig. 5. A chapel of rest. *Note:* Surrounded by many floral tributes a coffin is displayed in the chapel of rest at A. France & Son in Holborn. During the inter-war period the chapel of rest became an increasingly important feature of funeral directors' premises as families preferred to have the coffin accommodated away from the home in the interval between death and the funeral (Courtesy of A. France & Son).

A case recounted in 1933 by the Bishop of Southwark, Cyril Garbett, was even more dramatic:

> The ground floor of a house in London was recently occupied by two families, consisting of four adults and fourteen children. One family lived, fed, and slept in the front room, the parents and the two children on a mattress spread on the floor. The large family of ten had to itself the kitchen, a back room, and a small recess for furniture. This house was in a bad state of repair, damp, and overrun with rats. Measles broke out among the children, two of them died

---

documentary about the overcrowded housing conditions in Notting Hill, see *Kensington Calling* (1930).

from the complications that followed, largely due to the unhealthy house in which they had been living. When the undertaker came with the coffin for the body of one of the children he had to kill a rat that was trying to get at it.[37]

In 1937, the NAFD received a leaflet issued by the Housing Centre recognising the need for chapels but it was not envisaged that funeral directors be the providers: 'advocating the need of more Chapels of Repose and seeking to encourage their building by local authorities who already have power vested in them so to do, and also recommends the idea to church, chapel and councils.'

The editor of *TNFD* recommended thus: 'What we do wish to suggest, however, is that those who have made this provision should make the fact known widely in their area, realising that this service of theirs is an asset and that it doesn't want dissipating.'[38]

During the 1930s there was an increasing preference to use chapels when they were provided. In 1936, *The National Funeral Director* reported the opening of a chapel of rest by the Llandudno firm of W. Dobinson as 'one of the few, if not the only one in the whole of North Wales.'[39] In Leeds, William Dodgson included a chapel of rest in their new premises opened in 1938, but noted that:

> Customs died hard, and the public of the district have not looked favourably on mortuaries or mortuary chapels and the public mortuary facilities in the city leave much to be desired, but this new chapel of rest has been in almost continuous use since its completion, and this is surely a definite indication that the firm have provided something that has made a sure and speedy appearance, and also something that is proving of great utility and service to a community that has not hitherto found beauty and solace in the public accommodation provided.[40]

---

[37] Garbett C.F. (1933) *The Challenge of the Slums,* London: Society for Promoting Christian Knowledge, p. 5.
[38] 'Editorial Notes: Chapels of Rest' (1937) *TNFD,* April, p. 246.
[39] 'The Mortuary Chapel' (1936) *TNFD,* December, p. 129.
[40] 'The need for chapels of rest. Messrs Dodgsons' New Building at Leeds' (1938) *TNFD,* February, p. 193. For criticism of the mortuary at Southend see 'Inadequate Mortuary at Southend' (1925) *The Medical Officer,* 9 May, p. 209.

Similar sentiments were expressed when Seale & Sons of St Budeaux in Plymouth provided a chapel:

> Hitherto the idea of a rest room or chapel at St Budeaux was unknown to the people, and even today relatives, in the main, still prefer to have their dead till the day of burial. Under no circumstances does he [the funeral director] press the use of the chapel on relatives either before the funeral or for the funeral... After I have prepared a body and placed it temporarily in the chapel, relatives have come and seen, and have been so impressed as to ask that it should remain there till the day of the funeral. The chapel is being used more and more without any special advances on my part.[41]

In her study of laying-out women in Coventry, Sheila Adams attributes their decline to the arrival of the chapel of rest:

> Many working class families probably welcomed the introduction of the Chapels of Rest, attached to the undertaker's premises in the early 1930s. The body could be removed from the house and could remain at the undertaker's until the funeral. The final resting place of the body changed from the private sphere of the home, associated with the rationality of care, to the private sphere of the funeral director which was associated with scientific rationality.[42]

The above is confirmed by Roberts as he notes that it was a growing desire for privacy by working-class families that led to the breaking of the tradition of the coffin remaining at home.[43] A similar thought is expressed by an informant in Bolton to Christine Kenny:

---

[41] 'A Searle and Son, St Budeaux Plymouth: New Establishment on Modern Lines' (1938) *TUFDJ*, November, pp. 403–404. See also 'Two Undertakers' Chapels. How Undertakers are Giving the Public Service' (1930) *BUA Monthly*, September, p. 71.

[42] Adams S. (1993) 'A Gendered History of the Social Management of Death in Foleshill, Coventry, During the Interwar Years', in D. Clark ed., *The Sociology of Death: Theory, Culture, Practice,* Oxford: Blackwell.

[43] Roberts E. (1989) 'The Lancashire Way of Death', in R. Houlbrooke ed., *Death, Ritual and Bereavement,* London: Routledge.

> I think most people were relieved when the undertaker took over. I mean, it wasn't very nice was it, having a dead body in the house? It's morbid and I suppose it could be very frightening as well, especially if you were living alone.[44]

Although the public may have been reticent to embrace this change, as more funeral directors provided chapels their use became gradually accepted. But the shift also reflected the increasing preference for cremation. Phil Gore attributes the rise of use of the chapel of rest in Kent during the 1930s to delays in funerals taking place; in some cases this was due to the increasing use of one central cemetery rather than a multitude of parish churchyards, before the shift was made towards cremation.[45] It should also be noted that funeral directors were not alone in providing chapels of rest; they can be found is some crematoria. During the 1920s, Golders Green Crematorium advertised that it had a 'Private mortuary available for reception at any time pending the completion of funeral arrangements.'[46] South London (1936), St Marylebone (1938) and Mortlake (1939) also had chapels of rest, as did the new chapel at Gunnersbury Cemetery.[47]

Custody of the body and the establishment of chapels of rest were only one aspect of the funeral director's work that necessitated change to the premises. As Chapter 5 will detail, the gradual replacement of horse-drawn vehicles resulted in firms converting their stables into garages, while as Chapter 4 shows, mechanisation transformed the workshop as powered tools were increasingly utilised in the construction of coffins. Furthermore, the purchase of ready-made coffins reduced the need for timber storage. Additionally, the next chapter will indicate that custody of the body required room for its storage and treatment. Changes were also made to the front of house with dedicated space for receiving clients and a private office for arranging funerals. As was noted in Henry Sherry's premises mentioned above, a concerted effort was made to remove any overt reminders of death, although windows containing urns for ashes and smaller items of monumental masonry denoted the

---

[44]Kenny C. (1998) *A Northern Thanatology: A Comprehensive Review of Illness, Death and Dying in the North West of England from the 1500s to the Present Time*, Dinton: Quay Books, p. 75.
[45]Gore P. (2001) 'Funeral Ritual Past and Present', in J. Hockey, J.S. Katz and N. Small eds, *Grief, Mourning and Death Ritual*, Buckingham: Open University Press, p. 216.
[46]Advertisement (1924) *TUJ*, p. 87.
[47]See *The Builder*, 22 January 1937, Vol. CLII, No. 4903.

commercial activity. It was in this environment that strict demarcation ensured the areas required to be hidden remained inaccessible to the bereaved.

The Funeral Home Arrives

As has been indicated, from the 1920s funeral directors increasingly acquired custody of the body in the interval between death and the funeral. The chapel of rest replaced the family home as the place of repose while the task of preparing the body, formerly undertaken by the laying-out woman, now came within the remit of the funeral director. As the next chapter will outline, control of the body gave funeral directors greater opportunity to practise embalming. Meanwhile, a further opportunity to provide a greater level of client care was on the horizon: the construction of purpose-built funeral homes, with owners of funeral businesses looking to colleagues across the Atlantic for inspiration. The American funeral historians Robert Habenstein and William Lamers describe the rise of the funeral home as 'a consolidation of three functional areas, the clinic, the home, and the chapel, into a single operational unit' and for funeral directors in Britain they merged client care, body preparation and operational activities.[48] Laderman notes that as 'a domesticated space of death, the funeral home upset conventional boundaries between the religious and the profane, commerce and spirit, private and public'.[49]

Between 1925 and 1940, *TUJ* published many accounts by British funeral directors of their fact-finding visits to funeral homes overseas. During 1927, the London funeral director Stanley Leverton toured funeral homes in Chicago and New York and described the premises he encountered:

> The Americans are on a different footing altogether from us, because their funerals are very much more elaborate and very much more expensive. Their 'funeral homes' – as undertakers' establishments are called – have to be seen to be appreciated.

---

[48]Habenstein R.W. and Lamers W.M. (1995) *The History of American Funeral Directing,* third edition, Milwaukee: National Funeral Directors Association, p. 285.
[49]Laderman G. (2003) *Rest in Peace: A Cultural History of Death and the Funeral Home in Twentieth-Century America*, Oxford: Oxford University Press, pp. 24–25.

> I went to one in Chicago. On the first floor, in a great square lounge, were assembled between twenty and thirty people. It never dawned on me for a moment that I was in the presence of the dead, until I noticed, leading out of this central hall, eight or nine smaller rooms. Each one of these was tastefully decorated and furnished in a very definite period, and in several of them were bodies awaiting interment. They had been embalmed and, in many instances, were most beautifully dressed – some just reclining on couches before being coffined. And it was thus that they were viewed by the relatives and friends. The floral decorations were lavish, and the whole scene was a thing of exquisite beauty. Those little rooms are not called 'chapelles ardentes' but 'rooms of rest'.[50]

Joseph Heath visited America in 1929 (along with Stanley Leverton) and noted how the recent changes to his Sheffield premises were

> very similar in outward appearance to the famous Blair Funeral Home in Philadelphia. One might almost have thought we had modelled it on American lines. But that is not so; it is purely an English development made necessary by the requirements of modern business.

However, he conceded that his business in Earlham Street was 'the nearest approach to the American funeral home that I have seen in England, and yet it is essentially English and typically Yorkshire.'[51] The United States clearly impressed Joseph Heath as he made a return visit in 1938.[52]

---

[50] 'Funeral Homes and Rooms of Rest: The American Way. A Chat with Mr Stanley Leverton J.P.' (1927) *TUJ*, October, pp. 359–361. See also 'British Institute of Embalmers. Interesting Educational Meeting. Address by Messrs Stanley Leverton and G.H. Greene' (1928) *BUA Monthly*, January, pp. 159–161.
[51] 'An English Funeral Home. A Sheffield Firm's Enterprise – Mr Joseph Heath Compares Results after American Visit' (1929) *TUJ*, September, pp. 293–296 and 'British Institute of Embalmers. The Value of America to Britain in Sanitation Work' (1929) *TUJ*, December, pp. 381–384.
[52] 'Mr Joseph Heath's Busy Month. Return Trip to Texas' (1938) *TUJ*, December, p. 433. See also 'Educational Visit to America' (1930) *TUFDJ*, July, pp. 217–220 and 'Mr Kirtley Nodes' South African Tour' (1940) *TUFDJ*, November, pp. 285–287. See also 'Lessons from an American Tour. Mr John Summers of Cardiff Sees Ideal Funeral Home' (1940) *TUFDJ*, February, pp. 87–89. The first account in

Representatives of the BUA visited Canada and America in 1929 and were shown funeral homes, toured cemeteries, witnessed an embalming demonstration and attended the national convention.[53] *TUJ* published accounts of further trips; in 1935 W. Oliver Nodes returned to England and commented that he had been given 'every possible opportunity of learning from them, of showing all that there was to be seen, and encouraging us to go back and help in the development of the profession in our country'.[54] In 1938, the English embalming pioneer Arthur Dyer wrote of his experiences after touring American embalming colleges.[55]

While only a modest number of purpose-built funeral homes opened in the 1930s, many funeral directors were keen to adapt their premises. Heath's in Sheffield was one of a number of conversions of existing premises into a funeral home. Between the late 1920s and 1939 many others followed: Turner in Halifax,[56] N. Wheatley & Sons at Station Road in Birmingham,[57] N. & C.R. Windley in Sheffield,[58] Ingram's at Woking,[59] James Williamson of Perth in impressive premises overlooking the River Tay,[60] Summers in Cardiff (John Summers later wrote about 'The Ideal Funeral Home')[61] and Jennings of Wolverhampton.[62] In August 1937, the

---

English funeral publications of American funeral practices is by Dyer A. (1913a) 'American Methods and Some Suggestions for Adoption in the British Isles' *TUJ*, July, pp. 199–202.

[53]'The Canadian–American Tour. BUA Delegation's Enjoyable Time' (1929) *TUJ*, November, pp. 351–353.

[54]'Four Britishers Visit USA' (1935) *TUJ*, June, p. 175.

[55]'Arthur Dyer's Visit to the USA. His Attendance at Research Clinic' (1938) *TUFDJ*, September, pp. 429–431.

[56]'A Provincial Funeral Home. Mr Ernest Turner Sets a New Standard in Halifax' (1935) *TUJ*, November, pp. 373–374.

[57]'New Premises at Birmingham: N. Wheatley & Sons Ltd' (1938) *TUFDJ*, December, pp. 441–442.

[58]'Funeral Chapel Dedicated' (1936) *TUFDJ*, April, p. 125.

[59]'A Woking Funeral Service. Messrs Ingram & Sons' Establishment Described' (1937) *TUFDJ*, March, pp. 71–73.

[60]'The Establishment of James Williamson of Perth: A Scottish Funeral Home with Ideal Service in Charming Surroundings' (1939) *TUFDJ*, March, pp. 87–88.

[61]'Cardiff's Modern Funeral Establishment. Messrs J. Summers and Son Look Ahead' (1937) *TUFDJ*, September, pp. 301–303. See also Summers J. (1940) 'Lessons from an American Tour. Mr John Summers of Cardiff Sees Ideal Funeral Home', *TUFDJ*, February, pp. 87–89. See also 'James Summers & Son Ltd Open the First Funeral Home in Wales', (1954) *FSJ*, August, pp. 362–364.

[62]'F Jennings & Sons, Wolverhampton. A Century of Steady Service' (1946) *FSJ*, September, pp. 317–318.

Northover Funeral Service in Reigate, Surrey completed a conversion and its opening was featured in *The Times:*

> In days not too far distant most Englishmen died in their beds at home; the experience of funeral directors was that out of every 100 deaths 90 had so taken place. Now at least 50 per cent die in hospitals, nursing homes, or other institutions, and certain conventional usages with regard to funerals are becoming things of the past.
>
> Next month there will be dedicated here, in a Georgian house known as The Barons, a chapel which forms part of a modern funeral establishment designed by Messrs. Northover and Sons to meet the needs of a new age...There are reception rooms for the relatives, chapels of rest, and rooms set apart to meet the comfort and convenience of the mourners.
>
> Everything, including the religious service, can take place in this house... The body can be removed from the place where it lies, embalming – this is usual procedure – and placed in one of the chapels of rest in the building.
>
> Embalming is now advocated, particularly in cases where rooms in small or poor homes are used as death-chambers. In every large city and town, it is stated, this service is now available.[63]

The goal was for funeral directors to possess purpose-built funeral homes and in the late 1930s a small number of landmark premises were constructed. The year 1937 appears to be significant and four were featured in *TUJ*.[64] The first was for the Birmingham Co-operative Society, which built new offices, chapels of rest, a service chapel, mortuary, embalming

---

[63]'Modern Funeral Practice: Aid to Mourners' Comforts', *The Times*, 17 August 1937. See also 'Funeral Home at Reigate' (1937) *TNFD,* October, p. 94. The firm established Northover Funeral Airways in the 1950s (operating from Croydon Airport) and also the Northover Memorial Park for the scattering and burial of ashes (see *FSJ,* July 1952, p. 358). Their funeral home closed in 1978 and the park is now run by the local authority.

[64]One facility that was not featured in the *TUJ* during 1937 was the funeral home opened by the Huddersfield Industrial [Co-operative] Society Ltd. See 'A Huddersfield

room, workshops, garages, staff facilities and residential accommodation on a 1,500-square-yard site.[65] The second was a smaller facility comprising an office, chapels of rest and a preparation room opened by J.R. Holt Ltd at Rossendale in Lancashire in April 1937.[66] The third was for William Nodes Crouch End in north London. Although only comprising offices, a coffin display room and a service chapel – preparation room, coffin workshop and garages were at a different location – this imposing building was designed to match the progressive architectural vocabulary employed in the immediate vicinity, particularly the Scandinavian-inspired town hall. Externally, the ground floor was clad in black granite while the interior was panelled with walnut. A driveway at the side of the building eased the loading of the coffin onto the hearse.[67] In November, the Richmond-based firm of T.H. Sanders opened their purpose-built funeral home on Kew Road (Fig. 6).[68] It followed a similar scheme to Nodes and Holt as behind-the-scenes activities took place away from the site and the premises comprised a service chapel, two private chapels and offices. All were in the prevailing art deco style; a further smaller example is of W. Nodes' premises at Wood Green.[69] Those with embalming theatres were particularly highlighted as being up-to-date. Nodes' mortuary in Crouch End was fitted with white tiles, had direct lighting, ventilation, hot water, a cabinet

---

Chapel of Repose', *The Huddersfield Daily Examiner,* 15 April 1937 and 'A Local Chapel of Repose', *The Huddersfield Daily Examiner,* 19 April 1937.
[65]'Birmingham Co-operative Society's New Funeral Service' (1937) *TUFDJ,* April, pp. 105–107. The premises was demolished in the early 1990s. See *FSJ,* April 2007, pp. 94–96.
[66]'Rossendale's First Funeral Home' (1937) *TUFDJ,* May, pp. 141–142.
[67]'Funeral Directing in North London: Opening of William Nodes' New Premises' (1937) *TUFDJ,* October, pp. 339–341. See also 'The Funeral Home Comes to One of London's Most Densely Populated Boroughs' (1937) *TNFD,* October, pp. 108–109. For other chapels of the period see 'A Beautiful Building at Wood Green' (1933) *BUA Monthly,* December, pp. 117–118; 'A Private Rest-Room with Unique Decoration' (1933) *BUA Monthly,* December, p. 123; and 'Wood Green Chapel of Rest' (1934) *BUA Monthly,* October, p. 85. The decoration of this chapel at A.G. Hurry in St John's Wood High Street was carried out by his son, Leslie George Hurry (1909–1978), a theatrical designer. See Parsons B. (2014e) *The Undertaker at Work: 1900–1950,* London: Strange Attractor Press, p. 206.
[68]'Eighty Years' Progress: New Chapel and Premises for Old Established Business at Richmond, Surrey' (1937) *TUFDJ,* November, pp. 357–376. See also Parsons B. (2005d) 'T.H. Sanders: A History', *BIFD Journal,* Vol. 19, No. 1, pp. 28–31.
[69]Advertisement (1938) *TNFD,* January, p. 171.

Fig. 6. A funeral home. *Note:* A few purpose-built funeral homes were constructed in the UK during the 1930s. One of the few to survive is T.H. Sanders in Richmond, Surrey. The building to the left comprises two chapels of rest and a service chapel with staff offices above; to the right are the funeral arranging offices. Of the elegant design the *Richmond and Twickenham Times* commented, 'From outside, the brickwork of the new building harmonises with the older part, while the central tower and the plain cross in the brickwork are reminiscent of church architecture... Every night a warmly tinted light shines from the tower, being electrically regulated to start earlier as the days grow shorter, so that the dead will not seem to have been forgotten and left in darkness'. This image dates from the end of 1937 when T.H. Sanders acquired a Rolls Royce fleet (Author's collection).

for sterilised instruments and a 'valentine jar' (a receptacle containing embalming fluid suspended from the ceiling) for gravity injection.[70]

A number of comments can be made about the arrival of the funeral home in this country. First, funeral homes shared a key parallel with

---

[70]'Modern Preparation Room' (1935) *TUFDJ,* September, p. 293. See Parsons B. (2014e). *The Undertaker at Work: 1900–1950,* London: Strange Attractor Press, p. 210.

the early British crematoria: they were without architectural precedent. Although funeral directors would have had access to a limited number of illustrations of American funeral homes published in *TUJ*, they would have relied on their architect to interpret the brief. In each example above, they were designed by local architects who prepared successful schemes. Continuing the parallel, a second point was that crematoria and funeral homes have both public and private areas. In respect of the crematorium, the former is the chapel while the crematory the latter; in the funeral home the arrangement office and chapel are for the use of the public but access to the mortuary, embalming room, coffin workshop and garage must be restricted to staff. The delineation of space was essential to ensure that possible contact with the 'backstage' function, particularly body preparation, was eliminated. The third point was that some of the funeral homes had chapels in which a service could be conducted prior to burial or cremation. While clergy may have objected to their use on account of services not being held in a parish church this is not apparent from contemporary accounts. Indeed, the presence of clergy or particularly a bishop at the dedication could be identified as tacit approval of their provision. Although there was discussion in the trade press as to whether they should be dedicated or consecrated and thereby rule out use by those of other or no denomination, it would appear that the former did not have any bearing on their use.[71] However, one bishop did direct that the burial service should not be conducted in a funeral director's chapel.[72]

The final point was that although a small number of British funeral directors were inspired to innovate, they were keen not to be held responsible for the 'Americanisation' of funerals. There is much evidence to show, however, that they were clearly influenced by the progress of their transatlantic colleagues. The introduction and promotion of embalming, the opening of chapels of rest and the construction of funeral homes mirrored the development of the American industry albeit with an interval of three decades.[73] But while some British funeral directors were only too willing to make 'fact-finding' visits to funeral homes, embalming schools and conventions in their quest for professionalisation, others questioned the merit of changing traditions. One correspondent to *TUJ* stated that

---

[71]'Notes' (1936) *TUFDJ*, December, p. 384. See also 'Chapels of Rest' (1944) *TNFD*, October, p. 133. This was not always the case. See 'Chapels of Rest. Bishop of Wakefield's Direction to Clergy' (1944) *FSJ*, October, pp. 289–290.
[72]'Bishop and FD's Chapels' (1944) *TUFDJ*, October, p. 277 & 289–290.
[73]The costing of funerals can also be added to this list. See 'American Burial Methods of Costing' (1931) *TUJ*, November, p. 369.

> [I did] not admire American funeral trappings, and could see no reason for trying to secure their adoption in this country... It is true we are governed by tradition more than the Americans; but there is always the possibility that our traditions may be right. Let each nation follow its own genius and instincts. In these islands our traditions are based on simplicity, and where they have not been warped by town and city influences funerals are marked by reverence.[74]

Indeed, the funeral homes opened in Britain during this period mirrored the findings of those in America, as described by James Farrell:

> To induce people to patronize funeral homes, funeral directors tried to make our places of business as cheerful and pleasant as possible. They removed coffins and caskets from their show windows, and replaced them with flowers or potted palms. They divided the reception room from the show room, eliminating evidences of death from the first encounter with the client. And, when possible, they furnished the funeral parlor in the full fashion of the day. The result was 'well-fashioned', cheerful establishments where you will find well-appointed offices where business can be privately transacted [and] luxurious funeral parlors where funeral services can be quietly conducted. The cheerful luxury of these fine homes invited public patronage, even as it paralleled styles in cemetery and casket design, directing attention away from death and bereavement and towards the trappings of death.[75]

Following the opening of Williamson's premises in Perth during 1939, *TUFDJ* noted:

> Ten years ago any suggestion of establishing a funeral home in Britain would have been regarded as being ultra-modern,

---

[74]'American Methods' Letters to the Editor (1928) *TUJ,* March, pp. 87–88.
[75]Farrell J.J. (1980) *Inventing the American Way of Death 1830–1920*, Philadelphia: Temple University Press, p. 175. See also Salomone J.J. (2003) 'The Evolution of the Funeral Home and the Occupation of the Funeral Directors', in C.D. Bryant ed., *Handbook of Death and Dying. Volume Two: The Responses to Death*, Thousand Oaks: Sage Publishing, pp. 575–586.

with, perhaps, an expressed disapproval of the introduction of American ideas in funeral directing in a land steeped in tradition and custom that was entirely disinclined to change.

There has been a change. London first conceived a funeral establishment on modern lines followed with something that was typically a British creation; the provinces followed with something equally good but at the same time appropriate to the needs of their clients.[76]

Ironically, Williamson's had introduced the ultimate in American practices (noted by Stanley Leverton above) – viewing the body on a bed and not in a coffin was a concept hitherto unknown in Britain, certainly not widely replicated.[77] *The Journal* continued to publish photographs and descriptions of other overseas funeral homes; in 1938 the premises of David T. Cook in Johannesburg along with Human and Pitts in Cape Town were both featured.[78] Others not featured in *TUJ* but worthy of mention include Frederick W. Paine's large funeral home at Raynes Park in south-west London. The most substantial facility to be built in Britain was the Art Deco Scales Funeral Service in Blackburn, dating from 1940.[79]

The construction of funeral homes was effectively brought to a halt by World War II. Although funeral directors were encouraged to address changing needs towards the end of 1944, it was not until the 1950s when building restrictions were lifted that new premises began to be built.[80] The *National Funeral Director* responded by publishing plans and illustrations depicting the ideal funeral home; all were American in their conception.

---

[76]'The Establishment of James Williamson of Perth: A Scottish Funeral Home with Ideal Service in Charming Surroundings' (1939) *TUFDJ*, March, p. 87.
[77]'Editorial: Chapels of Repose' (1938) *TUFDJ*, March, pp. 99–100.
[78]'Two South African Funeral Establishment: Contrasts in Modern Style' (1938) *TUFDJ*, March, pp. 85–87. For an image of Human & Pitts premises in Cape Town in the 1970s see *TFD*, September 1974, p. 436.
[79]'The Scales Funeral Service Ltd Blackburn. Remodelled Premises Opened by the Mayor', *TUFDJ*, July 1940, pp. 191–193. The building has since been demolished. See also 'Blackburn's First Chapel of Repose' (1938) *TUFDJ*, February, p. 65; 'Editorial: Chapels of Repose' 1938 *TUFDJ*, March, pp. 99–100; and 'The Scales Chapel of Repose' (1938) *TNFD*, March, p. 223.
[80]'Reconstructing Your Premises. Be Equipped Ready for Fullest Service' (1944) *TUFDJ*, August, pp. 235–237.

For reasons of cost, the industry favoured the adaption of existing premises, although a modest number of funeral homes were constructed.[81]

In the years following the creation of the National Health Service in 1948 it was becoming evident that deaths were increasingly taking place away from the family home. From there the body went to the funeral director's premises. Custody of the body along with its treatment and presentation effectively dispensed with the female members of the community who undertook the task of laying out. Roberts discovered an increasing desire for privacy and a 'change in neighbourhood relationships' during the century, which led to people abandoning the services of this gendered responsibility.[82] One estimate was that by 1955, over 50 per cent of clients used the chapel of rest.[83] In 1969, a Croydon funeral director estimated that around 95 per cent of all who died in towns now lay at a funeral director's premises between death and the funeral. He also said that 85 per cent of deaths now took place in hospitals, although this figure is not supported by the data.[84]

The need for custody other than in the home can be seen to reflect changes that occurred in the 1950s with the building of new styles of residential accommodation. Smaller houses of open-plan design, as well as flats reached by comparatively narrow staircases and passenger lifts, prevented coffins being accommodated. The house was no longer compartmentalised with a 'best' room set aside for the reception of a coffin.[85] In 1962, the Birmingham funeral director Arthur Painter commented:

> The redevelopment of our Cities is bringing with it many problems for the funeral director. Old established firms in

---

[81] See 'The Modern Funeral Establishment' (1946) *FSJ*, January, p. 19; 'Everything on One Floor' (1947) *FSJ*, January, p. 16; 'Chapel of Rest and Preparation Room. Extensions to Todmorden Fd's Premises' (1949) *FSJ*, March, pp. 160–163; Scales W. (1949a) 'The Layout of Funeral Premises', *TNFD*, May, pp. 507–509 and June, pp. 571–573; Scales W. (1949b) 'When You Build a New Funeral Home', *TNFD*, August, pp. 66–68; and Hall A.C.A. (1949) 'When the Funeral Director Provides a Chapel', *FSJ*, June, pp. 352–353. See also 'Dedication of Chapel of Rest. Funeral Director Sense of Responsibility' (1949) *TNFD*, February, pp. 338–339.
[82] Roberts R. (1971) *The Classic Slum: Salford Life in the First Quarter of the Century*, Harmondsworth: Penguin Books, p. 197.
[83] 'Private chapels are in demand' (1956) *TFD*, May, p. 94.
[84] Ebbutt T.H. (1969) 'Planning a Generation Ahead for Funeral Requirements', *FSJ*, January, pp. 17–22.
[85] Jupp P.C. (1990) *From Dust to Ashes: The Replacement of Burial by Cremation in England 1840–1967*, The Congregational Lecture 1990, London: The Congregational Memorial Hall Trust, p. 24.

> thickly populated areas are being forced away from their locality, and no regard is given to the convenience of the public in these matters when building multi-storey flats in redevelopment areas. Modern multi-storey blocks of flats may be wonderful designs for living, but they won't make much provision for death. [86]

And this was endorsed in the 1970s by William Dodgson of Leeds:

> Friends and relatives used to be invited into the parlour to view the body; but few coffins are now taken into the home, due partly to the increase in the number of high-rise flats. 'You try getting a coffin up 17 storeys', said Mr Dodgson. From this springs the growth of chapels of rest in funeral parlours; though one funeral director reports that only about half of his clients wish to view the body.[87]

As will be highlighted in Chapter 3, custody presented the opportunity for embalming. Where this was not carried out it was necessary to keep the body in a chilled environment. Refrigerated mortuary accommodation was first advertised in the *FSJ* in 1952, while many funeral directors were keen to have their embalming theatres showing post-mortem tables, embalming equipment and body trolleys or hoists.[88]

Despite this increasing responsibility in the care of the deceased, the trade journals noted that in new towns there was plenty of room for the living but funeral directors' premises were not planned and no new cemeteries provided. There was a need for funeral directors to influence development corporations to incorporate fully equipped premises to service new communities.[89] Their provision was clearly a commercial activity and many experienced difficulties in obtaining permission to adapt premises.[90] Local regulation through the Huddersfield Corporation Bill of 1956 attempted to register funeral directors' premises, but this action was not

---

[86] Painter A. (1962) 'Many Problems' *FSJ,* July, pp. 343–344.
[87] Nicholson P. (1974) 'The British Way of Death', *The Illustrated London News,* Vol. 262, No. 6912, pp. 64–66.
[88] Advertisement for Frigidaire (1952) *FSJ,* January.
[89] 'NAFD Notes: Funeral Directors' Premises in New Towns' (1956) *FSJ,* November, pp. 498–499.
[90] 'Rest Rooms' (1961) *FSJ,* June, p. 255.

supported by the House of Lords.[91] Similarly, the siting of a crematorium in the basement of a funeral directors' in Leicester was not granted.[92]

From the 1950s, a small number of funeral homes were being built. The Enfield Highway Co-operative Society opened large premises in 1969.[93] Further Co-operative examples were at Leicester and Rochdale.[94] The Trinder Funeral Home at Banbury was built in 1973.[95] Other firms converted premises, such as C.W. Lyons occupying an old vicarage in Canterbury in 1966.[96] Others in the late 1960s included Deric Scott at Bournemouth in 1966, Hambrook and Johns in Dover, W. & F. Groombridge in Tonbridge and J.E. Gillman in Tooting.[97]

For the larger firm pursuing centralised operations, branch offices simply comprised an office with a chapel; some also had a general office and a small 'holding chapel' for the storage of coffins. F.W. Paine acquired large premises in Kingston to serve their network of branches in south-west London and north Surrey.[98] Comprising a garage for 20 vehicles, coffin store and workshop, mortuary and embalming theatre, service chapel and office accommodation it was more of an operational depot than a funeral home as clients seldom visited the premises. While most branches occupy 'high street' retail accommodation, funeral directors have found locations such as shopping centres have been successful, even if they are simply a satellite 'lock-up' office without a chapel.

---

[91]'Hygienic Standards for Funeral Premises. Huddersfield Corporation Seeks New Powers' (1956) *TFD*, January, pp. 14–15. See Huddersfield Corporation Act 1956, 4 & 5 Eliz, Ch. lxxiii. 'A Blow for Liberty!! NAFD Petitions Successfully' (1956) *TFD*, March, pp. 33–35.
[92]'Private Bill to Permit Crematorium' (1983) *FSJ*, February, p. 68; 'Private Cremation Bill Approved' (1984) *FSJ*, January, p. 16; and 'Setback for Ginns and Guttridge Bill' (1984) *FSJ*, May, pp. 191–192. See also 'Ginns and Guttridge Complain to Ombudsman' (1985) *FSJ*, February, p. 59.
[93]'Bishop Dedicates Co-op Chapels of Rest' (1969) *FSJ*, April, pp. 201–202.
[94]'New Landmark at Leicester' (1971) *FSJ*, October, pp. 515–516; 'A Leicester Landmark' (1972) *FSJ*, August, p. 399; and 'Striking New Home for Leicester Co-op' (1973) *FSJ*, December, pp. 562–563. 'New Co-op Chapel in Rochdale' (1971) *FSJ*, October, p. 519.
[95]'New Funeral Home – a Haven of Peace' (1973) *FSJ*, August, pp. 365–366.
[96]'Canterbury's New Funeral Home. Impressive Premises for C.W. Lyons' (1966) *FSJ*, August, pp. 418–419.
[97]'New Funeral Home for Deric S. Scott Ltd of Bournemouth' (1966) *FSJ*, September, pp. 476–477; 'New Funeral Home Opened in Dover' (1967) *FSJ*, October, pp. 518–519; and 'The House of Groombridge' (1968) *FSJ*, September, pp. 447–450. See also 'Funeral Home – Tonbridge, Kent' (1975) *FSJ* August, p. 353 and 'New Funeral Home in Contemporary Style' (1969) *FSJ*, June, pp. 296–298.
[98]'New Funeral Depot' (1963) *FSJ*, January, pp. 36–37.

Other large operational centres or 'hubs' (as they are termed by Funeralcare) can be found at Manor Park in east London and at Woolwich in south London. Purpose-built facilities include E. Wootten & Sons at Calne in Witshire and the large American-style funeral home in east London occupied by T. Cribb that opened in 1997.[99] Despite full-scale modernisation of branch offices, a number of 'heritage' premises remain.[100] The absence of modernisation can be reassuring to many who will identify and gain comfort from continuity even though it may be no more than a façade, with the services provided having a contemporary dimension.

---

[99] 'FSJ News' (1989) *FSJ,* August, p. 7 and 'Official Opening if Cribb's New Premises' (1997) *FSJ,* January, p. 13.

[100] Surviving examples in London (2011) include Frederick W. Paine, 24 Old London Road, Kingston-upon-Thames; F. Upson, 655 Tottenham High Road, Tottenham; W.G. Miller, 93–95 Essex Road, Islington; A. France & Son, 45 Lamb's Conduit Street, Holborn. Photos of the premises of Ernest Napier & Sons, Notting Hill (demolished in 1976) appear in Evans B. and Lawson A. (1981) *A Nation of Shopkeepers,* London: Plexus. The premises of Francis & C. Walters, Limehouse is depicted and mentioned in Fletcher G. (1962) *The London Nobody Knows,* London: Penguin. The premises was closed c.2005. See also the film *The London Nobody Knows* (1967) featuring the interior of the premises of H.M. Repuke in Islington.

Chapter 3

Caretaker of the Dead

While the previous chapter demonstrated how the new-found role for the funeral director as 'caretaker of the dead' led to the opening of chapels of rest, the focus here is preparation of the body for viewing and transportation. After reviewing the informal care extended to the body by the community, the introduction and progression of embalming is traced, followed by a determination of whether its development was led by demand from clients or supply by the funeral directors. The final section reviews some of the contemporary challenges to embalming.

Laying-Out

Prior to the involvement of the funeral director, it was the laying-out woman who was responsible for the preparation of the dead for burial.[1] This figure was present at terminal rites of passage of life; the beginning and end of life. On occasions these duties would coincide; when, for example, death occurred during childbirth. Laying-out was an informal

---

[1]Chamberlain M. and Richardson R. (1983) 'Life and Death', *Journal of Oral History*, Vol. 11, No. 1, pp. 31–43; Roberts E. (1989) 'The Lancashire Way of Death', in R. Houlbrooke ed., *Death, Ritual and Bereavement*, London: Routledge; Adams S. (1993) 'A Gendered History of the Social Management of Death in Foleshill, Coventry, During the Interwar Years', in D. Clark ed., *The Sociology of Death: Theory, Culture, Practice*, Oxford: Blackwell; Kenny C. (1998) *A Northern Thanatology: A Comprehensive Review of Illness, Death and Dying in the North West of England from the 1500s to the Present Time*, Dinton: Quay Books, p. 75; and Clark H. and Carnegie (2010) *She Was Aye Workin': Memories of Tenement Women in Edinburgh and Glasgow*, Dorchester: White Cockade Publishing.

system of neighbourhood care, commonly found in working-class areas.[2] Laying-out involved thoroughly washing the body and dressing it in clean nightclothes. Alternatively, the undertaker might supply a shroud or robe. Roberts notes that these women observed such rituals as placing pennies on the eyes of the deceased, the same pennies placed on the navel of newborn babies.[3] Similarly, the windows were opened to release odours in addition to the deceased's spirit.[4]

Through their contact with the newly bereaved, Naylor notes that these women were in a position to 'connect undertakers with their source of revenue'.[5] Although reward from families was usually non-financial, Adams points to the fact that it was the same individual who made a further contribution to the post-death arrangements by additionally preparing the funeral tea.[6] It does not appear that laying-out women were contaminated by their encounters with the body; they were honoured and respected by the community.[7] Death was not surrounded by mystique or isolation. This contrasts to the way in which the task is viewed by the hospital nurse.[8]

Funeral directors' records show that on occasions they organised and paid for this service. An entry in Maxwell Bros, Streatham, south London from January 1905 notes 'woman laying out body' at a charge of five shillings.[9] Others arranged by the Kensington firm C.G. Hatt around

---

[2] At least one religious order undertook the laying out of the dead. See Potter G. (1955) *Father Potter of Peckham*, London: Hodder and Stoughton, p. 35.

[3] Roberts R. (1971) *The Classic Slum: Salford Life in the First Quarter of the Century*, Harmondsworth: Penguin Books, p. 197. This was a practice decried when funeral directors assumed the responsibility of care, presumably as unprofessional. See *The Manual of Funeral Directing* (1998) Solihull: NAFD, Ch. 5, p. 3.

[4] A ritual confirmed to the writer by the owner of a nursing home in east Kent (October, 1994). See also Seabrook J. (1967) *The Unprivileged*, Harmondsworth: Penguin, p. 40.

[5] Naylor M.J.A. (1989) *Funeral Rituals in a Northern City*, Unpublished PhD thesis, University of Leeds, p. 55.

[6] Adams S. (1993) 'A Gendered History of the Social Management of Death in Foleshill, Coventry, During the Interwar Years', in D. Clark ed., *The Sociology of Death: Theory, Culture, Practice*, Oxford: Blackwell, p. 161. The author's interview with a funeral director working in the Scottish Borders between 1947 and 1977 confirms non-financial payment, including, in one instance, a pot of jam.

[7] Chamberlain M. and Richardson R. (1983) 'Life and Death', *Journal of Oral History*, Vol. 11, No. 1, p. 39.

[8] Blauner R. (1964) *Alienation and Freedom*, Chicago: University of Chicago Press and Blauner (1966) 'Death and Social Structure', *Psychiatry*, Vol. 29, pp. 378–394.

[9] Maxwell Bros entry no. 2440. Records held in the F.W. Paine museum, Kingston.

1900 give the name of the person engaged along with the amount paid (7 shillings and 6 pence); one entry from December 1898 reads 'To man and woman washing and dressing the body' of a 56-year-old male at a cost of 1 guinea. The presence of the 'man' may be due to the size of the deceased or request of the family.[10]

While the Midwives Act 1902 sought to provide registration and consequent regulation, particularly for childbirth, the work of laying-out women continued until around World War II, and even later in some areas. With the establishment of the National Health Service in 1948, however, in the post-war years care of the dying was transferred to the institution. Adams notes that for reasons of the unpleasantness of putrefaction many were only too glad to assign the responsibility of care and shelter to the funeral director.[11]

Although laying out gave the corpse a degree of dignity through presentation it did not, nor was it intended to, retard decomposition; this was an accepted eventuality over which there was no control.[12] It is plausible that such deterioration could be regarded as confirmation of death. The fear of premature burial (along with cremation and even embalming) was still a real concern until the early part of the twentieth century.[13] In one part this was attributable to a doctor not having to see the body prior to

---

[10]C.G. Hatt Entry 80. Records in the F.W. Paine Museum, Kingston.

[11]Adams S. (1993) 'A Gendered History of the Social Management of Death in Foleshill, Coventry, during the Interwar Years', in D. Clark ed., *The Sociology of Death: Theory, Culture, Practice*, Oxford: Blackwell, p. 164. The author Ayub Khan-Din includes a laying-out character in his play *East Is East*, based on life in working-class Salford during the early 1970s, a comparatively late date for this role.

[12]Conversation by the author in April 2013 with a male resident of Sturminster Newton in Dorset, who assisted his elderly grandmother to lay out people in the town when he was aged 10 years, revealed that during periods of warm weather blocks of salt were placed around bodies in coffins to absorb odours and leakage but potentially preserve the body.

[13]See Bondeson J. (2001) *Buried Alive: The Terrifying History of Our Most Primal Fear*, New York: W.W. Norton; Bourke J. (2005) *Fear: A Cultural History*, London: Virago, pp. 33–40; Dittrick H. (1948) 'Notes and Queries: Devices to Prevent Premature Burial', *Journal of the History of Medicine and Allied Sciences*, Vol. 3, pp. 161–171; and also Tozer B. (1906) 'Premature Burial and the Only True Sign of Death', *The Nineteenth Century*, October, pp. 544–559. TUJ recounts many cases of 'dead' waking up, for example, 'Notes' (1905) *TUJ*, February, p. 26 and 'The Accrington Catalepsy Case', p. xi. See Parsons (2017d) 'Premature Burial and the Undertakers', in S. McCorristine ed., *When is Death?* London: Palgrave Macmillan, pp. 69–85.

certification.[14] Active until the 1920s was the Society for the Prevention of Premature Burial, which called for strengthening of the law concerning death certification along with the building of 'waiting mortuaries'.[15] Life-saving coffins were available until around 1914, after which more sophisticated tests for death gradually became employed. At the BUA conference in August 1927, the 'infallible and harmless' Obiturin fluorescein-based test to prove the differentiation between living and necrose tissue was demonstrated. When it was injected into a living person, the area around the injection site turned green; in a deceased person no discolouration would occur. To the delight, or apprehension, of the conference delegates, James Hurry and Harold Kenyon (the national secretary and president) were both injected.[16]

Some attempts to control the unpleasantness of putrefaction were made by undertakers but these were largely ineffectual. Jack West mentions use of a 'pail of carbolic disinfectant placed under the coffin or a saucer of sliced onions laid on the table'.[17] Gore cites the use of a saucer of ammonia under the coffin and 'a sort of candle thing that burnt'.[18] The pages of trade periodicals published around 1900 advertise items such as disinfecting cones and antiseptic lozenges.[19] In addition, funeral furnishing manufacturers offered sanitary coffins, being an air- and watertight coffin and shell (see Chapter 4). The ice chest was also advertised.

---

[14]Fellows A. (1910) 'Death Certificates: The Weaknesses of the Present Law', *TUJ*, November, p. 266 and 'Death Certificates: Urgent Need of Reform of the Law' (1911) *TUJ*, November, p. 296. See also 'Fear of Premature Burial' (1931) *BUA Monthly*, April, p. 232.

[15]See Freeman A.C. (1906b) 'Waiting Mortuary for the Prevention of Premature Burial', *Burial Reformer*, Vol. 1, No. 5, April–June, pp. 37–39. See also 'Death Tests of a Blue Thread' (1926) *TUJ*, July, p. 209.

[16]'Lecture on Obiturin' (1927) *BUA Monthly*, August, pp. 44–46. For an earlier fluid see 'Notes' (1907) *TUJ*, March, p. 54. Severing an artery to prove death would be unnecessary if embalming was carried out. See 'Editorial Notes. Premature Burial' (1931) *BUA Monthly*, October, p. 89. See also Roe G.C.F. (1932) 'Tests for Cause of Death' *BUA Monthly*, February, p. 183.

[17]West J. (1988) *Jack West Funeral Director: Forty Years with Funerals*, Ilfracombe: Stockwell, p. 113. See also Parsons B. (2014a) *Bunny France: Memoir of a Holborn Funeral Director*, London: A France & Son, p. 15.

[18]Gore P. (1993) *From Undertaking to Funeral Directing – The Development of Funeral Firms in East Kent*, Unpublished MPhil, dissertation, University of Kent, p. 130.

[19]Dottridge Bros Advertisement (1904) *TUJ*, cover image.

Embalming Reintroduced

Although embalming was practised in England during the eighteenth century its commercial origins can be traced back to America where two events identified the efficacy of the treatment.[20] The first was the embalming of President Lincoln following his assassination in April 1865, followed by his transportation from Washington DC to Springfield in Ohio for burial.[21]

The second was the American Civil War, where Dr Thomas Holmes, proclaimed as 'The Father of Modern Embalming in the United States', capitalised upon earlier basic injection techniques used to preserve anatomical specimens as developed by Jean Gannal, William Hunter, John Hunter and others, and proceeded successfully to embalm the bodies of the battle-dead in preparation for transportation, invariably by rail, back to their hometowns.[22] At the end of the war the success of this preserving method brought attention to the fact that the technique might potentially be available for adoption on a commercial basis. Although Holmes, a physician by training, realised the commercial possibilities of embalming, he did not pursue the craft and he, like many other medically qualified practitioners, 'retreated from the field, leaving undertakers to advance into it'.[23] Embalming schools were opened and in classes lasting for three or

---

[20] See Quigley C. (1998) *Modern Mummies: The Preservation of the Human Body in the Twentieth Century*, Jefferson: McFarland & Co for contemporary information about arterial embalming. See also Howarth G. (1996) *Last Rites: The Work of the Modern Funeral Director*, Amityville: Baywood, pp. 95–109 and 147–170 and Bradbury M. (1999) *Representations of Death: A Social Psychological Perspective*, London: Routledge, pp. 113–139 for ethnographic accounts of the work of embalmers. In the US see Palmer G. (1993) *Death: The Trip of a Lifetime*, New York: Harper Collins.

[21] For Lincoln's embalming see Johnson E.C. (1975) 'Cattell's Skill with Lincoln's Remains Publicized Embalming', *Casket and Sunnyside*, Vol. 105, No. 9, September, pp. 16, 18, 20, 53–54 and see also Craughwell T.J. (2007) *Stealing Lincoln's Body*. Cambridge: Belhnap/Harvard.

[22] See Johnson E.C., Johnson G.R., and Williams M.J. (1990) 'The Origin and History of Embalming and History of Modern Restorative Art', in R.G. Mayer ed., *Embalming: History, Theory and Practice*, Stamford: Appleton & Lange; Metcalf P. and Huntington R. (1991) *Celebrations of Death: The Anthropology of Mortuary Ritual*, second edition, Cambridge: Cambridge University Press, p. 211; and Johnson E.C. (1983) 'Civil War Embalming', *The Embalmer*, Vol. 26, No. 4, July, p. 25. See also Faust C.D.G. (2008) *This Republic of Suffering: Death and the American Civil War*, New York: Knopf.

[23] Habenstein R.W. and Lamers W.M. (1981) *The History of American Funeral Directing*, second edition, Milwaukee: National Funeral Directors Association, p. 219.

four days of lecturers demonstrated undertakers about a simple injection technique. Most schools were owned by fluid and instrument manufacturers. One practitioner was Dr Auguste Renouard, who 'got his ideas concerning the best manner of preserving the dead... from the careless shipping of bodies from Denver to the East... which suggested... a more complete and certain preservation of the dead for transportation purposes'.[24] During the 1880s, Renouard established at least three embalming schools while also leading teaching tours.[25]

Concurrently, arterial embalming was being practised in England by physicians including Benjamin Ward Richardson and Professor John Struthers.[26] Their experiments, however, were for the preservation of anatomical specimens or bodies retained for lengthy periods in coroners' mortuaries rather than to fulfil commercial objectives.[27] George Smith, somewhat erroneously described as 'one of the first undertakers in London', advocated the use of Gannal's method of preservation in a pamphlet published in 1840.[28] The first embalmer offering a commercial

---

[24]'Interview with Professor Aug. Renouard' (1906) *TUJ*, September, pp. 241–243. See 'The Lives of the Teacher' (1987) *The Embalmer*, Vol. 30, No. 5, October, pp. 5–6.

[25]Habenstein R.W. and Lamers W.M. (1981) *The History of American Funeral Directing*, second edition, Milwaukee: National Funeral Directors Association, p. 225.

[26]Parsons B. (2005e) 'Benjamin Ward Richardson: A Forgotten Pioneer of Embalming', *The Embalmer*, Vol. 48, No. 4, pp. 16–20 and Struthers J. (1890) 'On the Preservation of Bodies for Dissection', *Edinburgh Medical Journal*, Vol. 36, September, pp. 297–303. See also 'Sir John Struthers on Embalming the Dead' (1898) *TUJ*, July, p. 112 and 'Through the Ages. Historical Survey of Embalming Ancient and Modern' (1942) *TNFD*, July, pp. 9–13. For previous centuries see Dobson J. (1953) 'Some Eighteenth Century Experiments in Embalming', *Journal of the History of Medicine and Allied Sciences*, Vol. 7, pp. 431–441. For a very brief account of the development of embalming in England see Cork N. (1930) 'The Practice of Embalming', *TUJ*, November, pp. 387–289 and December, pp. 422–424 and Swainson E. (1950) 'Embalming: The Scientific Approach', *TNFD*, July, pp. 671–672, August, pp. 713 & 716–717, and September, pp. 761–763. Parallels can be identified in the progress of embalming in Australia. See Chambers D. (1990) *No Funerals on Picnic Day! Victorian Funeral Industry Associations 1890–1990*, Melbourne: Australian Funeral Directors Association.

[27]For further examples of preservation processes see 'Editorial. Preservation of Dead Bodies. The So-Called New, Inexpensive, and Unencumbered Process' (1902) *TUJ*, January, pp. 15–16 and 'Patents Relating to Embalming' (1902) *TUJ*, February, pp. 38–39.

[28]Smith G. (1840) *The Gannal Process By Which the Progress of Decay is Arrested; The Cases of Contagion or Infection Prevented, and the Necessity of Embalming Superseded*. See also *The Times*, 22 January 1839 and *Literary Gazette*, 18 July 1840. See also 'The Embalmer Jean Nicolas Gannal (1791–1852)', *TNFD*, March, pp. 227–228.

service, listed in the 1874 edition of *Kelly's Post Office Directory for London*, was Peter Arthur Itzstein. The entry reads: 'Bodies embalmed and petrified – will keep indefinitely. Terms on application'. Others listed in the 1882 edition were Halford Mills of the Reform Funeral Co Ltd (Professor C. H. Garstin) of Baker Street and Dottridge Bros.[29] In the same year, a representative from Dottridge Bros had attended a convention of what today is known as the National Funeral Directors Association and had approached Dr Auguste Renouard to invite him to visit England on a $5,000-a-year contract over five years to teach embalming.[30] Renouard declined. However, there was increasing interest in embalming; articles, supportive editorials and advertisements for both fluids and practitioners can be found in the trade journals of the period.

In 1900, Dottridge Bros and the British Institute of Undertakers invited Dr Auguste Renouard to London to give undertakers a basic instruction in preservation techniques.[31] It was heralded as an 'Announcement Extraordinary' and undertakers were reassured that Renouard was not coming to England to 'revolutionize funeral customs', but simply to teach a technique of preservation. Classes commenced in August at the University College London with some 25 attending the first class. Popularity demanded a second session and over the one-month period some 48 people registered, with at least 30 graduating – that is being awarded a certificate of attendance, not passing a practical or theoretical examination. The US-based sponsoring company, OK Buckhout, then invited a Canadian, Professor Felix A. Sullivan, to continue the lecture tours.[32]

---

[29] Parsons B. (2006a). 'Halford Lupton Mills', *The Embalmer*, Vol. 48, No. 3, pp. 15–18 and 'A Famous London Firm. Messrs W. Garstin & Sons Ltd' (1936) *TUJ*, December, pp. 393–395. William Garstin & Co was responsible for embalming Lady Dilke, who was transported to Germany in 1874 for cremation. See Parsons B. (2005a) *Committed to the Cleansing Flame: The Development of Cremation in Nineteenth Century England*, Reading: Spire Books, pp. 37–38. See also 'Encouragement for the Embalmer: American Appreciation of English Embalming' (1921) *TUJ*, February, pp. 62–63.
[30] Johnson E.C., Johnson G.R. and Williams M.J. (1988) 'The Introduction of Embalming to England', *The Embalmer*, Vol. 21, No. 4, p. 16. See also Trompette P. and Lemmonier M. (2009) 'Funeral Embalming: The Transformation of a Medical Innovation', *Science Studies*, Vol. 22, No. 2, pp. 9–30.
[31] Parsons B. (2014e) *The Undertaker at Work: 1900–1950*, London: Strange Attractor Press, pp. 3–21.
[32] See Johnson E.C. (1974) 'Life and Times of Felix Sullivan, Noted Embalmer', *Casket and Sunnyside*, Vol. 104, No. 7, pp. 18, 20–21, 23, & 49; 'The Lives of the Teachers. Pioneer Embalming Educators of America. Prof Felix A. Sullivan' (1967) *The De-Ce-Co Magazine*, Vol. 59, No. 1, February, pp. 14 & 22; and 'The Late Professor F.A. Sullivan' (1931) *TUJ*, August, p. 262.

Between September 1900 and his departure two years later, he toured throughout the United Kingdom giving instruction classes to undertakers.

A major development arising mainly from Renouard's visit was the establishment of the British Embalmers' Society (BES) in November 1900 with Henry Sherry as its chairman.[33] The route towards professional status was immediately discernable:

> One of the great advantages from a trade standpoint connected with an association would be that only qualified embalmers be allowed to practice. The business of an undertaker in the ordinary sense of a word cannot be classified under any other heading than that of a trade, and for members of any trade there is no need for registration. But an embalmer, who is a professional man, should obtain some diploma or certificate of qualification which it would be the business of any Society to grant.[34]

The second progressive sign can be seen in the attention given to embalming in the pages of the trade periodicals, particularly *TUJ*, which since the 1880s has published in-depth technical articles, mainly penned by the US practitioners such as Renouard, Sullivan, Thornton Barnes, his brother Carl Lewis Barnes, H.S. Eckels, George B. Dodge and A. Johnson Dodge. A small number of British embalmers also made contributions.[35] From 1902, the short-lived *British Embalmer* was published. Monographs such as *The Art and Practice of Embalming* by Sullivan and *The Modern Funeral: Its Management* by Hohenschuh were also advertised in *TUJ*.[36]

---

[33] 'British Embalmers' Society' (1900) *TUJ*, November, p. 160. For Henry Sherry see 'Buarians of Note: Mr H.A. Sherry London' (1928) *BUA Monthly*, January, p. 138 and 'Interview with Mr H.A. Sherry' (1904) *TUJ*, March, pp. 61–62. For an obituary see 'The Late Mr Henry A Sherry. Father of the British Undertakers' Association' (1934) *TUJ*, January, p. 3.

[34] 'The Early History of Embalming in England. How the British Embalmers' Society was Formed' (1930) *TUJ*, October, pp. 334–335.

[35] For one of the first papers by a British practitioner see Lello S.B. (1902) 'Embalming', *TUJ*, October, pp. 96–98; Goulborn J. (1904) 'Anastomosis, Osmosis, and the Circulation of Fluid in Arterial Embalming', *TUJ*, February, pp. 32–33; and Foggart J. (1904) 'Embalming and Sanitation: Their Value to an Up-to-Date Undertaker', *TUJ*, October, pp. 205–206.

[36] See also Hohenschuh W.P. (1905) 'How to Conduct a Funeral', *TUJ*, September, p. 219. For biographical details see Johnson E.C., Johnson G.R. and Williams M.J. (1990) 'The Origin and History of Embalming and History of Modern Restorative Art', in R.G. Mayer ed., *Embalming: History, Theory and Practice*, Stamford: Appleton & Lange.

Accounts citing the efficacy of the treatment and the fluids used were also included, such as for Col Sir William Lanyon, who died in New York in April 1887 and was transported to London.[37] Halford Mills of the Reform Funeral Co was reputed to be the first American-qualified embalmer offering his services in England.[38] On the cover of *TUJ* in 1896 he included the photograph of a body six months after he had embalmed and transported it to New Zealand.[39]

There is little tangible evidence to show that embalmments were being regularly carried out. A few were reported in *TUJ*, such as those of Sir Arthur Sullivan in 1900, Sir Henry Irving in 1905 and General William Booth in 1912, and also a number of cases where the body was shipped abroad and later reported to be in a satisfactory condition such as that of the singer Madame Patti in 1919.[40] The London section of the BES calculated that its membership carried out a total of 91 embalmments from when Renouard commenced teaching to the end of 1902. The trade press reported that the south-east London undertaker Walter Uden was one of the most prolific embalmers, having embalmed some 45 cases since qualifying under Sullivan. By 1904, the BES had 89 full members, 4 associates and 4 honorary members. The records of J.H. Kenyon record 6 embalmments in 1900, when 659 funerals were undertaken. Although the figure rose to 32 in 1901 and 56 in 1902, in the following decade a steady decline is evident.[41]

One event did, however, assist in highlighting the value of embalming. On 1 July, a railway disaster occurred at Salisbury, claiming the lives of 27; apart from the driver and fireman all were American citizens.[42] Harold and Herbert Kenyon were summoned along with other embalmers. Seventeen cases were embalmed and then repatriated to the United States for burial.

---

[37] See 'Embalming of Col Sir William Owen Lanyon KCM GCB' (1887) *The Undertakers' and Funeral Directors' Journal* and *Monumental Masons Review*, 23 May, p. 53.
[38] Parsons B. (2006a) 'Halford Lupton Mills', *The Embalmer*, Vol. 48, No. 3, pp. 15–18.
[39] Advertisement (1897) *TUJ*, January cover image. Mid-late nineteenth century embalming fluids were arsenic-based; thereafter formaldehyde was the chief constituent. See Whorton J.C. (2010) *The Arsenic Century: How Victorian Britain was Poisoned at Home, Work and Play*, Revised edition, Oxford: Oxford University Press.
[40] Parsons B. (2009b) 'Embalming in the First Half of the Twentieth Century: A Few Notable Embalmments', *The Embalmer*, Vol. 52, No. 1, pp. 11–18.
[41] Parsons B. (2014b) *J.H. Kenyon: A Short History*, London: J.H. Kenyon.
[42] Parsons B. (2014e) *The Undertaker at Work: 1900–1950*, London: Strange Attractor Press, pp. 43–55; Pattenden N. (2015) *Salisbury 1906: An Answer to the Enigma*, third edition, Swindon: The South Western Circle; and Moody J.B. and Fleming G. (2006) *The Great Salisbury Train Disaster Centenary 1906–2006: Voices from the Boat Train*, Salisbury: Timezone Publishing.

From reflecting on the limited progress, it is necessary to ask what hindered the early British embalmers. First, there is evidence to show that the medical profession did not approve of undertakers carrying out embalming. Writing in *The Lancet* early in 1902, Dr John Garson declared:

> it will be seen that embalming is not a matter which should be relegated to the undertaker or someone employed by him to see to, as is too often done with unsatisfactory results. If it is to be practised successfully it calls for as much knowledge, judgement and skill as does the performance of a surgical operation and therefore it should always receive the direct attention of the qualified medical attendant of the deceased.[43]

A similar observation was made at the conclusion of a *BMJ* article appearing in 1898. After outlining the modern process, it stated that 'The methods of preserving corpses neither require unusual skill nor involve great expense'.[44] Although Garson was attempting to protect the physicians' monopoly over contact with the human body both dead and living, he nevertheless had a valid point, as the training of embalmers was brief; undertakers need only to have attended one of the embalming school classes to be awarded a certificate or diploma. As mentioned earlier, it was really a certificate of attendance rather than competence as no examination was held. There was, however, some support for embalming from figures such as the eminent physician, Sir Dyce Duckworth.[45]

A further hindrance was that when embalming was required, it invariably had to be undertaken at the place of death – usually the home. Although, as has been noted in the previous chapter, Dottridge Bros advertised their preparation room from 1903, such facilities were the exception.[46]

---

[43]Garson J.G. (1902) 'Embalming the Dead', *The Lancet*, Vol. 10, May, p. 1302. For a response to this article see Sullivan (1902) *The British Embalmer and Funeral Trades Monthly*, No. 4, June, p. 13. See also Garson J. (1909) 'Principles and Practices of Embalming', *TUJ*, April, pp. 80–81 and May, pp. 106–107 and McWalter J.C. (1907) 'The Prevention of Post-Mortem Putrefaction', *BMJ*, 14 September, pp. 673–674.
[44]'Embalming the Dead', *BMJ*, 28 May, 1898, pp. 1403–1404.
[45]'Shall We Embalm?' (1900) *TUJ*, September, p. 111. Sir Dyce Duckworth (1840–1928) was physician to Edward VII.
[46]An occasional task for undertakers was also the disinfection of the home. See 'Disinfection' (1923) *BUA Monthly*, April, p. 284. See also 'Disinfection and Fumigation' (1935) *BUA Monthly*, January, p. 160 and 'Disinfecting Rooms' (1936) *TUFDJ*, June, p. 182.

The cost of embalming was also no encouragement to its adoption. In 1900, Kenyon quoted the price of an embalmment as between £5 5s and £15 5s.[47] Even in 1920, the London Necropolis Company charged 15 guineas for temporary or permanent embalming.[48]

Perhaps the greatest hurdle, however, was the attitude of the undertaking trade, ultimately responsible for its advocacy.[49] If an undertaker could not accede to its advantages he would be unlikely to promote embalming to his clients. Even more so, how could an undertaker be convinced when he had little responsibility towards the deceased? With delays uncommon, especially in rural areas, and a reasonably steady climate, a mindset of 'out of sight, out of mind' can be detected. It is perhaps significant to note that many of the undertakers presenting themselves for embalming training were from urban areas where delays were likely to be encountered. Only in years to come, with bodies increasingly resting on the undertakers' premises, would the situation be reappraised.

TUJ charted the training given by British pioneers and was generous in its coverage of the subject.[50] For example, in March 1906, the south London funeral director Walter Uden led a three-week class in Preston under the auspices of the Anglo-American School of Embalming.[51] The last US pioneer to visit Britain was George B. Dodge, who gave a lecture tour in January 1910.[52] From then on a small group of British embalmers were responsible for its promotion. Arthur Dyer attended Professor Dodge's

---

[47]*Kensington News & West London Times*, 20 October 1899.
[48]Clarke J.M. (2006) *The Brookwood Necropolis Railway*, fourth edition, Usk: The Oakwood Press, p. 85. An advertisement in *TUJ* for Sullivan's book contained the copy 'Be Up-to-Date; Study Embalming; Make Money' (1914) *TUJ*, February, p. 39.
[49]H.K. Nodes believed the lack of progress was due to the inability to get a reliable embalming fluid. See Professional Progress in England' (1911) *TUJ*, January, p. 5. See also 'Editorial: To Embalming Aspirants' (1901) *TUJ*, February, pp. 35–36.
[50]See 'A London College of Embalming. Interview with the Founders' (1913) *TUJ*, November, pp. 319–321 and Sherry H.A. (1905) 'The Sanitary Advantages of Modern Embalming', *TUJ*, August, pp. 188–190.
[51]'Interview with Mr W. Uden' (1906) *TUJ*, April, pp. 105–106.
[52]'The Lives of the Teachers. Pioneer Embalming Educators of America. Prof A. Johnson Dodge' (1968) *The De-Ce-Co Magazine*, Vol. 60, No. 1, February, pp. 9, 20, & 30. See also Dodge G.B. (1909) 'Modern Embalming', *TUJ*, December, pp. 285–286; 'Interview with Professor George B. Dodge of Boston USA and Mr G.M. Bartlett' (1909) *TUJ*, December, pp. 291–292; 'Advertisement: Massachusetts College of Embalming' (1910) *TUJ*, January, p. 7; and 'Reception of Professor Renouard' (1906) *TUJ*, September, pp. 230–231.

class in London before studying in America.[53] He joined with W. Oliver Nodes to establish the London College of Embalming in October 1913.[54] Other pioneers include Morgan R. Morgan of Neath[55] and Joseph Heath of Sheffield, along with two from London, Albert J.E. Cottridge, a trained teacher and author of *Anatomy and Sanitation*, and James Goulborn.[56]

Following the end of the Great War the availability of embalming tuition proliferated. The BUA's Manchester Centre organised an 'Embalming Summer School' in June 1918, while in September the Northern College of Embalming opened, and Dyer and Nodes organised the first post-war 'Victory' class in Sheffield for ex-servicemen.[57] During the BUA conference in 1918, an embalming demonstration was given at Hull City mortuary.[58] By the 1920s a number of fluid and instrument suppliers were promoting their wares (Fig. 7). Following his visit to funeral homes and embalming colleges in the USA, Morgan R. Morgan wrote enthusiastically about them in *TUJ*. He also followed in the footsteps of Professor Sullivan by embarking upon an embalming lecture tour in Wales in 1917, then England in 1923 and 1925.[59] The link with the United States was

---

[53] See Dyer A. (1913b) 'Interview with Mr A. Dyer of Walthamstow', *TUJ*, April, pp. 109–110; Dyer A. (1914) 'Modern Embalming and the Undertaker', *TUJ*, February, p. 37; and Dyer A.B. (1949) 'On Ideals', *FSJ*, January, pp. 21–22. For an obituary see 'Mr Arthur B. Dyer' (1951) *FSJ*, p. 648.

[54] 'A London College of Embalming. Interview with the Founders' (1913) *TUJ*, November, pp. 319–321.

[55] 'Mr Morgan R. Morgan: A Character Sketch' (1914) *TUJ*, October, pp. 287–288.

[56] 'Death of Mr A.J.E. Cottridge' (1944) *TUFDJ*, April, p. 118. He died on 24 March 1944. See also 'The Passing of Mr A.J.E. Cottridge' (1944) *TNFD*, April, p. 385 and 'In Memory of A.J.E. Cottridge' (1944) *TNFD*, May, p. 430. Cottridge A.J.E. (1924a) 'Preservative Disinfectant', *BUA Monthly*, September, pp. 69–71; Cottridge A.J.E. (1924b) 'Signs of Death. Simple Tests Which Every Undertaker Should Know and Practice', *BUA Monthly*, December, pp. 159–160; For lectures by Cottridge see 'The Urgent Need of Post Graduate Tuition in Modern Embalming' (1924c) *BUA Monthly*, June, pp. 697–698; Cottridge A.J.E. (1925a) 'Anatomy and Post-Mortem Sanitation' *BUA Monthly*, June, pp. 311–312; Cottridge A.J.E. (1931) 'Signs of Death', *BUA Monthly*, pp. 82–83; Cottridge A.J.E. (1932) 'Medical Officers of Health', *BUA Monthly*, May, p. 252; and Cottridge A.J.E. (1943) 'Mr James Goulborn', *TNFD*, May, p. 416.

[57] 'Northern College of Embalming: Opening of First Course' (1918) *TUJ*, October, p. 259.

[58] 'The Demonstration and Lecture' (1918) *TUJ*, July, p. 177.

[59] Morgan M.R. (1919) 'American Impressions', *TUJ*, November, pp. 336–337 and December, p. 370 and (1920) January, pp. 25–26. See also 'Undertaking and Co-partnership' (1914) *TUJ*, August, pp. 218–219. See also 'M.R. Morgan's Lecture Tour' (1925) *TUJ*, March, 1925, p. 87. See also Morgan M.R. (1917) 'Lectures on Temporary Preservation' *TUJ*, November, p. 287 and December, pp. 314–315. For

DOTTRIDGE BROTHERS Ltd.
DORSET WORKS
EAST ROAD, LONDON, N.1

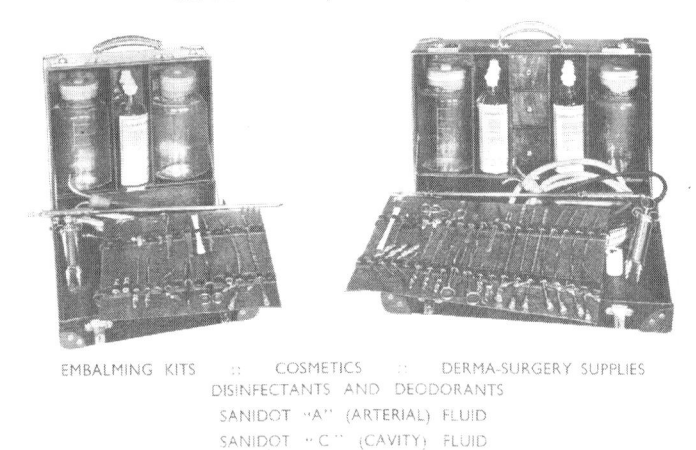

EMBALMING KITS :: COSMETICS :: DERMA-SURGERY SUPPLIES
DISINFECTANTS AND DEODORANTS
SANIDOT "A" (ARTERIAL) FLUID
SANIDOT "C" (CAVITY) FLUID

PRICES AND FULL PARTICULARS ON APPLICATION

Fig. 7. Embalming equipment. *Note:* Between its introduction around 1900 and the 1950s, little embalming took place in the UK and when it did treatment was usually in the home of the deceased. Suppliers such as Dottridge Bros marketed equipment in compact carrying cases through the pages of the trade journals, *The Undertakers' Journal* and the *BUA Monthly* (Author's collection).

made evident in 1924 when the Champion Chemical Co offered a scheme for six young men to travel to Cincinnati College of Embalming to study on a six-month course for $750.[60]

Although the BES continued its educational work post-World War I, the society was floundering, particularly as it had been marginalised by its 'parent' organisation the BUA and in 1916 had become a trade union.[61] As such it had 'lost its individuality and also its charter of incorporation'.[62] At a BUA council meeting in 1920, Morgan called

---

other material about M.R. Morgan see, 'Mr Morgan R. Morgan: A Character Sketch' (1914) *TUJ*, October, pp. 287–288; 'What Shall the Aims of the BUA Be? Mr Morgan R. Morgan's Views' (1916) *TUJ*, May, pp. 133–134; and Morgan R. Morgan (1916) 'Registration and the Needs of the Moment', *TUJ*, December, p. 326.
[60] Advertisement (1924) *BUA Monthly*, November, p. 123.
[61] 'Proposed Syllabus of Instruction in Sanitation' (1922) *BUA Monthly*, July, p. 2.
[62] 'Embalming in England' (1930) *TUJ*, August, p. 258.

for the BUA to refocus on post-mortem sanitation and at the annual conference; Cottridge proposed the adoption of a national programme of education involving lectures on sanitary knowledge, funeral management, legal issues and the history of funeral customs.[63] Three months later the association's membership had been galvanised into action with the appointment of lecturers who had placed their services at the disposal of the local BUA committees. The idea of an alternative association was also tabled in 1924, and then endorsed by the editor of *TUJ* the following year, mainly as a result of the likely demise of the BES.[64]

In February 1926, the London Area Embalmers' Section of the BUA called for a 'National Policy for Sanitarians', but still under the control of the BUA. Later in the year, the direction shifted as the London Area had decided to form a 'New and Progressive Society'.[65] In April 1927, the British Institute of Embalmers was founded, with W. Oliver Nodes as its first president.[66] The soon-to-be honorary secretary H. Kirtley Nodes commented:

> All qualified Embalmers and Undertakers throughout the Country, especially interested in the Sanitary Preservation of the Dead, will be most heartily welcomed.[67]

Education was the major focus of the Institute with studies comprising a minimum of 70 hours, including at least 10 hours' attendance at demonstrations and personal practice. The BIE ran classes for members of the BFWA in 1927 and also taught 'study circle' classes.[68] The first examination was held in 1928 and over the next decades a number of new embalming schools emerged to prepare students: the Metropolitan

---

[63] See also Cottridge A.J.E. (1924c) 'The Urgent Need of Post Graduate Tuition in Modern Embalming', *BUA Monthly*, June, pp. 697–698.
[64] 'Editorial: A Society of Scientific Morticians' (1924) *TUJ*, November, pp. 399–400' 'Editorial: Another Association?' (1925) *TUJ*, February, pp. 61–62; 'Revival of the British Embalmers' Society' (1925) *TUJ*, October, pp. 327–329; and 'Editorial. The BES. What of the Future?' (1926) *TUJ*, May, pp. 163–164.
[65] 'London Area Embalmers' Section. Decision to Form New and Progressive Society' (1926) *TUJ*, October, pp. 317–319.
[66] See 'History of the BIE' (1991) *The Embalmer*, Vol. 34, No. 1, pp. 14–20. See also Gaunt P. (1977) 'The British Institute of Embalmers', *The Embalmer*, Vol. 20, No. 1, pp. 7–12.
[67] 'British Institute of Embalmers (Incorporated) Proposed' (1927) *TUJ*, March, p. 81.
[68] 'British Institute of Embalmers. Sanitation Classes for Members of BFWA' (1927) *BUA Monthly*, November, p. 98, and 'Yorkshire Study Circle' (1935) *BUA Monthly*, July, p. 8.

School of Embalming conducted classes in 1933 with W. Oliver Nodes as its principal assisted by George D. Russell, L. Hodge and George Lear.[69] The latter would become a central figure to embalming.[70]

The BES and BIE overlapped by promoting the public health benefits of embalming and organising examinations; the BES finally disappeared in 1957.[71] In 1936 recognition of embalming was achieved when the Public Health Act gave the Secretary of State the power to make regulations 'as to the period of time a body may be retained after death on any premises, or with respect to embalming or preservation''.[72] With the treatment now endorsed by the state it is not surprising that local medical officers of health were often invited to BES/BUA conferences.[73]

---

[69] See 'Metropolitan School of Embalming' (1933) *TUJ*, September, p. 299.

[70] Parsons B. (2012a). 'George Lear Revisited', *The Embalmer*, Vol. 55, No. 4, pp. 19–25. See also 'British Institute of Embalmers' (1929) *TUJ*, November, pp. 341–342. For articles by George Lear see Lear G. (1933a) 'The Fundamental of Modern Embalming', *TUJ*, April, pp. 109–112 & 132; Lear G. (1933b) 'Raising the Standard', *TUJ*, May, pp. 147–149 & 164–165; Lear G. (1932a) 'What My Experiences in America Taught Me', *TUJ*, November, pp. 351–358; Lear G. (1932b) 'American Funeral Directing and Embalming', *TUJ*, December, pp. 387–388; Lear G. (1935a) 'A Go-Ahead and Practical Service', *BUA Monthly*, September, p. 77; Lear G. (1937a) 'Some Difficult Cases', *TUFDJ*, April, pp. 113–115 & 122; Lear G. (1937b) 'Stock-Taking', *TUFDJ*, November, pp. 367–370; 'Lear Embalming Service' (1938) *TUFDJ*, April, pp. 137–138; and 'A Dramatic Surprise! NAFD Film on Embalming Technique' (1953) *TFD*, July, p. 147. Latterly known as the Lear College of Mortuary Science, the school closed in 1996.

[71] 'The BUA and BIE' (1931) *BUA Monthly*, November, pp. 105–106; 'Proposed Merger of BES and BIE' (1956) *TNFD*, January, p. 5; and 'British Embalmers' Society' (1956) *TFD*, March, pp. 46–47. The first discussion about a merger took place in 1948. See 'NAFD and BIE' (1948) *TNFD*, July, p. 10 and 'BES Adopt Merger Plan. Single Organisation Approved' (1957) *FSJ*, June, pp. 265–267.

[72] Fellows A. (1952) *The Law of Burial and Generally of the Disposal of the Dead*, second edition, London: Haddon, Best & Co, p. 406. See also 'Editorial: Looking Ahead' (1938) *TUFDJ*, September, pp. 331–332 and Wilson G. (1938) 'Public Health Act and Embalmers', *TUFDJ*, June, pp. 203–206.

[73] Dr Alexander Wynter Blyth, the Medical Officer of the Borough of Marylebone, gave a paper at the inaugural convention of the BUA in 1905. See Wynter Blyth A. (1905) 'The Hygiene of the Death Chamber', *TUJ*, July, pp. 156–161. See also Barnes G.C. (1916) 'The Disposal of the Dead from the Public Health Standpoint', *TUJ*, September, pp. 242–246 (and 'Funeral Reform' (1916) *The Hospital*, 29 July, Vol. LX, No. 1573, p. 404); Forbes D. (1917) 'Public Health and the Disposal of the Dead', *TUJ*, July, pp. 182–184 (see also 'Disposal of the Dead' (1917) *The Medical Officer*, 1 September, pp. 66–71); Banks C. (1924) 'What Every Undertaker Should Know About Microbes', *BUA Monthly*, December, pp. 152–153; Johnstone Jervis J. (1924) 'The Disposal of the Dead', *BUA*

A notable guest in 1930 was the honorary pathologist to the Home Office, Sir Bernard Spilsbury.[74]

Embalming Progress: Supply or Demand?

Despite these progressive steps, until the 1940s the amount of embalming practised in Britain was still limited. But the period was a turning point as by this time the funeral industry was facing a number of challenges. The previous chapter outlined that the most important area of social change was the increasing number of deaths taking place away from the family home and the body being transferred to the funeral directors' premises to await the funeral rather than being returned home. This was a significant break in a long tradition and funeral directors responded by providing chapels of rest.

Routine embalming started to take place in the 1950s. A decade later, Habenstein and Lamers commented that embalming was now being practised 'far more than at any time in the past'.[75] They also cite the number of particularly large funeral firms employing full-time embalmers, the increase in trade embalmers and the number of dual-qualified embalmers/funeral directors. Some five years later, Pine among others quoted from a source that 'some firms embalm up to 80–90% of the dead they handle' – a figure confirmed

---

Monthly, February, pp. 567–570; 'The Institute of Embalmers: Dr Berkeley Way on Safeguarding Public Health' (1928) *TUJ*, February, pp. 45–46; Rose G.C.F. (1930) 'Forensic Medicine', *BUA Monthly*, December, pp. 135–136; Wray G.G. (1930) 'Smallpox', *BUA Monthly*, July, pp. 6–7; Taylor J.S. (1930) 'Ancient and Modern Methods of Disposing of the Dead', *BUA Monthly*, April, pp. 210–212; Newcomb W.D. (1931) 'Sanitary Preservation – Its Advantages and Disadvantages', *BUA Monthly*, January, pp. 150–153; Miller S. (1932) 'The Physiological Aspects of Death', *BUA Monthly*, February, pp. 176–177; Innes J. (1934) 'Public Health Services', *BUA Monthly*, January, pp. 148–150; Kitching W.C. (1935) 'The Observations of an Embalmer in the PM Room', *BUA Monthly*, May, pp. 238–239; Horder Lord (1936) 'The Public Health Aspect of the Disposition of the Dead', *TNFD*, September, pp. 67–68; Williamson A.B. (1937) 'What is the Place of the Funeral Director in the Health Services?' *TNFD*, August, pp. 45–47.
[74]Spilsbury B. (1930) 'The Sanitary Care of the Dead', *TUJ*, July, pp. 237–238. See also 'Sir Bernard Spilsbury Addresses the Conference' (1930) *BUA Monthly*, August, pp. 28–33; 'What Sir Bernard Spilsbury Said' (1937) *TNFD*, March, pp. 205–208; and Spilsbury B. (1929) 'Identification of a Dead Body', *TUJ*, December, pp. 399–400.
[75]Habenstein R.W. and Lamers W.M. (1963) *Funeral Customs the World Over*, Revised edition, Milwaukee: Bulfin, p. 560.

in 1966 as appertaining to the London area in addition to the estimate of over 50 per cent on a nationwide basis, although this cannot be substantiated.[76] By 1952, it was estimated that 15 per cent of all members of the NAFD practised embalming. A trend was discernible: 11.9 per cent were embalmed in 1949 and 14 per cent in 1951.[77] George Lear questioned why embalming was not more widespread, and noted that embalming was:

> greater in more thickly populated parts of the country, south Wales, the Midlands, London and the North... The more funerals undertaken by a firm, the more chance of embalming.[78]

In an article by the NAFD president, Lawrence Ashton, published in 1952, he tackled the issue of how the funeral director should introduce embalming with a client and in what circumstances it should be carried out.[79] This made little impact, however, and it is not surprising that in January 1953, when the BES embarked upon a census of embalming it was met with a lack of response.[80] The society proposed propaganda to encourage funeral directors to promote embalming as part of their services.[81] Another NAFD president, Col Durham Kenyon, called for 'all cases to be embalmed'.[82]

---

[76]Pine V.R. (1975) *Caretaker of the Dead: The American Funeral Director*, New York: Irvington, p. 57 and *Committee of the Work of the Committee on Death Certification and Coroners* (1971) Cmnd 4810, p. 329. In 1967, the NAFD recorded a national average of 52 per cent of bodies embalmed. See 'Analysis of Members' Answers to the Questionnaire: What the Public Wants (for 1967)', *TFD*, September, pp. 502–504. Regional differences are striking; in the London area 72 per cent is recorded, falling to 12 per cent in Scotland and 8 per cent in the western counties. Naylor details that by the 1980s, '25 per cent or 161,500 cases were being embalmed per annum, although the survey figures were not fully representative – with only a 29% return rate' Naylor M.J.A. (1989) *Funeral Rituals in a Northern City*, Unpublished PhD thesis, University of Leeds, p. 59.
[77]'BES Digest' (1952) *TNFD*, May, p. 524.
[78]Lear G. (1952) 'Embalming – Here, There – But Not Everywhere', *TNFD*, September, pp. 115–117.
[79]Ashton L.C. (1952) 'The Place of Embalming in Funeral Directing', *TNFD*, August, pp. 68–71.
[80]'A Census of Embalming' (1953) *TFD*, January, p. 8.
[81]'British Embalmers' Society' (1953) *TNFD*, May, p. 89. See also Davies T.A. (1959) 'The Centre of Funeral Service is Embalming', *TFD*, October, pp. 217–218.
[82]'Newquay Conference. The President's Address' (1956) *TFD*, June, pp. 112–118.

The growth of embalming stems from a period when greater responsibility for the body was acquired by the funeral directors. While custody did not automatically mean embalming would be carried out, its application was in the interests of the funeral director in contrast to the service being demanded by the bereaved. Evidence that embalming was carried out only relatively infrequently before the 1950s suggests that society was unaware of its existence and objectives, therefore unlikely to demand its application. As Lear suggested, however, funeral directors were not promoting the availability of the service, while advocates of embalming had difficulties advancing it within the trade, perhaps due to the fact that home was still the place of repose despite evidence to indicate that embalmments were carried out at home.

Although evidence exists to show that the science was brought to the attention of the public by the success of the embalming of Lenin in 1924 and that of Eva Perón in 1952, thus demonstrating the existence and efficacy of long-term preservation techniques, it is unfortunate that arterial embalming was then, as it often is now, confused with mummification.[83] It also underlined the misconception that embalming was something only for the rich and famous. The limited public awareness of the extent of embalming is confirmed by British anthropologist Geoffrey Gorer following his interviews with the bereaved in the early 1960s when he commented, 'as far as I can discover, this [embalming] is still an exceptional practice in Britain'.[84]

One problem was the word itself: embalming. As perhaps the most sensitive subject that a funeral director can discuss with the client, the deficiency of a suitable word or phrase to adequately describe it is probably the basis of this issue. The industry initially used the word 'sanitation', but has since adopted evasive terms such as 'hygienic treatment' and 'temporary preservation' along with the euphemistic 'care and preparation of the body'.

---

[83]For Lenin see 'The Secret of the Embalming of Lenin' (1940) *TNFD*, June, pp. 426–429. See also 'Stalin's Body Evicted – Lenin Now Lies Alone' (1962) *FSJ*, April, pp. 185–188 and Zbarsky I. and Hutchinson S. (1997) *Lenin's Embalmers*, London: Harvill, and for Perón see Johnson M.E.C and Johnson G. (1987) 'The Man Who Embalmed Evita: Dr Pedro Ara', *The Embalmer*, Vol. 30, No.1, pp. 14–26; and Lloyd Hughes D. (2007) 'Eva in the Shadows: The Partial Revenge of Dr Pedro Ara', *Hispanic Research Journal*, Vol. 8, No. 2, pp. 23–140; and Quigley C. (1998) *Modern Mummies: The Preservation of the Human Body in the Twentieth Century*, Jefferson: McFarland & Co, pp. 43–49.

[84]Gorer G. (1965) *Death, Grief, and Mourning in Contemporary Britain*, London: The Cresset Press, p. 45.

There is one area to which the actual demand for embalming can be directly attributed; the repatriation of human remains. In the days before airline travel many shipping lines insisted on embalming.[85] The transportation of coffins by air started in the 1920s and airlines soon introduced a requirement that arterial embalming be carried out to minimise the risk of problems occurring due to climatic or atmospheric changes during transit in addition to delay before final disposal. Consular regulations of many countries also insisted on embalming.[86]

From a supply-side perspective, however, it is more likely that funeral directors have been responsible for the increase in embalming for the following reasons: First, it is necessary to consider embalming in comparison to alternative methods of preservation. The first alternative was provided by developments in refrigeration. Cold storage for bodies started to be installed in coroners' mortuaries in London during the 1930s, but it was not until 1952 that such equipment was advertised in the *FSJ*.[87] However, refrigeration only provides preservation in a chilled atmosphere and before viewing, some superficial presentation must be executed on the features of the deceased. The installation of a refrigeration plant, although of long-term value, involves considerable capital expenditure and may necessitate the restructuring of premises. Many funeral directors would have hesitated before committing themselves to such expenditure, although the less-expensive Chillrest, a cooling device placed over a coffin, was available.[88]

Another method of preservation was dry ice: frozen blocks of carbon dioxide. In the mid-1930s Dottridge Bros marketed Drikold; another was called Cardice. It is available in blocks; it had a temperature of 110°F below zero and could be used to freeze the abdomen and other parts of the body.[89] However, when it evaporated, the blocks had to be replaced within 24 hours. As with refrigeration, the application of dry ice only arrested decomposition. In contrast to both methods, the process of

---

[85]See 'Transatlantic Shipment of the Dead' (1900) *TUJ*, November, pp. 169–171.
[86]Parsons B. (2017a) 'Funeral Directors and Distance Transportation of the Dead', *The Embalmer*, Vol. 55, No. 4, pp. 31–39.
[87]'A Model Public Mortuary' (1934) *TUJ*, March, pp. 91–92 and Townroe B.S. (1934) 'Westminster', *TUJ*, May, pp. 159–160.
[88]See Advertisement (1972) *FSJ*, August, p. 410.
[89]'Development in Pre-Burial Sanitation. A New Use for Solid Carbon Dioxide' (1935) *TUJ*, June, pp. 197–198 and Webb T.G. (1935) 'The Drikold Method for Pre-Burial Sanitation', *TUJ*, October, pp. 325–326.

embalming preserved the body, while on the completion of the task the embalmer also attended the presentation of features.

Second, although not proven by data, it is possible that the rapid growth in the preference for cremation in the post-war years increased the delay between death and the funeral. Building restrictions until the mid-1950s prevented new crematoria from being constructed, with the result that waiting times increased. Where delays occurred embalming could help prevent deterioration.[90]

Third, embalming could be offered by funeral directors as an additional service, thereby generating extra revenue. Although in the early days the cost of embalming was prohibitive, the increasing demand for embalming was met with a supply of 'trade embalmers' offering a freelance embalming service to funeral directors on a contractual basis.[91] The Lear Embalming Service served London and the home counties from the 1940s and George Lear advertised the year-on-year increase in the *TNFD*; between 1942 and 1948 it was significant.[92] Engaging a roving practitioner meant that the funeral director did not have to train as an embalmer or employ a full-time member of staff.

From the 1940s, the provision of embalming training was increasing and more funeral directors were becoming qualified. Two embalming schools emerged in 1946, the Dottridge School of Embalming and Funeral Hygiene (recognised by the Ministry of Labour as a training establishment) and the Lear School of Embalming, with others, such as the Midland School of Embalming, being established in the 1950s.[93]

The Essex funeral director Jack West noted that the NAFD embarked upon an extensive educational programme in the post-World War II years to encourage funeral directors to take a more responsible view of the need for thorough sanitation.[94] The BIE also created a research board in 1946

---

[90] See Lear G. (1948) 'Embalming and Cremation', *The Practitioner*, Vol. 161, pp. 94–100.
[91] *The Undertakers' and Funeral Directors'* (1896) *Journal and Monumental Masons' Review*, March, p. 4, contains an advertisement from undertaker/embalmer Halford Lupton Mills of 31 Cambridge Place, Paddington, offering an embalming service to the undertaking trade. For 'Temporary preservation, say for a week from 5 Guineas; Embalming for a long time, or for ocean voyage, from 10 Guineas; Complete Embalming, from 20 Guineas'.
[92] Advertisement (1950) *TNFD*, February, p. 372. See 'Lear Embalming Service Ltd. Annual Report' (1949) *TNFD*, February, p. 231. In 1949 the Lear Embalming Service embalmed 6,060 cases, being an increase of 798 over the previous year.
[93] Advertisement (1950) *TNFD*, January, p. 319.
[94] West J. (1988) *Jack West Funeral Director: Forty Years with Funerals*, Ilfracombe: Stockwell, p. 114.

to promote embalming.[95] Regular articles on technique and the treatment of different cases appeared in *The National Funeral Director*, many by Archibald Hall, while in 1953 the first book to include a section on embalming written by non-embalmers was published.[96] Embalmers were also encouraged to keep case notes.[97] A monthly series in the *FSJ* by Dr Charles A. Renouard entitled 'Thinking it Over' continued until 1951.[98] With an increasing number of practitioners in the field and as demand grew, the cost of embalming was subject to the advantages of price/supply competition. In short, embalming was becoming affordable for both funeral director and client.

---

[95]Gore P. (1991) 'Progress of Embalming Practice', *The Embalmer*, Vol. 34, No. 4, pp. 10–11. See also 'BIE's Council Five-Hour Session (1946) *FSJ*, February, p. 48.
[96]'Cerebral Accident' (1941) *TNFD*, December, p. 189; 'Beautifying the Dead' (1941) *TNFD*, May, p. 362; 'Protecting Public Health' (1942) *TNFD*, September, pp. 92–93; 'Are You Prepared for the Drowning Season?' (1938) *TNFD*, September, pp. 108–109; One of the Besetting Troubles of the Embalmer is – Pneumonia' (1938) *TNFD*, September, p. 140; 'Treating Severed Extremities' (1939) *TNFD*, November, p. 196; 'On the Treatment of Gunshot Wounds' (1940) *TNFD*, January, p. 264; 'On the Making of Death Masks' (1940) *TNFD*, March, p. 328; 'Drain for Safety' (1940) *TNFD*, April, p. 363; 'Preparing the Body for Post-Mortem Derma-Surgery' (1940) *TNFD*, September, p. 84; 'The Danger of Purging' (1940) *TNFD*, October, p. 115; 'Some Notes on the Embalming of Infants by a Practitioner' (1940) *TNFD*, November, pp. 146–148; 'Building a Complete New Face' (1940) *TNFD*, December, pp. 177 & 189; 'The Treatment of Jaundice' (1941) *TNFD*, April, pp. 316–317; 'Beautifying the Death' (1941) *TNFD*, May, p. 362; 'Strive for Naturalness' (1941) *TNFD*, July, pp. 7 & 11; and 'Are You Versed in Precautionary Methods?' (1942) *TNFD*, January, p. 231. See also 'Preparation Techniques' (1940) *TNFD*, July, pp. 16–17; 'A Memo on Imitating "Life"' (1942) *TNFD*, January, p. 236; 'Discolourations' (1943) *TNFD*, October, p. 142; 'Achieving the Effective Memory Picture' (1943) *TNFD*, pp. 144–145; and 'The Effect of the New Drugs on Embalming Technique' (1945) *TNFD*, February, pp. 284–285 & 301. See also Polson C.J., Brittain R.P. and Marshall T.K. (1953) *The Disposal of the Dead*, London: English Universities Press.
[97]'Case Report' (1935) *BUA Monthly*, May, p. 244. See also Case Analysis Record' (1942) *TNFD*, February, p. 257, and 'Notes on a case of embalmment or sanitary preservation' (1926) *TUJ*, May, p. 145. Cottridge had initially suggested this in 1925. See Cottridge A.J.E. (1925b). 'A New Campaign', *BUA Monthly*, April, p. 257, and 'That first entry in the 'Case Book''' (1941) *TNFD*, October, p. 113.
[98]Professor Charles A. Renouard' (1953) *FSJ*, August, pp. 367–368. For details of A.C.A. Hall see 'Mr Hall to Open His Own Business' (1955) *FSJ*, December, p. 572. For Scudamore see 'E.F. Scudamore, Master Fellow, Presidential Appreciation' (1974) *The Embalmer*, Vol. 17, No. 4, p. 16. Edwin Scudamore, author of *Embalming Theoretical and Practical* (1949), qualified as an embalmer in 1930. See 'Arthur Dyer's Embalming Class' (1930) *TUJ*, December, p. 407. See Scudamore E.F. (1935) 'Disinfectants' *TUJ*, August, pp. 261–262.

Fourth, in conjunction with the additional responsibility towards the body, it is likely that client expectations were increasing, with the funeral director being engaged as a specialist service provider. Whereas in the period when the body rested at home under familial care decomposition was accepted as inevitable, by entrusting it to a specialist the level of expectation increased. When clients view the body in a chapel, however, the expectation is that it will be presented decently without any leakage or odour. Although the bereaved are mostly unlikely to know exactly what 'care of the body' precisely entails, it is assumed that action will be taken to prevent the body being presented in an insanitary condition. Thus a standard of presentation and preservation can be presumed by the client when the funeral director is entrusted to 'take care of everything'. It is also interesting to note that the responsibility of care towards the body was becoming binding upon funeral directors who acquired the custody of the body. In 1935, George Lear brought to the attention of fellow funeral directors the position concerning a body that decomposed and caused illness, while in the care of the funeral director: 'The magistrate held that the funeral director was responsible for the condition of a body up to the time of burial'.[99]

Fifth, a number of funeral organisations were expanding through the acquisition of businesses and then servicing the needs of branch offices from one operational centre. Following the acquisition or development of a branch office all resources would be supplied by the operational centre, thus relieving the need for refrigeration, mortuary facilities and an embalmer at each unit. Some firms calculated that sufficient work existed for employing a full-time embalmer; the late Desmond Henley was engaged as Kenyon's first full-time embalmer in 1949. Other firms believed that economies of scale could be achieved by negotiating volume-rated embalming with contractors who would only embalm in one location. By providing embalming within the scope of centralised operation (see Chapter 6), embalmed bodies could be transferred to the branch offices without fear of decomposition, thereby reducing refrigeration and storage capacity at the head office.

Sixth, embalming must also be considered in the context of the professionalisation of the funeral director. While Chapter 8 will consider the contribution made by embalming towards the process, it is clear that the

---

[99]Lear G. (1935b) 'Post Mortem Sanitation: A Sheer Necessity', *BUA Monthly*, pp. 99–100. It is significant to note that all bodies that could not be buried during the Liverpool gravediggers strike in August 1987 were embalmed and then stored. See Taylor A. (1987) 'Report from Mersey District PRO' *TFD*, November, p. 13.

industry placed great emphasis on its practitioners possessing sanitary knowledge and exercising competence. Howarth believes that 'the pseudo scientific nature of the work such as embalming forms the basis for the industry's claim to professional respectability'.[100]

Although the precise extent of embalming in this country today is unknown, there are a number of indicators to suggest that its application is widespread.[101] Membership of the BIE with its constant flow of students (currently 1,230 subscribing members and 430 students),[102] at least 10 embalming schools and 4 fluid and instrument suppliers all suggest its reasonable widespread employment. In addition, the large firms, such as Dignity Caring Funeral Service, Co-op societies and many independent organisations advocate its practice.

Embalming Under Attack

In parallel with its progress since the 1950s has been criticism of embalming. The need for and purpose of sanitary treatment, the fluids employed and the commercial motivation of its advocates have come under increasing scrutiny. In the final part of this chapter, three strands where tensions exist are identified and discussed.

The first point is that embalming contributes towards the so-called 'denial of death'. Much of this rhetoric can be attributed to the commentary concerning the US funeral industry, although in 1955 anthropologist Geoffrey Gorer claimed that 'the art of the embalmers is an art of complete denial'.[103] Kearl deems that American embalmers are 'one occupation dedicated to the maintenance of the culture's death denial, as evidenced by its

---

[100]Howarth G. (1993a) 'Investigating Deathwork: A Personal Account', in D. Clark ed., *The Sociology of Death: Theory, Culture, Practice*, Oxford: Blackwell, p. 234.
[101]Only one unsubstantiated reference can be found to indicate the current extent of embalming. Pym D. (1990) 'Letters to the Editor', *FSJ*, January, p. 49 states 'in most parts of the UK the practice is approaching 90 per cent'. It is not known how the embalmer David Pym arrived at this figure.
[102]The gender split of the 2009 BIE membership list is 23 per cent female. For material relating to female embalmers see Cline S. (1995) *Lifting the Taboo: Women, Death and Dying*, London: Abacus, pp. 116–139 and Bradbury M. (1999) *Representations of Death: A Social Psychological Perspective*, London: Routledge, pp. 120–123.
[103]Gorer G. (1965) *Death, Grief, and Mourning in Contemporary Britain*, London: The Cresset Press, p. 51.

attempts to continue embalming the dead so as to create a "living memorial" for the deceased'.[104] Although disputed by Kellehear, Davies sees the obsession with hygiene, youth and beauty by Americans as continuing in death with sanitary treatment and cosmetisation of the body. Other writers see embalming as an attempt to make the corpse look 'life-like' or presented as 'sleeping death'.[105] Similarly, Elizabeth Kübler-Ross considers that 'the elaborate expensive display of an open casket with all the makeup in the slumber room enforces the belief that the person is only sleeping'.[106] Although Jessica Mitford was not explicit about it being responsible for denying death, she did question the public health value of embalming, the unnecessary use of cosmetics, its cost and funeral directors being evasive concerning whether it was required by state law.[107] Others mistakenly see embalming as one part of the 'Americanisation' of British funerals. In a review of the UK's National Funeral Exhibition held in 2000, Geoffrey Rowell commented that the American caskets and suchlike were part of a culture 'seeking to deny death in many ways'.[108] While it is a fact that the introduction of modern embalming can be attributed to the United States, the logic of it being a treatment to deny death can however be disputed. In her assessment of the work of the embalmer, Mary Bradbury notes that while such themes as hygiene and denial were apparent in the United Kingdom, they were 'probably less strongly articulated'.[109]

If denial is the refusal to acknowledge an emotionally challenging notion, just how does this relate to seeing an embalmed body? After treatment, the deceased is dressed in clothing supplied by the family; cosmetics

---

[104] Kearl M.C. (1989) *Endings: A Sociology of Death and Dying*, Oxford: Oxford University Press, p. 284.
[105] Davies C. (1996) 'Dirt, Death, Decay and Dissolution', in G. Howarth and P.C. Jupp eds, *Contemporary Issues in the Sociology of Death, Dying and Disposal*, Basingstoke: Macmillan, p. 60. It should be noted that Kellehear sees the creation of 'life-like corpses' as 'a logical continuation, of the cosmetics industry for the living and only sleeping'. See Kellehear A. (1984) 'Are We a "Death-Denying" Society? A Sociological Review', *Social Science and Medicine*, Vol. 18, No. 9, pp. 713–723.
[106] Kübler-Ross E. (1974) *Questions and Answers on Death and Dying*, New York: Collier Books, p. 101.
[107] Mitford J. (1963) *The American Way of Death*, London: Quartet, pp. 68–74 & 79–95.
[108] Rowell G. (2000) 'Tucked Up for Eternity', *Church Times*, 2 June, p. 12. See also Davies D.J. (1997) *Death, Ritual and Belief*, London: Cassell, p. 37.
[109] Bradbury M. (1999) *Representations of Death: A Social Psychological Perspective*, London: Routledge, p. 127. See also Hallam E., Hockey J. and Howarth G. (1999) *Beyond the Body: Death and Social Identity*, London: Routledge, pp. 128–131.

may too be provided for a female, but are used by British practitioners only in moderation. It is then placed in a coffin and presented in a chapel of rest – a receptacle and environment only associated with the dead. How does this deny the reality of death? Academic commentators offer no answers. Conversely, the presence of the body – whether embalmed or not – provides an opportunity to confront and acknowledge the fact of death.[110]

The second area is that the paucity of information about the history of arterial embalming, its objectives and the extent of its use has led to the circulation of much misinformation. The BIE cannot state with accuracy how much embalming is carried out and it is for this reason that writers such as Davies assert that embalming is virtually unheard of in this country.[111] This deficiency has resulted in inaccurate statements about its adoption in this country. For example, Chamberlain and Pearson mistakenly argue that it was the arrival in British funeral service of the American organisation Service Corporation International (SCI) that 'introduced an aggressive style of business, marketing expensive "hygienic" practices that included embalming and a widening choice of elaborate funerary fittings and services'.[112] As Chapter 6 indicates, SCI (now Dignity PLC) was the amalgamation of many companies that have been carrying out embalming for a considerable number of years; its approach towards preservative treatment is far from new. Furthermore, as noted above, although embalming was introduced in Britain by embalmers from America and Canada, those promoting its value were indigenous funeral directors.

Hailes states that the Co-op and Dignity carry out embalming as 'standard practice'.[113] Ken West also repeats this erroneous information.[114] The inference is that embalming has been introduced solely for commercial

---

[110]For literature on viewing the corpse, see Harper S. (2010b). 'Behind Closed Doors? Corpses and Mourners in English and American Funeral Premises', in J. Hockey C. Komaromy and K. Woodthorpe eds, *The Matter of Death: Space, Place and Materiality*, Basingstoke: Palgrave Macmillan. See also Harper S. (2010a) 'The Social Agency of Dead Bodies', *Mortality*, Vol. 15, No. 4, pp. 308–322 and Chapple A. and Ziebland S. (2010) 'Viewing the Body after Bereavement due to a Traumatic Death: Qualitative Study in the UK', *BMJ*, 340, c2032. doi:10.1136/bmj.c2032.
[111]Davies C. (1996) 'Dirt, Death, Decay and Dissolution', in G. Howarth and P.C. Jupp, eds, *Contemporary Issues in the Sociology of Death, Dying and Disposal*, Basingstoke: Macmillan, p. 60.
[112]Chamberlain A.T. and Pearson M.P. (2001) *Earthly Remains: The History and Science of Preserved Bodies*, London: British Museum Press, p. 173.
[113]Hailes J. (2007) *The New Green Consumer Guide*, London: Simon and Schuster, p. 224.
[114]West K. (2010) *A Guide to Natural Burial*, London: Shaw & Sons, p. 23.

motives and is carried out without the permission of the client. No reference is made to the overall efficacy of this preservative treatment, not to mention the requirement for overseas transportation. The charge for embalming represents only a small proportion of the overall funeral costs. In 2009, the NAFD found that the average cost was £75.[115]

The final area is the impact of embalming on practitioners and the environment. Concern over the effects of formaldehyde exposure upon practitioners has been apparent over the last 30 years.[116] While health and safety legislation has improved ventilation in the embalming theatre, the carcinogenic effect of formaldehyde led the European Commission in 1993 to introduce the Biocides Directive, which became law in 1998.[117] The ban will pose a severe problem for embalmers as a replacement is not available, although fluids for short-term preservation can be sourced. The health risk posed by blood-borne pathogens was also a concern when HIV/AIDS emerged in the 1980s; initially the BIE recommended that treatment was carried out, but this is no longer the case.[118]

Reservations about the cremation of embalmed bodies came from the cremation movement in the post-war years, but these were without rigorous research.[119] Other concerns were expressed, such as treatment being carried out before cremation certification had been completed, and the potential for disguising crime.[120] When the 1950 Home Office Interde-

---

[115]'NAFD Pricing Survey 2009 Results' (2010) *FDM*, March, p. 16.
[116]Korczynski R.E. (1996) 'Formaldehyde Exposure in the Funeral Industry', *Journal of Safety Research*, Vol. 27, No. 3, p. 198.
[117]Haler A. (2009) 'The Biocides Directive', *Pharos International*, Vol. 75, No. 1, pp. 10–12. See also King J.S. (2006) 'P45 and a Wooden Shovel', *Pharos International*, Vol. 72, No. 3, pp. 6–7.
[118]'AIDS Fears Dispelled – But Appropriate Precautions are Necessary' (1984) *FSJ*, January, p. 32; 'BIE Statement on AIDS Cases' (1985) *FSJ*, April, p. 144; and Inman R.J. (1988) 'Guidelines for Embalming an AIDS Body' (1988) *The Embalmer*, Vol. 31, No. 1, pp. 4–5. See also Troyer J.E. (2010) 'Technologies of the HIV/AIDS Corpse', *Medical Anthropology*, Vol. 29, No. 2, pp. 129–149.
[119]Nodes W.O. (1948) *'Period Between Death and Disposal'*, Report of the Conference of the Institute of Burial and Cremation Administration, pp. 29–31; 'Mr Costello Furthers the Case for Modern Embalming' (1955) *FSJ*, November, pp. 526–527; and Dodgson M.J. (1977) *'Embalming – Is it Necessary?'* Institute of Burial and Cremation Administration Conference Report, pp. 14–18.
[120]Haler D.C. (1969) 'The Pathologist's Objections to Embalming', *TFD*, February, pp. 90–91. See also 'Embalmed Before Inquest' (1944) *FSJ*, May, p. 149. The Secretary of the Cremation Society also argued that cremation should be promoted rather than embalming. See Noble G.A. (1924) 'Undertaking as a Profession: Its Problems and Responsibilities', *BUA Monthly*, September, pp. 67–68.

partmental Report on Cremation was published it stated that 'Cremation should not be permitted if a preserving fluid has been injected before the confirmatory certificate has been given or if the body has been embalmed', and treatment after certification remains industry practice.[121] The possible effect of embalming hindering the process of combustion was also expressed but there is no evidence to support this claim.[122]

Finally, attacks on embalming as part of the movement to reform funerals have been voiced in addition to concerns about the wider environmental consequences of the treatment. After making a number of unreferenced assumptions and giving a sensational description of embalming, *The Natural Death Handbook* suggests that 'Contrary to what some funeral directors believe, viewing experiences of these altered bodies can sometimes leave damaging last impressions on family and friends. A body that looks pink and vibrant may be very upsetting to relatives...'.[123] Morrell and Smith note that it is something to be avoided as 'an unnecessary expense and an unpleasant process',[124] while Gill and Fox declare that 'mainly on environmental grounds embalming is extremely bad news'.[125] In her 'green' consumer guide, Hailes terms the process 'grotesque' with the blood replaced by a 'poison' and claims that 'the formaldehyde leaches out into the soil'.[126] Similar claims are made by the pioneer of woodland

---

[121]'Council of British Funeral Services: Cremation Regulations' (1950) *TNFD*, November, p. 834. See also *Cremation Committee Report of the Interdepartmental Committee Appointed by the Secretary of State for the Home Department* (1950) Cmnd 8009, p. 21.

[122]Carter H.D.E. (1968) 'Does Embalming Affect Cremation?' *FSJ*, April, pp. 183–190 and 'Factors Influencing the Times of Cremations' (1975) *Resurgam*, Vol. 18, No. 3, pp. 64–66. See also Mallalieu A. (2009) 'Up in Smoke or Six Feet Under', *Pharos International*, Vol. 75, No. 2, pp. 4–9. See also 'Factors Influencing the Times of Cremations' (1975) *Resurgam*, Vol. 18, No. 3, pp. 64–66.

[123]Callender R. et al. (2012b) *The Natural Death Handbook*, fifth edition, London: Natural Death Centre and Strange Attractor Press, p. 136.

[124]Morrell J. and Smith S. (2006) *We Need to Talk About the Funeral*, Totnes: Alphabet and Image Publishers, p. 38.

[125]Gill S. and Fox J. (2004) *The Dead Good Funerals Book*, Ulverston: Engineers of the Imagination p. 30. See also Cowling C. (2010a). *The Good Funeral Guide*, London: Continuum, pp. 57–64.

[126]Hailes J. (2007) *The New Green Consumer Guide*, London: Simon and Schuster, p. 224. Only one reference can be traced regarding this matter and it appears to be inconclusive. See Spongbery A.L. and Becks P.M. (2000) 'Inorganic Soil Contamination from Cemetery Leachate', *Water, Air and Soil Pollution*, Vol. 117, pp. 313–327. See also Chiappelli J. and Chiappelli T. (2008) 'Drinking Grandma: The Problem of Embalming', *Journal of Environmental Health*, No. 71.

burial, Ken West.[127] The Charter movement of the 1990s had much to say about embalming; the *Dead Citizens Charter* held that everyone preparing for death 'had the right to choose... whether or not the body should be embalmed'.[128] Severe criticism of the process came from the ICCM's *Charter for the Bereaved*, which recognised that embalming was increasingly being carried out by unqualified practitioners and 'without express permission'. However, the dearth of evidence was acknowledged: 'one or two gallons of embalming fluid can be used and the effect of this on soil, soil organisms and air quality following burial or creations needs further independent research. Our ignorance of the consequences of using this chemical [formaldehyde] is a cause for concern. In particular, the chemical is used by funeral directors and embalmers who carry no responsibility for its impact on the cemetery, crematorium or community'.[129]

Despite these attacks and criticisms, embalming continues to be an important feature of British funeral service and is being widely practised.

---

[127]West K. (2010) *A Guide to Natural Burial*, London: Shaw & Sons, pp. 56–63. and Ball P. (1995) 'Ill Informed on Subject of Embalming' *FSJ*, January, p. 33.
[128] *The Dead Citizens Charter: The Complete Edition* (1998) Bristol: The National Funerals College, p. 20.
[129] *Charter for the Bereaved* (1996) London: Institute of Burial and Cremation Administration, p. 65.

Chapter 4

Furnishing the Funeral

> The undertaker's trade was the most conservative in existence. My grandfather said that he succeeded in building up the general carpentry business, but that the undertaking was withheld from him for so long as his predecessor was able to undertake it. Not only was it a rule that 'the man who made my father's coffin shall make mine'; but all details of its construction and the conduct of the funeral were required to be the same. So general and binding was this, that a full description of every undertaking was entered into the ledger, and reference made to it when the next need arise. Was the coffin of elm or oak? Was it single or double nailed? Was it covered with black material or linseed oiled? (We never polished them.) Was the furniture best or second class? The breastplate written in paint or gold leaf? Had it calico or swansdown lining, and what was the quality of the shroud? Each family had its own acknowledged order though varying in some small items, and it was unthinkable for us to suggest any change.[1]

Coffins represent death. Used exclusively as a receptacle for the dead body, they are the most visible reminder of mortality. Their provision is central to the work of the funeral director and it is from the craft of cabinet making or joinery that the undertaker originally emerged. While today few are hand-constructed, having been replaced by ready-finished coffins from the production line, it remains the principal item of 'hardware' supplied by the funeral director, but in an unprecedented range of designs and materials.

---

[1]Rose W. (1973) *The Village Carpenter,* Wakefield: EP Publishing, pp. 123–124.

The Evolution of the British Funeral Industry in the 20th Century:
From Undertaker to Funeral Director, 77–98
Copyright © Brian Parsons, 2018
All rights of reproduction in any form reserved
doi:10.1108/978-1-78743-629-920171004

Predominately descriptive, this chapter commences with an account of coffin making around the turn of the twentieth century before examining the factors that have impacted on coffin production during the twentieth century: cremation, technological advances and the introduction of non-solid coffins and materials other than wood. As will be seen, the supply of coffins has shifted from a skilled manual task to an 'off the shelf' activity.[2]

Coffin Making

In the latter part of the nineteenth century, the vast majority of coffins were hand-constructed by the undertaker. Coffins being 'made to order' necessitated the undertaker calling at the family home to measure the deceased and returning to the workshop to construct a coffin. Length of the deceased (lying down with toes pointing forward) and width of the shoulders were the two key measurements.

Undertakers would purchase boards from suppliers (see below) and these would be stacked to dry and season the wood. Elm and oak were the main woods used, although others were available, such as deal. Elm was particularly suitable on account of its bendable characteristic. Hasluck notes that there was a north/south difference in choice of wood; in Lancashire, common coffins were made of pitch pine and the better ones of oak, while in the southern counties English oak and elm were preferred.[3] Funeral accounts reveal that woods such as Canadian light wood, Canadian walnut, pitch pine and mahogany were occasionally used. For children's coffins, English woods such as alder or aspen were suitable.

---

[2] For texts on coffin making see Hasluck P.N. (1905) *Coffin-Making and Undertaking*, London: Cassell & Co.; 'Sable Plume' (1905) *Coffins and Coffin Making*, Uxbridge: *TUJ*. For chapters in books see Gore P. (2001) 'Funeral Ritual Past and Present', in J. Hockey, J.S. Katz and N. Small eds, *Grief, Mourning and Death Ritual*, Buckingham: Open University Press, p. 214. See also 'Grandfather's Coffin Shop' (1941) *TNFD*, December, p. 188. See also Coope R. (1928) 'The Troubles of Ye Olde English Coffin Maker', *TUJ*, October, pp. 247–248 & 351; Broome J. (1934) 'Reminiscences of Undertaking 50–60 Years Ago', *TUJ*, February, pp. 67–68; and Winter W.G. (1927) 'Early Days in Funeral Directing in England', *TUJ*, August, p. 281. See also 'The Evolution of the Coffin' (1943) *TNFD*, April, p. 367 and Routley A. (1993) 'Fashions in Coffins', *FSJ*, May, pp. 33–37. See also *The New Survey of London Life and Labour Vol II London Industries I* (1931) London: P.S. King, pp. 241–243.

[3] Hasluck P.N. (1905) *Coffin-Making and Undertaking*, London: Cassell & Co. p. 22.

The boards would be cut ¾ in. thick, although the width could be as much as 1½ in. or 2 in. Mouldings were purchased in 6–8 ft lengths and used to create a rim for the lid and also as a decoration for the side of the coffin. The sawing of wood on most undertakers' premises was a manual activity; mechanised equipment required significant investment and was largely confined to the suppliers.

A 'shell' or inner coffin was often provided, in which would be placed the outer coffin or 'case'. After the measurement had been obtained, a 'shell' was prepared in the same manner as a coffin but without any furniture such as handles. It would then be internally lined. The shell would be taken to the house, placed on trestles and the deceased placed inside. Hasluck suggests that before the undertaker took the coffin to the house an outline of the base of the shell should be taken in pencil on the board selected for the bottom of the outer coffin. The coffin should be 1/8 in. larger than the shell to ensure it was a good fit. The outer coffin or 'case' would be brought to the house at the time of the funeral. Webs would be used to lift the shell into the outer coffin; the coffin would then be sealed with closing screws topped with wreath holders.[4]

Some shells were lined internally or externally with lead; this arrangement would often be referred to as a 'triple coffin'. At the higher end of the market, they were used for burials in catacombs or vaults. Working with lead was a plumber's task and the material used would range from a thickness of 0.051–0.136 in. The lead would be rolled out on the floor, then cut and folded around the shell. The shell would be hermetically sealed with solder. Panelled coffins were constructed by fixing a frame over the sides of the coffin, thereby giving the impression of routed panels.

Once the coffin had been constructed it was necessary to seal the interior to prevent fluids leaking from the coffin. Holes would be filled with putty before boiling pitch was poured into the coffin at the breast and guided to the ends. Swedish pitch was considered the best as it set within minutes and would not crack. Bunny France of A. France & Son in central London recalls using paraffin wax for sealing coffins.

The covering of coffins was occasionally undertaken using an inexpensive fabric or velvet. Black was used for adult coffins and white or, occasionally, blue for children. After stillbirth registration was introduced in 1926, the number of small coffins increased dramatically; prior to this date such children were usually placed in the coffin of an unrelated adult.

---

[4]Thompson W. (1902) 'Funeral Management: The Coffin or Shell', *The British Embalmer and Funeral Trades Monthly*, No. 2, April, p. 15.

Nails kept the fabric in place and also for decoration. The coffin was then ready for lining. Sawdust, bran or cotton waste would be placed on the base, over which a sheet of calico would be secured with tacks. The sides would be lined with calico or flannelette or swansdown. Flannel and satin were used for the most expensive coffins.

After the coffin had been constructed, the sides and lid would be oiled with raw linseed oil to bring up the grain of the wood. An alternative was to 'blacken' the surface with a mixture of turps (white spirit) and lampblack to give it a dull and mournful finish. Covering the coffin in black cloth or velvet was a further approach. This had been done for the funerals of the nobility in the seventeenth and eighteenth centuries, and it was a convenient way of disguising poor quality boards and therefore ideal for 'parish' (pauper) coffins. Alternatively, coffins were varnished or French polished.[5] The former could be easily applied with a brush; the latter required skill to ensure that the polish was applied evenly. The best polishes comprised shellac dissolved in methylated spirits (Fig. 8).[6]

In his unpublished autobiography Desmond Henley, who worked for J.H. Kenyon in central London from 1948 to 1992, recounts his experience in the workshop:

> During 1943, it was suggested by Mr Arnold Kenyon that I might like to go to the works [of Kenyon's] in Westbourne Grove W2 to learn finishing coffins. 'Finishing' consists of polishing coffins that is french polishing, wax polishing, lining coffins, and fitting handles. There is certainly a skill to all these tasks, which I very soon came to learn.
>
> When the coffins were finally made – they were placed in the 'finishing shop'. Coffins were usually made of elm or oak. When I first started 'finishing' elm was usually considered the cheaper of the two, whilst mahogany the dearest.
>
> The bare elm coffin had all the nail holes at the side of the curving [kerfed] head, and foot 'stopped' with wax and yellow ochre. The wax was melted in a pot, and the yellow ochre was added, and stirred in, to obtain the correct

---

[5] For French polishing see 'Queries and Answers' (1932) *The Illustrated Carpenter and Builder*, No. 4 November, p. 896.
[6] For a photographic study of coffins being constructed see Parsons B. (2015) 'Coffin Making in the 1930s: A Unique Insight', *Archive: The Quarterly Journal for British Industrial and Transport History*, No. 87, pp. 57–63.

Fig. 8. Coffins being constructed. *Note:* Coffins in T.H. Ebbutt's workshop in West Croydon, 1937. Within 30 years such tasks would have largely disappeared as funeral directors purchased production-line coffins in veneered chipboard and more recently in foil covered MDF (Author's collection).

colour – sometimes a dark umber [sic] was added to tone the colour of the wax. Stopping, particularly, if the coffin was to be French polished – the brown umber was not added if the elm coffin was to be wax polished. Following 'stopping' the complete head, foot and sides including curving of the coffin were sand-papered to obtain a smooth finish. The coffin having been sand papered it was 'filled-in'. The outside area of the coffin was covered with hot tallow and plaster of paris, to fill in the grain. This was applied with a handful or two – a horse hair-like material. When this mixture had set it was scraped carefully (the residue being placed in the original pot – to save wastage). The out was again sand papered to smooth the grain. French polishing then began, using a rubber of cotton wool enclosed in a piece of soft domette and applied.[7]

Once lined, the coffin would be furnished externally. The type of fittings and material they were made from reflected the quality (and cost) of the coffin. For the lower end of the market 'common' or 'unregistered' furniture was used and was available in a few patterns and in large quantities; the opposite was 'registered', which was obtained in sets of a wide variety of styles. The sets comprised the breast-plate, lid ornaments and four pairs of handles and back plates or three pairs with two pairs of rings (for the head and foot ends of the coffin). They were often made from cast iron or solid brass. For cheaper-quality work, wire handles would be used. Plated nickel furniture gave a 'massive appearance'. Stamped tin plate was also available. Handles were often of the 'bar' variety, which permitted webbing to be passed through the projecting space and held secure when lowering the coffin into the grave.

In addition to the hand-constructed coffins, other types were available from suppliers. The first cremation at Woking crematorium took place in March 1885 and the records of William Garstin, a Marylebone-based undertaker with whom the Cremation Society of England had a close connection, show that many of the coffins were constructed from deal or elm. In a small number of cases, the body was taken out of the coffin and cremated, before the ashes were placed in a wooden casket. This was deposited inside the coffin and then buried. Cremation coffins constructed from pine were advocated by the founder of the Cremation Society of England, Sir Henry Thompson, although he also endorsed the use of woollen envelopes in which the bones would remain during the combustion process.

---

[7]Henley, D.C. (1997) '*Within my Preserve: An Autobiography*', Unpublished manuscript, pp. 4–5.

These were marketed by London funeral director Halford Mills, although their use was likely to have been limited.[8] An alternative idea of a cremation shell was devised by Mr Maw of Hull; the coffin had an opening at each end and when placed on the catafalque the body could be noiselessly drawn into the incinerating chamber during words of committal.[9] However, the efficacy of this arrangement was likely to be its downfall.

In a period before embalming and refrigeration, unpleasantness resulting from decomposition was inevitable. This resulted in a number of sanitary coffins appearing on the market, for example, Birch's mortuary shell of 1896, a sealed iron coffin with a glass face panel; on the side was a discreet tap attached to rubber tubing that could be led out of the window or up the chimney to permit the decomposition gases to escape.[10] Other niche coffins, including those with devices for clients concerned about premature burial, continued to be marketed until the 1920s.[11]

In contrast to the coffin, the rectangular-shaped casket was advertised in trade journals towards the end of the nineteenth century. Regarded as an American innovation, they were nevertheless embraced by the two largest suppliers, Dottridge Bros and Ingall, Parsons, Clive & Co Ltd, but their adoption was only modest.[12]

The Suppliers

Wholesale suppliers were essential to the funeral industry to provide wood for coffins along with external furnishings, linings and shrouds and equipment such as trestles and coffin biers. In many respects it was their range of products and services that influenced what funeral directors offered to their clients. At the turn of the century Birmingham was the centre of the coffin furnishing industry, comprising numerous small firms in addition to Ingall, Parsons, Clive & Co Ltd.[13] In London, the most important

---

[8]Parsons B. (2005a) *Committed to the Cleansing Flame: The Development of Cremation in Nineteenth Century England*, Reading: Spire Books, pp. 121–128.
[9]'A New Cremation Shell' (1900) *TUJ*, October, p. 130.
[10]'Birch's Mortuary Shell', *The Lancet*, 20 June 1896, p. 1728.
[11]'The Life-Saving Coffin' (1912) *TUJ*, February, p. 38. See also 'Life Saving Coffin' (1911) *Perils of Premature Burial*, Vol. 3, No. 27, October–December, p. 23. For an earlier example see 'The Month's Patents' (1910) *TUJ*, May, p. 120.
[12]Kiernan J. (2008) 'The Casket Story: History of the Modern Burial Box', *American Funeral Director*, Vol. 131, No. 6, pp. 18–20.
[13]Church R.A. and Smith B.M.D. (1966) 'Competition and Monopoly in the Coffin Furniture Industry, 1870–1915', *The Economic History Review (New Series)*, Vol. 19, No. 3, pp. 621–641.

general supplier was Dottridge Bros.[14] Henry Smith also operated in this market.[15] These suppliers were supplemented by smaller organisations that were often specialists in one particular item, or whose distribution was limited by locality, such as C.W. Waters in east London.[16] A review of supply companies operating at the end of the twentieth century reveals that none founded prior to 1940s were in existence. Dottridge Bros along with Ingall, Parsons, Clive, Newman Bros and Henry Smith have all disappeared. The industry is now supplied by organisations largely established since World War II including specialist coffin providers sourcing their products from abroad or making coffins as a sideline (Fig. 9).

Coffins in the Twentieth Century

During the twentieth century, three principal factors have had an impact upon the types of coffins used by funeral directors: increased mechanisation of coffin production and finishing; cremation; and the introduction of non-solid coffins and materials other than wood.

---

[14]Parsons B. (2009a) 'Unknown Undertaking: The History of Dottridge Bros Wholesale Manufacturers to the Funeral Trade', *Archive: The Quarterly Journal for British Industrial and Transport History*, No. 63, pp. 41–53. See also 'The Dorset Works of Messrs Dottridge Bros Ltd' (1921) *BUA Monthly*, November, pp. 106–108 and 'Company News: Dottridge Brothers Ltd' (1985) *TFD*, October, pp. 21–22.
[15]Following compulsory purchase, the business relocated from Battersea Park Road to Garrett Lane in Earlsfield where it remained until closure in 2005. See 'Farewell to Henry Smith Coffin Manufacturer' (2005) *FSJ*, August, pp. 70–71. For historical material about the firm see 'Standard Fleet of Modern Funeral Cars' Enterprising Development by Battersea Funeral Directors' (1925) *BUA Monthly*, February, pp. 209–210; 'Two Undertakers' Chapels. How Undertakers are Giving the Public Service' (1930) *BUA Monthly*, September, p. 71; 'Henry Smith (Battersea) Ltd: One Hundred Years of Pioneer Service' (1947) *FSJ*, April, pp. 191–192; and 'Henry Smith Stays in Battersea' (1967) *FSJ*, April, pp. 179–180.
[16]Charles W. Waters was an undertaker and coffin manufacturer in Bow, east London. (See 'A Well-Known Traveller's Autobiography. Who in London Doesn't Know E.W. Waters?' (1906) *TUJ*, November, pp. 296–298 and 'The Building Up of Messrs Waters Brothers' Business' (1921) *BUA Monthly*, December, pp. 135–136). He had a musical family and their ensemble entertained a number of BUA London Centre annual dinners. His daughter, Miss Elsie Waters, along with her sister, Doris, would form a duo that by the 1920s had acquired celebrity status in the music halls. Their brother Jack, who later changed his surname to Warner, became a familiar face as the policeman in the 1960s TV series, *Dixon of Dock Green*.

Fig. 9. Casket being constructed. *Note:* Despite the widespread use of mass-produced coffins, the demand for high specification coffins and caskets continues. Henry Smith in Earlsfield, south London, was one such supplier. These images of the workshop were taken in August 2005, one month before closure (Author's collection).

Increased Mechanisation of Coffin Production and Finishing

As the twentieth century progressed, the labour-intensive task of coffin making has changed through technological innovation. While the sawing of tree trunks into boards continued to be undertaken in the wholesalers' saw mills, undertakers would produce a range of basic coffins in their own workshops without the need for expensive equipment. However, more elaborate coffins such as those with panelled sides or with raised lids could be sourced from specialist suppliers.

Writing in *The Village Carpenter,* Rose notes the labour-intensive task of preparing coffin boards:

> For the making of the coffins large mellow butts of oak and elm were sawn at our pit, the oak always into one-inch boards and the elm into two thicknesses – some one inch, others three-quarters of an inch, the latter for cheap coffins for poor people. The sawing of a tree into coffin boards would often take two men the greater part of a week. After cutting, the boards were stacked outdoors with strips of wood laid between each to allow for ventilation. When sufficiently dry they were carried and stacked in a loft, this time without strips in between.[17]

Advertisements in *TUJ* provide an insight into the introduction of mechanisation; steam-driven bench saws appeared in 1913 but these were costly and a high volume of work would be necessary to justify investment. It was, however, the interwar years when relatively inexpensive electrically powered tools became widely available. Most were generic carpentry tools. In 1931, the British Equipment Co advertised three hand-held devices: the Skilsaw saw, the Skilsaw Sander and the Miami Polisher. The Skilsaw would be used for cutting and kerfing wood. The same firm produced an electric plane and an improved model, the 'tarplaner' in 1938. Other equipments included the 'crystal power' spray gun for spraying polish, varnish or paint onto coffins, which appeared in 1935, and the 'Jordan pistol tacker' for stapling linings to the sides of a coffin. Adverts made great play of the savings to be gained from acquisition of the equipment; some even provided quantification.[18] Of the tarplaner the copy read,

---

[17] Rose W. (1973) *The Village Carpenter*, Wakefield: EP Publishing, pp. 123–124.
[18] See 'Useful Tools for the Trade. Three New Labour Saving Devices' (1931) *BUA Monthly*, November, p. 119.

'It pays for itself in time saved' and 'Does 2 weeks work in a day. Saves up to 30s [shillings] an hour', 'This elm set, including ends, was cut by a Skilsaw in 3 mins 40 secs' and 'Electric planing does the work of 10'.

One labour-saving coffin which could be purchased in 'flat pack' from many suppliers was the 'set'. Also referred to as a 'knock-down' coffin, it comprised six pieces: the lid, base, foot, head and two sides, which required assembly. In 1927, Wybert Thomas & Son produced a quick-assembling set that would take only 25 minutes to construct, using four bolts. Time and efficiency were becoming the bywords.

Cremation

Perhaps the most influential factor in coffin production has been cremation.[19] The first regulations issued by crematoria can be traced to 1901 with the opening of Hull Crematorium, where their instructions stated:

> There is no smoke and little visible flame before the body is introduced, and if the coffin be made according to instructions (that is, preferably of dry oak boards, half an inch in thickness, without paint or varnish, and with no metal fixings of any kind, save under certain conditions, a thin zinc lining), there is practically no smoke during cremation.[20]

In 1909, formal guidelines were published by the London Cremation Company, the owners of London's Golders Green and also at Woking. Even at this stage only a modest number of cremations took place; in 1909 there were 855 at the 13 crematoria in operation in Great Britain. The regulations were announced in *TUJ*:

> The coffin should invariably be of some readily combustible wood such as cotton-wood, American whitewood, Canadian elm, thin pine or three-ply wood. English elm and oak being difficult to burn are most undesirable, and when their

---

[19]It can be argued that in the early years of cremation some undertakers were wary of this new form of disposal, as restrictions on the type of coffin that could be cremated reduced the possibility of the sale of a more expensive receptacle. See 'Interview with Mr George A. Noble. Secretary of the London Cremation Company Ltd' (1910) *TUJ*, October, pp. 249–250.
[20]'The Hull Crematorium' (1904) *TUJ*, February, p. 31. See also 'How to go about a Cremation' (1904) *TUJ*, April, pp. 74–75.

use cannot be avoided the board should be as thin as possible and well-seasoned and dry.

The notice continued:

a) There is no objection to the coffin used for a cremation being polished and having the usual furniture, but, unless made of special combustible metal (now obtainable from the wholesale manufacturers) the handles and breastplate should be so fixed as to be easily removed.
b) Any outer case or coffin not burnt with the body, and all handles and breastplates removed from a coffin, must be at once removed from the Company's premises by the undertakers in charge of the cremation.
c) There must be no cross-piece on the bottom of the coffin, and all screws and nails in this part of it should be carefully countersunk.
d) Pitch or sawdust in the coffin must be avoided entirely, as this will considerably retard cremation and cause black smoke. Other materials answering the same purposes should be used instead. The less lining, etc., inside the coffin the better.
e) The company will not cremate a body in a lead or iron coffin. Where it is desirable that the body should be cremated in a metal case, zinc only may be used as this metal is readily consumed.
f) An extra fee of 10s 6d will be charged if the coffin is not in accordance with requirements unless there is a valid reason for not providing a suitable coffin.[21]

Suppliers were aware that cremation would require a less substantial coffin and advertised appropriate examples. The London Necropolis Company offered 'special cremation shells' in 1900, while Dottridge Bros responded to the regulations by producing their 'City' cremation coffin constructed from 'three-ply birch upon a frame, waterproofed and lined completed with polished oak finish'. Using this coffin, they estimated, it would take 70 minutes for cremation to be completed. However, there was clearly disagreement among crematoria concerning which woods could be cremated. In 1938, the owners of the South London Crematorium wrote to *TNFD* to say, 'Please understand to us that it is immaterial what timber

---

[21]'Special Notice. Golders' Green and Woking Crematoria' (1909) *TUJ*, August, p. 199.

is used for coffins or caskets for cremation... with the exception of teak. We have no preference for soft over hard woods'.[22]

When Dottridge Bros published their *Cremation* brochure around 1925 they included further types of cremation coffins, including the 'Ilford', which was 'covered with grey felt, upholstered with silk cord and tassels, inscription plate and closing caps, waterproofed and lined'. Cloth-covered coffins were increasingly used during World War II when there was a shortage of quality timber.[23] Cloth-covered cremation shells remained in use until the 1980s. By this time the shells would have been chipboard. In addition to grey, coloured felt in purple, green, burgundy and black was also used.[24]

Of note in the above guidelines is that funeral directors could remove the outer case and also the non-combustible fittings from the coffin before cremation took place. The extent of this practice is not known but could well have given rise to folklore perpetuating the myth that bodies were not cremated in a coffin. Unfortunately, the removal and sale of coffin furnishings has not been merely myth, but fact, such as the 1944 case in Scotland.[25] The Federation of British Cremation Authorities (FBCA) responded with the launch of a Code of Practice. The London Cremation Company's guidelines became the basis of the first 'Code of Cremation Practice and Instructions for Funeral Directors', which was circulated by the FBCA at the end of 1945. Clauses 3 and 4 are similar to those published 36 years earlier.[26]

---

[22]'South London Crematorium' (1938) *TNFD*, November, p. 187.
[23]'Cremation in War Time. Superintendent's Review' (1943) *TUFDJ*, May, p. 135.
[24]See Doyle C.G. (1974a) 'Death in Modern Society', *TFD*, July, pp. 335 & 341–343.
[25]See McHale B. (2002) 'Cremation Lore and Law' in P.C. Jupp and H.J. Grainger eds, *Golders Green Crematorium 1902–2002: A London Centenary in Context*, London: London Cremation Company and Newall V. (1985) 'Folklore and Cremation', *Folklore*, Vol. 96, No. 2, pp. 139–155. See 'The Aberdeen 'Coffins' Case' (1944) *Pharos*, Vol. 1, No. 4, p. 2; Jupp, P.C. (2009) 'The Aberdeen Coffins Case and the Future of British Cremation', *Pharos International*, Vol. 75, No. 3, pp. 28–30; 'The Aberdeen Crematorium Case' (1944) *TNFD*, November, p. 177; 'The Coffins Case' (1944) *TNFD*, December, pp. 213–214; 'Lids Removed for Cremation' (1944) *TUFDJ*, November, pp. 331–332; '"Coffin Lids" Appeal Fails' (1944) *TUFDJ*, December, pp. 355–356; and Jupp J.C. et al. (2017) *Cremation in Modern Scotland: History, Architecture and the Law*, Edinburgh: Birlinn, pp. 141–146. For a further case at Darlington see 'Coffin Lid Case Result' (1945) *TNFD*, July, p. 6; 'Alleged Theft of Coffin Lids at Darlington' (1945) *FSJ*, March, pp. 83–85; and 'Coffin Lids Charge' (1945) *FSJ*, July, p. 207.
[26]'Code of Cremation Practice and Instructions for Funeral Directors' (1945) *TUFDJ*, November, p. 326. See also 'Federation of British Cremation Authorities. Instructions for Funeral Directors' (1945) *Pharos*, Vol. 11, No. 4, p. 4.

The Introduction of Non-Solid Coffins and Materials Other than Wood

The years following the end of World War II witnessed not only the dramatic increase in cremation (7.8 per cent in 1945, 24.35 per cent in 1955 and 44.28 per cent in 1965), but also a shift from the use of solid wood coffins. Veneered coffins were being advertised by the mid-1940s, and in the post-World War II years Dottridge Bros announced that they were producing veneers using glue developed for aircraft manufacturing.[27]

Woods other than English-grown oak and elm were increasingly available. From domestic sources came ash, chestnut and teak, while obeche and utile came from West Africa. Oak, elm and beech were also sourced from Japan.[28]

Some of the larger coffin manufacturers such as Dottridge Bros and L.T. & R. Vowles were adopting mass production techniques not only for coffin sets, but also for finished coffins. An advertisement in the March 1959 *FSJ* posed the question:

> Coffins or Set? In the past tradition and convenience have called for the large use of prepared sets. In the future funeral directors will increase the present trend to use the factory-made coffin which offers the convenience of wide variety and good finish, and economy in stock holding and high wages.

Relocation following bombing during World War II offered the opportunity to modernise. In 1950, Dottridge Bros purchased a seven-acre site in Hertfordshire. However, while this firm used advertising to compare their services and products with the magnificence of elm trees, a crisis was looming.

Elm has been in use as the principal wood used for the construction of coffins for many years, but two challenges emerged in the post-war years. In 1951, the Forestry Commission stated that the felling of elm trees must decrease by 50 per cent.[29] Although the Dutch elm disease *phelom necrosis* had been present in the United Kingdom since 1927, it was a particularly virulent strain, arriving 40 years later, that claimed an estimated

---

[27] See Advert by J. Nicholson & Sons for a ''Beresford' Veneered Coffin' (1946) *FSJ*, December, p. 458.
[28] See 'Coffin Timbers' (1938) *TNFD*, September, p. 118.
[29] Quoted in 'Are Funerals Too Expensive?' *Fifeshire Advertiser*, 1 September 1951.

25 million trees. Overnight the stock of domestic elm for coffins dried up.[30] Although solid wood from the home and overseas sources continued to be used, manufacturers also made use of other products. A three-layer formica wood chipboard coffin with an oak veneer appeared in 1964.[31] Chipboard was gradually adopted and by 1969 Dottridge Bros were advertising their 'Norwich' veneered oak casket, being a modern design slightly tapered at the shoulders.

During the 1980s, coffins made from medium-density fibreboard (MDF) were introduced. Produced by breaking down softwood into wood fibre, then bonding it with a wax and resin binder before being pressed into panels, it was considered ideal for coffins. Although much heavier than chipboard, it could be shaped and would not split, and was strong in addition to being ideal for veneering. By the 1990s, it was estimated that around 90 per cent of coffins used in the United Kingdom were veneered chipboard or MDF.[32]

As mentioned above, American caskets were introduced in the latter part of the nineteenth century and Dottridge Bros advertised various designs on the front cover of *TUJ* including their 'Norway' design in 1913. Some manufacturers, such as Henry Smith, produced their own distinctive range of rectangular caskets. Catalogues and advertisements showed the caskets (which were named after streets in the Earlsfield area of south London) such as the Garratt, the Soudan and Brocklebank. In 1932, the first all-metal British-manufactured 'American' style coffin was used in the United Kingdom. Made for the funeral of Mr William Simons, general manager of the British Iron and Steel Company Ltd, it was constructed of venetian bronze finished pressed steel with statuary bronze mountings and nameplate, and made by R.H. Coop & Sons of Oldham. The *Journal* somewhat righteously commented:

> Those people who can afford metal caskets of distinction never would care for the foreign made article, and experience has shown that the American-manufactured metal

---

[30] 'Notes' (1931) *TUJ*, December, p. 392.
[31] 'Wood Chipboard in Coffin Manufacture' (1964) *FSJ*, July, p. 400. There is evidence to show that veneered coffins were available by the end of World War II. See 'Veneers and Coffin Making' (1945) *TNFD*, December, p. 225. It should be noted that wood substitutes were marketed to the trade in the 1920s. See 'Imitation Oak' (1923) *BUA Monthly*, February, p. 244.
[32] Wilde B. (1992b) 'The History of Coffin and its Fittings', *FDM*, Vol. 72, No. 11, pp. 39–41.

casket available in this country has been almost solely used for wealthy Americans dying in the British Isles or on the Continent to be taken overseas for burial.[33]

In the 1980s, caskets in metal and wood were imported from US manufacturers such as Batesville. Others could be obtained from Bradnam Joinery and the London Casket Company, the latter marketing models from the York Casket Company of Pennsylvania. As time has passed the opportunity to use American-style caskets in metal or wood became increasingly limited. They were unsuitable for cremation and some cemeteries adopted an environmental policy that prevented the burial of metal caskets or coffins. However, the metal caskets were particularly suitable for the international transportation of human remains as they could be sealed airtight.[34]

Research reveals that a range of alternative coffins had come to the market, including those for removing bodies. In 1904, a wicker ambulance basket suitable for the removal of bodies was advertised, while in 1908 a concrete burial coffin appeared, and a rubber coffin was suggested in 1931.[35] Bakelite was developed between 1907 and 1909 by Dr Leo Baekeland and in the 1940s a coffin was marketed.[36] Although being advertised as 'eminently suitable for cremation', the cremation authority at Hull complained that one gave off a 'tremendous amount of smoke'.[37] It had a limited lifespan. In 1960, the coffin-shaped 'Primrose' fibreglass removal shell was designed. Being made of brown glass-reinforced plastic, it was ideal as a temporary receptacle to remove the body from the place of death to the mortuary and was particularly useful where death had occurred in distressing circumstances. It was light, tough and could be easily cleaned with water. These continue to be used by funeral directors, although more recently the collapsible wheel stretcher (a Washington, or sometimes called a gurney) has replaced the shell.

---

[33] 'The First All-Metal British Manufactured Casket Buried in this Country' (1932) *TUJ*, January, p. 23.
[34] See Parsons B. (2017a) 'Funeral Directors and Distance Transportation of the Dead', *The Embalmer*, Vol. 55, No. 4, pp. 31–39.
[35] 'The Imperishable Concrete Coffin' (1920) *TUJ*, January, pp. 23–24 and 'New Idea for Coffins' (1931) *TUJ*, September, p. 313. For an earlier example see 'Correspondence: A New Idea in Coffins' (1918) *TUJ*, October, p. 258.
[36] For an advertisement depicting the 'Halo' Bakelite coffin produced by the Ultralite Casket Company Ltd, see *TNFD*, March, 1941, p. 289. A Bakelite coffin was included at the plastics exhibition at London's Science Museum in 2008.
[37] 'Three-Day Cremation Conference' (1946) *FSJ*, August, p. 285.

Coffin Furniture

A wide range of coffin furniture has been available in a variety of metals and designs. However, as with coffins, the biggest influence on furnishings has been cremation. As noted above, brass and other cast metals could not be cremated so manufacturers had to create new designs. Although light metal was acceptable for combustion, the solution was found firstly with wooden items and then with plastic.[38] In 1946, the Universal Engineering Company was offering 'gravity and pressure die castings, and sand castings, in non-ferrous metals'. In the 1950s, Henry Smith offered a ring handle in English oak. Injection moulded handles also appeared in the 1950s. Designs and durability improved to the extent that by the 1980s most coffin handles, lid ornaments, nameplates, Masonic emblems and crucifixes were made of 'brassed' or nickel-plated coloured plastic.

Coffin Linings

Solid wood coffins always required sealing to prevent leakage. As already mentioned, usually pitch would be boiled and poured into the coffin, with wax being a substitute.[39] However, pitch was deemed unsuitable for cremation coffins, so alternatives emerged including 'Coffinseal' and 'Coffinex'. None required heating and they could be applied with a brush; they all provided an effective seal with the consistency of rubber for all joints, cracks and knots and also of MDF or chipboard coffins. The preparations were also approved by cremation authorities as they contained no tar or pitch.

As with other aspects of coffin preparation, cremation made an impact on linings. Polyvinyl chloride plastic replaced pitch and was cut from a roll and stapled to the sides of the coffin. However, the Environmental Protection Act 1990 caused the FBCA's 'Instructions to funeral directors' to prohibit the use of such material along with sawdust, wood shavings and any material that created unnecessary emissions.[40] Products such as

---

[38] See 'Post War Fittings' (1942) *TUFDJ*, November, p. 269.

[39] The author recalls sealing coffins with wax for a London funeral director in the mid-1980s.

[40] Wilde B. (1991) 'Materials Used in Coffin and Furnishing Manufacture', *TFD*, Vol. 71, No. 6, pp. 17–18. See also 'PVC and Cremation' (1976) *TFD*, January, p. 25; 'Our Place in the Environment' (1991) *FSJ*, Vol. 106, No. 4, pp. 47–61; and Wilde B. (1992a) 'The Role of the Manufacturers of Coffins and Furnishings in Responding to the EPA', *Pharos International*, Vol. 58, No. 4, pp. 132–141.

'Cremfilm', which was available in roll form from John Wilde & Co, were acceptable alternatives. Alternatively, one-piece coffin liners have also been produced.

Inscription Plates

Traditionally, the name of the deceased and other details such as age and date of birth and/or death have appeared on the lid of the coffin. Secured to the lid approximately in line with the widest part of the shoulder, the inscription plate was often referred to as the 'breastplate'. How the plate was presented was largely dependent on the cost of the coffin; those at the higher end of the range would have an engraved nameplate secured to a mount or plinth, while at the other end of the scale, on the lid of a coffin containing a pauper the initials would be painted by hand. When a coffin or casket was interred in a catacomb, a second eye-level inscription plate would be secured to the end panel of the coffin to facilitate easy identification when looking at a shelf or niche.

Nameplates could be prepared in the workshop or outsourced to a local engraver or one of the specialist suppliers. If the former, the method was to sketch the inscription with a crayon or sable pencil (a writer's pencil), varnish it and then dust bronze powder freely over the letters with a camel-hair brush. An hour later the surplus powder could be dusted off, revealing the inscription. The letters would be kept straight by chalking a piece of thread and stretching it across the plate. It was also possible to purchase ready-made black letters for adhering to the coffin lid.

As with coffin production, it was during the interwar years when technological innovations were adopted with respect to engraving. In 1931, the first pantograph engraver to cut coffin nameplates was advertised.[41] This machine involved loading and aligning brass stencil letters on a frame, then carefully tracing over them with a pointer. The latter was attached by a continuous belt to a revolving needle that cut the plate. A steady hand was required; one slip would result in the whole plate being ruined. A similar machine was the Gravograph, which also appeared around the late 1960s. Instant lettering and symbols using Letraset transfers were also advertised to the trade in the 1960s.[42] By the 1990s, computer engravers became available, thus eliminating the time-consuming setting-up of the

---

[41] Advertisement for Taylor Hopson Engraving Machine (1931) *TUJ*, April, p. 128.
[42] Advertisement 'Letraset' (1966) *FSJ*, June, p. 344.

pantographs. The cutting technology is much the same as the pantograph, but the inscription is typed and viewed on a screen before the plate is engraved.

Coffins for Children

There is much evidence to show that in the nineteenth and early part of the twentieth centuries the bodies of stillborn and young children would be placed in the coffin of an adult.[43] When a child's coffin was supplied it would often be covered with white domette.[44] A change in attitude towards children's funerals occurred in the late 1970s as the opportunity was given for the family to mourn the loss.[45] Today, funeral directors continue to offer white cloth-covered coffins in addition to coffins constructed from a variety of materials and decorated with teddy bears, flowers and nursery themes along with American-style caskets.

Coffins in the Late Twentieth Century

In the last two decades of the twentieth century the range of coffins available to funeral directors and their clients has never been so wide. While the Environmental Protection Act 1990 required manufacturers to ensure that their products gave off minimal emissions when cremated, the desire for greater choice stimulated by the funeral reform movement along with the 'green' credentials of those giving funeral instructions encouraged funeral directors to provide a range of coffins constructed from materials other than wood and also from sustainable sources.[46] Cardboard was one

---

[43] Parsons B. (2017b) 'Ninety Years On: The Registration of Births and Deaths Act 1926', *ICCM Journal*, Vol. 85, No. 2, pp. 56–59. See also Strange J.-M. (2005) *Death, Grief and Poverty in Britain, 1870–1914*. Cambridge: Cambridge University Press.
[44] For a scene of a child's coffin being constructed see *Kensington Calling* (1930) produced by Kensington Housing Trust.
[45] Kohner N. (2000) 'Pregnancy, Loss and the Death of a Baby: Parent's Choices', in D. Dickenson, M. Johnson and J.S. Katz eds, *Death, Dying and Bereavement*, second edition, London: Sage, pp. 355–359.
[46] Wilson P. (1991) 'The Impact of the Environmental Protection Act on the Funeral Service', *TFD*, Vol. 71, No. 7, pp. 12–13. See also Whiston R.W. (1976) *'Coffin Manufacture and the Use of Synthetic Materials'*, Institute of Burial and Cremation Administration Conference Report, pp. 40–44 and Mallalieu A. (2009) 'Up in Smoke or Six Feet Under?' *Pharos International*, Vol. 75, No. 2, pp. 4–9.

of the first alternatives to be marketed,[47] followed by bamboo and wicker. More recently, eco pod, banana leaf, dried grass and sea grass have also become available (Fig. 10). In many cases they are produced in sizes for children in addition to matching designs for urns. Coffins and ash caskets made from solid paulownia have also been advertised. It is extremely lightweight and a fast-growing sustainable wood that looks like oak when polished. Wool coffins have also appeared.[48]

Continuing the tradition of covering the exterior surfaces of coffins, computer printing technology has permitted coffins to be covered in vinyl and paper foil bearing pictures or designs such as football team colours, flowers and personal images. Concern over the cremation of coffins led

Fig. 10. An eco coffin. *Note:* The range of coffins available in the twenty-first century embraces not only MDF and solid woods, but also wicker, cardboard, bamboo and those with decorative transfers. A coffin made from sea grass is seen here at the opening of a woodland burial ground in 2009 (Author's collection).

---

[47]'Cardboard Coffin Project' (1983) *FSJ*, April, p. 165.
[48]The use of woollen shrouds at funerals has a long heritage that extended to a bill of 1678 'for the encouragement of the manufacturers of wool'. It was not repealed until 1814 See 'Notes' (1906) *TUJ*, February, p. 31; 'Burials Act', 1678 (1908) *TUJ*, September, p. 211; and 'Burial in Woollen' (1938) *TUFDJ*, December, pp. 449–450.

one firm to develop the 'coffin cover', comprising an external ornamental fold-up outer coffin that disguises an inner basic receptacle.[49] Perhaps the most novel range has been the 'crazy coffins' constructed by Vic Fearn & Co. These are produced in the shape of a skip, sledge, ski bag, canal barge or railway carriage (see Fig. 4).[50]

Urns and Caskets

The residue after cremation required the funeral director to offer a range of urns or caskets into which the ashes could be replaced and then be buried, deposited, transported or stored. The distinction between the two reflects the shape and material for construction; the casket being wood and generally rectangular or square, while an urn would be of non-wood construction and in a variety of shapes.

The ashes of the first person to be cremated at Woking in March 1885 were placed in a ceramic urn and then placed in a coffin that was then buried in the catacombs of Kensal Green Cemetery.[51] Other ashes were buried in caskets and interred in family graves. William Garstin provided a 'polished elm box with brass handles' and also a 'stained deal box, for ashes, with brass handles'. Suppliers such as Dottridge Bros soon realised that a choice of receptacle should be offered to clients and would be a source of income to funeral directors. Ingall, Parsons, Clive & Co advertised a stoneware urn and an oak casket in 1889, while in 1909 Dottridge Bros publicised their caskets and urns made from bronze, brass, porcelain, oak and mahogany. Caskets would have an engraved inscription plate mounted on the top. The casket would be accessible by unscrewing the base.

Plastic temporary urns, such as the 'polytainer', have been used extensively from the 1960s onwards. Being lightweight, inexpensive and durable, they were ideal for storing ashes before they were scattered or transferred to a more permanent receptacle. In parallel with contemporary coffins, urns have been made in a variety of materials such as cardboard, salt or gelatine (for dissolving in water), wicker (with an inner fabric lining), papier mâché and other biodegradable products.

---

[49]'Coffin Cover Launched' (2003) *FSJ*, August, pp. 10–12.
[50]*Crazy Coffins: Verrückte Särge aus England* (2005) Nottingham: Vic Fearn. Exhibition catalogue to accompany exhibition of the Museum für Sepulkralkultur, Kassel.
[51]See Parsons B. (2005a) *Committed to the Cleansing Flame: The Development of Cremation in Nineteenth Century England*, Reading: Spire Books, pp. 135–145.

Today, a visitor to a funeral director's workshop will find a supply of ready-finished coffins (complete with interior linings and handles) in a small range of sizes. This leaves the operative with the task of securing into the interior a coloured lining along with the engraving and fixing of the nameplate. Many coffins including large sizes and special orders are available within 24 hours from a supplier, negating the need for stocks to be maintained but also facilitating a wide range to be offered to the client from a brochure or the internet. Once a skill requiring specialist training, coffin preparation is now a relatively simple task that for many funeral directors can be efficiently 'undertaken' once the day's funerals have been completed.

Chapter 5

Transport to Paradise

The use of different forms of transport to move a coffin has largely been determined by the length and complexity of the journey. At the commencement of the twentieth century the horse and the railway were the principal modes of funerary transport; at its close these have been replaced by the motor hearse and aeroplane.

Supported by research from funeral directors' records, this chapter examines the differing forms of conveying a coffin, while the final section assesses transport in the context of the shift towards cremation and its impact on organisational change.[1]

Carrying the Coffin and Walking Funerals

At 1900, four modes of transport were utilised by undertakers: walking funerals, wheel bier, horse-drawn hearses and rail network. In addition, ships were used for overseas destinations. Irrespective of the mode employed, however, the bearing of coffins has been an important feature

---

[1]For general surveys of funeral transport see Parsons B. (2001) *The London Way of Death*, Stroud: Sutton Publishing; Parsons B. (2014e) *The Undertaker at Work: 1900–1950*, London: Strange Attractor Press, pp. 231–254; Reader D. (2008a) *A Pictorial History of the British Hearse 1800–2008*, privately printed by Dean Reader; and Scott N.M. (2011) *The British Hearse and the British Funeral*, Brighton: Book Guild Publishing. See also Mitchell S. and Reader D. (2012). *The British Hearse. Vol. 1: 1800–1920*, privately printed by Dean Reader; Mitchell S. and Reader D. (2014) *The British Hearse. Vol. 2: The 1920s*, privately printed by Dean Reader; and Reader D. and Mitchell S. (2015) *The British Hearse, Vol. 3: The 1930s*, privately printed by Dean Reader.

of British funerals. Funeral records in addition to photographic material shows the use of six or occasionally eight bearers carrying the coffin at shoulder height. This number was necessary not only for heavy solid (and sometimes triple-lined) coffins, but also when a distance had to be walked through a village to the church preceding burial. According to folklore, bearers were often matched to the age or marital status of the deceased. As will be discussed below, it is likely that agreements between the BUA and the BFWA negotiated the use of a minimum number of bearers and also that bearing staff were not permitted to drive vehicles. The latter was especially important at horse-drawn funerals as animals could not be left unattended.[2] The arrival of motor vehicles eliminated this issue and so drivers were increasingly deployed as coffin bearers.

In rural areas, funerals were often 'walked'; that is, carried the distance between the location where the coffin was resting to the place of service and/or interment. These involved the funeral director providing four or six bearers to shoulder and walk with the coffin; it may have been the case that two teams of bearers were utilised and that the coffin was conveyed on a frame at shoulder height. Such funerals were not entirely the prerogative of the rural community; the records of Frederick W. Paine in north Surrey note a number of walking funerals in the area between 1908 and 1940.[3]

Today, four bearers are generally used to shoulder coffins, unless it is particularly heavy or there is a long carry and possible steps leading into a church (Fig. 11). An increasing trend is for family members and friends to act as bearers under the guidance of the funeral director but with staff accompanying the coffin and to provide lifting assistance.

The Wheel Bier

Where there was a short distance between the deceased's residence, where the coffin rested between death and the funeral, to the place of burial, a wheel bier would sometimes be used. The historical use of hand and wheeled bier has been charted by Julian Litten.[4] Many different designs

---

[2]Unattended Coaches in Cemeteries (1914) *TUJ*, May, p. 141. See also Parsons B. (2014e) *The Undertaker at Work: 1900–1950*, London: Strange Attractor Press, p. 257.
[3]Parsons B. (2017c) *Frederick W. Paine Funeral Directors: A History*, London: F.W. Paine, p. 25.
[4]Litten J.W.S. (2002). *The English Way of Death: The Common Funeral Since 1450*, London: Robert Hale, pp. 119–134.

Fig. 11. A funeral director at work. *Note:* The funeral director at work: staff from Leverton & Sons carry the coffin containing Baroness Thatcher into the Church of St Clement Danes, London on 17 April 2013 (Author's collection).

have been used, from those that simply consist of a frame on which the coffin is secured and then carried by hand, to the more elaborate Stretton's Patent Improved Funeral Wheeled Bier and Grave Carrier, which dates from 1887.[5] As with other requisites, Dottridge Bros and Ingall, Parsons and Clive constructed and supplied a range of different wheel biers.[6] Many were of simple design and were usually often kept in the parish church or in a bier house.[7] A wheel bier drawn by fellow priests was used to transport the coffin of Fr Arthur Stanton from the church of

---

[5] Parsons B. (2006b) 'The Bier in Action', *FSJ*, June, pp. 101–105.
[6] For a curious case of funeral directors restricting the use of a wheel bier at a funeral see 'Funerals (Wheel-Biers)', *Hansard*, 29 July 1920, cols 1624–1626 and 'Monopolies and Combines (Undertakers)', *Hansard*, 28 July 1920, col. 1439–1440.
[7] For example, Ketton in Leicestershire 'Follow-up: Can you help? The Stretton Bier' (2008) *FSJ*, August, pp. 48–53. See also Mortimer J.G.M. (2004). *The History of the Funeral Bier: Exemplified by the Various Biers in Churches in North Herefordshire*, Leominster: J.G.M. Mortimer (Private publication). Bier houses can also be seen at Hardwick Cemetery in King's Lynn and in Margate Cemetery. Litten J.W.S. (2004). '*A Brief History of Hardwick Road Cemetery, King's Lynn, Norfolk*' King's Lynn: The Friends of Hardwick Road Cemetery.

St Alban the Martyr Holborn through the streets of central London to the Necropolis Station at Waterloo in April 1913.[8] Wheel biers were also used to move bodies to a coroner's mortuary; a framed compartment covered with fabric would conceal the body. Wheel biers continued to be advertised in *TUJ* until the late 1930s.[9]

A more contemporary version of the wheel bier is the collapsible trolley. First advertised in 1905, they were ideal for moving coffins around the funeral director's premises; and they have a metal concertina-style frame that compresses to enable the device to be kept in the lower compartment of a hearse or removal vehicle. They are also suitable for supporting large coffins and American-style caskets where weight prevents the coffin/casket being shouldered by bearers. More sophisticated body collapsible stretchers (sometimes called 'gurneys') for removals from hospitals have also been devised, and can be operated by one person.

The Horse-Drawn Hearse

While horse-drawn transport has a long connection with funerals, the introduction of the horse-drawn hearse can be attributed to the opening during the nineteenth century of out-of-town cemeteries.[10] Following the Burial Acts of 1852 and 1853 cemeteries were increasingly located at a distance from the living; the horse would have been the only viable way to efficiently convey a coffin and mourners. Kensington Burial Board opened its new cemetery at Hanwell some 6½ miles from the Kensington area in 1855 and the records of J.H. Kenyon show that two hours was allowed to reach the cemetery.

Towards the end of the nineteenth century the glass-sided hearse was introduced. Litten notes that 'It was lighter and far less sombre than the enclosed variety and it became an overnight success: the mourners – and the passers-by along the route – could now see the coffin, and therefore, the undertakers' handiwork.'[11] It was this design of hearse that was

---

[8]Parsons B. (2014c) *From Brook Street to Brookwood: Nineteenth Century Funeral Reform and St Alban the Martyr Holborn Burial Society*, London: Anglo-Catholic History Society.
[9]From the cover advertisement of trade periodicals *TUJ*. Such devices were still obtainable and continued to be utilised well into the twentieth century. For example, see *TUJ*, May, 1907 cover.
[10]Litten (2002) *The English Way of Death: The Common Funeral Since 1450*, London: Robert Hale, pp. 134–135.
[11]*Ibid.*, p. 136.

favoured by carriage masters and undertakers in urban areas. *Kelly's Post Office Directory* lists over 450 undertakers in the London postal area in the 1850s. Many only conducted a modest number of funerals, perhaps 50 or fewer, and could not justify the cost of maintaining a fully equipped stable. Such firms hired from a carriage master, who owned hearses specifically for hiring to undertakers. Henry Smith opened on Battersea Park Road in 1869 and became the dominant supplier in south London. Thirty years later he had a stable with 70 horses. James Harold Kenyon established himself as a carriage master on the Edgware Road in 1880; four years later, their records show the firm was supplying the transport requirements of 52 undertakers in and around central London.[12]

In the latter part of the nineteenth century a small number of firms had opened a network of branches and tended to possess their own stables and vehicles. By 1900, W.S. Bond had opened seven branches, which were served by stables at Shepherd's Bush.[13] The judicious use of capital-intensive resources would become a key concept in the development of branch networks.

Although, as noted below, the motor hearse started to appear on the streets within the first decade of the twentieth century, the ostentation generally associated with the so-called 'Victorian Celebration of Death' had disappeared, including mutes (engaged to stand at a front door to signify that a death had occurred) and feathermen (carrying trays of feathers).[14] In 1909, one London undertaker commented in The *Sunday Times*:

> The flashiness of funerals… is now a thing of the past. It only survives among the very poor, who still clamour for velvet palls. Black fringe and tassels, and other signs of mournful ostentation. The better class of tradesman… have done their best to dissuade their customers from indulging

---

[12]Parsons B. (2014b) *J.H. Kenyon: A Short History,* London: J.H. Kenyon, p. 34.

[13]'W.S. Bond. Funeral Directors & General Carriage Proprietor' (1907) *TUJ*, March, pp. 65–68. See also Parsons B. (2014d) *W.S. Bond: A Short History*, London: W.S. Bond.

[14]'The Feathermen' (1944) *TNFD*, January, p. 255. See also 'The Feathermen' (1944) *TNFD*, March, p. 330 and 'The Ancient Mute' (1935) *TNFD*, October, pp. 92–93. For illustrations see *The Daily Graphic*, 23 August 1899. See also Kellaway H.A. (1946). 'Mutes, Feathermen, Pages and Trappings', *FSJ*, December, pp. 463–464. See also 'The Mute' (1937) *TUFDJ*, December, p. 426. See also Gore C.G.F. (1846). 'The Mute', in *Sketches of English Character,* Vol. 2. London: Richard Bentley.

in these needless displays of finery, and they have in a large measure succeeded.[15]

Some developments had a welfare perspective. In January 1914, the Royal Society for the Prevention of Cruelty to Animals forbade the use of black ostrich plumes. They became heavy when they got wet and the strain on the horses' heads was immense.[16] Staffing levels and the appropriateness of a 'show' including the use of mourning wear during World War I further contributed towards an overall simplification of funerals.[17]

A further indicator of the anticipated move away from horse-drawn funerals was that *TUJ* ceased publishing 'The Stable' in October 1916. When the *BUA Monthly* commenced publication in 1921, a Motor & Engineering Section was included; increasing attention was given to the specifications and attributes of motor hearses, while advertisements for horse feed were replaced by those for rubber tyres and other motoring accessories.[18]

During the interwar years the horse-drawn hearse still had a presence on the streets, but there were increasing indictors that a transition had commenced. Fewer advertisements for horse-drawn hearses appeared in *TUJ* and the *BUA Monthly* from the mid-1920s. In December 1925, a four-page advertising feature for John Marston Carriage Works was illustrated by 12 motor vehicles but only three of the horse-drawn variety.[19] In the period up to the late 1930s funeral directors usually offered both

---

[15]'Funeral Reform' (1909) *TUJ*, December, p. 300. See 'Funeral Reforms: Some Healthy Changes', *The Sunday Times*, 28 November 1906.

[16]Parsons B. (2004) 'Farewell to the Appendages of Sorrow: The End of the Funereal Plume', *BIFD Journal*, Vol. 18, No. 3 September, pp. 13–15. See also 'Funeral Horses' Plumes' (1913) *TUJ*, March, pp. 80–81; 'Royal Society for the Prevention of Cruelty to Animals. Notice to Undertakers: Funeral Plumes on Horses' (1913) *TUJ*, September, p. 253; and 'The Passing of the Funeral Plume' (1914) *The Animal World*, p. 11; 'Funeral plumes' (1914) *The Animal World*, February, p. 22; and 'British Undertakers' Association (London Centre)' (1913) *TUJ*, November, p. 310; 'Feathers for Funerals' (1913) *TUJ*, November, p. 330; and 'No Funeral Plumes for Horses', *The Daily News and Leader*, 2 January 1914.

[17]Parsons B. (2014e) *The Undertaker at Work: 1900–1950*, London: Strange Attractor Press, pp. 74–79.

[18]Surprisingly, the *BUA Monthly* started to publish a similar column in the mid-1920s. See Wilson H.M. (1925) 'The Horse – His Home and Management 1', *BUA Monthly*, April, pp. 265–266.

[19]'John Marston's Carriage Works Ltd, Birmingham' (1925) *TUJ*, December, pp. 399–403.

modes of transport.[20] But it was clear that the motor hearse was increasingly preferred by clients and funeral directors.

Towards the end of 1935, the Minister of Transport, Leslie Hore-Belisha, announced that he was considering a scheme to exclude horses from London streets.[21] This was a response to those who believed that horse transport slowed down motor traffic and caused a loss of time and money to private passengers and business interests.[22] Despite much discussion, this was not pursued, mainly as the use of horses for commercial purposes was already declining; towards the end of 1935, it was reported that the number of funeral horses in South Shields had diminished from 85 to 12.[23] Further pressures against the use of horses occurred during World War II as feed was rationed, while there was concern that explosions would make horses difficult to manage.[24] Research has revealed the dates of the last horse-drawn funeral for three London funeral directors, all of whom adopted motor vehicles around 1913/1914: F.W. Paine, Kingston 28 December 1940; T.H. Ebbutt, Croydon 19 April 1932; C. Farebrother, Kingston; 5 October 1939.

Four years after the end of World War II *Picture Post* published a feature entitled 'A Coster's Funeral' with the following concluding words:

> There are left in London only thirty horses which are regularly used for funerals. Three undertakers have the monopoly on them and they find the expense so high that they are considering selling them in the next few months. When they do, the few features of London life that link the present with the past will have become one less, and the petrol-engine will have registered another triumph.[25]

---

[20]'J. Steadman & Sons of Doncaster' (1925) *TUJ*, July, pp. 233–235.
[21]'Bid to Retain Horse Traffic' (1935) *BUA Monthly*, November, p. 119.
[22]See 'Horse-Drawn Vehicles, London', *Hansard*, 5 December 1935, col. 313; 'Horse Traffic, London', *Hansard*, 12 December 1935, cols 1093–1094; 'Horse Traffic Limitations, London', *Hansard*, 16 December 1935, cols 1421–1422; 'Horse-Drawn Traffic, London', *Hansard*, 5 February 1936, cols 198–199; and 'Slow Moving Traffic Regulations', *Hansard*, 29 July 1936, col. 1519.
[23]'We hear' (1935) *BUA Monthly*, October, p. 89.
[24]'Use of Horses in Wartime' (1939) *TNFD*, October, p. 162; 'The War and the Funeral Trade' (1939) *TUFDJ*, October, p. 352. This is confirmed by West. See West J. (1988) *Jack West Funeral Director: Forty Years with Funerals*, Ilfracombe: Stockwell, p. 111. See also 'Air Raid Warnings' (1939) *TNFD*, October, p. 150, and also 'Securing of Horses (Defence) Order, 1940' (1940) *TNFD*, December, p. 174.
[25]'A Coster's Funeral', *Picture Post*, 23 April 1949, pp. 23–25.

In December 1951, the *FSJ* reported that Alfred Smith of Southwark Bridge Road in south London, who was the last London funeral director with working horses, 'had been compelled at last to dispose of his stable'. It was noted that:

> For some years now the horses have been kept at a financial loss especially to comply with the wishes of a few people. The loss of the old stables at Southwark, owing to the expiration of the lease at Christmas, has finally brought the end. Constantly increasing cost of oats and fodder as well as the impossibility of finding new stabling in London now makes it an economic impracticability to keep horses. Another problem is, of course, staff. Mr Smith pointed out that three men employed as stable staff are now getting old, and the younger men do not understand horses as they do.[26]

He watched 11 of his horses being auctioned at the Elephant & Castle horse sale for an average of 30 guineas each. Searle and Webb recorded that:

> I believe that Mr Alfred Smith... was the most distressed man in London that day. Standing forlornly between the stalls, before the auction began, he kept asking everyone in hearing what else he could do. For three years, he said, his horses hadn't earned a fraction of their keep. With food, stabling, grooming and exercise they cost him around £3,000 a year, and because they are stallions they can't be pensioned off to grass.[27]

Smith concluded, 'This is the saddest day of my life. I am a horse man and it breaks my heart to see them go like this.'[28] The horse-drawn funeral, apart from occasional appearances, was largely absent from the streets for around the next 30 years.[29] In 1984, T. Cribb & Sons reintroduced horse-drawn

---

[26] 'The Last Funeral Horses. Mr Smith Disposes of His Horses' (1951) *FSJ*, December, p. 729.
[27] Searle R. and Webb K. (1953) *Looking at London and People Worth Meeting*, London: News Chronicle, p. 35.
[28] 'The Last Funeral Horses. Mr Smith Disposes of His Horses' (1951) *FSJ*, December, p. 729.
[29] 'Horse-Drawn Hearse at Wisbech Funeral' (1965) *FSJ*, June, p. 333.

funerals and established a flourishing carriage master business (Fig. 12).[30] A number of notable funerals have given prominence to this type of transport, such as that of Ronnie Kray in March 1995, when a horse-drawn hearse with 6 horses followed by 26 Daimler limousines snaked their way through the streets of east London to Chingford Mount Cemetery.

In addition to the horse-drawn hearse, there are other instances where animate power has been used for funerary transport. These include coffins conveyed on farm carts and traps; in some cases they have been specially decorated for the occasion.[31] What was described as a horse-drawn 'car' decorated with flags and palms was used in August 1912 to convey the coffin containing the founder of the Salvation Army, General William Booth.[32] In 1923, the Duke of Somerset's coffin rested on a farm cart at his funeral at Maiden Bradley in Wiltshire.[33]

One other occasional mode of transport is the gun carriage. The tradition started in 1901 at Queen Victoria's funeral; since then it has been used extensively, during World War I for soldiers' burials and latterly

Fig. 12. A horse-drawn hearse. *Note:* A horse-drawn hearse on Charing Cross Road, London in September 2008. Horse-drawn vehicles disappeared from the capital's streets in the 1950s only to emerge three decades later (Author's collection).

---

[30]McGill A. (1990) 'A Black Plume for Duchess' *FDM*, November, pp. 20–21. See Venables Y. (2015). *Stan Cribb: An East End Farewell,* London: Simon & Schuster, pp. 229–242.
[31]Taylor L. (1983) *Mourning Dress: A Social and Costume History,* London: George Allen & Unwin, p. 266. For a further example see 'Country Carts at a Marquis's Funeral' (1911) *TUJ*, December, p. 321.
[32]Parsons B. (2001) *The London Way of Death,* Stroud: Sutton Publishing, p. 50.
[33]See also 'Farm Waggon for Hearse' (1911) *TUJ*, February, p. 31.

for state and ceremonial funerals including those of Diana, Princess of Wales and Margaret Thatcher.

'Place on Rail'

Since the construction of the rail network in the 1830s, trains have been used for the conveyance of all types of freight, including coffins. As an innovation of economic, social and technological importance, railways enabled the dead to be moved efficiently both in terms of cost and speed; there is considerable evidence to indicate extensive usage from around the 1850s until the early 1960s.[34] It was in 1988 when the national service stopped accepting coffins. Important factors in returning the dead to the place where they normally resided and therefore were entitled to be buried were not only the availability of space in a family grave and desire to be 'reunited', but also the financial penalty of being buried as a non-parishioner in a Burial Board Cemetery.

Elizabeth Hurren's research reveals the use of the railway between the 1850s and 1920s to transport from London to Cambridge the bodies of the poor destined for medical dissection.[35] At the opposite end of the spectrum, railways have conveyed monarchs, such as Queen Victoria in 1901, and also for many other state and high-profile funerals during the twentieth century.[36] With the limited number of crematoria in operation between Woking opening in 1885 and the 1940s, those desiring cremation would have to be conveyed by rail to the nearest facility, a factor that was largely responsible for the high cost of a cremation funeral.[37]

---

[34] Parsons B. (Forthcoming-a) 'Placed on Rail: Transportation of the Dead by Train in the UK'.

[35] Hurren E.T. (2012). *Dying for Victorian Medicine: English Anatomy and its Trade in the Dead Poor, c.1834–1929,* Basingstoke: Palgrave Macmillan, pp. 189–190.

[36] Keat P.J. (2001). *Goodbye to Victoria: The Last Queen Empress. The Story of Queen Victoria's Funeral Train,* Usk: The Oakwood Press. See also Packard J.M. (1995) *Farewell in Splendour: The Death of Queen Victoria and Her Age,* Stroud: Sutton Publishing; Parsons B. (2011b) 'The Funeral of Queen Victoria', *FSJ,* February, pp. 83–90; Bland O. (1986) *The Royal Way of Death,* London: Constable; and Hoey B. (2011) *The Royal Train: The Inside Story,* Sparkford: J.H. Haynes. See also Potts C.R. (1993) *Windsor to Slough: A Royal Branch Line,* Headington: Oakwood Press.

[37] Parsons B. (2005a) *Committed to the Cleansing Flame: The Development of Cremation in Nineteenth Century England,* Reading: Spire Books, pp. 128–155.

In the mid-nineteenth century two exclusive funerary trains running between fixed destinations were instigated. The London Necropolis and National Mausoleum Company transported mourners and coffins from their private station adjacent to Waterloo to the cemetery near Woking. The service commenced in the early 1850s and continued until 1941.[38] The second was from Belle Isle, north of King's Cross station, to the Great Northern Cemetery at New Southgate, which commenced in 1861. The short distance, only 7 miles from the capital, resulted in its underutilisation and abandonment after 2 years.[39]

In the early 1850s, the Railway Cleaning House stipulated that coffins conveyed countrywide would be charged at one shilling per mile. Funeral directors would be responsible for delivering and collecting coffins to and from stations and the registers of many firms records these; these were invariably entered as 'Place on rail at...'. Most coffins were transported a considerable distance between mainline termini, such as London to Edinburgh or to the West Country; some involved a change of trains. However, there is evidence to show that the rail service was also used for short journeys, which meant that staff and vehicles were not committed for a relatively lengthy period of time on conveyance rather than funeral work. At one shilling per mile, the charge for transporting coffins was also considerably lower than using animate power.

Depending on the destination, a combination of modes of transport was often deployed. For example, in July 1948, Frederick W. Paine was instructed to take a coffin by motor hearse to Euston and place it on a train destined for Heysham. A ferry then took the coffin to Belfast where a motor hearse completed the 56-mile journey to Five Mile Town.

Although motor hearses were introduced around 1900, the rail system continued to be used until the early 1960s. This lengthy transitional period was due to the reliability of early motor vehicles, the cost of

---

[38] Clarke J. (2006) *The Brookwood Necropolis Railway,* fourth edition, Usk: The Oakwood Press.
[39] See Curl J.S. (1986). 'Architecture for a Novel Purpose: Death and the Railway Age', *Country Life*, June 12, pp. 1716–1717 in respect of the railway from Belle Isle to the Great Northern Cemetery. See also Dawes M.C. (1999). 'The Great Northern London Cemetery and its Railway Service', *The London Railway Record*, No. 21, October, pp. 256–260; Dawes M.C. (2003) *The End of the Line: The Story of the Railway Service to the Great Northern London,* Cemetery Barnet: Barnet & District Local History Society; Kay P. (2009) 'The Great Northern Main Line in London: Cemetery', *The London Railway Record*, No. 59, April, pp. 182–193. A rail link to the City of London Cemetery at Ilford was proposed but not developed.

road transport compared to the railway and the long tailing-off of the widespread use of horses by funeral directors. The latter is likely to have occurred earlier in urban areas, as the level of work for rural undertakers often meant they also pursued a related craft such as carpentry or building and may have had less incentive to update their services as there was little or no competition. Furthermore, they may not have had the means of investment.

While by 1939 many urban funeral directors possessed a fleet of motor vehicles, restrictions on petrol and tyres during World War II brought a renaissance in the use of the train for the distance movement of coffins. However, by the 1960s, despatch by train had virtually ceased. This period coincided not only with intensive rationalisation of the rail network, but also the increasing reliability and speed of motor vehicles, improved road infrastructure and the dated image of using trains for freight, together with the lack of facilities for conveying coffins on modern trains and also at stations. Furthermore, the increasing preference for cremation and the portability of ashes meant that the need to transport a coffin for burial had declined significantly. These factors effectively consigned to history the transport of coffins by rail. When in March 1988 it was announced that coffins could no longer be taken on the national network it didn't even warrant a mention in the trade journals.

The Motor Hearse Arrives

Debate surrounds the first funeral director to use a motor hearse. Although Reuben Thompson of Sheffield is generally given this distinction, his Wolseley vehicle was used in 1900 for the distant deliveries of coffins rather than funerals.[40] Henry Smith of Battersea also made the claim to be the first, but in a later advertisement reference is made to this in fact being a removal vehicle. In the following decade there are a number of references to early motor hearses.[41] For example, in March 1903 *TUJ*

---

[40]Mitchell S. and Reader D. (2008) 'Transport to Paradise – Part 2: The Motor Hearse', *FSJ*, October, pp. 97–110; and Mitchell S. (2011) *British Hearses*, Leeds: Zeteo Publishing. See also 'The Motor Hearse. Its Arrival in England' (1910) *TUJ*, January, p. 10.

[41]'Standard Fleet of Modern Funeral Cars. Enterprising Developments by Battersea Funeral Director' (1925) *BUA Monthly*, February, pp. 209–210. See also 'The British Institute of Undertakers: The President' (1899) *TUJ*, September, p. 110; and 'Our Visit to Mr Henry Smith's Establishment at Battersea' (1922) *BUA Monthly*, May, pp. 254–255; and 'The First Motor Hearse!' (1928) *BUA Monthly*,

reported that 'For the second time to our knowledge in this country has the snorting motor car conveyed mortal remains. Recently a car, containing the coffin, was despatched from King's Lynn to Norwich, where the body was coffined and then conveyed to Hilgay Fan, on the other side of the county, for interment.'[42] Again, this was for a distance removal. In 1906, the *Motor Car Journal* noted that one had been used as a hearse with Sir Arthur Conan Doyle, himself a motorist, as a principal mourner at a funeral in Surrey. Certainly in Paris a hearse was displayed at the Auto Exhibition in 1905, while the first 'automobile funeral' in the United States was in March 1909.[43]

It was in 1910 that *TUJ* commented, 'The motor is entering so much into our daily life that it was inevitable that it should be eventually called in to serve the undertaker in his dealings with the dead.'[44] This article reveals that the first documented use of a motor hearse for a funeral was by Councillor Pargetter of Coventry. One of the strongest reasons put forward for its adoption was 'to do away with the great inconvenience connected with railway transit, as well as the objection of having the bodies conveyed in milk, fruit and other vans, used by railway companies for this purpose.'[45] By July 1911, Pargetter's hearse had completed over 10,000 miles.[46] *Punch* was minded to mock this development: 'Coventry now possesses funeral motor-hearse which is capable of travelling either at a walking pace or at such a speed that it can pick up customers as it goes along.'[47]

The infrequency of motor funerals in the early years warranted their mention in *TUJ*, but many were enclosed vehicles for removals rather than for use at funerals.[48] These were referred to as a 'handy', a term first appearing in *TUJ* around 1907.[49]

September, p. 78; and 'One Hundred Years of Pioneer Service' (1947) *FSJ*, April, pp. 191–192.

[42]'Notes' (1903) *TUJ*, March, p. 49.

[43]*Motor Car Journal*, 6 January 1906. See also 'Sixty Years Ago' (1966) *FSJ*, October, p 554; and 'The Automobile Funeral in America' (1911) *TUJ*, July, pp. 191–193.

[44]'The Motor Hearse. Its Arrival in England' (1910) *TUJ*, January, p. 10.

[45]'The Motor Hearse. Its Arrival in England' (1910) *TUJ*, January, p.10.

[46]'The Automobile Funeral in America' (1911) *TUJ*, July, pp. 191–193.

[47]*Punch*, 16 February 1910, p. 109.

[48]'Motor-Car Funeral' (1910) *TUJ*, October, p. 239. Advertisement (1911) *TUJ*, January, p. 20.

[49]See 'Messrs Longhurst & Sons New Motor Handy' (1911) *TUJ*, October, p. 283.

Although the complete transition to motor hearses proved to be slow, the process was eagerly anticipated. In 1914, *The Daily News and Leader* commented that the motor hearse was:

> now an everyday feature of the modern funeral. It is usurping the ancient prerogative of the horse; invading the most cherished and sacred traditions... With the advent of the motor... the tedium of long-distance funeral is avoided... A speed of 15 miles an hour is regarded as the maximum rate of progress, but the smooth gliding motor of the cars, the absence of beat of hoof and rattle of wheels, and the only sounds an occasional hoot on the hearse horn, do not suggest an impression of unseemly hustle as would be created by a horse-drawn funeral travelling at the same rate.[50]

The carriage builders soon responded to the shift towards motor vehicles that started in earnest around 1910. For example, John Marston's last full-page advertisement for a horse-drawn hearse appeared in *TUJ* in April 1914. Thereafter they described themselves as:

> The Pioneers of Modern Hearse Building – Designers, Patentees, and Builders of Hearses, Funeral Cars, Clarence Coaches, Undertakers' Broughams, Handy's Patent Hearses, and every description of Carriage used in the Trade. Also Motor Hearses, Funeral Buses, and every kind of Motor Car and Van Bodies.

By the start of the interwar period, carriage masters in the urban areas had recognised the potential of possessing a motorised fleet. London firms such as J.H. Kenyon and W.S. Bond promoted their motor fleet in the local and trade press from the early 1920s.[51] Henry Smith in south London pre-dated them by advertising the availability of motor vehicles from December 1916. The name of the manufacturer was usually revealed, such as Leyland, Rolls-Royce, Austin or Armstrong Siddeley, effectively becoming a symbol of identity for the undertaker.

Much editorial space was allocated to news of firms receiving their first fleet.[52] The *BUA Monthly* appeared in 1922 and regularly featured

---

[50]'Disappearance of the Horse in Modern Funeral' (1914) *TUJ*, January, p. 9.
[51]'The Motor Hearse' (1915) *TUJ*, April, p. 101.
[52]For example, 'Messrs English & Sons Motor Hearse' (1916) *TUJ*, February, p. 51.

a 'Motor & Engineering Section'. In the same year a debate took place at the BUA conference concerning suitable vehicles for funerals. It was reported that coffins had been transported in open touring cars, furniture vans and landaulettes. The following resolution was adopted: 'That carriage masters and undertakers do refuse to furnish supplies for, or assist in any way, adult funerals conveyed by road in other than recognised funeral conveyances used for the conveyance of a corpse.'[53]

Not all clients appreciated motor vehicles. When the Essex firm of West & Coe purchased their first hearse during the interwar years, Jack West commented:

> I was quite keen to introduce it to the families, sometimes to receive a rebuke of 'I suppose you want my neighbours to think I am rushing him away', and so we were content to leave it to the distant funerals to introduce the motors.[54]

In March 1930, it was reported that the last horse-drawn funeral had taken place in Portsmouth. In attributing this to the change in the character of funerals since World War I, one funeral director commented:

> I tried a motor hearse in the first instance not meaning it to supersede horses entirely, but found it such favour that the demand for horse hearses dwindled and fell away to practically nothing... It is only the older generation who still cling to the old-fashioned ideas of a funeral... The young people have changed entirely. They seem to appreciate the fact that no amount of sorrow or weeping will bring back the departed, and that no good can be done by making themselves more unhappy than can possibly be helped. No doubt they feel the sadness of it just the same as ever.[55]

During World War II rubber tyres were rationed, leading the NAFD to make representations that funeral directors should receive special treatment. It was, however, the need to conserve petrol supplies that had the biggest consequences.

---

[53] 'Recognised Funeral Conveyances' (1922) *BUA Monthly*, July, pp. 54–55.
[54] West J. (1988) *Jack West Funeral Director: Forty Years with Funerals*, Ilfracombe: Stockwell, p. 110.
[55] 'Brighter Funerals in Portsmouth' (1930) *BUA Monthly*, March, p. 189.

Walking funerals (presumably with the motor hearse) were disallowed while a 30-mile fixed radius for funeral vehicles was imposed; for longer trips coffins would have to be taken by rail unless the journey involved many changes. The most dramatic scheme was to reorganise funerals to take place throughout the working day rather than all concentrated in the afternoon.[56] In the post-World War II years this scheme would be employed to great effect as large organisations increased their network of branch offices.[57] In addition, hearse production had halted during the war as manufacturers such as Thomas Startin of Birmingham and Lancefield Coachworks in London had their production lines requisitioned for the war effort.

When production recommenced post-war, the range of hearses increased dramatically. Designs appeared in *TNFD* and vehicles constructed in the period 1950–1970 largely followed the models and styles of vehicles used on the domestic market.[58] Some hearses were fitted with a removable deck to convert them into passenger vehicles; others, such as the 'bearer' hearse, were capable of accommodating four bearers and the conductor.[59] Conversions into hearses of Daimler, Austin Sheerline, Princess, Rolls-Royce and Humber vehicles, and matching limousines, were supplied in the 1950s and 1960s by a seemingly large number of coachbuilders; Alpe & Saunders, Simpson & Slater and Woodall Nicholson were the most prominent.[60] Alongside these British vehicles were a limited number of foreign imports: Mercedes, Peugeot, Citroën and a few Cadillacs. In the late 1960s, the Daimler DS420 hearse and limousine built by Woodall Nicholson appeared and has generally been held by funeral directors to be the all-time classic hearse. Ford's became popular in the 1970s, while in the following decades conversions of Vauxhalls, Volvos, Jaguars and Mercedes vehicles became available. While black has been the traditional colour, various firms have made departures including silver, silver-grey, 'Midnight Blue', adopted by Hodgson Holdings in the 1980s and two-tone liveries, such as black and grey, or black and maroon.

---

[56] Parsons B. (2014e) *The Undertaker at Work: 1900–1950*, London: Strange Attractor, p. 180.
[57] See also 'There's Something to be Said for Leadership' (1943) *TNFD*, October, p. 133.
[58] 'Tomorrow's Style of Funeral Hearse' (1945) *TUFDJ*, April, p. 105.
[59] Polson C.J. and Marshall T.K. (1975) *The Disposal of the Dead*, third edition, London: English Universities Press, p. 375.
[60] 'Popularity of the Funeral Motor' (1925) *TUJ*, March, pp. 103–104. Between 1910 and 2008 over 150 coachbuilders have been traced in the UK. See Reader D. (2008b) 'Coachbuilders', *The Mourning News*, Issue 32.

In their section on English funerals in *Funeral Customs the World Over*, Habenstein and Lamers note that replacing the horse-drawn hearse with the streamlined fleet meant fewer heads turned when the cortège passed.[61] While this is debatable, the more recent use of vehicles other than hearses to convey coffins does attract attention. More accurately, this should be described as a 'reappearance', as evidence shows occasional use throughout the twentieth century of vehicles such as lorries, traction engines, buses, fire engines and farm carts.[62] Contemporary vehicles include specially constructed vehicles such as the motorcycle hearse (with the coffin in the side compartment) and the trikehearse (pulling the coffin compartment), along with others representing an interest or occupation, such as a canal barge (Fig. 13).[63]

Fig. 13. A motorcycle funeral. *Note:* The range of vehicles to convey a coffin has never been so broad and includes not only the motor hearse, but a vintage lorry, Land Rover, VW camper van and a motorcycle hearse, as seen here (Courtesy of Sergio Ramazzotti/Parallelozero).

---

[61]Habenstein R. W. and Lamers W. M. (1963) *Funeral Customs the World Over*, Revised edition, Milwaukee, WI: Bulfin, p. 565.
[62]Parsons B. (2008b). 'Transport to Paradise – Part 3: Unusual and Novel Funeral Transport', *FSJ*, November, Vol. 123, No. 11, pp. 80–99; and Parsons B. (2014e) *The Undertaker at Work: 1900–1950*, London: Strange Attractor, pp. 231–154.
[63]See *Hearse and Rider: The Official Publication of Motorcycle Funerals Limited* (2010) first issue. 'Boat Lover Makes Unique Voyage' (1999) *FSJ*, July, p. 8.

Distance and International Transportation

A final area that has only been an occasional task for the funeral directors has been the distance and overseas movement of coffins.[64] Until the 1920s, the sea was the only means to reach not only different parts of the world but also many locations around the United Kingdom. For example, in March 1913, F.W. Paine delivered a coffin to the Dundee & Perth Shipping Company's Limehouse-based warehouse for a journey by sea to Arbroath in Scotland. Both J.H. Kenyon and W. Garstin's records contain details of international transportations.[65]

To prevent leakage and to withstand multiple handling, the coffin was substantially constructed and often lead lined. Furthermore, a rectangular packing case would be used to contain the coffin; it would also disguise the fact that a deceased person was on board ship. Externally the case would be marked with the initials of the deceased or labelled 'Biological Specimen'.[66]

As Chapter 3 has indicated, embalming was not only essential, but usually required by shipping lines and/or consulates. For these reasons, such shipments were costly.

The first documented occasion of a coffin being moved by air was in 1924, with the flight being from Cologne to Croydon.[67] Although Imperial Airways advertised in 1936 that flying was up to 50 per cent less expensive than surface travel, from examining funeral directors' records there's little evidence to show that air travel to move coffins was used to any great extent until the post-World War II years. Funeral directors soon embraced this modern and efficient mode of transport. In 1948 Moreton Air, operating from Croydon, offered a 'funeral flight'. Initially flights were used only for short distances, but soon they started to cover greater distances. F.W. Paine arranged a UK transportation in

---

[64]Parsons B. (2017a) 'Funeral Directors and Distance Transportation of the Dead', *The Embalmer*, Vol. 55, No. 4, pp. 31–39.

[65]Parsons B. (2014e) *The Undertaker at Work: 1900–1950*, London: Strange Attractor, pp. 34–35.

[66]Parsons B. (2014a) *Bunny France: Memoir of a London Undertaker*, London: A France & Son, p. 24.

[67]'An Aeroplane Funeral. An Interesting Experience for Warrington Undertakers' (1924) *TUJ*, February, p. 89. See also First Air Funeral from Switzerland' (1927) *TUJ*, September, p. 303. For details of early aircraft to convey coffins see Baer B.A. (1971). 'The World's First Flying Hearse', *Casket & Sunnyside*, Vol. 101, Centennial Issue, pp. 44 & 46; and Hathaway W.S. (1970) 'When to Use an Air Hearse', *Casket & Sunnyside*, Vol. 100, No. 3, pp. 18–19 & 24.

January 1949 when a coffin was flown from Croydon to the Isle of Islay in Scotland, while a year later a Pan Am flight to New York became the firm's first transatlantic consignment. By the late 1940s some organisations, such as the Northover Funeral Service at Reigate, owned their own aircraft and advertised its availability to colleagues. A photograph dated 1948 in the F.W. Paine collection shows a Miles M57 Aerovan owned by the firm that was used for transporting coffins, although no references can be found in their records.

With an increase in leisure and then medical tourism, a whole section of the funeral industry has emerged to manage the specialist and complex activity of the global movement of deceased persons.[68] Depending on the destination, documentation issued by the coroner and consular, health and overseas officials has to be obtained, while the deceased usually has to be embalmed, and then sealed in an invariably metal-lined coffin before delivery to the airport. Many of the specialist transportation companies have contracts with insurance companies to arrange the flight, documentation and final delivery of the coffin to a firm of funeral directors nominated by the next of kin.

Transport, Cremation and Organisational Change

The shift towards cremation combined with the adoption of motor transport opened the way for efficient and economic working practices to be adopted by the funeral director.[69] Utilising such vehicles not only reduced travelling time, but also permitted the conveyance of coffin-bearing staff in the hearse rather than in an additional vehicle. Furthermore, while horse-drawn hearses necessitated the driver remaining with the horses during the funeral rather than be part of the bearing team, using a motor vehicle meant that the driver could act as a bearer. With an increasing number of funeral services being conducted solely in the crematorium chapel and not at a church, this enabled the hearse to be released for another funeral as soon as the coffin had been carried into the chapel and the floral tributes offloaded. In addition, while the journey to the place of disposal would be

---

[68]For Rowlands see 'A Century of British Funerals' (1978) *FSJ*, August, p. 323; 'Firm 108 Years Old and Still Expanding' (1984) *FSJ*, April, p. 153; and 'Company News' (1984) *TFD*, July, pp. 28–30.
[69]See Parsons (2014f) *Abandoning Burial. Explaining a Regional Shift Towards Cremation*, Paper presented at the 15th Cemeteries Colloquium, University of York, 16 May 2014.

taken at an appropriate pace, the return would not be so restricted, thus further reducing the overall time engaged on a funeral. This contrasts with burial, where the service took place in the cemetery chapel prior to interment. Only after the service at the graveside had concluded could the hearse and staff be released. It was particularly the case at a burial that took place during a 'public reading time', where a communal service was conducted in the cemetery chapel with multiple unrelated families present. As has been noted in Chapter 1, these continued until the 1960s. An account of the format and the delay that could be experienced is provided in the memoir of a central London funeral director:

> If Church of England, the duty clergyman would use the 1662 *Book of Common Prayer* 'Order for Burial of the Dead'. This was often, but not always, read at what was known as the 'Public Reading Time' when up to seven funerals would arrive at the chapel for a communal service. The bearers would carry the coffin into the chapel through the left hand door and place it on a semi-circular catafalque. At the conclusion of the service the cemetery superintendent would then tell the funeral directors the order in which the coffins should be removed from the chapel via the right hand door. The first funeral to leave would convey the minister to the grave in the hearse where he would conduct the committal service. The same vehicle would then take him to the next grave where the family and funeral director would be waiting.[70]

In contrast and as noted above, cremation enabled vehicles and staff to be released more promptly and therefore be available for another funeral. Furthermore, the increase in the number of service times created by the opening of new crematoria, particularly in urban areas, aided this situation. Eleven were opened in south London during the 1950s; in the Manchester area 9 of the 12 crematoria were built in the same period. Whereas a horse-drawn hearse could undertake a maximum of two funerals in a day depending on the location of the cemeteries, a motor hearse owned by a firm situated near a crematorium could cope with three or four local funerals without too much difficulty. Just as carriage masters in

---

[70] Parsons B. (2014a) *Bunny France: Memoir of a Holborn Funeral Director*, London: A. France & Son, p. 17.

the nineteenth century optimised the use of their hearses, carriages and horses, funeral directors operating a network of branches utilised vehicles to a similar level through careful fleeting. This enabled a series of funerals to 'work-over' from one to another, particularly if funeral directors' offices and crematoria were in a small radius. Such management of the fleet ensured the maximised use of capital resources.

The final section of this chapter draws on research utilising the records of F. W. Paine. The firm was founded in the 1880s and its move to Kingston in 1908 was followed by the opening of a network of branches during the interwar years, by which time motor transport had replaced horse-drawn vehicles.[71] The data indicate that Paine's promotion of cremation together with the provision of local crematoria created a regional shift in preference that is at considerable variance to that recorded nationwide.

F.W. Paine and Cremation

By the 1930s, F.W. Paine was well established, with a network of branch offices in south-west London and north Surrey served from the head office in Kingston.[72] In 1938, the firm was responsible for 1,803 funerals; 20 years later the 14 branches carried out 2,550 funerals. No other funeral director operated on such a scale and a competitive analysis reveals that Paine's were the dominant business in the area. For example, when they opened in Kingston there were 15 funeral directors trading; by the 1930s this was reduced to Paine's and one other firm. A similar situation can be found in other areas where branches had been established. The number of funerals carried out indicates the strength and reputation of the organisation.

Historically, north Surrey has an important place in the development of cremation: the first crematorium in this country was established in Woking in 1879. It has also been an area particularly well served by facilities during the twentieth century.[73] Operating under the auspices of the Cremation Society of England, the first cremation took place in March 1885. By the time Frederick Paine had established his office in Kingston

---

[71]Parsons B. (2001) *The London Way of Death,* Stroud: Sutton Publishing, pp. 114–127.
[72]Parsons (2017c) *Frederick W. Paine Funeral Directors: A History,* London: F.W. Paine.
[73]Parsons B. (2005a) *Committed to the Cleansing Flame: The Development of Cremation in Nineteenth Century England,* Reading: Spire Books.

there were 14 crematoria operating, with Woking being just under 19 miles from the head office. The second nearest facility opened in 1902 at Golders Green in north London at a distance of around 16 miles. The next in London was 2 years later when the City of London Crematorium opened at Ilford, while West Norwood followed in 1915. The late 1930s witnessed a concentrated growth of crematoria in the south London area: Streatham Park (1936), Croydon (1937), Putney Vale (1938), Mortlake (1939) and Honor Oak (1939). Wartime building regulations prevented further facilities from opening, although fortuitously Kingston (1952) was among the first followed by South-West Middlesex at Feltham (1954), North-East Surrey at Morden (1958) and Lambeth in Tooting (1958). Randalls Park at Leatherhead (1961) was the final facility to be erected in the area. By the early 1960s, there were 16 crematoria within an 18-mile radius of the firm's head office in Kingston.

Table 1 indicates the number of cremations carried out by Paine's at decade intervals between 1918 and 1968. In 1918, the firm managed only two cremations. Ten years later cremations had increased to 2½ per cent, a figure above the overall proportion for Great Britain of 0.7 per cent. By 1938, the preference for utilising a facility closer to the Kingston area was apparent as 67 of the total of 158 cremations took place at South London Crematorium, which had opened towards the end of 1936. With a round trip to Streatham of 18 miles, this clearly impacted on the demand and desirability to travel further afield, such as to the more distant Golders Green.

In the post-war years, the move towards cremation in the area was dramatic. For example, in 1948 there was an increase to 36.16 per cent in

Table 1. F. W. Paine and Cremations: 1918–1968

Year/Number of Frederick W. Paine Offices	Number of Cremations	Number of Funerals Managed by F.W. Paine	Percentage of Funerals to Cremations	Percentage of Deaths in England and Wales to Cremations and Number of Crematoria in Great Britain
1918 (4 offices)	2	1,034	0.02	0.3 (14 crematoria)
1928 (4 offices)	27	1,102	2.45	0.7 (18 crematoria)
1938 (11 offices)	158	1,803	8.76	3.0 (47 crematoria)
1948 (14 offices)	515	1,424	36.16	14.9 (58 crematoria)
1958 (14 offices)	1,409	2,550	55.2	31.5 (120 crematoria)
1968 (15 offices)	2,036	3,207	63.4	52.6 (203 crematoria)

Source: F.W. Paine archive and The Cremation Society of Great Britain

the preference for cremation, in contrast to the national proportion of less than 14.9 per cent. By this time Mortlake Crematorium had opened, 5.5 miles from Kingston, along with Putney Vale at 5.2 miles. However, South London Crematorium continued to be the most utilised, with the nearer Putney Vale in second place.

By 1958, the proportion of cremations arranged by F.W. Paine had exceeded burials. While nationally it was 31.5 per cent, for the firm it was 55.2 per cent. Kingston Crematorium along with South-West Middlesex had opened in 1952 and 1954 respectively, then North-East Surrey in May 1958. Of note is the high number of services taking place at crematoria near Paine's head office; at Kingston Crematorium a total of 503 cremations were recorded during the first full year. A similar situation of high usage is discernible at South-West Middlesex, which handled over 1,500 cremations in its second complete year of operation and over 2,000 in its fifth complete year. By 1968, the proportion of cremations managed by Paine's had reached 63.4 per cent, a figure some 11 per cent higher than the average for England and Wales.

From the perspective of the funeral director, two key factors can be identified as contributing to the shift towards cremation. First, although records prior to 1918 show the use of animate power to travel the considerable distance to Woking, Golders Green or West Norwood for the occasional cremation, Paine's started to utilise motor transport around 1913/1914. This transition was timely. In the two cremations managed during 1918, both involved the use of such vehicles for the round trip from Kingston of over 30 miles to Golders Green and 22 miles to West Norwood. By the mid-1920s, horse-drawn funerals had virtually been replaced and in 1928 Paine's used motor hearses for all 27 cremations. However, their use declined and the firm's last horse-drawn funeral took place in 1940.

The opening of new crematoria impacted upon existing facilities by enabling advantage to be taken of time and mileage savings. For example, when South London Crematorium opened the number of cremations at Golders Green decreased, with the distance to travel being nearly halved. This factor is further discernible from those crematoria opening in the post-war years. For example, following the construction of Kingston in 1952, the number of funerals managed by Paine's at South London Crematorium reduced from 161 in 1948 to 107 in 1958. The accessibility of a facility about half a mile from the head office eliminated the need for an 18-mile round trip to Streatham. Once the hearse had departed from Kingston Crematorium it could reach another branch within half an hour in readiness for the next funeral. This trend continued; the figures for

10 years later show most cremations taking place locally, such as at South-West Middlesex, North-East Surrey and also Randalls Park. Curiously, those at Woking remained relatively stable. By this stage, 63.4 per cent of Paine's funerals were cremations, in contrast to 52.6 per cent in England and Wales.

Although most took place locally, cremations in the years 1958 and 1968 show the firm's willingness to travel to crematoria outside the immediate trading area. For example, in 1958 funerals were taken to three other London crematoria, in addition to Charing (Kent) and Southampton (Hampshire), both around 65 miles from Kingston. A similar situation can be found in 1968, with the greatest distance travelled to a crematorium being Northampton. Although this meant that a hearse was committed for a longer period than at a local funeral, the firm would have charged additional time and mileage for this service. Furthermore, when travelling to a crematorium at a distance from Kingston, staff supplied by a funeral director in the area or the chapel attendant at the crematorium would have been engaged as coffin bearers, eliminating the need for two or three of Paine's employees to be away for a lengthy and unproductive period of time. Instead, they could be more cost-effectively utilised as drivers or bearers on local funerals.

Secondly, there is the issue of funeral directors contributing to the public awareness of cremation. Although the number of cremations until the 1940s were modest, it was in the interest of all funeral directors to secure funeral instructions *per se* and there is evidence to show that many firms fully embraced this alternative to burial by specifically advertising that they made arrangements for both 'funerals' and 'cremations', the inference being that a funeral was a burial. Including the word 'cremation' indicated that the firm was fully conversant with documents and procedures.

From the time Paine's opened in Kingston, cremation was promoted.[74] Photographs of the exterior of the head office show prominent window lettering bearing the legend 'Cremations at Woking and Golders Green', while branches displayed ceramic and wooden urns. Furthermore, advertisements published in local newspapers from the early 1920s onwards specifically mention cremation; Paine's regularly included a separate advertisement for cremation in the twice weekly *Surrey Comet* in addition to their main, more general box-type classified advertisement.

---

[74]Parsons B. (2014a) *Bunny France: Memoir of a Holborn Funeral Director*, London: A. France & Son, p. 20.

Although the Cremation Society of England (later, Great Britain) published leaflets such as *Leading Questions about Cremation Answered by a Cremationist* (1935) and the location guide entitled *Crematoria in Great Britain* (1934), it is not known how widespread was the distribution and if these were available in F.W. Paine offices. Opened by a private company in 1936 and run by directors with a background in funeral directing, South London Crematorium issued its own promotional material, such as leaflets, calendars and framed photos for display in reception areas. In addition, the crematorium had sustained advertising in many local newspapers and church magazines, an acknowledgement of the high level of readership and also church attendance. The crematorium also offered a pre-payment scheme, where the cremation fee could be paid to the company in advance with nothing further to pay when cremation took place. Acknowledging that contact with and helpfulness towards funeral directors would increase business, particularly as competition increased following the building of further facilities in the south London area, the company offered the collection of statutory documentation and delivery of ashes. The payment of commission for all cremations brought to the crematorium was also made to funeral directors; the same applied for burials taking place in the company's cemetery at Streatham Park. The combination of these strategies was clearly advantageous to the provider as well as Paine's; 67 of the 158 cremations handled in 1938 took place at South London Crematorium.[75]

Although Frederick W. Paine recorded a shift in preference away from burial that differed significantly from the national figures, they were neither alone as this was noted in research carried out at other funeral directors in the London area, nor was the increase in cremation only encountered by firms operating a group of branches; those with a single office would have noted the same situation. It was, however, the shift to motor vehicles coinciding with the increase in the number of crematoria that enabled this large organisation to benefit from the more efficient use of their resources. The operational benefits would be central to the growth of the large organisation, a development explored in the following chapter.

---

[75]Parsons B. (2017e) Funeral Directors and the Promotion of Cremation: A Regional Perspective, *Pharos International, 83*(3), 32–41.

Chapter 6

Organisational Change

> We are born in organisations, educated by organisations and most of us spend our life working for organisations. We spend much of our leisure time paying, playing and praying in organisations and when the time comes for burial the largest organisation of all – the State must grant official permission.[1]

Introduction

Change during the period 1900–2014 indicates that in organisational terms, it is the emergence of the management of funerals on a centralised basis that can be identified as the most strategic development encountered by the industry. As small family firms have faced increasing problems, specialist funeral organisations have sought to make acquisitions in recognition of the economies of scale gained through large-scale operations, as discussed in the previous chapters. During the last four decades considerable acquisitional activities have restructured the organisational composition of the industry. These developments must be considered from a broad perspective, however, as the independent firm still continues to dominate the industry in terms of percentage market share.

---

[1] Etzioni A. (1964) *Modern Organisations,* London: Prentice Hall, p. 1.

The Funeral Industry 1900–1960

In his assessment of the funeral industry during the nineteenth century, Julian Litten identifies three types of undertaking organisation:

> ...coffin-maker did as the title suggests: he made coffins. He might have also performed funerals, but not necessarily so. The undertaker was a coffin maker and performer of funerals, whereas the funeral furnisher did not make coffins, but bought them in ready-made, dressed them, and in addition performed the funeral. This, then was the hierarchy of the trade.[2]

At the beginning of the twentieth century a similar typology can be applied to the industry as analysis from data, such as from *Kelly's Post Office Directory for London* or the British Undertakers' Association *Year Book and Diary*. For 1919, the latter records 750 members.[3] First, the dual-activity (or non-core) undertaker who supplied a coffin and arranged the timings of the funeral. This type of organisation would hire the means of transportation from a carriage master. Level of work was usually the decisive factor between full- and part-time operations. From examination of the *Post Office Directories,* the department store could also be classified in this manner as many were involved in the provision of funerals. The Army & Navy Co-operative Stores, Maples, Harrods and William Whiteley (all in central London) are examples not essentially of diversification into funerals, but fulfilment of the philosophy of the department stores: providing for all aspects of life. An additional point is that all these stores would have had extensive clothing and drapery departments that could supply the necessary attire for the period of mourning.[4] These organisations sub-contracted resources from the third type of funeral firm outlined below. The involvement of department stores in undertaking appears to have ceased by the 1920s, although Harrods continued to offer this service through a sub-contracting arrangement with a Knightsbridge firm of Birch and then J.H. Kenyon until the 1970s.

---

[2]Litten J.W.S. (2002) *The English Way of Death: The Common Funeral Since 1450*, London: Robert Hale, p. 26.
[3]Figures from the British Undertakers' Association *Year Book and Diary*, 1919.
[4]Taylor L. (1983) *Mourning Dress: A Costume and Social History,* London: George Allen & Unwin, pp. 191 & 266.

Secondly, the specialist or sole-activity undertaker existed whose work level was as such to warrant full-time employment in the occupation. His functions mirrored those of the non-core undertaker except that he may well have also possessed animate transport and manpower instead of hiring from the third category.

Thirdly, the carriage master who would supply on a contractual basis to an undertaker lacking capital-intensive resources such as the hearse, carriages and manpower required for the funeral. The latter would also undertake funerals.[5]

Although no figures can be located, the vast majority of business organisations in operation during the eighteenth and nineteenth centuries were family owned and managed, that is to say, 'patrimonial' organisations.[6] In respect of the funeral industry, throughout history the family has contributed in differing ways to the disposal of the dead; when the occupation first emerged it was the patriarchal family that sought to provide the goods and services on a commercial basis. It is only during the twentieth century that the presence of the family has declined; it has not, however, been replaced. As figures later presented in this chapter reveal, although concentration has had the effect of attempting to replace the family in this occupation, such organisations are today still the dominant type in the industry. Such a situation therefore prompts an examination as to why a connection exists between the family and the occupation of undertaking.

In the nineteenth century, trades such as building and distribution as well as craft-based, low-capital sectors tended to be founded by the lower middle classes. Due to the low social status possessed by the industry, undertaking can certainly be deemed part of this category. While actually establishing an undertaking firm involved comparatively little capital due to the sub-contracting to the carriage master, diversification into the trade, especially if the core occupation was carpentry-related, probably required even less initial capital.

Donnelley identifies six characteristics as strengths of the family business; (i) the availability of otherwise unobtainable financial and management resources due to family sacrifices; (ii) important community and business relationships stemming from a respected name; (iii) a dedicated and loyal internal organisation; (iv) an interested, unified

---

[5]The records of J.H. Kenyon (1874 to c.1910) indicate that they supplied carriages and resources to at least 16 firms in the central and west London areas.
[6]Kerr C. et al. (1974) *Industrialism and Industrial Man*, Harmondsworth: Penguin.

management-stock-holder group; (v) a sensitivity to social responsibility; (vi) continuity and integrity in management policies and corporate focus.[7]

The following illustrates the first and fifth points. Although the undertaker operating at the turn of the century would not have offered a 24-hour service (a significant characteristic of the industry today), due to the fact that bodies were retained at the place of death and not on the undertaker's premises, it is likely that members of the family would be used for duties in the stables or in the coffin workshop.[8]

The family would have been utilised during busy periods to supply additional support, especially with labour-intensive coffin making. Such flexibility and use of part-time resources is still apparent within the independent sector of the industry. While it is likely that the male gender would have been employed, the wife of the proprietor would have provided a 'collaborative and supportive' role.[9] It is clear that personal demands made of those engaged in funeral service are reflected in skills such as sensitivity and tact acquired through family mentoring. In respect of social responsibility, Essex funeral director Jack West notes the almost philanthropic nature of some undertakers.[10]

It is particularly important to note that the craft-based enterprise of undertaking was suitable for succession to a male sibling. Personal contact with the community encountered by the nature of the occupation leads to the creation of customer loyalty. As recommendation from satisfied clients is the most effective form of advertising, future funerals will be forthcoming as long as appropriate contact is maintained. The weight of such continuity can be increased if a male sibling enters the family business and succeeds the paternal line. This lineage can frequently be seen in

---

[7]Donnelley R.G. (1964) 'The Family Business', *Harvard Business Review*, July–August, p. 97.

[8]When writing her book in the early 1960s, Jessica Mitford interviewed Lawrence Charles Ashton of Ashton Funeral Directors in Clapham, south London to learn about English funeral rituals, and the issue of a 24-hour service emerged. She notes: 'I asked him what happens when a person dies at home in the middle of the night. American undertakers, to a man, take the greatest pride in rushing to the scene at no matter what hour; in fact on their list of "essential services" – and a major justification for their high charges – is maintenance of a 24-hour operation, their ability to remove the deceased any time of the day or night within minutes of death. "I'd send along in the morning," said Mr Ashton.' Mitford J. (1963) *The American Way of Death*, London: Quartet, p. 214.

[9]Blood R.O. and Wolfe D.M. (1960) *Husbands and Wives*, Glencoe: Free Press, p. 91.

[10]West J. (1988) *Jack West Funeral Director: Forty Years with Funerals*, Ilfracombe: Stockwell, p. 115.

firms indicated by the appending of '& Sons' (or 'and daughter') to the family trading name.

The maintenance of the trading name is of immeasurable value in generating work. In addition, continuity of the name is also of considerable importance. In conjunction with this point it is important to note that accommodation for the owners of most craft-related trades was at the place of work. Activities such as coffin construction would have taken place in workshops adjoining living space and it is likely that siblings were exposed to the work of the undertaker at an early stage in their own lives. The duties involved in undertaking would be very visible to any sibling.[11] West recalls how a child's coffin was brought into the living room for completing (c.1920). It is also likely that siblings would be given small tasks around the workshop.[12]

The commercial transaction of funeral arrangements involves entrusting the body to functionaries willing to take responsibility for this rite of passage. As a funeral is a highly personal event affecting and involving the whole family, it is thus appropriate that a family dedicated to the provision of funeral service participates and interacts with the bereaved at this time.[13]

The Co-operative Movement

During the 1920s, the Co-operative movement became involved in the provision of funerals.[14] Through the Co-operative Insurance Society a death benefit was payable depending on the level of purchases at Co-operative stores. For example, in 1935 if a husband died and a wife made a claim, then the payment was calculated on 4 shillings per £1 purchased to a maximum value of £40.[15] It was a sure way of preventing a pauper's

---

[11]Dyer, W.G. (1956) 'The Interlocking of Work and Family in Social Systems among Lower Occupational Families', *Social Forces,* Vol. 34, No 3, pp. 230–233.
[12]West J. (1988) *Jack West Funeral Director: Forty Years with Funerals*, Ilfracombe: Stockwell, p. 108.
[13]For a discussion on the different types of firms in operation in the early part of the twentieth century, see Cottridge A.J.E. (1918) 'What is an Undertaker? Who Shall Be Admitted as Association Members?' *TUJ,* July, p. 186.
[14]Parsons B. (2014e) *The Undertaker at Work: 1900–1950*, London: Strange Attractor Press, pp. 113–131.
[15]Carr-Saunders A.M., Sargant Florence P. and Peers R. (1938) *Consumers' Co-operation in Great Britain: An Examination of the British Co-operative Movement,* London: George Allen & Unwin Ltd, p. 175. If a wife died, the husband claims

funeral. However, the societies questioned why they were paying out money after the death of a member only for the family to then use the services of a private undertaker to supply a funeral. The Co-operative was in an ideal position to enter the market and barriers to entry were particularly low. First, societies with members who obtained the death benefit policy had a captive audience and a guaranteed income. Secondly, in addition to those who had a death benefit policy, the Co-operatives had a loyal clientele who were likely to use another service provided by the Co-operative, especially if a dividend was obtained. Thirdly, it is likely that the family would also spend money purchasing mourning wear or food for post-funeral refreshments at the Co-operative stores. The supply of funerals also encouraged diversification into the monumental masonry business along with the supply of wreaths.[16] Fourthly, many societies had premises that could be adapted to accommodate a small funeral office. Behind-the-scene activities could also be serviced, including stabling or a garage for animate power or motor hearses, and a joinery shop that could be used to construct coffins. Furthermore, where a Co-operative hall existed, it could be used for the post-funeral refreshments. Fifthly, economies of scope could be achieved as staff could be drawn from other departments such as deliveries or the joinery department to act as drivers or bearers. Furthermore, limousines could be hired out for weddings. Sixthly, Co-operative departments already in existence could be utilised for supplies such as timber for coffin construction. At one stage the CWS motor body department even designed and made a motor hearse. The CWS timber works in Norfolk could supply wood for coffins, while the fabric for coffins interiors could be sourced from their own textile mills. Seventhly, a loan could be obtained from the Co-operative bank to establish a funeral service. Lastly, societies with only a small membership could federate with other local Co-operatives to create a funeral service.

In the post-World War I years many societies established a funeral service. The Nelson Society was reportedly carrying out half the funerals in the Lancashire town by 1919; the society in Pendleton started a year

---

were calculated on 2 shillings per one pound purchased to a maximum of £20, and for a single person 5 shillings to a maximum payout of £50. In 1935 the total paid out for life assurance was £440,000.

[16] 'Funeral Furnishing' (1932) *The Producer,* June, p. 185. See also 'Memorials to the Departed. The New Funeral Furnishing Department of the CWS' (1934) *The Producer,* December, pp. 373–374.

later.[17] By 1922, Sunderland and Newcastle were involved in funerals.[18] Some smaller societies joined forces as a federation to supply services such as laundry and simply extended this to funerals; Beswick, Droylesden and Failsworth federated in 1926.[19] The first in London was the Royal Arsenal Co-operative Society, which opened a branch at Plumstead in March 1929. Birmingham was opened in 1935. The Birmingham Industrial Co-operative Society had a funeral department just prior to World War I.[20] By 1935, there were 122 societies engaged in funerals.[21]

Initial reaction by the existing industry to the Co-operative was antagonistic, as can be seen from one of the first references in the trade press, dated 1922:

> We read in the *Northern Echo* that owing to the refusal recently of livery stable keepers to supply carriages and horses to convey a coffin which was made by the Sunderland Co-operative Society, it has been decided to establish a complete funeral furnishing department. The decision has come to be representative of practically the whole of the Co-operative societies in the Sunderland district, and a committee has been appointed to work at the details of a scheme.[22]

It is apparent that with a Co-operative society entering the industry a threat was presented to existing firms in the market. As the above illustrates, the Co-operative, itself a heavily unionised organisation, could not hire from carriage masters. The latter were members of the BUA and

---

[17] 'Co-operative Societies as Funeral Furnishers' (1926) *TUJ*, May, p. 165, and 'Sixteenth Annual Convention of the British Undertakers' Association' (1919) *TUJ*, July, p. 194.
[18] 'Retirement of Mr H.D. Webster' (1950) *FSJ*, October, p. 576.
[19] 'Co-operative Societies as Funeral Furnishers' (1926) *TUJ*, May, p. 165. See also 'Co-operative Societies and the Funeral Trade' (1926) *BUA Monthly*, May, pp. 246–247.
[20] 'Notes' (1935) *TUJ*, September, p. 282.
[21] Carr-Saunders A.M., Sargant Florence P. and Peers R. (1938) *Consumers' Co-operation in Great Britain: An Examination of the British Co-operative Movement*, London: George Allen & Unwin Ltd, p. 413. The precise number of societies with a funeral department is uncertain. A *TUJ* correspondent writing in May 1934 said that there were 60 towns 'with full funeral facilities, including vehicles, mourning outfits available, as well as cafes at which funeral parties can dine'. 'The Battle with the Co-operatives' (1934) *TUJ*, May, pp. 147–148.
[22] 'Co-operative Undertakers' (1922) *BUA Monthly*, August, p. 86.

negotiated rates and working practices and forbade members to deal with the societies.[23] Nevertheless, by extending funerals to its existing portfolio of retail goods and service, the organisation prospered.

Not only does the entrance of the Co-operative movement into funerals append a further category to the 1900 typology advanced above, but it also represents the first departure from the funeral organisation being owned and managed by the same individual. Thus in contrast to the small family firm, the owner's was not the name that appeared above the door. Although similarities can be drawn with the department store, unlike the latter it did not sub-contract hire of vehicular resources. Furthermore, through owning and providing a network of branches it represented an integration of carriage master and small firm, operating on a centralised basis.

As undertakers' responsibility towards the dead body increased during the twentieth century they responded by providing custody and then preservation. In addition, it was during the slightly later period that other societal changes occurred, such as the increase in cremation that developed in parallel to the transition to motor power and the adoption of mass-produced coffins. The level of additional responsibility gave funeral firms the ability and opportunity to centralise their high-cost capital resources. While from an organisational perspective improved telecommunications aided the process, in sociological terms population changes also contributed through suburbanisation. Firms in such areas expanded to meet the demands of new areas while benefiting from centralised operations. For example, population migration from the south-eastern areas of inner London to the outer southern suburbs, such as Bromley, Orpington and Addiscombe, can be seen to have occurred in the 1930s – a time when centralisation was in its initial stages. As the services of funeral directors were required, firms like Francis Chappell in south-east London and Frederick W. Paine in north Surrey and south-west London expanded their operations to meet the growing market opportunities.[24] During the period 1922–1973, Francis Chappell increased its number of branch offices from 3 to 17. By 1962 the firm had 24 branches.[25] In the case of an acquisition by Francis Chappell a change in trading name usually followed soon afterwards. As Crichton noted:

---

[23]'Co-operative Societies as Funeral Furnishers' (1926) *TUJ*, May, p. 126.
[24]Parsons B. (2017c). *Frederick W. Paine Funeral Directors: A History*, London: F.W. Paine.
[25]Crichton I. (1976) *The Art of Dying*, London: Peter Owen, p. 126.

the firm had begun with one branch in Deptford in 1840. Then it grew through the generations of the Chappell family. As South-east London developed and the population passed out of the inner suburbs, Chappell's went with it... We spread to places like Bromley and Orpington, and by the mid 1930s we were doing about 3,000 funerals a year... In 1950 a local mason gave up the trade, and then in Woolwich a funeral director retired, and we succeeded to their business.[26]

He continues:

But in going to a new town you have to wait and be patient. The population there is essentially young and the death-rate is very low. When we started in Crawley we were doing only about forty funerals a year. Now it's up to 300.[27]

Just as Chappell's expanded, so did firms like Paine's in the interwar years as a result of the expansion of the suburbs.[28] Likewise, the Co-operative societies such as the Royal Arsenal established branch offices in south-east London and exploited the virtues of centralised working practices.[29]

Following a brief review of the developments occurring as a result of the ability to apply centralisation and organisational growth, the management of funerals under this system will be considered.

Expansion, Acquisition and Organisational Developments 1960–1994

Data detailing the precise number of funeral-directing organisations in England and Wales do not exist. However, in the following sections figures relating to the expansion of Kenyon, Great Southern Group and Hodgson have been made possible due to their status as public limited

---

[26] *Ibid.*
[27] *Ibid.*
[28] Parsons B. (2017c) *Frederick W. Paine Funeral Directors: A History,* London: F.W. Paine.
[29] Parsons B. (2014e) *The Undertaker at Work: 1900–1950,* London: Strange Attractor Press, pp. 124–128.

companies. Further disclosure has also been possible through information contained in the MMC Report (1995). Although the media have drawn considerable attention to the acquisitions by these three organisations, even by 1994 (by which times these three firms had amalgamated) it was estimated that SCI controlled a total UK market share of only 12.7 per cent. When the MMC reported in 1995, the Co-operative societies possessed 'few formal links, but a strong sense of common identity...' but through merger the situation has now changed and collectively they have just over a quarter of the market share.[30] It is the independent funeral sector, however, that continues to possess the largest proportion.

The growth of the branch office network sought not only to change the complete management of funerals in terms of organisation, but also caused realignment of the structure of the industry.[31] A snapshot of the industry at 1960 reveals the following:

1. Non-core or dual-activity funeral directors. Such organisations would usually be located in rural areas and undertake funeral performance as a 'sideline' to building, cabinet-making, vehicle hire or retailing. Such an organisation would be family owned and managed, but may well utilise the vehicular resources of a neighbouring funeral director or carriage master.
2. The family-owned and managed core-activity specialist funeral directing firm arranging between 150 and 250 funerals a year from a single premise. This type of organisation would conduct sufficient funerals to enable the purchase of a hearse and limousine and removal vehicle. The organisation would also possess coffin storage and preparation facilities, a mortuary, chapel and office accommodation. Such an organisation would probably be in the second, third or fourth generation of succession and heavy reliance would be placed on survival through the maintenance of a reputation with the community.
3. The medium-sized firm utilising the principles of centralisation with perhaps 4–10 branch offices. This type of organisation would probably be family owned and managed. Some branches would have been acquired non-aggressively, such as firms the new owner previously supplied as a carriage master. It is also likely that the trading name of each

---

[30]Monopolies and Merger Commission (1995) *Service Corporation International and Plantsbrook Group PLC – A Report on the Merger Situation*, Cm2880, London: HMSO, p. 9.
[31]For a brief survey of the industry see Farthing D.S. (1978) 'The Organisation of Funerals in Great Britain', *FSJ,* September, pp. 367–370.

acquired organisation would have been retained. Others would have been established organically where the demand was apparent and there was an absence of competition.
4. The Co-operative societies and large firms. Operating a centralised working system that often covers considerable geographic – usually urban – areas, the latter type of organisation will have grown predominantly through acquisition, while the former organisation will have grown almost exclusively by establishing new branches.

Funeral Partners, C.P.J. Field and the former Yew Holdings (now part of Dignity) are all examples of organisations that have grown through acquisition. Dignity Caring Funeral Service (the funeral division of Dignity PLC) has made acquisitions but has also opened a large number of new branches on 'brownfield' sites. Firms such as the family-owned Lodge Bros are also a combination of both strategies, as is Funeralcare (part of the Co-operative Group), which has expanded by opening new branches, although acquired established businesses become part of its Fairways subsidiary and trade under their original identities. In all these organisations there is significant separation of ownership from control and all would be seeking opportunities for business expansion.

The four categories are essentially distinguished by ownership and consequently reflect the financial objectives of the owners. The dual-activity firm provides a service in response to local demand while their non-core activity supplies the mainstay. The objectives of the small firm, like the dual-activity, centres around survival while again meeting the financial needs of the owner.

For the medium-sized business, however, economies of scale gained through limited centralisation would be a positive source of revenue for expansion and provide greater rewards for the shareholding family likely to be actively involved in the business. Finally, the management of the PLC and to a certain extent the Co-operatives will have a brief to match the expectations of their shareholders with those of profits. In addition, retained finance will be used to acquire firms and also open new branches. Like the three other classifications, turnover reflects mortality and client preference. With recently fluctuating death rates and newly emerging market opposition, the resultant need to achieve economies through control of operational costs may underline conflict of objectives between management, staff and the bereaved. It is these latter points that will be discussed below.

Although there is evidence to show that some firms acquired neighbouring organisations in a non-aggressive fashion, others such as the

Co-operative preferred to establish branch offices organically. As had already been mentioned, the period 1960–1996/1997 witnessed growth of the large organisation primarily through acquisition. As the vast majority of firms acquired in the last 30 years were family owned and managed, it is therefore necessary to examine why such a situation occurred.

Problems Facing Small Funeral Organisations

The family-owned firm has been a characteristic of the funeral industry for many years. Like other small businesses, however, it has faced increasing problems as a result of social, economic and technical changes. Two major areas specifically relating to funerals can be identified. The first concerns the dilemma of succession, particularly following the retirement or death of the owner when no family member is willing or able to manage the business. Acquisition provides a solution to the problem of succession, particularly in the case of retirement where no provision has been made for a pension. It is perhaps significant to note that even in the pre-industrial era the funeral industry had always been dominated by the male gender. Although this could stem from the tradition of the male working in craft-related occupations such as carpentry, it could also be from the fact that in some communities, such as certain regions in Wales, females do not attend funeral rituals. However, a not inconsiderable number of examples can be cited of female relations in senior positions with firms.[32] Although a male (or female) may be available to enter the family business, several factors can be identified that prove to be stumbling blocks to business lineage. While there is the stigma attached to occupations that deal with the dead, the commitment of providing a 24-hour service can also act as an effective deterrent to entering the industry. The increased opportunities of intragenerational mobility may also be seen to lead siblings away from funeral directing as a career. The responsibility of managing a small business may also discourage entry. Goss identifies that small businesses generally 'offer fewer promotion prospects, less job security and lower wages'.[33] Unresolved conflict and tensions between family members can be a further factor in deciding to dispose of the business.

The second problem relates to the evidence demonstrating that the economic viability of many small funeral organisations had become suspect.

---

[32]Larner A. (1992) 'The Role of Women in the Funeral Profession', *Pharos International,* Vol. 58, No. 2, pp. 48–50.
[33]Goss D. (1991) *Small Business and Society,* London: Routledge, p. 56.

Essentially, the viability of a funeral organisation rests not only on the reasonably secure number of deaths occurring in the locality, but also on the reputation of the organisation generated by the years of service to a community. However, the effects of this perceived market stability resulted in funeral directors believing that their organisation was immune to the myriad of environmental changes. Two examples underpin this argument.

First, evidence indicating increasing consumer awareness of price coupled with a tendency to 'shop around' has challenged the reliance on past customer loyalty.[34] Although precise figures detailing the increase in telephone quotations do not exist (they appear to be as closely guarded as the number of funerals actually undertaken), discussion with funeral directors particularly in urban areas reported an increase in this trend within the last three decades. Consumer decisions are based on price in addition to the manner in which the encounter is handled.[35] The second aspect is change in the social composition of an area through population dispersion and the fact that fewer people are dying in a community. Hodgson gives the example of Handsworth in Birmingham; London's East End can be cited along with other inner city areas.[36] With geographic mobility, siblings returning to arrange a funeral may not know who is the established or 'usual' firm in the area. They may well look to those occupying an important role in the disposal process, such as hospital administrators or coroner's offices, rather than neighbours. Furthermore, an internet-savvy generation, perhaps also influenced by the quantity of death-related material appearing in the media, have become more aware of choice. This has required funeral directors to adopt a broader approach to their range of services and also marketing opportunities. However, willingness to reposition the business or adopt a new range of facilities or services requires a widening of perspective. It would be fair to say that the vast majority of funeral directors have not had business training and it is only in very recent years that aspects such as strategy, finance, marketing and personnel matters have been included in national qualifications. Those who have succeeded into family firms would often have had little opportunity to

---

[34]Parsons B. (2011a) 'A Dying Business? Mortality and Funeral Directing in West London', Paper presented at the Tenth International Conference of the Social Context of Death, Dying and Disposal, Nijmegen, 9–12 September.
[35]Hopwood D. (1996) 'Funeral Marketing in the 1990s', *Pharos International,* Spring, Vol. 62, No. 1, p. 15.
[36]Hodgson H.O.P. (1992) *How to Become Dead Rich,* London: Pavilion, p. 11. See 'Lack of Custom in the Dying Business', *Manchester Evening News,* 12 August 2004. See also 'Buried Like Kings', *The Economist,* 21 December 2013, pp. 79–82.

broaden their commercial awareness and experience. It is thus likely that the effects of competitive and commercial influences may not always be recognised. Evidence of this myopic vision towards change is provided by Howard Hodgson. He wryly comments:

> the whole profession while being extremely decent, honest and hardworking always damaged itself by its small-minded obsession with its local competitor. I never visited a funeral director in order to acquire him, without having to listen to the "disgusting behaviour" of his competitor down the road for at least two hours before we could turn our attention to the business in hand – theirs. The vast majority of funeral directors are wonderful with their clients but if they bit their tongues while talking about their competitors they would probably die from septicaemia.[37]

The literal effect of such inertia was to reduce the overall long-term profitability of organisations operating, particularly in urban areas. As owners sought to maintain a steady return from their business, despite the decline in available funerals they were caught by two problems. First, the amount of retained profit declined for capital improvements and investment, such as the purchase of new vehicles, modernisation of premises or investment in staff or IT. If the business was operating against a competitor that was owned by a large organisation and had, for example, invested in premises refurbishment, the small business would be at a strategic disadvantage, particularly if a carefully managed public relations programme had accompanied the refurbishment and strong community-based activities were undertaken by staff. Secondly, as the margin of profitability declined, owners would be forced to seek ways of sustaining a standard of revenue by cost-cutting. By disposing of capital assets, such as vehicles, and hiring all resources from other firms, a reduction in expenditure could be achieved. Working in conjunction with another possible rival firm, however, meant that the availability of resources was reduced and as control passed to a different organisation the risk of standards falling could not be ruled out.

For the small business facing these problems a number of options are available for survival in the face of a declining market: rationalisation, specialisation and diversification. Although a limited amount of diversification

---

[37] Hodgson H.O.P. (1992) *How to Become Dead Rich*, London: Pavilion, p. 98.

took place, such as with Hodgson marketing financial services and offering pre-paid funeral plans and Great Southern Group through their ownership of crematoria, the specialised nature of the industry with its capital equipment such as hearses or refrigeration being used for specific tasks meant that the scope to adopt any of these three strategies is almost nil.

In the face of a decline in the number of deaths in predominantly urban areas and the fact that such areas have remained competitive, it is clear that a realistic option open would be for owners to sell their business. The trend in mergers and acquisitions that occurred from around the late 1960s is noted by the Acton Society, which detected that industries in a declining market faced with a falling demand for their product or service tended to sell so that horizontal or vertical integration could bring economies of scale.[38] While in wider business terms the 1960s and 1970s were decades of merger mania, in funerals a number of non-aggressive acquisitions occurred between neighbouring firms that had formed and maintained a relationship through hiring resources from each other. It was soon clear, however, that funeral firms were a lucrative source of income and became sought-after economic units.

Mergers and Acquisitions 1970–1995

From the 1970s, the most significant characteristic of the UK funeral industry has been acquisitional activity.[39] In the initial period of expansion (1970–early 1980s) firms without a previous record of involvement in funerals were active, such as Musical and Plastic Industries acquiring Francis Chappell and Gerrard and National Temple Securities in respect of J.H. Kenyon.[40] Dealings were usually short-term and in the latter case involved asset-stripping by the disposal of property. It was during the 1980s that specialist funeral companies commenced an acquisition contest financed chiefly by share issues and operating profits resulting from the

---

[38] Goodman E. (1969) *The Impact of Size,* London: The Acton Society Trust, pp. 54–55.
[39] An assessment of this period is made by Smale but there are many inaccuracies in the text. See Smale B. (1997) 'The Social Construction of Funerals in Britain', in K. Charmaz, G. Howarth and A. Kellehear eds, *The Unknown Country: Death in Australia, Britain and the USA,* Basingstoke: Macmillan.
[40] Crichton I. (1976) *The Art of Dying,* London: Peter Owen, p. 126. See also Parsons B. (2014e) *The Undertaker at Work: 1900–1950,* London: Strange Attractor Press, p. 22.

centralised management of funerals. Three PLC organisations emerged to dominate the period 1982–1994: the Great Southern Group, Hodgson Holdings and Kenyon Securities. In addition, various Co-operative societies and other organisations also made acquisitions. As it was the three former organisations that pursued acquisition, integration and rationalisation on an unprecedented scale, analysis is warranted here. The large organisations identified the possibilities resultant from centralisation and also the increasing availability of independent firms for acquisition. More importantly, they required capital specifically for this purpose and became public limited companies to secure investment from external sources. Before looking in detail at the rationale and developments underlying this period, it is worth briefly considering the primary developments of the three organisations mentioned above. Each organisation had been involved in funeral directing for some time prior to the heady period of the 1980s.

The Great Southern Group started as a cemetery and then crematoria operator, diversifying backwards into funeral directing in 1972 with the portentous acquisition of London Necropolis, which included some 20 branches of F.W. Paine along with other trading names.[41] By 1975, the group had acquired a total of 32 funeral branch offices and at the end of five years a further 37 had come under their ownership, mainly the substantial firm of Francis Chappell in south-east London and north Kent in 1977. In 1983, the Great Southern were floated on the Unlisted Stock Market (USM). Three years later the group's retail outlets totalled 92, which between them in the year ending December 1985 had carried out 22,000 funerals.[42] By this time the group also controlled nine crematoria, responsible in 1985 for 22,640 cremations and 516 burials.

---

[41]Ibid, p. 127. It should be noted that the holding company of the Great Southern, J.D. Field, were originally funeral directors, owning the firm of Bedford & Slater in Blackfriars Road, London. It is a business that goes back to 1690. The organisation was sold at the time of World War II. The Great Southern Cemetery, Crematorium and Land Company was formed in 1907 with the opening of Streatham Park Cemetery in January 1909. Three of the original directors of the company were funeral directors. The South London Crematorium opened in the grounds of the cemetery in 1936. See 'Great Southern Group PLC. Placing by Hill Samuel & Co Ltd' (1986); and '*FSJ* takes a look at the Great Southern Group PLC' (1987) *FSJ,* December, pp. 484–488. See also 'Three Centuries of History from Family Funeral Firm' (2009) Company Newsletter. See also Parsons B. (2012c) 'A Nineteenth Century Initiative Continued: London Proprietary Cemeteries in the Twentieth Century', *Journal of the Institute of Cemetery and Crematorium Management*, Vol. 80, No. 2, pp. 62–81.
[42]'GSG plans to enter USM' (1986) *FSJ,* October, p. 383.

James Harold Kenyon moved from Brighton to commence trading in central London in 1875 predominantly as a carriage master. The location of the firm resulted in the undertaking of many prestigious funerals, which led to Kenyon's becoming firmly established as the funeral director to London society.[43] In the 1960s and 1970s the firm acquired a number of funeral firms in west London and in 1975 a subsidiary company, Kenyon Air Transportation, was established to provide a worldwide repatriation service, along with Kenyon Emergency Service to deal with mass fatalities. Somewhat smaller than Great Southern, by 1984 it had 22 branches and a coffin manufacturing business. Kenyon's was listed on the USM in 1983.[44]

Like Kenyon and Great Southern, Hodgson Holdings was a family organisation that had grown through acquisition after Howard Hodgson had purchased his father's ailing firm in 1975.[45] Hodgson recognised the market-related problem and sought to increase turnover by integrating an acquired local business in his 'cluster'. Other acquisitions soon followed, particularly that of the funeral assets of the House of Fraser, which in 1987 was responsible for 13,000 funerals.[46] By 1988, Hodgson possessed 263 branches managing over 40,000 funerals a year. Hodgson Holdings went on the Unlisted Securities Market in 1986.[47]

---

[43] Although the press stated that Kenyon's subsequently lost the 'royal contract', this is inaccurate as no 'contract' ever existed and they simply supplied services when requested. See *The Daily Telegraph* (5 January 1993) 'New Men for that Last Delicate Task'.

[44] 'Kenyon Securities on USM' in December 1983 see *FSJ,* September 1986, p. 344 and 'USM Placing for Kenyon Securities' (1984) *TFD,* January, Vol. 64, No. 1, p. 26.

[45] Horbury J. (1987) 'A Personal Profile of Howard Hodgson', *FSJ,* August, pp. 312–316. See also Townsend E. (1987) 'Hodgson Expands Funeral Empire', *The Embalmer,* Vol. 30, No. 3, p. 27.

[46] 'Hodgson and CWS take over Ingalls' (1987) *FSJ,* June, p. 209. The deal cost £15.5M. Ingall industries sold light engineering and focused on acquiring funeral directing businesses. See 'Ingall Industries More Acquisitions' (1984) *TFD,* January, p. 26. 'House of Fraser offers £9.6M for Ingall' (1985) *FSJ,* June, p. 239 and this was successfully cleared by the Office of Fair Trading. At this stage House of Fraser carried out 9,000 funerals in Scotland and Ingall carried out 15,000 funerals. The deal was then referred to the MMC ('Proposed Ingalls Buy by CWS referred to Monopolies Commission' (1987) *FSJ,* July, p. 250 and *TFD,* August, p. 13). The MMC required the CWS to sell half of the House of Fraser branches. ('Monopolies Commission force CWS to sell half of Acquisitions' (1987) *FSJ,* November, p. 410).

[47] 'Hodgson Holdings Go Public on USM' (1986) *FSJ,* July, p. 254, and 'Second Funeral Group Joins USM' (1986) *TFD,* July, p. 10.

The flotation by Great Southern, Kenyon and Hodgson gave each organisation funds to reduce borrowing by lowering their gearing ratio but also capital with which to acquire more funeral businesses.[48] With all three organisations possessing capital for expansion opportunities existing in the market for acquisition, and all now conscious of the additional need to satisfy shareholders, it was clear that a race had begun to acquire funeral directing firms. All three organisations were aware of the problems facing small operators, as outlined in the previous sections. Hodgson in particular believed that it was the inefficient operational basis on which the small firms were managed that made them ripe for acquisition. In a share-placing prospectus he stated, 'The existence of economies of scale in the industry (because of the high cost of fixed assets required) means that these smaller firms are often uneconomic.'[49] Hodgson later stated:

> Why should I watch small independent businesses struggling in competition with each other, all of them having highly valuable vehicles, refrigeration units, embalming facilities and staff, when I was sure that by amalgamating some of those assets I could run perhaps five of them as cheaply as one? At current prices, the half-dozen funerals a week that a small business might expect to handle would bring in about £3,500, and involve about forty man hours each, but five firms could bring in £15,000 for the same amount of equipment and hardly any increase in staff. This would make possible improvements in standards of service, which could not otherwise have been achieved and enable those improved standards to be offered more cheaply.[50]

To increase profitability, Hodgson and the other organisations rationalised immediately upon acquisition. This usually, but not always, involved the centralisation of operations. The origins of this strategy can be found in the work of the nineteenth-century carriage master supplying transport requirements to a number of small businesses. Since the 1920s, however, societal and technical developments have considerably assisted in the growth of centralisation, such as the shift from animate to motor power and custody of the body on the funeral director's premises. In conjunction

---

[48] For a general review of this period, including an interview with Colin Field, see Jeffreys S. (1987) 'Queuing Up at Death's Door', *TFD*, January, pp. 10–11.
[49] *Share Placing Document* (1986) Hodgson Holdings PLC, p. 8.
[50] Hodgson H. (1992) *How to Become Dead Rich*, London: Pavilion, p. 36.

with the increase in responsibility assigned to the funeral director, the latter has been able to capitalise upon this control of funerals in an effective manner. The growth of the large organisations since the 1950s indicates that principles of centralisation can be applied successfully to manage funerals. It is therefore not surprising that some organisations manage up to 30 branch offices from one centralised unit.

Centralisation controls resources to an optimum level of productivity. With the integration of acquired branch offices into a centralised area of operation, the necessity for each branch to operate as an independent self-sufficient economic unit is removed and responsibility for provision of all resources is shifted to the operational centre.

Centralisation in the funeral industry essentially manages funerals on what appears to be a production or assembly line; it is a 'Fordist'-style approach to internal funeral administration. Each task that comprises the work of the funeral director, from arranging the funeral through to its performance, is divided among a number of specialist functionaries and departments. In a similar manner to the motor vehicle being constructed as it moves through the assembly line, so when a funeral is arranged the body becomes the unit that is progressed through the departments at the centralised operational nucleus and emerges to occupy the most important position at the funeral.[51] The centralised system commences with the client's first contact to arrange the funeral in the branch office. A date and time for the funeral is organised through liaising with the administration office and when all external and internal documentation has been completed, full funeral details are forwarded to the head office. The administration office then becomes responsible for channelling appropriate information to departments, such as embalming and the coffin workshop.

After the administration has organised the conveyance of the body to the centralised premises, a process of embalming, coffin preparation, encoffining and transport to the branch office is completed in turn. On the day prior to the funeral an administrator generates a work programme detailing the vehicles and manpower required for each funeral. Each one is booked to 'work-over' from one funeral to another so that all resources are utilised to their optimum potential without the need for hired-in additional assistance or slack. At any given time the administration will have knowledge of the movements of all personnel, vehicles, stock and at which stage the body is within the custody of the organisation.

---

[51]Naylor M. (1989) 'Opening Geoffrey Gorer's Door: A Personal Overview of Funerals 1983–2003', *Pharos International*, Vol. 70, No. 3, pp. 17–23.

In respect of Hodgson Holdings, the implementation and centralisation was supplemented by other managerial strategies:

> The policy of your company is expansion through acquisition – a philosophy which to date has been put successfully into practice by the purchase of small and medium sized businesses.
>
> The formula used is simple but effective with three ingredients being critical to its success. Firstly, the business acquired is brought swiftly and efficiently into the Group structure by means of detailed check lists containing over 150 procedures and operating methods to be implemented. Secondly, economies of scale are made (without detriment to the high standard of service expected by the Board) as soon as practicably possible. Finally, and in conjunction with the first two steps, rigorous and regular reporting requirements applied consistently throughout the Group are introduced.[52]

The advantages to funeral organisations of centralised management are two-fold. First, economies of scale can be gained from the bulk purchase of coffins and other variable-cost items, such as coffin linings and embalming supplies along with fuel, uniforms and other items where the possibility exists to negotiate favourable prices with the vendor. Only one garage, embalming theatre, mortuary and coffin workshop and store has to exist to serve the branches. Secondly, centralisation allows for control over resources, so that costly fixed overheads such as vehicles and staff can be utilised in the most cost- and time-effective manner. Both bring benefits to the organisation through the cost-effective running of the operation. It can, however, be argued that a centralised operational style leads to depersonalisation and deskilling of staff.[53] The former can be from a lack of continuity between funeral arranger and conductor/director. When clients arrange a funeral they meet a member of staff exclusively committed to arranging and administering the funeral. Through the interview conversation a rapport is frequently generated with the arranger. On the

---

[52] Hodgson H. (1992) *How to Become Dead Rich,* London: Pavilion, p. 73.
[53] Parsons B. (1997) '*Change and Development of the British Funeral Industry in the Twentieth Century, with Special Reference to the Period 1960–1994*', Unpublished PhD thesis, University of Westminster, London.

day of the funeral, however, a different employee arrives to supervise the ritual as conducting/directing is not within the employment ambit of the first employee. Thus through demarcation staff are not in a position to manage the funeral as a continuous event and in a manner that would extend the maximum level of personal support to the bereaved.

On balance it is appropriate to point out that this can be the same in a busy independent/family firm with an employee arranging the funeral and the owner conducting/directing the funerals. Deskilling results from breaking down the funeral process into manageable tasks performed by operatives in defined capacities. This strategy effectively deskills through not exposing staff to the many and varied tasks that comprise the overall work of funeral directing. Funeral arrangers only have experience of client-facing matters, embalmers of sanitary matters, chauffeur bearers of driving and carrying coffins, etc. While it could be argued that this has created the role of specialists in these tasks, the notion of the funeral director also having a comprehensive knowledge and portfolio of the other roles that represent the whole funeral as a complex event is not apparent as most employees are trained in one specific task, rather than progressing through a broad employment experience.

More recently, the issue of centralisation has provoked a reaction from commentators on funeral service. Storing the deceased in what is perceived to be a 'warehouse' away from the branch where the funeral was arranged, which is, in fact, a purpose-designed facility with walk-in refrigeration unit, is perceived to be deceptive as clients are not informed of this intermediate transfer between the place of death and the chapel of rest. One documentary focused on Funeralcare.[54] This operational strategy, however, is utilised by many organisations irrespective of ownership.

Expansion through acquisition has limitations. First, some funeral directors were not interested in selling their business. Reasons for non-sale include the availability of succession, ideology towards the large organisations or insufficient price offered. In addition, the low cost of their funerals in comparison to the purchasing firm's prices could be considered a problem as an increase in price may take the newly acquired firm significantly out of line with existing competitors. Conversely, maintenance of the acquired firm's original charges may make an insufficient contribution towards the organisation's centralised overheads. Secondly, in circumstances where the business only undertakes a modest number of funerals, the potential for future growth may be limited. Some firms, such as those

---

[54] *Dispatches: Undercover Undertaker* (Channel 4, 25 June 2012).

in urban areas, also found that their property was more valuable than the funeral business. Thirdly, from the perspective of the purchasing organisation, an operational centre or 'cluster' might not be within a convenient radius. Thus a prospective firm, although viable, could only be managed as a 'mini-cluster' with reduced profit margins. Despite this issue, some successful 'standalone' firms have been acquired by the large organisations and maintained as such with minimal corporate intervention.

Fourthly, some funeral directors have been unwilling to sell their business due to the perceived loss of 'personalisation'. Not only was this from loss of continuity when dealing with a large organisation, but through staff not being rooted in the community in the same manner as an owner/manager. In McFarland's research among funeral directors in Scotland, a respondent highlighted a clear distinction between the location and the service perceived to be provided by the large/small firms:

> Our job is very, very different from an inner city funeral director because we know the people and we are not salesmen [...] I am able to sit here with my friends and I'll be honest and say, "Oh, come on. Your mother wouldn't have wanted that, your mother would have liked something plain and simple, good quality. Your mum wasn't a fancy person" because I know them. You wouldn't get that working for a big company in Glasgow.[55]

And as Saunders states, 'Some small funeral directors already have an indirect label for the large group: "Hodgson? He is not a proper funeral director, gives the trade a bad name through his impersonal approach."'[56]

During the 1980s, the effects of rationalisation upon the funeral industry were becoming apparent as acquisitions continued. For example, in 1987 the Great Southern Group acquired 17 funeral businesses, adding 20 further branches to the existing 92. Hodgson pursued the same policies and from June 1986 to May 1987 a 70 per cent increase in number of funerals from 5,600 to 9,500 per annum was recorded as a result of adding 52 outlets to the organisation. These complemented the current geographical areas of operation in addition to new ones. Hodgson warned at the end of 1988 that, with concentration occurring on such a considerable

---

[55] McFarland E. (2008) 'Working with Death: An Oral History of Funeral Directing in Late Twentieth-Century Scotland', *Oral History,* Vol. 36, No. 1, p. 72.
[56] Saunders K.C. (1991) 'Service Without a Smile: The Changing Structure of the Death Industry', *The Service Industries Journal,* Vol. 11, No. 2, p. 206.

scale, the number of acquisitions could not be maintained and predicated a slower rate of expansion in 1989. Attention was then turned to medium- and large-sized organisations. For example, Kenyon acquired the six branches of W.S. Bond in 1987,[57] then the substantial east London- and Essex-based group Dottridge Brothers for £11.5M, adding 5,750 funerals.[58] As mentioned above, Hodgson purchased part of the House of Fraser's funeral directing assets, being some 13,000 funerals per annum.

Further rationalisation of the industry intensified when Hodgson Holdings merged with Kenyon Securities PLC to form PFG Hodgson Kenyon International PLC, with a 25 per cent stake in the business from French investment.[59] The effect of this newly formed alliance was to create a funeral directing firm carrying out approximately 65,000 funerals a year and controlling an estimated 20 per cent of the market in the United Kingdom. Hodgson expressed the logic of the deal:

> The total market was flat, even declining, and would be for another ten years. Funeral prices had not risen, and were still not rising, as fast as inflation. Over 80% of the cost of funerals was fixed, and therefore the opportunities for economies of scale were overwhelming.[60]

Although Hodgson and Kenyon did have relatively distinct trading areas, the aftermath of the merger led to intense rationalisation of resources, including redundancies. In addition, the organisation was now in a position to obtain greater purchasing discounts of coffins, soft furnishings, vehicles, etc. Howard Hodgson remained chief executive at PFG Hodgson Kenyon International (as it had become after an investment by Pompes Funerabres Generales) until the end of 1990.[61] It was renamed the Plantsbrook Group in 1992 (Plantsbrook being the name of the river running under the head office).[62]

In August 1994, the American funeral organisation Service Corporation International (SCI) acquired the Great Southern Group, followed a month

---

[57]'£3M Acquisitions by Kenyon' (1987) *FSJ*, September, p. 326.
[58]*The Daily Telegraph*, 16 January 1988.
[59]'Hodgson's and Kenyon's Merger' (1989) *TFD*, October, pp. 18–19. 'Hodgson and Kenyon Merge with French' (1989) *FSJ*, August, p. 5.
[60]Hodgson H. (1992) *How to Become Dead Rich*, London: Pavilion, p. 117.
[61]'The Surprise Departure of Howard Hodgson' (1991) *FSJ*, February, p. 11.
[62]'Change of Name for PFG Hodgson Kenyon International' (1992) *FSJ*, April, p. 9.

later by the Plantsbrook Group.[63] Established in Texas in 1962, SCI owned funeral directors, cemeteries and crematoria in the United States, Canada and Australia. It also acquired a proportion of the French, Spanish, Portuguese, Dutch, Swiss, Italian, Belgian and German funeral markets, although these were subsequently sold.[64] As a result of the merger, total market share was in the region of 14 per cent with the number of branches aggregating 520. The second acquisition was followed by an investigation by the Monopolies and Mergers Commission.[65] Their report of May 1995 concluded 'that the merger may be expected to operate against the public interest'.[66] The report offered the following reasons as detrimental to the supply of funerals arising from the merger: that SCI would raise prices excessively; lack of true ownership identified to clients and the choice of firms in 10 areas being restricted. The principal recommendations were the sale of 12 branch offices, ownership disclosure and pricing transparency.[67] Although SCI challenged these decisions in the Court of Appeal, the MMC believed that as SCI crematoria and funeral branches were in the same areas this would result in funerals being deliberately directed to their own facilities, thereby restricting choice. The firm agreed to give an undertaking that 'it would post details of competing crematoria at every SCI funeral directing branch in the area of an SCI crematorium'.[68]

---

[63]'Great Southern Fights off US 'predator' (1994) *FSJ*, July, p. 11 and 'GSG Remains Firm against Hostile Bid from SCI' (1994) *FSJ*, August, p. 11; 'SCI adds Plantsbrook Group to its Collection' (1994) *FSJ*, September, p. 19, 'SCI Chief Delivers A Categoric No to the Americanization of Funerals' (1994) *FSJ*, December, p. 12, Horbury J. (1995) 'How are Things Settling Down at SCI?' *FSJ*, February, pp. 33–40. See also *The Sunday Telegraph*, 17 July 1994; *The Daily Telegraph*, 10 June 1994; 3 August 1994; 7 August 1994; 8 August 1994; 11 August 1994; 12 August 1994; *Financial Times*, 2 August 1994; 16 August 1994.
[64]See MMC (1995) p. 33 for a brief history of SCI.
[65]The acquisition of both companies attracted considerable coverage in the trade press in addition to the national press. For example, see 'Little Southern Comfort for US Undertaker', *The Daily Telegraph*, 10 June 1994; 'Why SCI wants Great Southern', *The Daily Telegraph*, 10 June 1994; 'Panel Green Light for SCI', *The Daily Telegraph*, 11 August 1994; 'Rival to Appeal on Great Southern Bid' *The Daily Telegraph*, 9 August 1994; 'SCI buys Stake in Second British Funerals Group', *The Daily Telegraph*, 12 August 1994; 'The Great American Burial Plot', *The Guardian*, 25 October 1995.
[66]Monopolies and Merger Commission (1995) *Service Corporation International and Plantsbrook Group PLC – A Report on the Merger Situation*, Cm2880, London: HMSO, p. 4.
[67]Ibid, p. 4. 'SCI told by MMC to sell off Businesses in Certain Areas' (1995) *FSJ*, June, p. 13, and for a list of the 12 branches see 'Funeral Branches to Change Hands' (1997) *FSJ*, January, p. 36.
[68]Ibid, p. 5.

Developments Post-SCI

There is little doubt that the presence of SCI and other large operators has had a lasting impact on the landscape of British funeral service. While SCI in America faced lawsuits concerning trading information, in February 2001 the opportunity arose for a management buy-out by the UK management.[69] One journalist remarked:

> it was difficult to find any positive impact made by SCI in Britain. They changed the culture in the funeral industry and created a new type of competition to drive up prices, which put great pressure on the rest of the industry.[70]

While there is no doubt that this period raised the profile of the industry, the claim that SCI's presence changed the culture of funerals and fuelled price increases is not supported by evidence; a more accurate assessment would be that it stimulated competition in an environment where funerals were already being reformed.

Following a management buy-out by the UK board in September 2001, SCI's holdings in the United Kingdom has traded as Dignity PLC. The company was floated on the London Stock Exchange in 2004 and is now a FTSE 250 listed company.[71] As of December 2016, Dignity has over 792 branches, 44 crematoria and 5 cemeteries, along with manufacturing and pre-need divisions. In 2016, they managed 70,700 funeral and have nearly 12 per cent of the market share of funerals in the United Kingdom.[72]

Other structural changes have occurred since 1995. The Loewen Group of Canada made their first acquisition in 1998, followed by others.[73] It became Alderwoods in December 2001, while two years later a management buy-out formed Alderwoods UK.[74] The business was renamed the Fairways Partnership in 2003. It possessed 49 funeral businesses before

---

[69]'US Lawsuit Against SCI' (2000) *FSJ,* March, pp. 72–78.
[70]'Few Mourn as US Funeral Group Departs', *The Times,* 15 January 2001.
[71]'SCI UK Partial Sale' (2000) *FSJ,* December, p. 5, and 'New-Look SCI Pushes for Higher Industry Standards' (2001) *FSJ,* September, p. 5, 'Dignity Buy-Out for £220M' (2001) *FSJ,* March, p. 7.
[72]http://www.dignityfunerals.co.uk/corporate/investors/results-and-reports/shareholders/. Accessed on 20 May 2017.
[73]'Loewen Announces its First Affiliation in the UK Funeral Sector with the Purchase of JNO Steel & Sons' (1998) *FSJ,* January, p. 5. See also Harr J. (2001) *Funeral Wars,* London: Short Books.
[74]'Alderwoods breaks away from US Parents' (2003) *FSJ,* December, p. 5.

86 per cent of the share capital was purchased in 2006 by the Co-operative Group Ltd. Maintaining the Fairways brand, it represents the 'private name' section of the Co-operative Funeralcare, although this distinction was dropped in 2015. This acquisition resulted in an OFT investigation to assess the share of funerals in an area, rather than a 25 per cent or greater share of deaths and a 'fascia count', as used in the MMC's report into SCI (1995).[75] Disinvestment was required in five areas, with the branches being purchased by Funeral Service Partnership (now Funeral Partners, see below). Although the criteria used by OFT to assess whether an acquisition is likely to reduce competition was not limited to the tests applied in the above, Funeralcare and Dignity are now required to seek OFT approval where an acquisition is likely to cause a breach. This was the case in January 2013 when Dignity acquired the two crematoria and some of the funeral directing assets owned by Yew Holdings (formerly the Warburton Group of Companies).

During the 1980s Co-operative societies started to merge with a notable example between the Co-operative Retail Society and the Co-operative Wholesale Society to become the Co-operative Group (CWS) Ltd.[76] As of January 2015, there were only 12 societies offering funerals remaining in the United Kingdom.[77] The Co-operative Funeralcare is the largest society with around 800 branches. Collectively, the Co-operative societies have approximately 25/26 per cent of the market share of funerals in the United Kingdom. However, apart from a common heritage, there is no financial link between the societies; the tendency for researchers, journalists and commentators to see the Co-operative movement as one entity is erroneous. In locations such as Edinburgh, Scotmid and Funeralcare compete against each other.

Other organisations have grown by acquisition since the 1980s. Some, such as Lodge Bros (Funerals) Ltd, A.W. Lymn and C.P.J. Field (formerly the Traditional Family Funeral Company Ltd), are family owned

---

[75] *Competition Acquisition by the Cooperative Group (CWS) Limited of Fairways Group UK Limited* (2006) Office of Fair Trading, p. 9.

[76] For example, 'Co-operatives Merger Approved' (1995) *FSJ*, April, p. 8. There was also an attempt to purchase the Co-operative. See 'Andrew Regan – Dead and Buried? by FD Forthright' (1997) *FSJ*, June, pp. 43–44. 'Merger get Nearer' (2000) *FSJ*, March, p. 5 and 'CWS-CRS Merger' (2000) *FSJ*, April, p. 5.

[77] Co-operative societies with funeral divisions are: Funeralcare (including the former Fairways branches); Southern; Anglia; Scotmid; Clydebank; Mid Counties, Heart of England, Lincoln, Chelmsford Star; Midlands, East of England and Tamworth.

and managed.[78] Others, such as Funeral Partners (and the former Laurel Funerals), are supported by asset management companies.[79] A feature of all these organisations is that they have retained the original identities of acquired businesses.

The 1990s in Focus

Towards the end of the 1980s, a reaction began against the large organisations operating in funeral service. In 1989, the National Society of Allied and Independent Funeral Directors (SAIF) was founded to protect the interests of family-owned and managed firms who claimed the NAFD, which embraced the key large organisations in their membership, could not represent their interests. At an early meeting of SAIF it was stated that:

> For the past few months there has been a strong groundswell of opinion that views with 'considerable apprehension' the growth of the big conglomerate funeral groups – and particular their activities in the promotion of their own pre-paid funeral schemes. Such schemes, say the independents, unlike the NAFD Windsor life scheme, are 'redeemable' only at branches of the group which issued them, and so preclude independent funeral directors carrying out a funeral, even though the deceased may have lived in their particular area and the funeral group which sold the plan may not have an office in that area.[80]

SAIF declared that their objectives were 'to promote, protect and assist the rights of independent funeral director', concerning both pre-need and at-need funerals.[81] Its formation led to a number of independent/family firms withdrawing from membership of NAFD to join SAIF; some were embraced in both organisations. In 1993, a number of Co-operative

---

[78]'Traditional Family Funeral Company in Top Five' (2003) *FSJ,* May, p. 5.
[79]'Laurel Management Buy-Out' (2003) *FSJ,* November, p. 5 and 'FSJ Interviews Funeral Service Partnership' (2008) *FSJ,* February, pp. 62–64.
[80]'Formation of the Society of Allied and Independent Funeral Directors' (1989) *FSJ,* October, p. 13.
[81]'Clive Leverton Delivers a Progress Report on the Society of Allied and Independent Funeral Directors' (1989) *FSJ,* November, p. 17.

societies then departed from NAFD to form a Funeral Standards Council (FSC). Membership was regulated through a 'Client Pledge', not dissimilar to the NAFD's Code of Practice.[82] In May 1994 the Funeral Ombudsman Scheme (FOS) was launched to deal with complaints about FSC members and also the Funeral Planning Council that represented some pre-need organisations.[83] SAIF joined the FSC/FOS in 1998.[84] At its height, the FSC/FOS claimed to represent 60 per cent of funeral directors in the United Kingdom.

Plantsbrook also withdrew from membership of the NAFD and established its own code, called 'The Oaktree Charter'.[85] This was a short-lived move and the firm returned to membership of the NAFD in January 1995 only for its new owner, SCI, to resign again from the NAFD in May 1998.[86] SAIF then left the FOS at the end of 2001 and the FOS ceased shortly after.[87] After the FSC departed from the FOS in August 2002 to form its own arbitration scheme the latter ceased.[88] In December 2003, the FSC amalgamated with the NAFD.

An unfortunate consequence of this period was the conflict between the contrasting sectors of the industry, essentially representing deep division between competing organisations. From an external perspective, while the profile of funeral service was raised, it is questionable whether the period enhanced the image of the industry, particularly as tensions were exploited by the media. The expansion and operational style of the large organisation, funeral costs, standards of standard, marketing activities and alleged manipulation of client preference were some of the issues focused upon. Many sensationally worded headlines appeared in both the regional and national press, particularly between 1995 and 2000. The findings of the 1995 MMC report provided much ammunition, while 2 years

---

[82]Gornall L. (1993) 'The Departure of the Co-operatives', *TFD*, August, p. 27, and 'Co-operative Funeral Businesses Resign from NAFD' (1993) *FSJ*, July, p. 19.
[83]'Ombudsman Scheme for UK Funerals' (1994) *FSJ*, June, pp. 74–75.
[84]'The Society of Allied and Independent Funeral Directors joins Funeral Ombudsman Scheme' (1998) *FSJ*, June, p. 17.
[85]'Plantsbook Group Pulls out of NAFD' (1994) *FSJ*, February, p. 5 and 'Plantsbrook Quits NAFD and Opts to Abide by its Own Charter' (1994) *FSJ*, February, pp. 26–31.
[86]'SCI's Ex-Plantsbrook Firms Re-admitted to NAFD' (1995) *FSJ*, January, p. 7; 'SCI Leaves NAFD' (1998) *FSJ*, June, p. 5; and 'SCI Joins Funeral Standards Council' (1998) *FSJ*, October, p. 5.
[87]'SAIF to Leave FOS' (2001) *FSJ*, December, p. 68 and 'Former Ombudsman Hits Out' (2003) *FSJ*, September, p. 41.
[88]'FSC to Leave Ombudsman Scheme' (2002) *FSJ*, August, p. 5.

later SAIF released a dossier of negative press cuttings about SCI's Age Concern Funeral Plan.[89] A price survey conducted on behalf of SAIF in 1999 found that SCI tended to charge more than any other funeral director; the same exercise was conducted in 2010. It received little attention from the media and simply antagonised Dignity.[90] TV documentaries focused on funeral directing with the intention of portraying SCI in a poor light. Matters came to a head when Channel 4 broadcast *Undercover Britain – Last Rights* on 12 May 1998.[91] Lawyers for SCI attempted to prevent its transmission by applying to the High Court for an injunction. Mr Justice Lightman refused and undercover reporter Ben Anderson's portrayal of activities at H.A. Harold funeral directors of Salisbury was revealed to the nation. This became a turning point as it was realised by many in the industry that all funeral directors were being viewed negatively.

The trade press was also not reticent in its coverage of these tensions. One example was the particularly vocal anonymous correspondent called 'F.D. Forthright' who made contributions to *FSJ* from February 1994.[92] These prompted many letters regarding the sentiments expressed and also other matters, such as SCI being awarded a contract for providing bereavement services in a hospital and its nursing-home educational initiative entitled Quality in Focus, which gave staff an insight into the work of the funeral director.[93]

---

[89]'The Age Concern Funeral Plan. A United Cause for the Independent Sector' Issued by SAIF. See also *Summary of the UK Funeral Profession* (1997) Edinburgh: Golden Charter.
[90]'Nationwide Funeral Price Survey' (1999) *FSJ,* January, p. 17. See also Hindley P. (1999) 'Is the Price Right?' *FSJ,* February, p. 42. 'Funeral Cost Comparison Research. Report prepared for SAIF' (2010) Ipsos MORI.
[91]Channel 4, *Undercover Britain- Last Rights* (Broadcast on 12 May 1998). See 'Undercover Britain' (1998) *FSJ,* June, pp. 20–23. One-page advertisements placed by SCI in national newspapers in the aftermath of the programme reassured the public of the organisation's commitment to standards when dealing with clients and the deceased. For example, see *The Sun,* 13 May 1988. See also Granada, *World in Action* (broadcast on 19 January 1998). See 'Media Attention' (1998) *FSJ,* February, p. 7. See also 'Broadcasting Complaint Not Upheld' (1999) *FSJ,* March, pp. 30–31 and 'Broadcasting Standards Commission and Service Corporation International', *Pharos International,* Vol. 65, No. 1, pp. 52–53.
[92]For a rebuff of 'F.D. Forthright' see Bailey C. (1997) 'A View from the Front', *FSJ,* April, pp. 35 & 39.
[93]'Central Middlesex NHS Trust' (1997) *FSJ,* June, p. 6 & 9 and 'SCI Wins NHS Contract' (1997) *FSJ,* August, p. 12; 'Anger over US Funeral Firm's Hospital Deal', *The Guardian,* 3 July 1997. See also Lymn Rose N. (1997) 'Legislation', *FDM,* October, pp. 8–12. A similar contract was also acquired by the Co-operative for Northampton.

It was an ugly period. One journalist even commented, 'It is a pity that a profession whose role is to offer comfort to the bereaved cannot behave with more dignity when speaking as an industry.'[94] *The Economist* wistfully noted that, 'To some extent, SCI is a whipping-boy for discontent about the sleepy, and sometimes sleazy, funeral industry in Britain'. It also speculated: 'Anyone planning to organise a funeral in the developed world has to ask himself whether the American companies will succeed in dominating the business.'[95] In the event, SCI did not come anywhere near domination of the UK funeral market as the largest share continues to be held by independent/family businesses.

Further negative publicity occurred in 2012 through the screening of two television programmes that focused on the operations of the large organisations. The first took the view that the strategy of running branches from a 'hub' was of no benefit to the bereaved and purely of convenience to the organisation. Specifically naming Funeralcare, the programme made no mention that this operational method was also used by organisations of other sizes and ownerships.[96] The other highlighted unethical behaviour of staff within branches of Funeral Partners.[97]

The Independent/Family Funeral Business

One of SAIF's initiatives was to reinforce the sector's independent identity. In 1997 they instigated a 'Campaign for Fair Funeral Practices'.[98] The purpose was to create awareness of coroners' removal contracts being awarded to one funeral director; to ensure the OFT's recommendations are fair to independent funeral directors and to give freedom over choice of funeral director for Age Concern funeral plan holders.[99] The underlying theme was to promote the idea that the independent/family-run

---

[94]'Funeral Rights and Wrongs', *The Sunday Telegraph*, 23 March 1997.
[95]'The Business of Bereavement: An Expensive Way to Go' (1997) *The Economist*, 4 January, Vol. 342, No. 7998, pp. 75–77. For a study of the American industry see Smith R.G.E. (1996) *Death Care Industries in the United States*, Jefferson: McFarland & Co.
[96]*Dispatches: Undercover Undertaker* (Channel 4, 25 June 2012). See Hutsby B. (2013) 'Dispatches: The Outcome', *FDM*, September, pp. 12–13.
[97]*Exposure: The British Way of Death* (ITV, 26 September 2012).
[98]'Independents' Day: The Launch of the Campaign for Fair Funeral Practices', (1997) *FSJ*, October, pp. 73–74 and West J. (1997) 'Campaign for Fair Funeral Practices', *FSJ*, November, pp. 53–56.
[99]'Saifview' (2001) *FSJ*, February, p. 83.

organisation offered a higher level of personal service in contrast to that of a large firm. Although highly subjective and impossible to quantify, this argument arises from the notion that the personally vested interest of independent ownership is likely to generate more individual commitment as survival is dependent upon a combination of recommendation, reputation, price, promotion and standard of service.[100] Thus the owner of an independent business is likely to possess a higher level of motivation to promote his/her firm than those who are merely employed in a branch of a large organisation. It is certainly significant that a former director of the Great Southern Group commented:

> arguably the quality of service is reduced when a paid member of staff replaces the owner whose income is directly related to the success of the business, for he always gives that little bit more and, indeed, this will always be the case and, therefore, one will never see the demise of the traditional family funeral director.[101]

While issue can be taken with this statement – a highly motivated workforce in a large firm may have the same or a greater level of commitment – it is the final phrase that is of significance as since the 1990s the number of funeral directors opening for business – both independent and branches of large organisations – has been significant. In recognition of this it is appropriate to review the predictions proposed in an article by Saunders that appeared in 1991 when he advanced a six-year cycle of 'disintegration [of the large group] and reversion back to small units...'.[102] His understanding was that this could be achieved through the following stages:

> [The]... large firm absorbs smaller businesses, cuts out competition; rationalises staff, services and assets; increases the cost of funerals to cope with mounting overheads; injects a greater element of impersonality; message gets around to the public that this or that small funeral director gives a much nicer funeral; future clients revert to small family business and the number of their funerals grows; more of

---

[100] See 'Are Independents Better?' (1999) *FSJ*, April, p. 35.
[101] Field C.P.J. (1989) 'Funeral Directing – The Next Decade', *Pharos International*, Vol. 55, No. 3, p. 99.
[102] Saunders K. (1991) 'Service Without a Smile: The Changing Structure of the Death Industry', *The Service Industries Journal*, Vol. 11, No. 2, p. 205.

the experienced managers, retirees and their offspring set up new small businesses to meet the demand and so drain away or draw custom from the larger groups. Result: large groups diversify to survive...[103]

Reviewing this statement in 2014, Saunders' forecast has only been partially accurate. Although the thrust is underpinned by evidence – that staff leave an acquired business then set up in competition – other claims are questionable. First, large groups had already diversified by the 1990s. The Great Southern Group had long been involved in crematoria management and all organisations offered pre-need funeral plans.[104] Beyond these the opportunities for diversification are limited. Secondly, when in more recent years acquisition of independent businesses has taken place by large organisations, there has been a tendency to resist 'corporatising' by enforcing a standardised decoration of premises, adoption of a uniform coffin range and enforcement of one make of vehicles, etc. This preserves the pre-acquisition identity, and takes a *laissez-faire* approach to change. In this way existing staff are less likely to be alienated, a situation that could lead to them leaving and opening in competition. This acknowledges that entering an acquired organisation with 'guns blazing' to change working practices is not a successful strategy. Thirdly, it is unclear how the large organisation 'cuts out competition'. Rather than contracting the market, acquisitions have fuelled the opening of new businesses. Lastly, the industry has not seen the 'collapse' of the large organisations, as Saunders predicted. Indeed, the situation is far from that; the large organisations have maintained their trading position and continue to make acquisitions. A survey of businesses trading in the west London area between 1995 and 2010 reveals the presence of many new independent organisations in addition to branches of large firms.[105] It is not confined to the capital, as revealed by the large number of regular applications for new branch offices to be members of the NAFD.[106] In some cases the perspicacity of the owners of some firms has recognised a

---

[103] *Ibid.*, pp. 205–206.
[104] The Great Southern Group had long been involved in crematoria management, while Dignity have significantly increased their portfolio.
[105] Parsons B. (2011a) 'A Dying Business? Mortality and Funeral Directing in West London', Paper presented at the Tenth International Conference of the Social Context of Death, Dying and Disposal, Nijmegen, 9–12 September. See also Gould G. (1996) 'Letter from America: Local Ownership as a Competitive Advantage', *Insight Special Edition,* May, Issue 13.
[106] These are listed each month in the *FDM.*

niche market and the needs of specific religious or social groupings, such as Afro-Caribbean communities or by specialising in Asian or Muslim funerals.[107] In addition, some firms have responded to the needs of those wanting an 'alternative' funeral such as a 'green' burial, or support for a self-managed funeral or offering a 'direct cremation' service. A funeral 'supermarket' opened at Walthamstow in February 1996 and a similar 'Funeral Centre' in Catford five months later.[108] Other types of operation have also emerged. There are internet-based funeral directors, who have no premises and who, after receiving instructions (and payment), sub-contract the funerals to a firm near to the client or where the funeral is to take place. In addition, there are direct disposal services that will collect the deceased, arrange cremation without any ceremony and return the ashes to the client. The role of 'funeral advisers' can be added to this list. In some cases, endorsement is made by the Natural Death Centre and/or *The Good Funeral Guide*.

The presence of new independent firms indicates that two major barriers to entry traditionally understood to exist by the industry must be reappraised. First, the capital cost of establishment is the primary barrier to entry, as confirmed by firms contributing to the 1987 MMC report.[109] However, from the number of independent businesses that have emerged, a proportion appear to have started with minimal capital investment, have only basic facilities and hire vehicular resources from a carriage master. Investment is then dependent on growth. It is interesting to note that an organisation giving evidence to this first report – the Co-operative Wholesale Society – stated that no 'substantial' barriers to entry existed and in confirmation cited evidence concerning the number of entrants in Scotland.[110] The second barrier is the absence of reputation. Recommendation as a result of past funerals is important to success and essentially stems from a combination of individual competence, sensitivity and organisational efficiency. Those establishing their own business have generally

---

[107] It should be noted, however, that some religious groups, such as Orthodox Jews, have always provided for their own community members.
[108] 'Funeral Supermarket Opens' (1996) *FSJ,* March, pp. 70–71 and 'The Funeral Centre, Catford' (1996) *FSJ,* March, p. 73. The Funeral Supermarket is now owned by Funeralcare and operates in the same way as any other funeral director; the Funeral Centre has since closed.
[109] Monopolies and Mergers Commission (1987) *Co-operative Wholesale Society Limited and House of Fraser PLC: A report on the acquisition by the Co-operative Wholesale Society Limited of the Scottish funerals business of House of Fraser PLC*, Cm229, London: HMSO, p. 35.
[110] Ibid, p. 29.

had experience in the industry and often capitalise upon existing personal reputation in an area. As the author of *The Good Funeral Guide*, Charles Cowling, wryly notes, 'We must backhandedly bless the Co-operatives, in particular, for unintentionally breeding some of our best born-again independent funeral directors.'[111]

However, this poses the question: is it the firm or the individual that is being recommended? A definitive answer is impossible, but it is likely to be the firm for two reasons. First, as it may be years between usage and recommendation there is no guarantee the member of staff will still be there, and secondly, the client may well have received good service from more than one person. In this respect it is akin to any other service organisation, such as a solicitor.

A key feature of promotion is through reinforcement that 'small is beautiful'. However, the large organisations have similarly been engaged in marketing strategies, such as forming associations with bereavement support groups and through linking charities with pre-paid funeral plans.[112] The coverage afforded to Co-operative Funeralcare in the pages of *FSJ* and *FDM* indicate the extent of their external activities. Heritage attached to many of the trading names has also been capitalised upon through the publication of company histories.[113]

---

[111] Cowling C. (2010a) *The Good Funeral Guide,* London: Continuum, p. 154. See also 'F.D. Forthright' (1994) 'The Atlantic Invasion, 1994', *FSJ,* July, p. 25.
[112] See 'Age Concern and SCI Launch New Funeral Plan' (1997) *FSJ,* March, p. 9.
[113] For histories of funeral directing firms see: For J.H. Kenyon see Parsons B. (2014b) *J.H. Kenyon: A Short History,* London: J.H. Kenyon. For Leverton see Leverton B. (1982) 'A Family Undertaking: Memoirs of a St Pancras Funeral Furnisher', *Camden History Review,* No. 10, pp. 10–12, and 'Leverton & Sons Ltd' (1994) *FSJ,* October, pp. 65–71. (For additional material on Leverton & Sons see 'Funeral Home and Rooms of Rest. The American Way. A Chat with Mr Stanley Leverton JP' (1927) *TUJ,* October, pp. 359–361, 'How Burial Customs Have Changed Since the Time of Dickens. Messrs. Leverton & Sons, Ltd' (1941) *TUFDJ,* June, p. 155. For C.T. Butterfield, see: Wyatt K. (2003) *A Yorkshire Undertaking* (C.T. Butterfield), Yorkshire: K. Wyatt. For Banting see: Banting D. (1998) 'The Life of William Westbrook Banting – Undertaker to the Crown', *FSJ,* May, pp. 78–85; Woodall R.D. (1993) 'The Undertaker Who Taught Slimming', *FSJ,* September, pp. 60–61; Van Beck T. (2006) 'Legacy of a Fat Undertaker', *TFD,* February, pp. 30–33. For F.W. Paine see: Parsons B. (2017c). *Frederick W. Paine Funeral Directors: A History,* London: F.W. Paine. For Field see: 'Three Centuries of History from Family Funeral Firm' (2009) Company Newsletter; For John Nodes see: 'The Nodes Family History and the Funeral of an Undertaker', (1995) *The Friends of Kensal Green Cemetery's Quarterly Newsletter,* March, Issue 14, pp. 8–11; For Tovey see: *Tovey Bros: A 150 Year History in Newport* (2010) Newport: Tovey Bros; for F.A. Albin see: Albin-Dyer B. and Parsons B. (2011). *Up and Down Like Tower Bridge,* London: Strong Shoulders Press.

The industry-generated gulf that has opened between the independent sector and large organisations raises three important issues and in this final section the definition of the family and/or independent firm, retention of the trading name and funeral directors as owners of crematoria are discussed.

What is an Independent/Family Firm?

The definition of both a family and/or an independent funeral organisation becomes unclear when the sector is examined closely. If that of a family firm is one where there is no familial separation of ownership from that of control, does this equally apply to firms owned by a family but managed entirely by employees? Similarly, can family status be applied to firms owned by an individual with all non-familial assistance? Further permutations raise additional questions. As the family funeral firm is claimed by many to be one offering a higher level of personal service than that of the large organisation, it is necessary to consider the definition from an operational perspective. While a family firm may be run by a husband and wife team, a similar situation can be found in many large firms employing this combination to manage branch offices. Under these circumstances an equal or greater familial presence may exist than in an independent family-owned firm managed by a number of unrelated employees. Furthermore, family-owned firms operating a number of branches, for example six to eight, from a centralised unit exhibit essentially the same characteristics as a large organisation of similar proportions. Branches staffed by funeral arrangers with funerals directed from a 'pool' of conductors may be found in both organisations. Thus continuity of contact at all stages of the funeral may equate to or be greater than the level found in a large organisation.

The term 'independent' is perhaps less problematic. Essentially it acknowledges an autonomous status: that the firm is not owned by another funeral organisation. However, can a firm run by family members, an individual or employees, but financed by part-ownership or by investment capital from another (not necessarily large) organisation be classified as independent? Independent status is taken a step further when the smaller Co-operative societies are examined. Edinburgh-based Scotmid Co-operative and also Lincoln Co-operative Society are both small funeral operations with ownership the prerogative of local members and profits reinvested in the business. Is this not an independent business? While the minutiae of these definitions may appear to be pedantic, in view of the strategies adopted by the independent sector such as SAIF's 'Campaign for Fair Funeral Practices', a more realistic definition of 'family' and 'independent' would be firms not owned specifically by Dignity or a Co-operative society.

Retention of the Trading Name

If one aspect can be highlighted that has provoked considerable controversy, it is the issue of retention of a trading name after acquisition. The name is maintained due to the strength of the trading identity and hence reputation. Smale sees trading identity as 'the most marketable commodity he [the funeral director] possesses'.[114] In the interest of retaining consumer loyalty the impression is given of the personality and individuality associated with the small family firm being retained although it is owned by a large organisation.

Although there is evidence to show that over many years trading names have been retained, such as F.W. Paine in south-west London being owned by a number of organisations from the 1950s, the issue came to the forefront during the 1980s. In the 1987 MMC Report the following can be found:

> Nearly one-quarter of the adverse comments we received about the supply of funeral undertaking services related to an alleged CWS policy of giving the public an illusion of undiminished choice by omitting to trade openly as CWS after taking over independent funeral directors.[115]

The strong feelings were made clear by a communication the Commission received from one funeral director: 'In failing to make it plain that a formerly family-owned business was now operated by CWS it was guilty

---

[114]Smale B. (1985) *Deathwork: A Sociological Analysis of Funeral Directing*, Unpublished PhD thesis, University of Sussex, p. 235; Hennessy P.J. (1980) *Families, Funerals and Finances – A Study of Funeral Expenses and How They Are Paid*, London: HMSO, p. 44 and Foster K. (1987) *A Survey of Funeral Arrangements* (OPCS), London: HMSO, p. 13.
[115]Monopolies and Mergers Commission (1987) *Co-operative Wholesale Society Limited and House of Fraser PLC: A report on the acquisition by the Co-operative Wholesale Society Limited of the Scottish funerals business of House of Fraser PLC*, Cm229, London: HMSO, p. 35.

of calculated deception and many bereaved persons were unaware that they were employing CWS.'[116]

This issue, along with price increases after acquisition and the 'sure and methodical Americanisation of our industry' was the thrust of a bill to regulate funeral directors in 1991 by the MP for Leigh, Lawrence Cunliffe. In an interview he conducted with Howard Hodgson Mr Cunliffe asked, 'How on earth can you reconcile the increased demand for your services with your masquerade of using the name of local family undertakers?'[117] Not all Members of Parliament agreed with this attempt to regulate the sector. One argued that:

> there is a principle that crosses professions, including bankers. For example, there is no longer a Mr Coutts at Coutts and Co., and the same is true of soap powders, bookshops and Fox's glacier mints. Fox's was taken over by Rowntree, which was taken over by Mackintosh. The change of name is not important, but... it is important that the standard of service continues irrespective of ownership.[118]

The issue was thoroughly discussed in the 1995 MMC report, with the recommendation that SCI branches in certain areas disclose ultimate ownership through 'prominent plaques on the wall at the branch reception'.[119] Indeed, the MMC report went a step further by suggesting that SCI and all funeral firms with branch offices operating under different trading names:

> disclose its ownership of funeral directing businesses in the determined areas prominently in all documentation presented to customers and in all advertisements or other promotional material used in connection with those businesses. We believe it is highly desirable that the disclosure of ultimate ownership of funeral directing branches should be general practice throughout the UK.[120]

---

[116] *Ibid.*, p. 40.
[117] 'Funeral Industry', *Hansard,* 22 April 1991, col. 794.
[118] 'Funeral Industry', *Hansard,* 22 April 1991, col. 795.
[119] '*Funerals: A Report of the OFT Inquiry into the Funeral Industry*' (2001) London: Office of Fair Trading, p. 16.
[120] Monopolies and Merger Commission (1995) *Service Corporation International and Plantsbrook Group PLC – A Report on the Merger Situation*, Cm2880, London: HMSO, p. 5.

The CEO of SCI (UK) confirmed that they 'liked to retain the names of established firms that join our company' and 'prominently display a plaque featuring the SCI company logo, plus a declaration of ownership inside the home.[121] This strategy was recognised by MP David Chidgey in 1997, although he still believed that there was an overall lack of transparency.[122] In 1998, SCI attempted to give greater transparency to ownership by changing the names of its four trading divisions, with Associated Funeral Directors becoming SCI Funerals Ltd.[123] The 2001 OFT report recommended that the ultimate ownership was displayed 'on the outside of the building'.[124] Although not compulsory for the industry, it was indirectly and voluntarily achieved by SCI/Dignity and Funeralcare through the use of a corporate identity. What the reports did not, and could not, stipulate was for any funeral organisation to change its trading name after acquisition, as there is plenty of evidence to indicate that many family and/or independently owned firms also operate branches under the pre-acquisition identity. Examination of trade association membership lists indicates this; similarly, the branches acquired by the Co-operative from SCI after the MMC's 1995 report have mostly retained their original trading identity. From the consumer perspective, revelation of the ownership can indicate the density of ownership in a locality. It can also discourage families from choosing funeral directors for whom there is a legitimate reason for avoidance, for example if a funeral in the past had not been managed to the family's satisfaction, and reduce the number of firms from which a family may obtain funeral quotations. However, the significance of this aspect of transparency to the consumer over other related issues identified by Brown (see Chapter 7) such as choice and information requires clarification.[125]

It would appear that little empirical research has been carried out to detect the consumer's opinion, with the exception of a small-scale survey by Hopwood, who found that: 'the actual ownership of the chosen funeral service centre was of little interest to the respondents'.[126] He goes on to report, 'You just want what seems to be a caring dignified organisation

---

[121] Hindley P. (1998) 'A Vision for the Funeral Industry', *FSJ,* December, pp. 88–96. See also Farrin J. (1999) 'A British Way of Death?' *FSJ,* October, pp. 77–92.
[122] 'Funeral Services', *Hansard,* 17 December 1997, cols 297–300.
[123] 'Corporate Identity – News from SCI' (1998) *FSJ,* November, p. 24.
[124] *Funerals: A Report of the OFT Inquiry into the Funeral Industry* (2001) London: Office of Fair Trading, p. 17.
[125] Brown C. (1995) 'Funerals – The Consumers' Perspective', *Pharos International,* Vol. 61, No. 4, p. 163.
[126] Hopwood D. (1996) 'Funeral Marketing in the 1990s', *Pharos International,* Spring, Vol. 62, p. 15.

who go and organize it for you, and you are really not that bothered who the actual owner is.'[127]

Similar findings are reported by the OFT in 2001:

> Many people genuinely seem to have a preference for either large or small businesses. Our survey showed that large businesses were often seen as offering experience and professionalism, more choice and options, with greater capacity to handle requests, while small family firms were seen by many as offering a more personal touch.[128]

As earlier surveys along with those carried out by funeral organisations indicate, repeat usage (albeit frequently with an interval of many years) is the primary reason for selecting a funeral director.[129] Hopwood confirms that clients will return to a firm without any contemplation of ownership provided a satisfactory standard of service has been received in the past. A supplementary line of investigation could have been to ascertain if the respondent would choose another firm if the one used in the past has been acquired by a large organisation and retained the original trading identity.

It would appear that in both MMC reports the issue of ownership is almost exclusively the prerogative of funeral directors from the independent/family sector. In some cases rival firms have taken the matter into their own hands by publishing advertisements to create awareness of ownership. In February 1998, the *Richmond and Twickenham Times* published the following:

> When choosing a funeral director, do you know who you're dealing with? In recent years the funeral profession has changed significantly with many long established funeral directors being taken over by multi-national conglomerate firms or the Co-operative movement. Unfortunately, they do not change the name above the door making it hard for you to distinguish between the truly independent family owned firms and those who are now part of a chain.

---

[127] *Ibid.*
[128] *Funerals: A Report of the OFT Inquiry into the Funeral Industry.* (2001) London: Office of Fair Trading, p. 16. See also *Consumer Experiences of Arranging Funerals: A Report* (2001) Office of Fair Trading, pp. 26–27.
[129] Hennessy P.J. (1980) *Families, Funerals and Finances – A Study of Funeral Expenses and How They Are Paid*, London: HMSO, p. 44 and *Funerals: A Report of the OFT Inquiry into the Funeral Industry.* (2001) London: Office of Fair Trading, p. 28.

Your local owned SAIF independent family owned funeral directors is [list of branches of a family owned firm] Those business connected with the American Company SCI [Service Corporation international] are [list of SCI branches][130]

Similar advertisements also appeared in the regional press during 2010 to highlight this issue in addition to research from an Ipsos MORI report to 'investigate if there is a consistent difference in the cost of funerals provided by independent funeral directors, funeral directors which are part of Dignity, and Co-operative Funeralcare branches'.[131]

Funeral Directors as Owners of Crematoria

The issue of funeral directing firms owning and managing crematoria (a 'vertical monopoly') is one that has emerged only in recent years. The dilemma appears to pivot around a conflict of interest where a funeral director would 'channel funerals to its [his] own crematoria'.[132] Today, Dignity own 44 crematoria, some acquired from Great Southern with others being former local authority or private enterprises and the remainder being newly built facilities.

A number of points can be made about this issue. First, it is the timing of this argument that is curious as it was three decades after crematoria owners Great Southern diversified backwards into funeral directing in 1972 that the first indication was expressed of the possibility of subverting client preference. Indeed, there is evidence to indicate a long relationship between funeral directors and the owners of private crematoria.[133] As a matter of history private enterprise was responsible for operating the first

---

[130] For an earlier example see 'Ownership Transparency in Cardiff' (1996) *FSJ*, December, p. 18.
[131] 'Funeral Cost Comparison Research. Report Prepared for SAIF' (2010) Ipsos MORI, p. 2.
[132] Monopolies and Merger Commission (1995) *Service Corporation International and Plantsbrook Group PLC – A Report on the Merger Situation*, Cm2880, London: HMSO, p. 4.
[133] For example, the chairman of the General Cemetery Company owning the West London Crematorium also owned John Nodes Funeral Directors, although the former was sold in 2014. Birkbeck Securities Ltd who owned Beckenham Crematorium prior to its acquisition by SCI in 1998 also owned local funeral director H. Copland. Following an MMC ruling the crematorium was retained by SCI and Copland's was sold to Co-operative Funeralcare. Harwood Park Crematorium at Stevenage is owned by Austin Funeral Directors.

three crematoria in this country; many opening in the last two decades have been by the private sector, including funeral directors.[134] As already mentioned, the Great Southern Cemetery, Crematorium and Land Company opened Streatham Park Cemetery in 1909 and South London Crematorium in 1936. When in 1972 Great Southern Group acquired the funeral directing establishments in the south London area, many branches had regularly utilised this crematorium over a sustained period. With the acquisition of these branches by SCI, the status quo was maintained. It was, however, only at this point that the MMC expressed the possibility of subverting client preference, but no direct evidence was offered.

Secondly, emphasis is placed on the notion that staff will manipulate client preference by directing them to their own crematoria. Not only must the branch be in the catchment area of the crematorium but employees must be complicit in this activity. This is hardly a sustainable practice.

Thirdly, SCI crematoria exist in areas with many non-SCI funeral directors who, through client instruction, utilise the facility. It would not be in SCI's economic interests to deter their business. Jupp has suggested that ownership of a crematorium by a funeral director 'may give the company an advantage that keeps competition at a distance.'[135] Such an argument, however, is flawed as it is in SCI's interest (or the owner of any private crematorium) to maintain good relations with all funeral directors in an area served by an SCI crematorium. Indeed, it could be argued that non-SCI funeral directors could dissuade potential clients of SCI crematoria from using the facility, as part of their anti-large-organisation tactic. Although unconfirmed, the former could well have occurred at Brighton following SCI's acquisition of the Downs Crematorium, as the number of cremations fell a dramatic 49 per cent between 1994 and 1999. In this case the local-authority-owned Woodvale Crematorium adjacent to the Downs Crematorium experienced an increase in cremations.[136]

Acquisition of one crematorium by SCI did become a matter for the OFT when in 1998 Birbeck Securities, owning Beckenham Crematorium and H. Copeland funeral directors, in the same area was sold. The MMC gave SCI the ultimatum of owning either the funeral directing firms or the crematorium

---

[134]'So You Want to Build a Crematorium' (1993) *FSJ*, December, pp. 45–50. See also Hussein I. (1997) 'The PFI from a Public Sector Manager's Perspective', *Pharos International*, Vol. 63, No. 1, pp. 19–21.

[135]Jupp P.C. (1997b) 'The Dead Citizens Charter', *Pharos International*, Vol. 63, No. 4, p. 23.

[136]Figures from *Pharos International*. See also 'Crematorium's Sales Ploys Condemned as Tasteless', *The Daily Telegraph*, 15 December 1996.

but not both, despite a close financial relationship having existed between the two for many years. In the event, SCI retained the crematorium while the funeral directing assets were acquired by the Co-operative Funeralcare.

While it could be argued that in an area where two or more crematoria are in close proximity a competitive environment exists and they therefore rely on funeral directors for the generation of their work, familial past association and geographic proximity indicate that clients have a location in mind when arranging a cremation. Indeed, the increasing preference towards cremation that has occurred during the twentieth century has engendered considerable loyalty to a particular crematorium – a situation encouraged by the tradition of scattering cremated remains for each member of the family in the same position within the Gardens of Remembrance. Thirdly, to influence clients would be a public relations scandal waiting to happen. As mentioned above, the presence of SCI attracted considerable unfavourable media coverage, with competitors and the press looking for any opportunity to criticise their activities. If, for example, an SCI crematorium had adopted a strategy to give preferential rates to their own funeral directors or to reserve popular cremation times such as between 11.30 am and 2.00 pm, this would soon be detected by competing funeral directors.

During the 1990s, local authorities were encouraged to sell their crematoria in the interests of cost savings.[137] Jupp points out that the central government-led Private Finance Initiative of 1995, which enabled local authorities to sell their crematoria, would place funeral directors in a strategic position of acquisition.[138] Yet, conversely, the MMC (1995) report repeatedly points to the monopoly control situation that would arise.[139] In the event few crematoria actually sold their facilities, although in more recent years a few have entered into a long-term management contract with a private organisation, such as Dignity operating the London Borough of Haringey's Enfield Crematorium. In this respect funeral directors could be considered to be in an ideal position to manage crematoria as through their interaction with the bereaved they may have a greater appreciation of changing needs and demands than local authority administrators.[140]

---

[137]'Privatisation of Crematoria', (1995) *FSJ,* November, pp. 10–11.

[138]Jupp P.C. (1997c) 'The Context of Funeral Ministry Today', in P.C. Jupp and T. Rogers eds, *Interpreting Death: Christian Theology and Pastoral Practice,* London: Cassell, p. 10.

[139]See Voytal J. (1996) 'Cremation and the Private Sector Finance Initiative', *Pharos International,* Vol. 62, No. 3, pp. 133–139.

[140]Parsons B. (2003) 'Conflict in the Context of Care: An Examination of Role Conflict between the Bereaved and the Funeral Director in the UK', *Mortality,* Vol. 8, No. 1, pp. 67–87.

Chapter 7

Funerals and Finance

Despite the lack of rigorous evidence, nineteenth-century funeral directors have been stigmatised by allegations of manipulation of the bereaved, a position largely attributable to the claims of Charles Dickens. While these are outside the scope of this study, there is, however, evidence to indicate that in the early years of the twentieth century some funeral directors engaged in the unscrupulous practice of touting for funerals. Furthermore, registration of the BUA as a trade union gave the opportunity for restrictive practices to operate among members, thereby controlling funeral charges. With the anxiety to prevent a pauper's funeral still in evidence, however, this period coincided with increasing interest in funeral costs by social reformers who called for regulation of the industry through municipalisation and even nationalisation. While the introduction of the Death Grant helped to reduce financial concerns for the bereaved and also criticisms of funeral directors, these were short-lived as from the 1970s on, investigations into funeral costs coincided with the funeral reform movement, which increasingly brought the industry under the spotlight.

'The Fat Atmosphere of Funerals': The Legacy of the Nineteenth Century

Although the nefarious activities of burial clubs, the disgrace of a pauper burial and the exploitation of the bereaved by the undertaker continue to be themes associated with Victorian funerals, little evidence has been published to confirm these allegations. The commencement of a new century did not also eradicate the belief that the undertaker should be responsible for encouraging excessive funereal expenditure.[1] In 1903, a judge at Lambeth County Court gave vent to this notion:

> My experience for many years on the Bench, is that there is no more dangerous man than the undertaker. He takes mean and wicked advantage of the sorrow and suffering of people – and especially the poor and ignorant people – to induce them to indulge in reckless extravagance at funerals. Far too much money is spent of funerals by the poor, but the fault lies with the undertaker.[2]

Bishops too raised their voice to the issue of particularly the poor spending on funerals.[3] The industry did itself no favours when in January 1901 the editor of *TUJ* accused funeral reformers of being 'wreckers' while also observing that the cost of funerals had diminished through the disappearance of mutes, durable coffins, special mourning attire, scarves, funeral trappings and requests for no flowers. He believed that the way to tackle criticisms of overcharging was through organisation.[4] Although the BUA gave its membership a collective voice on issues of mutual concern, it could exercise little control over one important issue that was plaguing the industry: touting. The giving of rewards to those referring a family to use an undertaker was highlighted in 1906 when the MP for Birkenhead, Henry Vivian, spoke of the alleged secret commission between medical men and undertakers.[5] The secretary of the Liverpool and Birkenhead centre of the BUA, Chas Porter, attributed the blame elsewhere:

> If he had made himself thoroughly acquainted as to who the real culprits are, and where this wretched evil principally exists – in so far as the practice of giving and receiving secret commission exists between a *certain class of*

---

[1]For a broad historical review of funeral expenditure see Hennessy P.J. (1980) *Families, Funerals and Finances-A Study of Funeral Expenses and How They Are Paid*, London: HMSO, pp. 5–14. See 'Editorial: Illicit Commissions' (1899) *TUJ*, May, pp. 55–56.
[2]'Notes' (1903) *TUJ*, June, p. 127.
[3]'Extravagant Funerals' (1905) *TUJ*, April, p. 83. See also 'Elaborate Funerals' (1910) *TUJ*, November, p. 267.
[4]'Editorial: The Queen's Funeral' (1901) *TUJ*, January, pp. 13–14.
[5]'Prevention of Corruption Bill', *Hansard*, 3 April 1906, cols 428–429.

undertaker [emphasis added] and the recipients – he would have ascertained that the principal offenders are hospital porters, workhouse porters, and club collectors.[6]

Touting in the Liverpool area made headlines the following year with correspondence in the *Daily Mail* and the *Daily Despatch*. Porter wrote to say:

> the BUA has been formed with the object of making these practices more difficult to carry out... It seems impossible to persuade a certain section of the trade of the heinousness of these offences against common decency where the sacred dead are concerned.[7]

Porter hoped that the forthcoming Prevention of Corruption Act 1906 would stop the touts; if convicted they would receive a £500 fine.[8] However, this made little impact; a case before the police court at Wigan in 1907 only resulted in a very modest fine.[9] By way of insight, when asked about the 'special troubles you have to contend with' Mr R. Horlock, an Edmonton undertaker, revealed the methods employed:

> Many of the so-called undertakers – painters, wheelwrights, plumbers, bricklayers, upholsterers – all parlour window men – tout and even knock and ask for a funeral, which no self-respecting man would do... Those I have named of course compete unfairly with firms, say like our own, for which these men 15s out of each funeral would pay them for the two half days' work they would lose; and in this district many of the poor hawk their order from place to place for the sake of saving a shilling or two.[10]

Touting was highlighted in the *Yorkshire Evening Post* in 1911 when publication coincided with the BUA's conference in Leeds. Despite a

---

[6]Letter: Porter C. (1906a) 'Parliament and the Undertaking Trade', *TUJ*, April, p. 110. See also Porter C. (1906b) 'Past, Present and Future', *TUJ*, pp. 190–194.
[7]'Liverpool Centre and Touting' (1907) *TUJ*, May, p. 112.
[8]'Secret Commission' (1907) *TUJ*, June, pp. 140–141.
[9]'Touting for Funerals at Wigan' (1907) *TUJ*, August, pp. 190–191.
[10]'Interview with Mr R. Horlock of Railway Approach, Edmonton' (1910) *TUJ*, December, pp. 301–302. See also 'A Ghoulish Undertaker. A Scandal Calling for Redress' (1911) *TUJ*, November, p. 294.

clause included in the Code of Ethics, the association was powerless to prevent such behaviour.[11] A notable case emerged later that year in Birmingham when an undertaker called at a lady's house to tout for a funeral before she knew her husband was dead.[12] Even in the late 1920s there was evidence to indicate the practice still persisted.[13]

During the nineteenth century the need to save money to prevent the disgrace of a pauper's funeral was an activity to which most working-class families subscribed. The proportion of money budgeted each week from a pay packet had been highlighted in 1913 by the publication of *Round About a Pound a Week* by Maud Pember Reeves, the founder of the Fabian Women's Group. In analysing the weekly expenditure of a family she found that in 1910 a printers' warehouseman jobbing hand had an average wage of thirty-two shillings a week, and of this one shilling was spent on burial insurance.[14] A further example from the following year notes this to be two shillings a week.[15] Pember Reeves summed up the situation and offered the solution:

> The small proportion which does come to him is swallowed up in a burial, and no one but the undertaker is the better for it. As a form of thrift which shall help the future, or be a standby if misfortune should befall, burial insurance is a calamitous blunder. Yet the respectable poor man is forced to resort to it unless he is to run the risk of being made a pauper by any bereavement which may happen to him... The only real solution of this horrible problem would seem to be the making of decent burial a free and honourable public service.[16]

Two points are discernable from this statement. First, Pember Reeves is probably the first woman to comment on funeral expenditure. This is

---

[11]'Sixth Annual Convention of the British Embalmers' Society and the British Undertakers' Association' (1911) *TUJ*, June, pp. 148–150. See also 'Ethics of Undertaking', *Yorkshire Evening Post*, 24 May 1911, p. 4.
[12]'Touting in Birmingham' (1911) *TUJ*, October, p. 268.
[13]'Can Touting be Suppressed?' (1929) *TUJ*, April, p. 107.
[14]Pember Reeves M. (1913) *Round About a Pound a Week* (1979 edition), London: Virago, p. 82.
[15]*Ibid.*, p. 86.
[16]*Ibid.*, pp. 73–74. For a review of the book see Harrison A. (1914) 'The State and the Family', *English Review*, January, pp. 278–284. See also 'Notes' (1914) *TUJ*, March, pp. 62 & 65.

significant as it was a female who had to budget the household finance to ensure that burial insurance was paid. Failure to do so would reflect on her ability to manage the family purse. As will be seen, over the next four decades a number of female commentators highlighted the issue of funeral expenditure and how it could be controlled. Secondly, the suggestion of a 'free' funeral – or more accurately one paid for from taxation and provided through a public organisation – would be a reoccurring theme that only diminished after the introduction of the Death Grant in 1949. The suggestion of a funeral benefit – rather than a publically organised funeral – predates Pember Reeves by one year as in 1915 *The New Statesman* published a 'Supplement on Industrial Assurance', which recommended that 'In many respects the simplest, the most economical, and the most desirable method of providing Funeral Benefit would be simply to add this to what is provided under the National Insurance Acts of 1911 and 1913...'[17] The report also thought that the Co-operative movement, trade unions and friendly societies should:

> ...extend their practice of paying respect to the funerals of their members. It would be a good thing if, following the example of the mediaeval guilds, these societies each maintained a bier or hearse, a pall or other suitable trappings, possibly even carriages and horses, to be lent for the funeral of every deceased member, as a mark of sympathy and respect.[18]

As noted in Chapter 6, it was around this time that the Co-operative societies became involved in the provision of funerals, especially as the death benefit money paid to their members would be spent within the society; within a decade the movement had made a considerable impact on the funeral industry.[19]

The issue of industrial insurance would occupy the minds of Arnold Wilson (later the MP for Hitchin) and Professor Hermann Levy.[20] Their 1938 volume *Burial Reform and Funeral Costs* called for control of burial

---

[17] 'Special Supplement on Industrial Insurance', *The New Statesman*, Vol. IV, No. 101, 12 March 1915, pp. 30–31.
[18] *Ibid.*
[19] Parsons B. (2014e) *The Undertaker at Work: 1900–1950*, London: Strange Attractor Press, pp. 113–131.
[20] 'Burial Reform and Funeral Costs' (1938) *TUFDJ*, May, pp. 157–158. See also 'Letters to the Editor' (1938) *TUFDJ*, June, p. 207.

fees and funeral charges through the establishment of a Commissioner for the Disposal of the Dead.[21] Their key question was the extent to which undertakers encouraged lavish expenditure on funerals.[22] None of Wilson and Levy's recommendations were explored further. Wilson had already provoked the ire of London funeral directors when, during the second reading of the Workmen's Compensation Bill, he had suggested that if payment included burial expenses of £20 rather than £15, funeral directors would increase their charges accordingly so they '...would take the lot'.[23]

With the outbreak of World War II in 1939, the threat of mass civilian deaths led Wilson to call for a maximum funeral charge to be fixed to discourage unnecessary expenditure. He also called for metal embellishments on coffins and the use of expensive woods to be prohibited; wheel biers should also replace motor hearses wherever possible.[24] Wilson died in May 1940, but Levy continued the reforming calls; in 1942 he argued again that industrial insurance must disappear, funeral money should become a statutory social insurance benefit and that '...funerals should be standardised, and democratic equality should be regarded as a fitting honour to the dead'.[25]

The calls for regulation in the early part of the twentieth century must be viewed against the way the industry exercised control over funeral directors. First, in the latter part of 1916, the London Funeral Carriage

---

[21] Wilson A. and Levy H. (1938) *Burial Reform and Funeral Costs*, Oxford: Oxford University Press, p. 194. See also 'Burial Reform and Funeral Costs' (1939) *TUFDJ*, May, pp. 147–158; Day R.E. (1939) 'Letters to the Editor: Burial Reform and Funeral Costs', *TUFDJ*, June, p. 207; and Wilson A. (1939) *More Thoughts and Talks*, London: The Right Book Club, pp. 131 & 206. Wilson also took an interest in cemeteries. See Wilson A.T. (1933) 'Public Cemeteries and Cremation. A Layman's View', *TUJ*, February, pp. 61–63.

[22] Wilson A. and Levy H. (1938) *Burial Reform and Funeral Costs*, Oxford: Oxford University Press, pp. 85 & 88.

[23] 'Parliament and Undertakers. MP's Allegations Challenged' (1937) *TUFDJ*, December, pp. 415–416. See also 'Compensation Bill', *Hansard*, 19 November 1937, cols 767–773.

[24] 'Burials', *Hansard*, 28 September 1939, cols 1463–1465 and 'In Parliament: Prohibition of Metal Coffin Furniture' (1939) *TUFDJ*, October, p. 352. See also 'Royal Air Force. Casualties (Funeral Expenses)', *Hansard*, 26 September, col. 1226.

[25] Levy H. (1942) 'Funeral Waste', *The Spectator*, 4 December, No. 5971, p. 525 and *Journal of the National Association of Cemetery and Crematorium Superintendents* (1943), Vol. 19, No. 1, February, pp. 5–7. See also Letter 'Funeral Waste' (1942) *The Spectator*, 25 December, No. 5974, p. 600. The only funeral-related assurance that was launched was for cremation. See 'Cremation Assurance. The Scheme Launched' (1936) *TUFDJ*, February, pp. 30–31.

Proprietors' Association (LFCPA) was formed with an objective of supplying BUA members with vehicles at a standardised minimum charge; similar arrangements were then established throughout the country.[26] The following year, having abandoned their attempt to become incorporated, the BUA registered as a trade union. Under legislation passed in 1913, they were permitted to require members to adhere to a minimum charge for funerals; an elm coffin provided for an adult would be charged at £8.10s.[27] Not all undertakers were in agreement; a Highgate undertaker, George Swan, believed it forced many people to have their relatives buried at the public expense. He challenged the BUA's control by asking for twelve funeral directors to conduct a simple funeral for £6.10s.[28] Secondly, responding to the BUA status as an employers' union, those engaged in coffin preparation, bearing and driving vehicles formed the British Funeral Workers' Association (BFWA) to facilitate collective negotiations on wages and conditions.[29]

The hold the BUA had on its members was tested in 1920 when the case of Miller v Hurry and Repuke came before the court. An ex-soldier, William Miller returned to Islington to establish a funeral business. Mindful of the need to be a member of the centre before a carriage master would supply funeral vehicles, he applied for BUA membership only

---

[26] See 'London Funeral Carriage Proprietors' Association' (1916) *TUJ*, September, p. 253; October, pp. 275–276; November, p. 302; and December, p. 330. For an example of the charges see Brown E.W. (1917) 'Hull on the Upgrade', *TUJ*, October, pp. 273–274.

[27] 'Report of the Committee on Amalgamation of the British Undertakers' Association and the British Embalmers' Association' (1915) *TUJ*, July, pp. 182–183; 'Working out the Amalgamation' (1915) *TUJ*, August, pp. 209–212; 'The Proposed Amalgamation' (1915) *TUJ*, October, p. 273; 'Amalgamation of the BES and BUA' (1915) *TUJ*, November, pp. 299–303; 'The New Association' (1915) *TUJ*, December, pp. 337–338; and 'British Undertakers' Association' (1916) *TUJ*, April, pp. 96–99. For the formation of a trade union see 'Fourteenth Annual Convention' (1917) *TUJ*, July, p. 175. See also Cole P. (1921) 'Incorporation and Registration', *BUA Monthly*, June, pp. 338–340. See also 'The British Undertakers' Association. London Centre' (1918) *TUJ*, April, pp. 93–94 and 'British Undertakers' Association. London Centre' (1918) *TUJ*, October, p. 253. For the full list see 'British Undertakers' Association and FCP Section' (1919) *TUJ*, December, pp. 353–354.

[28] 'Funeral Profiteering', *The Daily Chronicle*, 16 October 1918. See also 'London Undertakers. Accusations of Profiteering' (1918) *TUJ*, November, p. 288.

[29] A rival organisation also emerged, the National Union of Funeral Workers. The BFWA later became the National Union of Funeral and Cemetery Workers. 'Interview with Mr Thomas W. Kingston' (1918) *TUJ*, January, pp. 19–20. See also 'The National Union of Funeral and Cemetery Workers. A Review of its Growth, Scope and Objects' (1950) *FSJ*, June, pp. 325–326.

to be rejected. After accepting an order for a child's funeral and finding it impossible to hire vehicles, Miller alleged that the secretary of the London Centre of the BUA, J.R. Hurry, had 'induced, coerced and intimidated one of the plaintiff's customers for carrying out a contract with him'. The BUA's defence was that there were sufficient undertakers already in business in Islington; indeed, research reveals that 22 firms traded in the vicinity. Lord Darling found for the plaintiff and awarded Miller £150.[30] Although this case did not generate nationwide publicity, dubious activities continued to be reported in the press during the 1920s; a 'body-snatching' case at Sheffield, along with touting in Liverpool and Wigan.[31] It is of little surprise that a year later Viscountess, Lady Astor commented in Parliament: 'Undertakers ought to be looked at more than others, for they certainly have you at their mercy. Undertakers, doctors, and plumbers all get you.'[32]

While Wilson and Levy were agitating for changes to industrial insurance payments in an effort to reduce funeral expenditure, other ideas for reforms were being voiced. One of the most prominent was that the state should take over management of the disposal of the dead and in the ensuing years, municipalisation and the nationalisation of funeral directors were discussed in addition to a municipal funeral scheme.

Municipalisation

The idea to municipalise funeral services can be attributed to such systems employed on the continent. The matter had been briefly discussed by the Committee on Death Certification in 1893,[33] while the author of a letter in *The Daily Telegraph* in 1906 enthused about municipal funerals carried out in Paris. A Colonel Mapleson commented, 'How different are

---

[30]'Undertakers' Action over Alleged Intimidation. Milller v Hurry and Repuke' (1920) *TUJ*, December, pp. 373–375. For a full account see Parsons B. (2014e). *The Undertaker at Work: 1900–1950*, London: Strange Attractor Press, pp. 99–110.
[31]'Body Snatching at Sheffield' (1912) *TUJ*, March, p. 72 and 'Touting. An Ever-Present Evil' (1925) *BUA Monthly*, October, p. 90. See also 'St Helens Undertakers Protest against Funeral Touts' (1933) *TUJ*, April, p. 127 and 'Ghoulish Touting Practices' (1932) *TUJ*, December, p. 404.
[32]'Ministry of Labour Vote', *Hansard*, 4 August 1921, cols 1721–1722. See also 'Lady Astor and the Undertakers' (1921) *TUJ*, August, p. 261.
[33]'Analysis of the Evidence and Findings of the Committee on Death Certification' (1906) *TUJ*, June, pp. 163–165.

funerals conducted with us [in Britain]. The enterprise of private individuals who are only in the business to make money, they lack all that is reverential and decorous.'[34] Writing in *The Lancet* in 1907, Stephen Wills endorsed the appointment of a local authority burial official to arrange a simple funeral for all.[35] However, it was Thomas W. Kingston, Secretary of the BFWA, who was the first within the industry to voice the need for radical intervention by the state:

> We have municipalised many things – trams, electric lighting, gas, in some place, the treatment of infectious diseases; we shall eventually nationalise railways. And my opinion is that until the burial of the dead is managed by the State, or municipality, we shall never get rid of some of its objectionable features.[36]

Kingston highlighted the waste of using so many men in carrying coffins when there could be sufficient staff at each cemetery to act as bearers. He also outlined a scheme for district funeral offices with fixed prices. Touting would be eliminated, while 'barbaric splendour abolished… all unnecessary expense avoided'. He also warned against the Americanisation of the industry and claimed that '…embalming will never be general in England'.[37]

Following a touting problem in south London during 1906, the remedy of municipal funerals was explored by one unspecified borough.[38] In responding to a newspaper's call for the government to arrange a compulsory burial for everyone, the editor of *TUJ* questioned '…if everything connected with human life that is of a compulsory nature – like coming into the world for instance – is to be made a "civil or government" affair, where in the end is individual and moral responsibility to come in?'[39]

---

[34]'Notes' (1906) *TUJ*, September, p. 222.
[35]Willis S.P. (1907) 'Burial by the State', *The Lancet*, 16 February, Vol. 169, No. 4355, p. 463. See also Wills S.P. (1910) 'Burial by the State', *Perils of Premature Burial*, January–March, p. 64.
[36]Kingston T.W. (1906) 'Funeral Reform', *TUJ*, May, pp. 127–128.
[37]*Ibid*. See also "Ubique" 'Undertakers and Municipal Control' Enforced Sanitation' (1906) *TUJ*, May, pp. 135–136. For a response to Kingston see 'Letter: J.R. Hurry Mr Kingston and his Ideas' (1906) *TUJ*, June, pp. 165–166. See also 'Interview with Mr T.W. Kingston' (1907) *TUJ*, December, pp. 295–296.
[38]'Undertakers and their Methods' (1906) *TUJ*, October, pp. 259–260.
[39]'Editorial: Burial by the State' (1906) *TUJ*, December, pp. 319–320.

In 1914, Isabel Basnett raised the issue of municipal funerals in the *Englishwoman*. After reviewing the situation in France, Italy, Germany and Switzerland she asked why local authorities in Britain should not follow their example and assume the burden of funeral expenditure.[40] Two years later the *Manchester Daily Despatch* asked the same question. Although it stated that 'There is a rapidly-growing feeling in this country that funerals ought to be all conducted by the municipalities', substantiation was not provided.[41]

The chairman of the Liverpool Burials Committee suggested a scheme in 1916 to enable the local authority to make arrangements for the 300 funerals taking place each week in the area. After death had been certified, the body would be removed to prevent an unnecessary display to curious sightseers; the system would also eliminate any 'show' at a funeral. Noting that the average cost of a funeral was £10, the scheme would reduce it to £5.[42] A similar proposal was tabled in 1930 at Hull where the Public Assistance Committee decided to carry out the funerals of destitute persons. The Hull and District Undertakers' and Carriage Proprietors' Association protested against the decision of the Committee to have all coffins made in the council's workshops, leaving the undertakers to provide the hearse. Undertakers refused to hire out their vehicles if they could not supply the coffin as well.[43]

By the mid-1930s, calls for municipal funerals started to come from cemetery superintendents. The first that can be traced was from the registrar at Stretford Cemetery, J.V. Sullivan. In a paper entitled 'Cemetery Ethics' delivered at the NACCS and FBCA Joint Conference in 1936, he suggested that 'Local authorities could act as complete undertakers, providing both the coffin and the grave, as it would be the duty of the community, through the local authority, to see that the bodies of the deceased persons were disposed of.'[44]

---

[40]Basnett I. (1914) 'Municipal Funerals', *The Englishwoman*, Vol. XXIII, No. 67, pp. 23–28. See 'Municipal Funerals' (1914) *TUJ*, August, pp. 220–221.
[41]'Costly Funerals. Necessity for a Municipal Undertaker' (1912) *TUJ*, June, p. 159.
[42]'Municipal Funerals: A Liverpool Scheme' (1916) *TUJ*, June, p. 145 and 'Alderman Taggart on £5 Funerals', *TUJ*, July, p. 172. See also 'Funeral Reform' (1916) *The Hospital*, Vol. LX, No. 1566, 17 June, p. 252. See also 'Funeral Reform (1916) *The Hospital*, Vol. LX, No. 1573, 29 July, p. 404.
[43]'Municipal Funerals at Hull' (1930) *TUJ*, November, p. 393.
[44]Sullivan J.V. (1936) '*Cemetery Ethics*' Fifth Joint Conference of Cemetery and Crematorium Authorities: A Report of Proceedings with Addresses and Papers Read NACCS/FBCA, p. 68.

The call for reform from a cemetery official could be motivated by their distaste for private (and some local authority) cemeteries paying commission to undertakers under the guise of being 'appointed agents'. Under a municipalised funeral service this would not be necessary. Percy Benson, the superintendent of Tottenham Cemetery, believed commission gave the opportunity to divert preference and was simply another form of touting.[45]

The calls continued during World War II, despite the likelihood of implementation being minimal. The editor of *TUJ* warned:

> The danger is much more evident in England today by the threat of municipalised funerals... With this danger of municipalised funerals looming to the fore the industry must take notice of it for the standardization of funerals under official control (apart from the unjust interference of private enterprise and service about which much can be said) will have no regard for the personal, deeply significant, individual ceremony.[46]

In 1940, a significant development occurred under the wartime Defence Regulations as a payment of £7.10s was made by local authorities towards the cost of burial of a civilian. It was only intended to be a contribution to funeral costs; an assessment of F.W. Paine's funeral records shows that the average charge for a burial in 1940 (excluding disbursements) was in the region of £18. From January 1944 the payment was increased to £10.[47]

Allegations that funeral directors touted for work and submitted exorbitant bills to relatives of bombing victims in Weston-super-Mare were aired in the press and discussed in parliament in 1942.[48] An investigation

---

[45]Benson P. (1937) 'What We Would Like', *TUFDJ*, December, pp. 427–432. See also Wilson A. and Levy H. (1938) *Burial Reform and Funeral Costs*, Oxford: Oxford University Press, pp. 157–158; 'British Undertakers' Association. London Centre. The Question of Commission: Is it Legal?' (1908) *TUJ*, February, pp. 41–42; and Broome J. (1908) 'Relationship of Undertakers, Their Clients, and Burial Authorities', *TUJ*, March, pp. 63–64.

[46]'Editorial: Specialised Service' (1940) *TUFDJ*, November, pp. 295–296.

[47]'London Mayor's Tribute to Funeral Directors. No Overcharging for Burial of Bomb Victims' (1944) *TUFDJ*, December, p. 350 and '£10 Funeral Grant Now' (1944) *TNFD*, February, p. 288. See also Bermondsey Borough Council Minutes, 23 May 1944, p. 21.

[48]'Weston-super-Mare' (1942) *TNFD*, September, p. 110. See also 'Touting by Weston Undertakers Alleged', *The Weston Mercury and Somersetshire Herald*,

ently revealed these to be without foundation, but it fuelled the ...alisation argument, as did a strongly argued article in *Justice of ...e and Local Government Review* encouraging an 'Enabling Bill', to which *TNFD* issued a rebuff.[49] As will be discussed below, this matter coincided with the release of the Beveridge Report recommending the introduction of a Death Grant. However, it did not prevent a further call by the MP Frederick Cocks requesting an investigation into the excessive cost of funerals.[50] Support for state action came from the Social Security League, whose president was Sir William Beveridge. In its 1944 pamphlet *Funeral Reform*, the author and League's secretary, Joan S. Clarke, proposed that undertakers' maximum charges be fixed by a statutory authority; legislation to allow local authorities to provide a funeral service including the standardisation of coffins, the area pooling of vehicles and labour and compulsory itemisation of funeral accounts. Burial and cremation charges were also to be fixed nationally.[51] The NAFD issued a robust response in *TNFD* (calling the material 'slanderous innuendo'), where it revealed that the thrust of the Social Security League was to '…promote the Principles of the Beveridge Report'.[52] However, these proposals were far in excess of the recommendation contained in Beveridge's report, which simply suggested a grant of £20 while upholding choice of undertaker and no standardisation of funerals.[53] A Tory Report Committee pamphlet dealt with the same issue but said that the maximum grant should be £15, while also claiming that there was a 'close corporation of undertakers'.[54] *Funeral Reform* had

---

25 July 1942, p. 5 and Air-Raid Victims, Weston-super-Mare (Funeral Charges)', *Hansard*, 30 July 1942, Vol. 392, No. 96, cols 671–673. See also 'House of Commons. Alleged Coffin Touting After Raid' (1942) *TUFDJ*, September, p. 203. See also *The Times*, 31 July 1942.
[49]'Municipal Funerals' (1945) *Justice of the Peace and Local Government Review*, 5 May, Vol. CIX, pp. 206–207. See 'Another Big Attack' (1945) *TNFD*, July, pp. 12–16 & 29.
[50]'Funeral (Cost)', *Hansard*, 31 May 1945, col. 405.
[51]Clarke J.S. (1944a) *Funeral Reform*, London: Social Security League, p. 9. For a summary see Clarke J.S. (1944b) 'Funeral Reform', *TUFDJ*, August, pp. 229–230.
[52]Passmore Bishop B. (1945a) 'Response. A Reply to the Pamphlet Entitled "Funeral Reform" Issued by the Social Security League', *TNFD*, February, p. 2. See also Passmore Bishop, B. (1945b) 'Getting in Front of Our Shadows', *TNFD*, August, pp. 70–73.
[53]Beveridge W. (1942) *Social Insurance and Allied Services*, London: HMSO, Cmd: 6404, pp. 65–67.
[54]'Industrial Life Assurance', *The Times*, 13 January 1944, and 'Cost of Funerals', *The Times*, 14 January 1944. See also 'Response. A Reply to the Pamphlet

its foundation in an article of the same title published in January 1943 in the *Fabian Quarterly*.[55] Although anonymous, the research secretary of the Fabian Society was Joan S. Clarke. The paper demanded that '...every Borough Council or other Local Government Authority should have included in its staff an expert in the arrangements for funerals in exactly the same way as it has its Medical Officer, Food and Sanitary Inspectors...'[56]

The society believed that eliminating all 'private profit should halve the cost of funerals'. A paper given by Clarke at the NACCS conference in 1947 reiterated the call for a free disposal service administered by the local authority or a voluntary body as '...competition – seeking of custom of bereaved relatives for the financial profit of a group of industrialists – is ethically unsuitable'. She also called for a Royal Commission on funeral costs.[57]

Further support for municipal funerals came from the MP Peter Freeman in 1946, then from the another MP, Garry Allighan, who reiterated this demand along with the abolition of privately owned burial grounds and crematoria.[58] He also prepared a paper for the 1947 NACCS conference in which he expanded his ideas in addition to calling for rationalisation of all disposal-related legislation, the state registration of funeral directors and regularisation of charges.[59] But no legislation was forthcoming and at a NACCS conference a decade later the MP George Thomas expressed his frustration at the situation:

Entitled "Funeral Reform" Issued by the Social Security League', *TNFD*, March 1944, and 'Cost of Funerals' (1944) *Journal of the National Association of Cemetery and Crematorium Superintendents*, Vol. 20, No. 2, February, p. 15.

[55]'Funeral Reform' (1943) *Fabian Quarterly*, January, pp. 23–29. See also 'Funeral Reform' (1944) *Journal of the National Association of Cemetery and Crematorium Superintendents*, Vol. 10, No. 3, August, pp. 6–9.

[56]'Funeral Reform' (1943) *Fabian Quarterly*, January, p. 28. A review of the wartime reports appeared as 'Publicity Campaign Threatens Private Enterprise' (1944) *FSJ*, February, pp. 49–50.

[57]Clarke J.S. (1946) '*Funeral Ethics in a Modern State*', Report of the Conference of the National Association of Cemetery and Crematorium Superintendents, June, pp. 18–23. A similar call had been made in 1940 by the superintendent of Shrewsbury Cemetery. See Willis, A.G. (1940) 'Modern Rules and Regulations for Cemeteries', *TUFDJ*, May, pp. 139–145. This was also a theme taken up by the MP for Blackburn in 1936 when addressing the Fifth Joint Conference for Cemetery and Crematorium Authorities. See Elliston G.S. (1936) 'The Disposal of the Dead from the Health and Economic Standpoints', *TUFDJ*, October, pp. 337–342.

[58]'Funeral Furnishing Services (Local Authorities)', *Hansard*, 4 July 1946, col. 2302 and 'Burial Grounds and Crematoria', *Hansard*, 21 January 1947, cols 29–30.

[59]Allighan G. (1947) '*Burial and the State*', Report of the Conference of the Institute of Burial and Cremation Administration, pp. 33–42.

> Surely it is a fantastic anachronism that in 1959 there is still no registration or even inspection of those engaged in undertaking. It is hard to believe that any Tom, Dick or Harry, who has the necessary cash can push his way into this profession. Be assured of this, any new Act of Parliament dealing with the disposal of the dead will have to deal with this aspect of the problem... I want to see the incentive to profit taken out of funerals, I want to remove the temptation to exploit the grief of bereaved people. That's why I am a great believer in public ownership and control at least of all crematoria.[60]

In 1944, the memorandum issued by NACCS's post-war planning committee believed that the proposal Death Grant required '...contemporaneous legislation to guide the expenditure of it' while also recommending '...free disposal by compulsory state insurance or by national or local taxation'.[61] However, not all within NACCS agreed with this proposal. The superintendent of Hammersmith Cemetery, F.G. Herbert, commented in 1947 that:

> The question of instituting and operating a single comprehensive funeral service under a Local Authority... would be folly, even if it were practicable, to try to buy out all the undertakers, close up their businesses and operate only a Municipal Funeral Service... To be a success a funeral service operated by a Local Authority would require to be managed by an expert, a man with wide experience of funeral service, fully qualified as an embalmer... With the right man in this job, with the Cemetery or Crematorium being serviced with the fullest efficiency, and the two combined imbued with the spirit of giving the public the best services at the lowest possible cost I for one have no fear of its future.[62]

---

[60]Thomas G. (1959) *Parliament and the Disposal of the Dead*, Report of the Institute of Burial and Cremation Administration/Federation of British Cremation Authorities 39th Conference, pp. 11–15.
[61]See also 'Municipalised "Free Funerals" Superintendents Issue Recommendations for Post-War Reform' (1944) *TUFDJ*, June, pp. 201–203.
[62]Herbert F.G. (1947) 'Post-War Reform', *Journal of the National Association of Cemetery and Crematorium Superintendents*, Vol. 13, No. 2, May, pp. 9–10.

Nevertheless, speaking at the conference a year later, C. Humphrey from Crewe Cemetery proposed a local authority-run service or the compromise of one contracted out to undertakers to supply a standard price for coffins and vehicles. The cost would be paid for by the employers and employees as a part of the National Health and Social Services Scheme. He stated that 'The local Authority would be the controlling body for the disposal service, acting as agents for the Government and to receive grants from the State in proportion to the number of disposals undertaken.'[63]

William Horridge of Hastings Cemetery went a step further by suggesting that local authorities should consider constructing municipal funeral homes, not just chapels of rest or mortuaries for use by funeral directors who did not possess such facilities.[64] Despite there being little chance that such plans would ever come to fruition, cemetery superintendents have continued to recommend this strategy; Walter Pearson from Leeds in 1957 and, after an absence of over 40 years, Ken West.[65] Although the Localism Act 2011 gives local authorities in England the power to trade as a funeral director, a survey carried out by the ICCM in 2016 revealed only two carrying out a direct service to the public, while some have a contract with a funeral director.[66]

Nationalisation

The possibility of nationalisation of the funeral industry, although never a serious threat, was raised in 1946 when the government proposed bringing inland transport services under public ownership.[67] The matter was not settled by 1950 when the Conservative peer Lord Mancroft, who

---

[63]Humphrey C. (1948) 'Disposal of the Dead by the State', *Journal of the Institute of Burial and Cremation Administration*, Vol. 15, No. 2, May, pp. 9–10.
[64]Horridge W. (1948) 'Mortuaries, Chapels of Rest or Funeral Homes', *Journal of the Institute of Burial and Cremation Administration*, Vol. 24, No. 3. August, pp. 26–29. See also Horridge W. (1943) 'Municipal Funeral Homes?' (letter), *Journal of the Institute of Burial and Cremation Administration*, Vol. 19, No. 2, May, pp. 12–13.
[65]'The IBCA Conference' (1957) *FSJ*, September, p. 411 and West K. (2010) *A Guide to Natural Burial*, London: Shaw & Sons, pp. 265–274. See also 'NAFD. The Presidents' Speech' (1957) *FSJ*, June, p. 257.
[66]'Municipal Funeral Service', Email to ICCM Members, 17 February 2017.
[67]'Nationalisation of Transport Threat' (1946) *FSJ*, April, pp. 131–132; 'The Shadow of Nationalisation' (1946) *FSJ*, November, p. 422; and 'Public Ownership of Transport' (1946) *FSJ*, December, p. 443. See also 'Road Nationalisation' (1946) *TNFD*, December, pp. 115 & 123.

was anxious to prevent implementation of this policy, addressed funeral directors. He detected a '...natural antipathy...' towards the occupation and that accusations of overcharging continued to be aired.[68] However, the Conservative MP for Billericay, Bernard Braine, reassured LAFD members that nationalisation was unlikely. He also encouraged every funeral director to belong to the NAFD.[69] In 1952, Bournemouth funeral director Deric Scott gave an interview to the town's *Daily Echo* in which he noted:

> There had been threats of nationalisation put out against the funeral directing business... the personal nature of the work and the fact that every funeral was different from every other. It followed that bureaucratic methods could have no place in funeral directing... The bereaved are in no fit state to fill in forms... Nationalisation was totally unsuitable to the specialised service of funeral directing.[70]

The Transport Bill was presented to the House of Commons in July 1952, but funeral directors were exempted.[71] Four years later the Huyton Division of the Labour Party presented a resolution to the National Executive calling for nationalisation by bringing funeral directors within the scope of the National Health Act.[72] The NAFD national secretary, Florence Hurry, defended the NAFD's position. Since that time nationalisation of the funeral industry has not been an issue for discussion.[73]

---

[68]'Close the Ranks! Lord Mancroft Speaks to London' (1950) *TNFD*, February, pp. 362–363. See also 'The Fear of Nationalisation. Lord Mancroft Speaks Frankly to Funeral Directors' (1950) *FSJ*, February, pp. 76–78 and 'Lord Mancroft on Public Service and Private Enterprise' (1950) *TNFD*, June, pp. 598–599. He also contributed on pauper funerals and the Death Grant. See Mancroft Lord (1950) 'Funerals are Private Affairs: Intrusion Cannot be Tolerated', *FSJ*, July, pp. 395–296.
[69]'LAFD. Annual General Meeting. Nationalisation Address by Mr B. Braine MP' (1950) *FSJ*, November, pp. 617–620.
[70]Scott D. (1952) 'Funeral Directing is a Family Business. Unsuited to State Control', *TNFD*, September, p. 125.
[71]'The Transport Bill' (1952) *TNFD*, October, pp. 172–173.
[72]'NAFD Notes: Nationalisation' (1956) *FSJ*, September, pp. 420–403.
[73]There is a reference to nationalisation in the 1959 film *Billy Liar* by the journalist Keith Waterhouse, who started his working life with a funeral director in Leeds.

The Death Grant

The 1942 White Paper *Social Insurance and Allied Services* represents a high watermark in the state's care for the bereaved.[74] *TUFDJ* noted how it generated letters to the press calling for municipalisation or state control of funerals.[75] In 1944, the document went before the Cabinet where it was estimated that the total annual expenditure for pensions, sickness, maternity and death grants was in the region of £700,000,000.[76] It was not until June 1949, however, that the Death Grant was introduced. No statutory control of funeral directors' charges was proposed. However, the Central Price Regulation Committee made an arrangement between the NAFD and the Parliamentary Committee of the Co-operative Congress, which provided that a funeral director should charge no more for a funeral than that charged in February 1949, and that the maximum for a simple earth burial or cremation was £20 (exclusive of clergy and interment fees). The specification of a simple funeral was a coffin, hearse, four bearers and one following car, with distance not exceeding 10 miles. Charges for additional mileage, extra following cars, the use of a chapel of rest and removal of the body before the funeral were also negotiated. Funeral directors were also required to make available in their establishments an itemised list of their charges for all their services.[77] The charge was based on information given by the BUA to the Cohen Departmental Committee report of 1932; the average cost of an adult funeral (excluding disbursements) in London was £15 and £13 in industrial centres.[78] Allowing for inflation, £20 was not considered unreasonable. The payment was titled a 'grant' so as not to be benchmarked against funeral costs.[79]

The arrival of the Death Grant coincided with the National Assistance Act 1948, which gave local authorities the duty to pay for the burial or cremation where no funeral arrangements had been made. Authorities negotiated contracts with funeral directors to carry out a funeral at an

---

[74] See 'The Beveridge Plan' (1943) *TNFD*, January, p. 246.
[75] 'Beveridge Funeral Grant' (1943) *TUFDJ*, April, p. 89.
[76] 'The Proposed Ministry of Social Security' (1944) *TNFD*, August, p. 48.
[77] 'Funeral Charges', *Hansard*, 3 June 1949, col. 201. See also 'From Hansard', *TNFD*, July 1949, p. 18. See also 'Funeral Prices Regulated' (1949) *FSJ*, June, p. 321; Howell D.V.P. (1949) 'National Health Insurance', *TNFD*, April, pp. 450–452; and 'Funeral Prices Regulated' (1949), *FSJ*, June, pp. 321–322. See also Ferran W.H. (1984) 'The Death Grant', *Pharos*, Vol. 50, No. 2, pp. 55–65.
[78] 'Government Social Insurance Proposals' (1944) *TUFDJ*, October, p. 294.
[79] Hennessy P.J. (1980) *Families, Funerals and Finances-A Study of Funeral Expenses and How They Are Paid*, London: HMSO, p. 11.

agreed price; in effect this became the 'pauper's funeral' and remains in place today under the Public Health (Control of Disease) Act 1984.

Beyond Beveridge: Developments from 1949

Despite the Death Grant and a price agreement with the NAFD, there were still calls in Parliament for enquiries into funeral costs along with a more wide-reaching review of disposal.[80] The NAFD appointed a public relations agency to help disseminate balanced information through its 'Aims of Industry' campaign.[81] In 1952, the grant was increased to £22 even though the NAFD said the average cost was now £35.[82] The voluntary agreement ceased in 1956, although the NAFD encouraged members to make available a minimum priced funeral for £25.[83] But criticisms of funeral costs continued in the national press while questions were asked in Parliament.[84] An increase to £25 was made in 1958 and then by £5 in 1967 until its withdrawal 20 years later. Nine years after the Death Grant was introduced, *The Economist* noted that the number of burial insurance policies had dropped, but then recovered. This was attributed to strong working-class traditions and that the grant of £25 was insufficient to cover an average funeral. An amount of £60 was estimated to be the likely cost of an unostentatious funeral.[85]

During the 1960s repeated accusations of overcharging were followed by calls for enquiries into funeral costs. Despite investigations and sensationally worded allegations in the media, there was little substantiated evidence of exploitation. Nevertheless, agitation continued for local authorities to establish a municipal funeral service. What finally emerged were agreements with funeral directors to provide a fixed-price funeral.

---

[80]'Funeral Charges', *Hansard*, 2 June 1949, col. 201 and 'Cremation Bill', *Hansard*, 23 March 1952, cols 843–846. See Rolph C.H. (1949) 'The High Cost of Dying', *The New Statesmen and Nation*, 2 April, p. 319.
[81]Nesfield M. (1952) 'Does it Cost Too Much to Die?' *TNFD*, September, p. 112.
[82]'Valuable Public Relations Work' (1952) *TNFD*, November, p. 217 and 'The Modified Voluntary Agreement' (1953) *TNFD*, May, pp. 85–87.
[83]'End of the Voluntary Agreement' (1956) *FSJ*, April, pp. 155–156 and Neal W.E. (1953) 'State Funerals? The Dead End', *TFD*, August, p. 163.
[84]'Putting Them Right' (1953) *TNFD*, September, p. 181 and letter in *The Daily Telegraph*, 31 August 1953. 'Funeral (Costs)', *Hansard*, 18 February 1971, col. 551.
[85]'The Business of Burial', *The Economist*, 5 April 1958, Vol. 187, No. 5980, pp. 8–10.

The real issue, however, was that the government failed to keep the Death Grant in line with funeral costs.

As with proposals for the municipalisation of funeral service, it was from politicians that demands came for an alternative scheme. In July 1966 the Greater London Council member for Brent, Illtyd Harrington, surveyed London councils to see whether they wanted to go into business as funeral directors; it was believed that they could carry out a funeral for under £30.[86] Harrington also claimed that, 'American Funeral directing techniques are coming to Britain' but did not qualify his statement.[87] James Crook, a funeral director local to Harrington, said that a funeral costing £30 would have to be subsidised from the rates. A year later one publication appeared that supported funeral directors' opposition of local authority involvement in funerals. It dryly commented:

> In short, a municipal funeral service would be unlikely to save anyone any money, and might well add to the sum of human misery by confronting the bereaved with a council official. Most local authorities are already subsidising the cost of burials, and are subsidising cremations quite considerably. If it saved the bereaved money, a municipal funeral department would add to the burden borne by ratepayers who in many cases are already paying the losses on direct labour, municipal catering, municipal entertainments, and other services which are irrelevant to the role of government.[88]

Nevertheless, enthusiasm for the scheme continued. In 1968, Slough Council of Social Services suggested that hire purchase loans should be available and that funeral firms should amalgamate to cut costs.[89] Allegations in *The People* in February 1968 about backhanders to matrons, coroner's offices, mortuary attendants, etc, and other 'sharp practices' by funeral

---

[86]'Municipal Funerals. Labour Group Sounds Out London Boroughs' (1966) *FSJ*, July, pp. 359–360.
[87]Harrington I. (1972) 'Solemn Undertaking', *New Statesman*, 22 December, Vol. 84, No. 2179, pp. 940–941. See also Harrington I. (1973) 'Solemn Undertaking', *FSJ*, February, pp. 65–66 and Coates D.R. (1973) 'The Price of Dying', *FSJ*, February, pp. 66–67.
[88]Dunstan R.E. (1967) *Government: Wise Parent or Tycoon* (An Aim of Industry Publication), pp. 9–10. See also 'Costly Irrelevant Side-Lines' (1967) *FSJ*, July, pp. 343–344.
[89]'Social Service Council Wants Hire-Purchase Funerals' (1968) *FSJ*, February, pp. 71–72.

directors led one MP, William Price, to claim that registration was necessary or the trade must devise safeguards.[90] *The Daily Mirror* urged referring funeral bills to the Prices and Incomes Board; it also voiced approval of Illtyd Harrington's municipal funeral scheme.[91] An increase in the Death Grant was requested on at least three occasions during the 1970s, while in 1971 the request for an enquiry on funeral costs was rejected by the MP Nicholas Ridley.[92] Illtyd Harrington repeated his plea to local authorities in 1972; three years later Lambeth Council announced that they were pressing ahead for statutory powers to carry out a funeral service as they wanted to give people a choice; the Royal Arsenal Co-operative Society said the scheme would reduce standards.[93] Coincidentally, the NAFD president was Geoff Mitchell of the Lambeth-based Ashton Funeral Service. At that year's conference he described municipal funerals as 'undesirable' and said that proponents relied on poorly researched material from newspapers.[94] In 1975, Greenwich Council was said to be exploring a 'package deal' burial and cremation service being provided by the borough; there would be no cost to the ratepayer and a profit could be generated to help relatives.[95] Hull revisited the idea of council funerals in 1974, but the matter did not progress.[96]

The Birth of the Municipal Funeral and the Death of the Grant

By the start of the 1980s there was a high probability of local authorities embarking upon some form of funeral service. Although Sheffield abandoned their proposals in 1980, in the decade that followed many authorities gave consideration to the matter.[97] Liverpool, Stockton, Bolton,

---

[90]'*The People's* Probe' (1968) *FSJ*, March, pp. 123–124 and 'The Great Funeral Ramp', *The People*, 11 February, 1968, 18 February 1968, and 25 February 1968.
[91]'National Association Replies to Another Attack on Funeral Charges' (1969) *FSJ*, February, pp. 71–72 and 'The Final Reckoning', *The Daily Mirror*, 22 January 1969.
[92]'MP says 'Increase the Death Grant', (1970) *FSJ*, January, p. 124; 'Death Grant', *Hansard*, 29 January 1970, col. 399; 'Death Grant – A Plea for the Elderly Poor', (1974) *FSJ*, February, pp. 59–62; 'Death Grant', *Hansard*, 22 January 1974, col. 1427; and 'Funerals (Costs)', *Hansard*, 13 February 1971, col. 551.
[93]'A New Meaning to 'Council Undertaking'' (1973) *FSJ*, March, p. 107.
[94]'Municipal Funerals are Undesirable – Will Add to Rate Burden – Says NAFD President' (1975), *FSJ*, May, pp. 203–204. See also 'Raise Your Voices Now' (1975) *FSJ*, August, p. 355.
[95]''Package Deal' Funeral Plan for Greenwich' (1975) *FSJ*, November, pp. 496–497.
[96]'Council Funeral Scheme Under Fire' (1974) *FSJ*, September, pp. 383–384.
[97]'No Municipal Funerals' (1980) *FSJ*, February, p. 68.

Manchester, Islington, Camden and Wolverhampton, along with authorities in Wales, all explored the idea.[98] When Sandwell Borough Council revealed its intention, the ever-entrepreneurial funeral director Howard Hodgson counterbalanced the strategy by proposing an alternative scheme costing £280–£350K to establish, with running costs of £150K per year; to break even it would require 20 funerals a week charged at £350 each.[99]

What was unclear, however, was the legal position of a local authority to establish and run a funeral service. Nottingham Council was advised that they did not have sufficient powers.[100] Others pressed ahead and by mid-1985, 18 councils considered joining a consortium to share the cost if one was involved in legal action. Manchester City Council even suggested adapting the mayor's Rolls-Royce as a hearse.[101] A year later Leeds was advised after legal counsel that it had no power to operate a funeral service.[102] Other authorities such as Blackburn soon abandoned the idea.[103]

The NAFD took Counsel's opinion on the matter while Lord Graham, speaking at the Association's seminar, called for authorities to exercise caution.[104] He observed:

> The prime culprit for increasing costs of funerals has not been the businesses; many of the costs are outside their control, the capital costs for vehicles and labour have escalated, while the level and range of disbursements figure largely in

---

[98]'Funeral Directors Set to Oppose Liverpool 'Municipalisation' Scheme" (1983) *FSJ*, July, p. 307; 'Reservations About Municipal Funerals' (1985) *FSJ*, August, p. 319; 'Manchester Plans Contracted Out Service' (1987) *FSJ*, January, p. 12; 'Islington Council Enter Funeral Business' (1987) *FSJ*, September, p. 326; 'Municipal Service Idea Dropped' (1986) *FSJ*, November, p. 425; 'Wolverhampton Considering Municipal Funeral Service' (1986) *FSJ*, November, p. 424; and 'Welsh Call for Council-Run Funerals' (1986) *FSJ*, September, pp. 341–342.
[99]'Funeral Firm Suggests an Alternative to Municipal Funeral Service' (1983) *FSJ*, December, pp. 539–540.
[100]'"No Lawful Way of Operating a Municipal Funeral Service' States Report" (1984) *FSJ*, January, p. 15 and 'Municipal Funerals Decision' (1986) *FSJ*, October, p. 387.
[101]'Municipal Funerals: Councils Asked to Form Consortium to Fight Legal Action' (1985) *FSJ*, July, pp. 276–277.
[102]'Funeral on the Rates Plan Dropped' (1986), *TFD*, July, p. 10.
[103]'Another Council Interested in Municipal Funeral Service' (1984) *FSJ*, October, pp. 397–398. See also 'Municipal Funerals Plan Shelved' (1984) *FSJ*, November, p. 443 and 'Light-Hearted Look at Municipal Funerals' (1984) *FSJ*, November, p. 459.
[104]'Pledge to Oppose Municipal Funerals' (1984) *FSJ*, June, p. 238. See also 'Campaign Against Municipalisation' (1984) *FSJ*, December, p. 484 and 'Municipal Funerals: Legal Battle Warning' (1985) *FSJ*, May, p. 188.

the costs. The real culprit is the disgraceful way the government has dragged its feet in substantially increasing the Death Grant. A 1967 grant of £30 should be well over £200 in 1984, yet many thousands of the elderly population live their last days full of worry that they will die without the means to be buried with dignity and respect.[105]

Despite the query over the legal position, Liverpool Council said their scheme was to start during 1986.[106] Lambeth Council circumnavigated this hurdle by negotiating with a funeral director for a funeral costing £295.50 with the following provided: collection of body within ten miles, embalming, robe, use of chapels of rest, a coffin, hearse and one limousine.[107] Thirty-five funerals were carried out between February and May.[108] Southwark and Lewisham's contract with the Co-op was for £380, to include the funeral director's charge and the cremation fee.[109] However, in 1989 the Co-op withdrew from the Southwark scheme claiming that its popularity necessitated much more work than expected; a reported 460 funerals were carried out in 1988.[110] An agreement with funeral directors across the London Borough of Hounslow to supply a funeral for residents at £280 plus disbursements started in 1987 and the arrangement continues.[111] Similarly, in 1995 Nottingham City Council and CWS agreed on a fixed-price funeral for £995.[112]

From 1967, the Death Grant remained at £30 despite attempts to increase the allowance, with amounts between £200 and £300 suggested.[113]

---

[105] Graham L.T. (1984) 'Funeral on the Rates – No Answer to the Problem of Increasing Funeral Costs', *TFD*, December, pp. 22–23.

[106] 'Liverpool Council May Start Municipal Funeral Service Next Year' (1985) *FSJ*, August, p. 318. See also Connett D. (1985) 'Fight to the Death on Council Funerals', *The Embalmer*, Vol. 28, No. 3, p. 48.

[107] 'Lambeth Council Signs Contract for Fixed Price Funerals' (1986) *FSJ*, March, p. 91. See also 'Letter: How Lambeth Contract Operates (from E.E. Field)' (1986) *FSJ*, April, p. 129. See also 'Letter: Lambeth's Municipal Funeral Service (from J.C. Day)' (1986) *FSJ*, August, p. 311.

[108] Day J.C. (1986) 'Lambeth's Municipal Funeral Service', *FSJ*, August, p. 311.

[109] 'Lewisham Negotiations for Funeral Service' (1986) *FSJ*, May, p. 173. See also 'Lewisham Funeral Deal with Co-op' (1986) *FSJ*, August, p. 301 and "Interim' Municipal Service' (1987) *FSJ*, May, p. 175.

[110] 'Co-op Caned for Wanting Increase' (1989) *FSJ*, February, p. 4.

[111] 'Cheaper Funeral Plan for Hounslow' (1987) *TFD*, December, p. 16.

[112] 'The Nottingham Funeral' (1995) *FSJ*, December, p. 9.

[113] 'Death Grant Scandal' (1979) *FSJ*, January, pp. 15–17; 'The High Cost of Dying. A Bad Time to Phase out Death Grants' (1979) *FSJ*, October, pp. 429–431;

A Green Paper published in 1985 recommended that it be abolished as each payment cost £20 to administer.[114] Finally withdrawn on 31 March 1987, it was replaced with a means-tested benefit.[115] Ten years later, the DSS (now DWP) Funeral Expenses Payment, a £600 contribution towards funeral directors' costs and the minister (with certain disbursements also paid), was established.[116] This was increased to £700, where it remains, out of step with actual funeral costs and leaving a shortfall between the amount awarded and the total cost of the funeral.

Pre-Paid Funeral Plans and Consumer Interest

From the 1960s, funeral costs increasingly came under the spotlight through a series of investigations and reports. The Consumers' Association published their first survey in 1961 and noted that although the Death Grant was £25, the basic funeral that members of the NAFD agreed to supply was £29.5s.0d. Overall it recorded satisfaction with service by clients, although some complained that '…undertakers tried to do too much for them'.[117] Six years later, the Consumers' Association published the first consumer orientated guide *What To Do When Someone Dies*.[118]

The Price Commission's report *Funeral Charges* appeared in 1977.[119] Findings indicated that there was no evidence of abusive practices as found

---

'Death Grant', *Hansard*, 25 June 1979, cols 253–260; '£250 Selective Death Grant Urged' (1984) *FSJ*, September, pp. 359–360; 'Government's New Death Grant Proposals'; (1982) *FSJ*, May, pp. 206–207; 'Death Grant', *Hansard*, 3 December 1984, col. 72; 'Death Grant' (1985) *TFD*, January, p. 8; and 'Funerals', *Hansard*, 28 January 1986, col. 498.

[114]'Abolition of the Death Grant' (1985) *FSJ*, July, p. 281.

[115]'Reform of Social Security' (1987) *TFD*, April, p. 4.

[116]'Submission to the Social Security Advisory Committee relating to The Social Fund Amendments Regulations 1997' (1997) *TFD*, January, pp. 11–16. See also 'DSS Funeral Payment Proposals – 1997' (1996) *TFD*, December, pp. 10–14. See also 'Funeral Payments', *Hansard*, 9 January 1996, p. 11. See also 'Brief Synopsis of the Social Funeral Payment Changes to be Introduced on the 7 October 1996', *TFD*, July, p. 5. See also Gormley R. (1995) 'Social Funds and Unreal Expenses', *Pharos International*, Vol. 60, No. 2 pp. 103–104.

[117]'Funerals' (1961) *Which?* February, pp. 43–45. The NAFD produced a survey of funeral costs in 1970 that related to the cost of funerals. See 'Spending on Funerals' (1970) *TFD*, April, pp. 215–218 and September, pp. 502–504.

[118]Rudinger E. (1967) *What To Do When Someone Dies*, London: Consumers' Association.

[119]*Funeral Charges* (1977) Price Commission Report No. 22.

in north America, and while funerals may be a real burden on the poorer people, funeral costs '…are low compared with elsewhere';[120] Furthermore, there was little or no complaint about standards. While the owners of small businesses received 'reasonable remuneration', for the large firms, profits were considered 'generous or even high'. Among the Commission's recommendations were that funeral directors always give a written estimate, display the set price for a basic funeral, provide itemisation of funeral costs and devise a complaints procedure. They also suggested that there was room for reduction in charges by large organisations.[121] Taking the lead from Canada and the United States, the Commission also suggested the establishment of memorial societies to facilitate a simple funeral.[122]

The response by the industry to concern over the costs of funerals was met by the introduction of pre-paid funeral plans.[123] In contrast to policies sold by insurance companies, a funeral plan secures future market share for a funeral director while giving the purchasers a guarantee of full or part payment of the funeral costs. The Great Southern Group's Chosen Heritage plan was launched in 1985 and a year later the NAFD announced their Windsor Life scheme.[124] The other large organisations soon followed: Kenyon's 'Forethought', Hodgson Holdings with 'Dignity in Destiny' and the Co-operative with their Funeral Bond. Golden Charter plans were devised for the independent sector, while a proportion of other companies have their own schemes. Two charities, Age Concern and Help the Aged (now Age UK) also have links with plan providers.[125]

---

[120]'Funeral Costs Inquiry' (1975) *FSJ*, May, pp. 203–204. A typical burial was £177 and £166 for cremation. See also 'Prices Survey will Prove Funeral Directors Profit Margins are Not Excessive' (1976) *FSJ*, June, pp. 249–251 and Blair A.O.H. (1977) 'The Price Commission's Inquiry into Funeral Charges', Cremation Society Conference Report, pp. 63–69 and 'Comments on Price Commission Study of Funeral Costs' (1978) *FSJ*, June, pp. 253–254.

[121]*Funeral Charges* (1977) Price Commission Report No. 22, p. 1. See also 'Price Commission Exonerates British Funeral Service' (1977) *FSJ*, April, pp. 145–148. See also 'The High Cost of Dying' (1977) *Labour Research*, July, pp. 146–147.

[122]For an examination of the industry in America see Chapter 8 and for Canada see 'Coriolis' (1967) *Death Here is Thy Sting*, Toronto: McClelland and Stewart; Fric L. (1997) 'The Economics of Death', in J.D. Morgan ed., *Readings in Thanatology*, Amityville: Baywood; and Flynn D. (1993) *The Truth About Funerals*, Burlington: Funeral Consultants International Inc.

[123]The first reference to such plans in the UK trade journals was in 1939. See 'Pre-Arranged Funerals' (1939) *TUFDJ*, December, pp. 425–427 & 433.

[124]'NAFD Announces Pre-Planning Scheme for Funeral Expenses' (1986) *FSJ*, February, p. 47.

[125]'Funeral Planning Societies on the Way?' (1983) *FSJ*, April, p. 163.

Such has been their popularity that by the mid-1990s it was estimated that approximately 5 per cent of funerals in the United Kingdom were prearranged.[126] Regional TV advertising was used for Chosen Heritage plans and more recently Funeralcare has embarked upon the same medium. As with at-need funerals, pre-need came under scrutiny from the OFT in 1995 and the Consumers' Association in 1999.[127] The OFT raised a number of concerns about this unregulated market, including sales practices, and among the recommendations were transparency in contract conditions and trust arrangements. The Financial Services and Markets Acts 2000 contained provisions for the sector, which is self-regulated by the Funeral Planning Authority (FPA). This organisation operates a Code of Practice for member firms, some also being members of the National Association for Pre-Paid Funeral Plans. However, not all pre-paid plan providers are registered with the FPA. This factor along with aspects of transparency and value for the consumer were highlighted in a report published in 2017 by Fairer Finance in partnership with Dignity.[128] Being outside the scope of this study, a comprehensive analysis of the workings and future of pre-paid market is awaited.

As noted in Chapter 6, structural changes during the 1980s and 1990s refocused attention on the industry, spurring a number of investigations. In addition, reports appeared, mainly concerning funeral costs. The Consumers' Association's second investigation was published in 1987, and revealed that most clients were satisfied with the service received, but recommended consultation with more than one firm to assess price and the level of helpfulness.[129] As will be outlined in Chapter 8, with the introduction of the NAFD's Code of Practice in 1979, it is not surprising that adherence to its clauses was a feature of Kate Foster's *Survey of Funeral Arrangements* carried out in 1987. Of the 893 interviewed who had arranged a funeral, she found that written estimates were not always given.

---

[126] Meek H. (1995) 'The Funeral Services Market: Strategies for the 1990s', *FSJ*, January, pp. 62–69.

[127] *Pre-Paid Funeral Plans: A Report by the Office of Fair Trading* (1995), London: OFT; 'OFT Director General Urges Law to Cover Pre-Paid Funerals' (1995) *FSJ*, June, pp. 45–55; Humphreys J. (1995) 'Pre-Paid Funeral Plans', *Pharos International*, Vol. 60, No. 3, pp. 136–127; and 'Funeral Plans – The *Which?* Report' (1999) *FSJ*, February, p. 5.

[128] 'Is the Prepaid Funeral Planning Market Working Well for Consumers?' (2017) Fairer Finance/Dignity PLC. https://www.fairerfinance.com/assets/uploads/documents/Funeral-plan-report-FINAL-6-July-2017.pdf. (Accessed 25 July 2017).

[129] 'Funerals' (1982) *Which?* November, pp. 653–655. See also Adams C. (1989) 'Funerals – A Report by the OFT', *Pharos International*, Vol. 55, No. 4, pp. 133–143.

This research formed the basis of the OFT's report issued two years later, which reiterated the issue of 'poor' compliance with the code. Lapses in service were also noted, but so too was the tendency for people not to complain. Its conclusions were that the public needed more information about funeral costs and that: 'Demand is shaped by the industry. There are formidable barriers, of ignorance and reticence, which prevent people from considering the kind of funeral they really want.'[130]

The issue was seized upon by Lawrence Cunliffe, MP for Leigh, who in a Parliamentary debate revealed that he secured employment with two funeral directors so he could undertake his own investigations. Particularly enraged by the mark-up differential of a coffin purchase from a manufacturer by a funeral director and sold to the client, he expressed concern about the '...big businesses that are creating monopolies'.[131] In 1991, he called for a thorough investigation of the funeral industry with a view to seeking a bill to establish a funeral industry registration council.[132] The MP for Edinburgh South, Nigel Griffiths, supported this position by claiming that '...the public is demanding regulation of the trade...' although, like so many other such statements, it was not substantiated.[133]

By the time the Consumers' Association's third report appeared it was taking a more combative approach towards the industry. Published in 1992, investigations found wide variations in the cost of the NAFD basic funeral, while no price list was available at over two-thirds of the 59 funeral directors visited by mystery shoppers. Consumers were again urged to 'shop around'.[134] Colin Brown, Deputy Director of Research at the Consumers' Association, used these findings supplemented by additional investigations to express disappointment at the level of adherence before going a step further:

> Our conclusion is that the industry as a whole is still unable, completely unable, to guarantee the most basic of consumer/ customer information on funerals and I would go further to suggest, although we didn't say this in the magazine, that many funeral directors think it wrong to offer the information and that the customer has no right to it.[135]

---

[130]*Funerals: A Report* (1989) London: The Office of Fair Trading, p. 1.
[131]'Funeral Costs', *Hansard*, 6 February 1989, cols 776–782.
[132]'Funeral Industry', *Hansard*, 22 April 1991, cols 788–818.
[133]'Funeral Industry', *Hansard*, 22 April 1991, col. 813.
[134]'Funerals' (1992) *Which?* February, pp. 112–116.
[135]See also Brown C. (1995) 'Funerals – The Consumers' Perspective', *Pharos International*, Vol. 61, No. 4, pp. 162–166.

The Consumers' Association's fourth and fifth reports continued its critical stance by accusing funeral directors of not giving sufficient information while pressurising the bereaved into choosing something they don't want and 'dodgy selling'.[136] It also observed that the newly founded Funeral Standards Council was making no impact in trying to enforce adherence to the NAFD Code of Practice. Funeral plans were also discussed, as they were in a 1999 report.[137] A further call for regulation of funeral service and pre-paid plans came from MP David Chidgey in December 1997; the following year he issued a report recommending a single code.[138] By this time the phrase 'funeral poverty' had started to be used as research indicated that there was an increasing problem in paying for funerals.[139] However, while some of the data are certainly questionable, what is clear is the rise in the number of public health funerals arranged and paid for by the local authority.[140]

At a conference entitled 'Redress and the Funeral Profession' held in 2000, the Office of Fair Trading announced a second investigation and its report appeared the following year.[141] It said that adherence to the NAFD Code was 'patchy' and recommendations included displaying price lists

---

[136]'Finding the Right Funeral Director' (1995) *Which?* February, pp. 26–29 and 'Which? Investigates Funeral Directors' (2012) *Which?* February, pp. 68–70.

[137]'Funeral Plans – How Much Peace of Mind?' (1999) *Which?* January, pp. 24–27.

[138]'Funeral Services', *Hansard*, 17 December 1997, cols 297–300. See 'Adjournment Debate' (1998) *FSJ*, January, pp. 32–34 and 'The UK Funeral Industry – A Case for Reform' (1998) *FSJ*, September, p. 8.

[139]Drakeford M. (1998) 'Last Rights? Funerals, Poverty and Social Exclusion', *Journal of Social Policy*, Vol. 27, No. 4, pp. 507–524. See also 'Funeral Poverty: A Plan for Managing the Impact of Funeral Costs' (2013) Wiltshire: Citizens Advice Centre. http://cabwiltshire.org.uk/phocadownload/funeralpoverty_feb2013.pdf. (Accessed 5 January 2015) and Gregory (2014) 'Future Consideration in Paying for Funerals. Briefing Paper', Centre on Household Assets and Savings Management. http://www.birmingham.ac.uk/Documents/college-social-sciences/social-policy/CHASM/briefing-papers/2014/Future-Considerations-in-Paying-for-Funerals—LG.pdf. (Accessed 5 January 2015). See Woodthorpe K., Rumble H. and Valentine C. (2013) 'Putting "The Grave" into Social Policy: State Support for Funerals in Contemporary UK Society', *Journal of Social Policy*, Vol. 42, No. 3, pp. 605–662. See also Valentine C. and Woodthorpe K. (2014) 'From Cradle to the Grave: Funeral Welfare from an International Perspective', *Social Policy and Administration*, Vol. 48, No. 5, pp. 515–536.

[140]*Public Health Funerals* (2010) Local Government Association. https://inews.co.uk/essentials/news/uk/worrying-picture-isolation-numbers-paupers-funerals-soar/. (Accessed 17 May 2017).

[141]Bridgeman J.S. (2000) 'The Way Forward for the Funeral Profession', *FSJ*, February, pp. 57–70.

and written estimates. It also called for details of the organisation having ultimate control of the business to be revealed and for industry code to have the approval of the OFT.[142] The Consumers' Association followed with another undercover investigation, which found that although three codes of practice existed, compliance was patchy and service variable. The association endorsed the need for a single code of practice embracing minimum levels of service and training.[143] As will be discussed in Chapter 8, the industry still has two codes operated by NAFD and SAIF, although in April 2017 discussions were under way to achieve a consensus.

The last decade has seen the publication of many surveys and reports on funeral costs; the University of Bath has been commissioned by Sun Life to assess average charges,[144] and also examine the gap between costs and payments from the Social Fund,[145] while the ICCM has worked in conjunction with Royal London to endorse the need for an increase in the Social Fund contribution to costs along with the reuse of old graves.[146] The NAFD has also surveyed its membership to assess funeral charges.[147] However, some of these reports continue to provide no clear distinction between third-party costs (particularly cemetery and crematorium charges) and those of the funeral director.

Concern over funeral costs has resulted in at least one local authority negotiating specifications with funeral directors, while the Consumers' Association continues to offer advice to those making funeral

---

[142] *Funerals* (2001) London: Office of Fair Trading, pp. 2–3. See also *Survey of Funeral Directors. A Report of the Results* (2001) London: Office of Fair Trading and *Consumers Experiences of Arranging Funerals: A Report* (2001) London: Office of Fair Trading.

[143] 'Funeral Directors Investigated' (2002) *Which?* March pp. 8–11.

[144] For example, see 'Cost of Dying 2014: The Eighth Annual Report' (2014) file:///C:/Users/sutherland/Downloads/SunLife-Cost-Of-Dying-Report-2014.pdf. (Accessed 5 January 2015).

[145] 'Funeral Poverty in the UK: Issues for Policy' (2014) http://www.bath.ac.uk/ipr/pdf/policy-briefs/affording-a-funeral.pdf. (Accessed 5 January 2015). See also *Support for the Bereaved* (2016) House of Commons Work and Pensions Committee. Ninth Report of Session 2015–2016.

[146] 'Are We Losing the Plot?' (2014) Royal London/ICCM. http://www.iccmk.com/iccm/library/2758%20Royal%20London%20Funeral%20poverty%20report%20V3%2001.12.14.pdf. (Accessed 5 January 2015).

[147] 'NAFD Pricing Survey 2014'. https://gallery.mailchimp.com/91a20d214f6f0a4fb90c5b3ee/files/NAFD_Pricing_Survey_2014_FINAL.pdf?utm_source=NAFD+e-newsletter+MEMBER+listing&utm_campaign=f0658c7341-NAFD_April_Newsletter4_17_2013+2&utm_medium=email&utm_term=0_e7810c9bed-f0658c7341-92620425. (Accessed 6 January 2015).

arrangements.[148] In 2011 Quaker Social Action instigated a 'funeral mentor' scheme to help plan funerals for low-income families.[149]

As this chapter has revealed, repeated demands for schemes to control funeral costs have all been unsuccessful. Although there has been evidence to show that questionable practices have occurred, the reasons for the absence of price control require assessment. First, the assumption is made that funeral directors deliberately exploit the bereaved by overcharging. However, in the absence of rigorous and impartial research, including the assessment of charges based on the comparison of like-for-like funeral specifications, such claims are largely subjective. Although a number of websites provide this information, it is too early to assess their efficacy, while funeral directors have doubted the accuracy of their information. Furthermore, isolated incidents do neither represent a pattern, nor can anecdotal information be taken as evidence of a wide-scale problem. Indeed, accusations of overcharging cannot be ascertained without the scrutiny of a firm's statement of income and expenditure or a detailed comparative survey of competitors' costs. The lack of consistent and definitive data along with the issue not being sufficiently vote-winning explains the unwillingness of central or local government to become involved in the control of what has historically been a private business function. That said, an indication that funeral directors may be subjected to some form of regulation has been through the Burial and Cremation (Scotland) Bill 2016. At the time of writing there are no details of the scheme, although an inspector has been appointed.[150] It is too early to speculate on the scope of regulation along with whether the legislation will be introduced into England and Wales.

Secondly, being only too aware of the ease of being accused of profiteering from the bereaved, deliberate overcharging by funeral directors not only affects reputation, but also increases the potential for bad debt. Evidence from funeral directors indicates that a proportion of funeral accounts remain unpaid, while some debts can lead to what has been called

---

[148]'Hounslow Community Funeral Service'. http://www.hounslow.gov.uk/community_funerals_may14.pdf. (Accessed 5 January 2015) and 'The Nottingham Funeral'. http://www.nottinghamcity.gov.uk/article/22195/The-Nottingham-Funeral. (Accessed 5 January 2015). See also '10 Things You Should Know About Funerals'. http://www.which.co.uk/news/2012/01/10-things-you-should-know-about–funerals-277448. (Accessed 4 January 2015).
[149]https://www.quakersocialaction.org.uk/taking-social-action/our-practical-work/funeral-poverty/down-earth. (Accessed 7 May 2017).
[150]Burial and Cremation (Scotland) 2016 Bill, Part 5, Sections 65–70.

'funeral poverty'. Although without clear definition (and also re-termed as 'funeral affordability' by the NAFD), this is a topic that has generated considerable discussion, but ultimately can only be addressed by an increase in the DWP payment or funeral directors lowering their costs.[151] Although an increasing number of firms ask for third-party payments to be paid in advance of the funeral, there is little means of redress if the balance is not paid as debt collection is a difficult task. As Dom Maguire, the former public relations officer for the NAFD, noted in 1996:

> I don't know any other profession or any other occupation where someone can walk in unannounced off the street into an office, sit down and arrange for the provision of services and merchandise to the tune of £1000 or £1200, or even £1500, and then on top of that expect the funeral director to commit his company to paying disbursements or outlays for another three or four hundred pounds [at 2015, at least £900]. These people have no banker's reference, they have no credit reference of any type, they sign a piece of paper, they are given an estimate and they get up and leave.[152]

Research by the NAFD reveals that the bereaved were very happy with the service provided by a funeral director and that costs coincided with expectations.[153] Furthermore, data published in Dignity's annual report confirm that over 90 per cent of clients would recommend the organisation.[154] Taking this to its logical conclusion, if funeral directors were deliberately exploiting their clients this would not be the case.

Lastly, critics seem to be unwilling to accept that expenditure by the bereaved can often be attributed to a desire to 'do their best' for the deceased. In a response to an article about East End funeral costs published in 1916 in the *Daily Mail,* one undertaker said he '…believed that

---

[151]Corden A. and Hirst A. (2015) '*The Meaning of Funeral Poverty: An Exploratory Study*', University of York Working Paper WP 2668.
[152]Maguire D. (1996) 'The Role of the Modern Funeral Director', *Pharos International*, Vol. 62, No. 3, p. 144.
[153]*Funerals Matter: How the British Public Views the Funeral Profession in 2016*, Solihull: NAFD.
[154]http://www.dignityfunerals.co.uk/media/2366/dignity_annual_report_and_accounts.pdf p16. (Accessed 27 May 2016).

people thought a handsome funeral is still a debt to be paid to the dead... We do not force the fashions in funerals; we simply execute orders'.[155] A century later, with greater consumer awareness and industry codes requiring the issue of an estimate before the funeral, many wish for more than a 'basic' funeral, a term with a variety of meanings.[156] As Ann Clarke observed in respect of contemporary funerals in east London: 'Mourners desire to give one last thing to the deceased; the more expensive the better because it shows just how much you care; and the need to celebrate the deceased's life in a very visible way.'[157]

---

[155]'Simpler Funerals' (1916) *TUJ*, September, p. 232. See also Howarth, G. (2007) 'Whatever Happened to Social Class? An Examination of the Neglect of Working Class Cultures in the Sociology of Death', *Healthcare Sociology Review*, Vol.16, No. 5, pp. 425–435.
[156]For a discussion on the possible future direction of the industry see Walter T. (2017) 'Bodies and Ceremonies: Is the UK Funeral Industry Still Fit for Purpose?', *Mortality*, Vol. 22, No 3, pp. 194–208.
[157]Clarke A. (1996) 'Where, Oh Death, Is Now Thy Sting?' *The Friend*, 13 September, pp. 13–14.

Chapter 8

The Newest Profession?

> My daily woman was grumbling one day that her daughter didn't speak to her any more since she'd married into the professional classes. What did her son-in-law do, I asked. 'Oh', said my daily woman. 'He's an undertaker.'[1]

The pursuit of professional recognition has been an ambition of the funeral industry since the end of the nineteenth century. Through utilising all the established characteristics such as the formation of an association, promoting education, embarking upon registration and adopting a code of practice, the occupation has also redefined its role from undertaker to funeral director being an advisor to the living on all matters funereal. However, the extent to which these attributes have resulted in professionalisation is a matter of debate. Using the chapter title that Jessica Mitford adopted when surveying the same subject in *The American Way of Death*, an assessment is made of why and how the British funeral industry has sought to professionalise.

The desire for an occupation to be classified as a profession can chiefly be attributed to the degree of status and prestige such a conferment provides. Although the characteristics of a profession and the process of the professionalisation is the subject of much debate and, along with a theoretical assessment, has been well covered in other texts, for the purpose of this study the definition used is: 'A profession is an occupation in which people use specialised knowledge to perform an exclusive service, and for which they receive occupational autonomy, income, status and powers, including

---

[1]Cooper J. (1979) *Class,* London: Eyre Methuen, p. 98.

the power to set standards of admission and practice.[2] Furthermore, the 'temporal sequence of professionalization' that moves through the 'life history' of the occupation is as follows: a full-time activity in the performance of a bundle of necessary tasks; establishment of a training school; formation of a national professional association; redefinition of the core task, giving dirty work over to subordinates; conflicts between the home guard and the profession-orientated newcomers; hard competition with neighbouring occupations, especially at the later stages of professionalisation; political agitation in order to win support of law for protection of the job territory and its prerogatives, and rules and ideals embodied in a formal code of ethics.[3] This suggests a sequence of events that an occupation must pursue to be designated as a profession.[4] In other words, 'What are the circumstances in which people in an occupation attempt to turn it into a profession, and themselves into professional people?'[5] The objective of this chapter is neither to discuss the well-rehearsed theories dealing with this issue nor to arbitrate as to whether funeral directing is or is not a profession, but to examine the industry's approach to the acquisition of such status.[6]

The Desire to Professionalise

For funeral directing, professionalisation can be seen to be an important objective, if not a preoccupation. In the early years of the twentieth century, British undertakers looked to their American counterparts for inspiration and to gauge their progress and success.[7] As will be discussed, in the first half of the century British undertakers attempted to promote

---

[2]Farrell J.J. (1980) *Inventing the American Way of Death 1830–1920*, Philadelphia: Temple University Press, p. 152.
[3]Wilensky H. (1964) 'The Professionalization of Everyone?' *American Journal of Sociology*, Vol. 70,September, pp. 137–158.
[4]Abbott P. and Wallace C. eds (1990) *The Sociology of the Caring Professions*, Hampshire: Falmer Press, p. 25.
[5]Hughes E.C. (1958) *Men and Their Work*, Glencoe: Free Press.
[6]For other assessments of the professionalisation of the funeral director see Smale B. (1985) *Deathwork: A Sociological Analysis of Funeral Directing*, Unpublished PhD thesis, University of Sussex; Naylor (née Page) M.J.A. (1989) *Funeral Rituals in a Northern City*, Unpublished PhD thesis, University of Leeds; and Howarth G. (1992) *The Funeral Industry in the East End of London: An Ethnographic Study*, Unpublished PhD thesis, University of London.
[7]See Leavitt B. (1915) 'Lifting a Business into a Profession', *TUJ*, December, pp. 329–332 and Lady W.W. (1926) 'Our Mission as Funeral Directors', *BUA Monthly*, July, pp. 4–5.

embalming as the key to professionalisation in the same way that their transatlantic colleagues had achieved.[8] Huntington and Metcalf identify that the adoption of embalming strengthened funeral directing in the United States in two ways. First, a system of state licensing, 'designed… no doubt to protect the public from charlatans, [which thus] created a controlling professional *élite,*' while technical apparatus necessitated that the body be moved to their premises, thus giving greater control.[9]

Professionalisation is a continually evolving process. As has been indicated, the concept is without precise definition and just as occupations change and develop so too do the reasons to seek professional status. Developments occurring during the ensuing life history of the occupation may necessitate reaffirmation or refocusing of the professional objective. With this in mind, it is necessary to consider the work of the undertaker operating in the latter part of the previous century to locate primary evidence of the desire to professionalise. Similarly, it is also necessary to consider changes occurring to the occupation during this century that can be seen as reaffirmation of the need for professional recognition. Four reasons can be attributed to the desire for the funeral industry to embark upon professionalisation: distancing from unscrupulous behaviour and myths; the increasingly complex funeral and disposal environment;

---

[8]For the American funeral director see Bowman L. (1959) *The American Funeral: A Study in Guilt, Extravagance and Sublimity,* Washington: Public Affairs Press; Habenstein R.W. (1962) 'Sociology of Occupations: The Case of the American Funeral Director', in A.M. Rose ed., *Human Behaviour and Social Processes,* London: Routledge & Kegan Paul; Porter W.H., Jr (1968) 'Some Sociological Notes on a Century of Change in the Funeral Business', *Sociological Symposium,* Vol. 1, pp. 36–46; Kastenbaum R.J. and Aisenberg R. (1976) *The Psychology of Death,* New York: Springer; and particularly Pine V.R. (1975) *Caretaker of the Dead: The American Funeral Director,* New York: Irvington; Farrell J.J. (1980) *Inventing the American Way of Death 1830–1920,* Philadelphia: Temple University Press; Kearl M.C. (1989) *Endings: A Sociology of Death and Dying,* Oxford: Oxford University Press; Thompson W.E. (1991) 'Handling the Stigma of Handling the Dead: Morticians and Funeral Directors', *Deviant Behaviour: An Interdisciplinary Journal,* Vol. 12, pp. 403–429; Laderman G. (2003) *Rest in Peace: A Cultural History of Death and the Funeral Home in Twentieth-Century America,* Oxford: Oxford University Press; Kalkofen R.W. (1989) 'After a Child Dies: A Funeral Director's Perspective', *Issues in Comprehensive Paediatric Nursing,* Vol. 12, No. 4, pp. 285–297; and Hoy W.G. (2013) *Do Funerals Matter? The Purposes and Practices of Death Rituals in Global Perspective,* New York: Routledge.
[9]Metcalf P. and Huntington R. (1991) *Celebrations of Death: The Anthropology of Mortuary Ritual,* second edition, Cambridge: Cambridge University Press, p. 197.

relations with allied occupations; and stigmatisation through body-handling in addition to the economic environment of funeral directing.

Distancing from a Legacy of Unscrupulous Behaviour and Myths

As identified in Chapter 7, allegations of impropriety have underpinned the desire for twentieth-century funeral directors to distance themselves from the conduct of some of their forebears. One commentator states:

> The trade in the nineteenth century does not stand up to close examination. In the main they were a semi-educated band with neither trade nor union affiliation, and greedy – the occasional client was brought to financial ruin by undertakers charging over-inflated and extortionate prices for an unnecessary spectacle that few could either afford or understand.[10]

Writing in the 1930s, Albert Cottridge considered how a previous generation perceived the need to improve the image of the industry:

> a growing section of undertakers... [have sought] to cut themselves off as completely as possible from the bad old traditions of their class, and to endeavour to create in our own generation a new and better type of public service such as will entitle them to the recognition and protection afforded to other professions.[11]

From this statement it is clear that these undertakers were anxious to depart from an industry besieged by allegations of corruption and poor ethical practices. In order to elevate the status in the eyes of the bereaved, undertakers looked to professionalisation and the necessity of refocusing on the whole nature of the service being provided.

In conjunction with the increasing complexity of funerals, this shift from merely selling goods to providing an essential service in an altruistic framework became the prevailing objective. No longer was the undertaker

---

[10]Litten J.W.S. (2002) *The English Way of Death: The Common Funeral since 1450*, London: Robert Hale, p. 31.
[11]Cottridge A.J.E. (1933a) 'The Professional Undertaker and the Public Health', *Public Health*, January, pp. 132–134. See also Cottridge A.J.E. (1933b) 'The Professional Undertaker and the Public Health', *TUJ*, February, pp. 57–58.

merely a purveyor of goods; they were a specialist service provider. Being recognised as a professional is perceived by the industry as a means of elevating the image by demonstrating severance from unprincipled connections.

Increasing Complexity in the Environment of Disposal

A second reason can be linked to the changing environment of disposal. From the 1830s, matters concerning burial, death registration, the function of the coroner and public health all became enshrined in legislation. For the undertaker operating around the turn of the century, and particularly those located in urban areas, this increasing regulation necessitated possession of a considerable body of knowledge of both law and practice. Individual cemetery regulations and growing bureaucracy required the undertaker to be in a position to advise the bereaved with authority. Although the undertaker was utilised to carry out virtually all funerals, as gatekeepers to a specialist knowledge base they became exclusive intermediaries between the bereaved and those responsible for the ultimate disposal of the dead. As other responsibilities were gradually acquired during the twentieth century, such as care of the body, in addition to widening the scope of services it is appropriate that an all-embracing definition of the role of the funeral director has come to be offered by the NAFD: 'technical adviser, agent, contractor, master of ceremonies and custodian of the dead'.[12] Thus the management of funerals became a technical and specialist function that legally takes the form of a contract. The role of the undertaker therefore changed from merely selling or hiring goods to offering a complete service that essentially represented the overall direction and responsibility of funeral performance. In 1948 Clifford Ellis noted that:

> The calling of a funeral director today is in no way less important than in the ages now long past, and our public rightly demand that every avenue should be explored whereby we who are called upon to render this very necessary service should be fully conversant with all the intricate details of funeral directing, and for this service we shall be recognised internationally.[13]

---

[12] *Manual of Funeral Directing* (2009) Solihull: NAFD, Ch. 18, p. 2.
[13] Ellis C. (1948) 'The Age-Long Profession of Funeral Directing', *TNFD*, March, pp. 235–237.

It is certainly this change through increasing complexity to which we can largely attribute the renaming of the occupation from undertaker to funeral director, as will be discussed later in this chapter.

The growing complexity of funerals had other effects on the undertaker/funeral director. In organisational terms, urbanisation led to an increasing number of deaths to be managed and organisational intricacy of operation demanded increased managerial and coordination skills, for example by carriage masters supplying resources to small firms of undertakers. The economic and efficient allocation of such resources has to be carefully regulated to avoid errors and failure to fulfil commitments. In this respect there is also evidence to show an increase in the number of undertakers beginning to specialise in funeral directing. Exclusive activity in one occupation signified not only sufficient trading demand but also a commitment to the occupation, especially if financial investment was involved. Again this particularly applies to urban areas, where there is clear evidence to denote a decline in the number of non-core-activity undertakers.

As further societal and technical developments have occurred during the twentieth century so too have different areas of funereal complexity. Although the acquisition of responsibility for care of the body will be discussed below, it is societal changes such as the emergence of ethnic groups with funeral demands in contrast to traditional rituals that have had an impact upon the work of the funeral director. In encountering these groupings, funeral directors have had to respond to their needs by providing goods and services that conform to the seemingly bewildering parameters of law and regulations that now surround disposal of the dead. In addition, the increase in international transportation of the dead has led to specialist organisations taking responsibility for the management of these complex operations. Thus the desire to seek professional status can be seen to stem from the opportunity presented to the undertaker/funeral director to become an expert service provider.

The increasing complexity of the disposal environment has led the undertaker to possess great power and control over the system of funeral management. Control of the body can be attributed to the source of this power.[14] The provision of custody and the application of a preservative craft in the form of arterial embalming has reaffirmed the definition of the funeral director to include custodian of the dead. While this has given the occupation justification for its claims for professional recognition, it can however be argued that control hinders professionalisation.

---

[14]Howarth G. (1993b) 'AIDS and Undertakers: The Business of Risk Management', *Critical Public Health,* Vol, 4, No. 3, pp. 47–53.

Walter argues the body is 'the key to commercialisation and professionalisation of death'.[15] While possession of the body is seen to be the locus of control, it nevertheless prevents mourners from becoming actively and fully involved in ritual preparation – an important issue to funeral reformers. Walter further argues that repossession of the body will facilitate the regaining of funereal control. If the funeral director is to maintain the quest for professional recognition and still possess a measure of control over the funeral, the role may well have to change to that of facilitator rather than director, as mentioned in Chapter 1. However, while this may apply to those desirous of performing a self-managed funeral, as the vast majority of funerals are undertaken by funeral directors they continue to provide a necessary and indispensable service.

Relations with Allied Occupations

Through the increasing complexity of funerals and responsibility for the funeral director, it is clear that the latter has greater involvement with two occupations already acknowledged to be professions; medicine and the Church. During the nineteenth century undertakers would have had comparatively little occupational proximity with physicians. As the undertakers had minimal contact with bodies there was no common ground for meeting, although there is evidence of irregular financial transactions occurring between undertakers and physicians when recommending clients.[16] As the legislative formalities surrounding death certification and disposal – especially cremation – increased, scope for communication was augmented, particularly when funeral directors became responsible for the provision of custody.

The Church has also played a central role in death and funerals and although their power has decreased – for example the physician replacing the clergyman at the deathbed and the abandonment of urban churchyards for the proprietary cemeteries – their role during the funeral ritual is still of strategic importance. In the case of the latter, funeral directors have an unwritten obligation to contact Church of England clergy to perform funerals for those professing allegiance to this denomination.[17] The undertaker/

---

[15]Walter T. (1994) *The Revival of Death,* London: Routledge, p. 17.
[16]Morley J. (1971) *Death, Heaven and the Victorians,* London: Studio Vista, p. 24.
[17]Rowell G. (1977) *The Liturgy of Christian Burial,* London: Society for Promoting Christian Knowledge. See also Jupp P.C. ed. (2008b) *Death Our Future: Christian Theology and Funeral Practice,* London: Epworth. For an exploration of the role

funeral director would be responsible for securing the services of a cleric and in effect the funeral director – occupying the role of master of ceremonies – would hand over control to this functionary at the time of the funeral.

In working alongside two occupations that appear to enjoy a high degree of professional status, the funeral director occupies an almost subservient and possibly inferior role. Although pertaining to funeral directors in America, Porter's observations could well apply in this country: 'There is also some indication that the inordinate number of contacts of the funeral director with two recognized categories of professionals, the minister and the physician, contributes to his feelings of inferiority and increases his desire for comparable status.'[18]

In addition, funeral directors have an increasing link with solicitors, for example in the payments of accounts, the swearing of statutory declarations for certain formal transactions and the increasing necessity of knowledge of specialist matters such as wills and probate.

Occupational Stigmatisation: Body-Handling

As has been noted in Chapter 2, the undertaker operating around 1900 had comparatively little contact with the dead body. From the 1930s, however, a shift occurred in the place of repose as undertakers in urban areas in particular increasingly provided chapels of rest. This area of supplementary responsibility gave the funeral director further ability to provide facilities and services, specifically being the chapel of rest and embalming. While it can be seen that supply of these services presented the impetus to professionalise, it is argued here that the responsibility of body-handling has caused the funeral director to become stigmatised. Consequentially, professionalisation is recognised as a technique to overcome such tainting.

Custody of the dead can be seen as part of what Clark terms the wider 'professionalization of death' in society.[19] As care passed from the local,

---

in the US see Bradfield C.D. and Myers R.A. (1980) 'Clergy and Funeral Directors: An Exploration in Role Conflict', *Review of Religious Research,* Vol. 21, No. 3, pp. 343–350.

[18]Porter W.H. Jr (1968) 'Some Sociological Notes on a Century of Change in the Funeral Business', *Sociological Symposium,* Vol. 1, p. 39.

[19]Clarke D. (2002) 'Death in Staithes', in D. Dickenson, M. Johnson and J.S. Katz eds, *Death, Dying an Bereavement,* second edition, London: The Open University/Sage, p. 8.

informally organised laying-out female to the commercial services environment dominated by the male funeral director and/or embalmer, a degree of this 'professionalization of death' occurred. This development can be seen as confirmation of a process in which 'the male-dominated professions gain control over and subordinate female-dominated occupations'.[20] A similar situation occurred in the professionalisation of nursing when: 'male midwives (obstetricians)... claim[ed] to have scientific knowledge and technical expertise not possessed by female midwives'.[21] These laying-out women were honoured and respected by the community.[22] However, through the institutionalisation of the dead in the commercial environment and in conjunction with the prevailing attitudes towards the dead body as a source of pollution and contamination, the occupation of funeral directing has become stigmatised. Grainger refers to the people carrying out body-handling tasks as 'dealing in an official way with those aspects of life and death that society has structured itself specifically to avoid'.[23] They possess the 'taint of death', are 'unclean' and have become the 'untouchable' professionals.[24] Spencer Cahill notes that 'funeral directors' pecuniary dependence upon and intimacy with death made them seem polluted, callous, and strange'.[25] Although Harrah and Harrah go too far by aligning funeral directors with criminals, the latter part of their analysis expresses the occupational dilemma:

---

[20]Abbott P. and Wallace C. eds (1990) *The Sociology of the Caring Professions*, Hampshire: Falmer Press, p. 3.
[21]*Ibid.*, p. 18.
[22]Chamberlain M. and Richardson R. (1983) 'Life and Death', *Oral History*, Vol. 11, No. 1, p. 39.
[23]Grainger R. (1988) *The Unburied* Worthing: Churchman Publishing, p. 142.
[24]Charmaz K., Howarth G. and Kellehear A. eds (1997) *The Unknown Country: Death in Australia, Britain and the USA*, Basingstoke: Macmillan, p. 182; Sudnow D. (1967) *Passing On: The Social Organization of Dying*, Englewood Cliffs: Prentice-Hall, pp. 51–64; Fulton R. (1961) 'The Clergyman and the Funeral Director: A Study in Role Conflict', *Social Forces*, Vol. 39, pp. 317–323; and Bradbury M. (1999) *Representations of Death: A Social Psychological Perspective*, London: Routledge, pp. 135–138. It is worth noting that stigmatisation appears to also apply to those employed in the funeral industry without direct contact with dead bodies, for example gravediggers. See Terkel S. (1974) *Working*, Harmondsworth: Penguin, p. 416 and Saunders K.C. (1995) 'The Occupational Role of Gravediggers: A Service Occupation in Acute Decline', *The Service Industries Journal*, Vol. 15, No. 1, pp. 1–13.
[25]Cahill S.E. (1995) 'Some Rhetorical Directions of Funeral Direction: Historical Entanglements and Contemporary Dilemmas', *Work and Occupations*, Vol. 22, No. 115, p. 125.

> Funeral Directors do the dirty work that literally 99% (or more) of society would not do. They perform an absolutely vital service. Society might be grateful. Instead, it heaps abuse on him or her, higher than on sanitation workers, pornographers, or child molesters. Why? People tolerate (more or less) pollution, dirty pictures and rape because they think they can escape them. But death-defying, death-denying syndromes notwithstanding, deep down, everyone knows he's going to die and he doesn't like it. Funerals remind him he's mortal. He doesn't like to shake hands with a mortician. [26]

With this transition occurring in America, funeral directors became stigmatised due to the fact that they were 'linked to the American death orientation whereby the industry is the cultural scapegoat for failed immortality'.[27] It is presumably for this reason that the industry experienced problems in advancing its status in the 1920s when Farrell stated 'the American public may have been reluctant to bestow the mantle of "professionalization" on a group of people who worked with the dead'.[28] Yet to the industry professionalisation is viewed as one of the key techniques in overcoming stigmatisation, or of 'doing death work'.[29]

The claim for professional status appears to take two dimensions. First, the role of the funeral director is re-emphasised as a caregiver to the living and is therefore distanced from the dead. Secondly, the adoption and practice of the craft of embalming is seen as a foundation for the claim of professional respectability. Thompson further argues that role-distancing, redefinition of work and cloaking in a 'shroud of service' are other methods for achieving this objective.[30] The utilisation of both of these stigma-alleviating devices will be considered below.

---

[26]Harrah B.K. and Harrah D.F. (1976) *Funeral Service: A Bibliography*, Metuchen: The Scarecrow Press, p. xi.
[27]Kearl M.C. (1989) *Endings: A Sociology of Death and Dying*, Oxford: Oxford University Press, p. 278.
[28]Farrell J.J. (1980) *Inventing the American Way of Death 1830–1920*, Philadelphia: Temple University Press, p. 155.
[29]Pine V.R. (1975) *Caretaker of the Dead: The American Funeral Director*, New York: Irvington, p. 28.
[30]Thompson W.E. (1991) 'Handling the Stigma of Handling the Dead: Morticians and Funeral Directors', *Deviant Behaviour: An Interdisciplinary Journal*, Vol. 12, p. 421.

Occupational Stigmatisation: Profit from Loss?

In the agreement negotiated between the bereaved and the funeral director a coffin, along with services and use of facilities, is purchased as part of a commercial contract.[31] In this transaction as in most business activities the price charged covers overheads in addition to a margin of profit. It is, however, in the context of funeral directing that the notion arises that profits are gained from the misfortune of others. In his research among American funeral directors, Thompson found the following general opinion prevalent among interviewees:

> Many of the funeral directors... believed the major reason for negative public feelings towards their occupation was not only that they handled dead bodies, but the fact that they made their living off the dead, or at least, off the grief of the living.[32]

From the perspective of the bereaved it is possible to see how funeral directors can be accused of profiteering from their loss, and three strands can be highlighted. First, the provision of a funeral can be identified as a seldom welcome, but inevitable service. As Brown notes: 'There is no doubt in our minds that it is appropriate to deal with these things – but they are not things any one wants. They are a service, which as you know, people would rather not have to call upon.'[33]

From this statement a number of observations can be made. It is possible to discern that the funeral director operates in a market with a seemingly endless source of supply; death will always occur and funerals will always be required. While this notion does not recognise the fact that funeral firms are subject to commercial influences including competitive and demographic, in the immediate stage of loss such rationality is probably far removed from those entering into a contract for a funeral. The second observation is that the funeral director occupies a monopoly position, not necessarily in a competitive sense but because to most prospective purchasers it is not perceived feasible to circumnavigate use of

---

[31]Parsons B. (2003) 'Conflict in the Context of Care: An Examination of Role Conflict between the Bereaved and the Funeral Director in the UK', *Mortality*, Vol. 8, No. 1, pp. 67–87.
[32]Thompson W.E. (1991) 'Handling the Stigma of Handling the Dead: Morticians and Funeral Directors', *Deviant Behaviour: An Interdisciplinary Journal*, Vol. 12, p. 422.
[33]Brown C. (1995) 'Funerals – The Consumers' Perspective', *Pharos International*, Vol. 61, No. 4, p. 162.

their service. Although self-managed funerals are a possible alternative, for most it is not a realistic option as few are willing or able to undertake comparable tasks at a time of bereavement. While sourcing a coffin and securing appropriate transport are feasible, the issue of body-handling and storage can be a deterrent. A YouGov survey carried out in 2015 by the NAFD and Cruse Bereavement Care revealed that only 8 per cent of Britons would be likely to arrange a funeral themselves rather than go through a funeral director.[34] Lastly, selecting the service of a funeral director is not something that people usually shop around for, unlike consumer durables or other services.[35] Although there is anecdotal evidence to suggest that this is increasing, the perceived need not to delay the funeral, the notion that 'it is not the done thing' and the 'distress purchase' element are largely responsible for the reticence to contact different funeral directors. Although some clients do price match in person, on the phone or using websites, it can equally be argued that the vast majority would not wish to shop around as evidence indicates that they return to a funeral director with whom they have had a satisfactory experience in the past or utilise the services of one they have been recommended. Of the 73,500 funerals during 2015 by Dignity PLC, 92 per cent of their clients only approached one funeral director, while 72 per cent chose their funeral director based on personal experience or recommendation.[36]

In 2016, shopping around was actively promoted in the Fair Funerals Pledge launched by Quaker Social Action.[37] While it is too early to comment on its effectiveness, the encouragement for funeral directors to place their charges online, along with the creation of funeral comparison websites, indicates that there is transparency in pricing in at least a proportion of funeral directors. Evidence would suggest, however, that price is not the only criterion for selection when prospective clients obtain alternative quotes; the manner in which the enquiry is dealt with, the degree of empathy and sensitivity and ownership have also been cited.[38]

The second point is the nature of 'hidden' funeral costs. The vast majority of tasks carried out by the funeral director, such as body-handling,

---

[34] 'Funerals Matter. How the British Public Views the Funeral Profession in 2016' (2016) NAFD/Cruse Bereavement Care, p. 4
[35] Brown C. (1995) 'Funerals – The Consumers' Perspective', *Pharos International*, Vol. 61, No. 4, p. 162.
[36] *Dignity PLC Annual Report and Accounts 2015*, p. 6. www.dignityfunerals.co.uk. (Accessed 2 September 2016).
[37] www.quakersocialaction.org.uk (Accessed 5 September 2016).
[38] Brown C. (1995) 'Funerals – The Consumers' Perspective', *Pharos International*, Vol. 61, No. 4, pp. 162–166. See also 'Funerals Matter. How the British Public Views the Funeral Profession in 2016' (2016), NAFD/Cruse Bereavement Care, p. 8.

coffin preparation, administration and liaising with third parties, are not witnessed by the client. Effectively, they are paying the funeral director to not be exposed to these functions. This lack of 'dramatic realisation' results in a situation where a service purchaser may not be fully aware of what is actually involved and thus how and where the funeral director's charges are being spent.[39] The many, particularly cadaver-related, tasks are completed in non-public areas of the premises, often in an environment where there has been a high level of investment along with running costs. Irving Goffman expresses the dilemma: 'the proprietor of a service establishment may find it difficult to dramatize what is actually being done for clients because the clients cannot actually "see" the overhead costs of the service rendered them'.[40]

Addressing issues, handling queries and finalising details may take several days, but the actual funeral ceremony is completed within an hour and a half. Although Hodgson points to the fact that the average funeral takes about 40 hours to complete, it is of little surprise to find statements such as 'the public's great misconception that making several hundred pounds is not bad for a couple of hours' work'.[41] It is somewhat ironic that the NAFD's public relations film produced in the 1980s was entitled *An Hour on the Day.*

However, as funerals are often purchased under an 'inclusive charge' tariff, due to the varying complexity of preparation and involvement with some funerals it could be argued that some clients pay for services not utilised. Nevertheless, due to the unpredictable nature of the service funeral directors are obliged to have facilities and staff in readiness. Lastly, there is the nature of the purchase itself. The funeral is a 'distress purchase *in extremis*.'[42] As an advocate for consumer rights, Brown sees the interaction as a purchase quite unlike other consumer transactions: 'the bereaved are likely to be completely unfamiliar with the market; they think it is distasteful to argue about money in the circumstances; they will have no idea about what their rights are and what to expect'.[43]

---

[39] Goffman E. (1959) *The Presentation of Self in Everyday Life,* Harmondsworth: Penguin, p. 40.
[40] *Ibid.*, p. 4. Berridge articulates this situation as 'The undertaker's riddle': 'The man that makes it doesn't want it, the man that buys it has no use for it, the man that's in it doesn't see it'. See Berridge K. (2002) 'Coffin Fits', *The Spectator*, 9 November, pp. 72–73.
[41] Hodgson H.O.P. (1992) *How to Become Dead Rich,* London: Pavilion, p. 97.
[42] Brown C. (1995) 'Funerals – The Consumers' Perspective', *Pharos International,* Vol. 61, No. 4, p. 163.
[43] *Ibid.*

In contrast to other contracts it can be seen that the purchaser of this service occupies a position of inequality: 'in the relationship between the funeral director and client, the former has a marked psychological and commercial advantage, so that the balance of bargaining power is tilted in his favour'.[44]

Youngson expresses this more forcefully:

> The funeral director is engaged in a business for profit and, like all businessmen, aims to make as large a profit as possible ... the director has a unique psychological advantage over you. Your resistance is low. You may be shocked out of your normal disturbance of judgement so far as matters connected with your loved one are concerned. The experience of the ages has shown that when people have this sort of power over others, there is a strong tendency for it to corrupt. The director is certainly entitled to a fair profit, but he is not entitled to manipulate you ruinously for his advantage.[45]

Kübler-Ross suggests that funeral directors may take advantage of the guilt experienced by the bereaved as a result of loss 'in order to commercialise their products and to have greater profits in their business'.[46] As previously pointed out, like many such statements, no evidence is offered to underpin this allegation. Indeed, it may be that expenditure on the funeral helps resolve the feelings of guilt.[47] As one widower stated, 'Her death left unfinished business between us and it comforted me to spend more than I could afford on the funeral.'[48] Thus without influence from the funeral director the bereaved may commit themselves to purchasing services beyond their means. From a commercial perspective the encouragement of overspending, whether induced or not, is of no advantage to the funeral director; in the short term it may well lead to a bad debt while risk of loss of reputation or the decline of future usage also arises.[49]

---

[44]*Funeral Charges* (1997) Price Commission Report No. 22, p. 37.
[45]Youngson R.M. (1989) *Grief: Rebuilding Your Life After Bereavement,* Newton Abbot: David & Charles, p. 120.
[46]Kübler-Ross E. (1974) *Questions and Answers on Death and Dying,* New York: Collier Books, p. 102.
[47]Pine V.R. and Phillips D.L. (1970) 'The Cost of Dying: A Sociological Analysis of Funeral Expenditures', *Social Problems,* winter, pp. 405–417.
[48]Taylor C. (1979) 'The Funeral Industry', in H. Wass ed., *Dying: Facing the Facts,* Washington DC: Hemisphere, p. 379.
[49]Bradbury M. (1999) *Representations of Death: A Social Psychological Perspective,* London: Routledge, p. 74.

Although performance-related pay, such as coffin commission, could benefit both employer and employee, they are not strategies utilised by Dignity, the Co-operative Funeralcare or the vast majority of independent or family-run funeral businesses.

From one perspective, it could be argued that as funeral firms have considerable client loyalty, the opportunity exists for exploitation through the inflation of prices in the knowledge that the bereaved will not make comparisons and thus possess a yardstick to measure overcharging. This was an argument put forward by the 2001 report issued by the Office of Fair Trading, but it offered no evidence to support this claim.[50]

In respect of professional status and profits, such a situation raises the issue of manipulation for gain. Johnson notes that such a consideration occupies second place for true professions. He states, 'The professional performs his services primarily for the psychic satisfactions and secondarily for the monetary compensations.'[51]

Although the issue of making a profit from funerals could be considered a problem for funeral firms of all types, it can be argued that it is a greater dilemma for organisations with shareholders to satisfy. As Chapter 6 revealed, there was much adverse reaction to the presence of SCI in the UK market, resulting in debate over the issue of the retention of trading names and the alleged 'Americanisation' of funeral service, in addition to the belief that SCI's investment must yield a favourable return. This gave rise to concerns over sales tactics and growth policies. While researchers such as Smale may state that British funeral directing businesses are 'dedicated to commercial profitability', evidence supporting allegations of manipulation and overcharging are absent from the rhetoric.[52]

Professionalisation in Practice

The perception of an occupation as a profession is ultimately judged by those coming into contact with it in addition to society at large. In the same way that a single definition does not exist, neither does the existence

---

[50] *Funerals* (2001) London: Office of Fair Trading, p. 9.
[51] Johnson A. (1944) 'Professional Standards and How They Are Obtained', *Journal of American Dental Association,* No. 3, September, pp. 1181–1189.
[52] Smale B. (1977) 'The Social Construction of Funerals in Britain', in K. Charmaz, G. Howarth and A. Kellehear eds, *The Unknown Country: Death in Australia, Britain and the USA,* Basingstoke: Macmillan, pp. 125–126.

of one route to the goal of professionalisation. This section considers ways in which the occupation has attempted to acquire professional status. Seven areas are discussed: the formation and role of occupational associations; registration; education; codes of practice; presentational changes: language, dress and premises; change in occupational title and role redefinition and finally, public image. As the previous section outlined, stigmatisation is the key area that the occupation has sought to address and correspondingly many of the strategies are concerned with this issue.

The Occupational Association

The formation of an association contributes in a major way to the process of professionalisation. Following its establishment, the organisation then pursues a change of name or occupational description, the construction of a code of ethics and political agitation for legal constraints on who may or may not perform a service. The regulation and education of practitioners then follows. As will be seen below, there were two attempts at registration, with the most significant event being in 1935 when the BUA ceased to be a trade union while also changing its name to the NAFD. This new identity effectively repositioned the occupation by emphasising the 'directional' function rather than simply 'undertaking' funeral instructions.[53] Its objectives also became more focused:

> To secure state registration of funeral directors; to protect its members in the proper conduct of their business and to deal with all matters affecting their interests; to afford facilities for intercourse among members, and for the collection and dissemination of useful information; to secure a definite standard of qualification for all who seek to practise (sic) as funeral directors and the recognition of a code of professional conduct.[54]

---

[53]This took effect on 1 November 1935. See 'Editorial: The Reorganization of the BUA' (1935) *TUJ*, February, pp. 55–56; 'Draft Rules: National Association of Funeral Directors' (1935) *TUJ*, July, pp. 218–222; 'Editorial. The New Machine' (1935) *TUJ*, July, pp. 231–232; 'Editorial: What's in a Name?' (1935) *TUJ*, October, pp. 335–336; and Perritt J.D. (1935) 'The National Association of Funeral Directors. The National President on the New Constitution', *TUJ*, November, p. 371.
[54]'British Undertakers' Association. National Executive and Reorganization' (1935) *TUJ*, March, pp. 75–76.

Membership of the NAFD is voluntary and entirely corporate as it represents the interests of those owning funeral-directing organisations rather than individual funeral directors. The association can discipline members, including expulsion. This does not, however, prevent them from operating as funeral directors. It seeks to improve the image of member funeral directors through its public relations function and parliamentary representation. It issues press releases, comments on incidents and investigates complaints against members. It also publishes a monthly periodical, arranges an annual conference at which a president is appointed and operates a code of practice. At local level and now only in a few geographic areas it is also involved in collective bargaining. The NAFD also examines and awards the Diploma in Funeral Arranging and Administration and the Diploma in Funeral Directing.

The National Society of Allied and Independent Funeral Directors (SAIF) has parallels with the NAFD, but as its name suggests represents only the interests of funeral directing firms not owned by the larger organisations, such as the Co-operative societies or Dignity. Its date of establishment is significant on account of the changing structure of the industry: the late 1980s. SAIF operates in exactly the same manner as the NAFD. It maintains a code of practice similar in scope to the NAFD's code, runs an educational programme through the IFD College and membership is entirely voluntary.

Individual funeral directors who possess the NAFD Diploma in Funeral Directing (and other qualifications such as NVQ, BTEC and overseas credentials) may join the British Institute of Funeral Directors (BIFD).[55] Founded in 1981, it is a multi-grade qualifying association offering the following post-nominals: MBIFD, FBIFD and hon MBIFD (there being no student category). The BIFD holds business/educational meetings, publishes a journal, organises and awards its own qualifications and awards membership certificates. Reflecting its individual rather than corporate membership, the BIFD possesses a Code of Ethics to which all members are obliged to adhere. Its clauses include personal integrity and care for the dead. The BIFD also issues a licence to members who have completed 12 hours of continuing professional education (CPD) in a one-year period, but this is a voluntary requirement.

The British Institute of Embalmers (BIE) was formed in 1927 after the BES, being part of BUA, had become a trade union. The BIE is a qualifying association with the International Examinations Board of Embalmers (IEBE), administering entrance examinations. It has grades

---

[55] Liddell C. (2007) '25 Years with the BIFD', *The BIFD Journal,* Vol. 21, No. 1, pp. 22–25.

of membership for students, honorary members, full members and fellows. Like the BIFD, the BIE has a Code of Ethics, which comprises five clauses, such as a belief in the objectives of embalming, confidentiality, respect of the dead, etc. Of note is that at the presentation of certificates to newly qualified embalmers the Code of Ethics is repeated by all present at the ceremony, thus reaffirming individual members' allegiance to professional standards.

The above four organisations each represent a different sector within the industry, be it individual or corporate. Each has differing entry requirements and inevitably in such a small sphere there is a degree of overlap. For example, many firms are members of the NAFD and SAIF while a number of individuals are members of both BIE and BIFD; a business owner could be in all four. Although all organisations have the power to discipline or suspend from membership, the fact remains that membership of any of the above four groups is voluntary. Individuals may practise as funeral directors and/or embalmers without any experience or qualification and also continue to operate after expulsion. Thus self-control has its limitations. Nevertheless, each occupational organisation strives to proclaim its presence by encouraging firms or individuals to embrace membership and through the means of distinguishing between members and non-members, for example by the display of logos, letters of affiliation and the code of practice. To the public these act as proof of the firm and/or individual's commitment to a professional ideal and the desire for its occupational profile to be reassessed.

Registration

The registration of funeral directors has been an objective of the BUA/NAFD since 1905. It has been debated on numerous occasions in addition to two serious attempts to establish a scheme for achieving this status, but to no avail. After disappearing from the agenda it has re-emerged through the Burial and Cremation (Scotland) Act 2016.[56]

Prior to the BUA there is evidence to indicate that this subject occupied the minds of a number of undertakers; an editorial in the *TUJ* in May 1898 asked why, if registration was achievable in the United States, it was not here. The point was made that sanitary knowledge was essential to

---

[56]A review of registration attempts is contained in 'President Robb's Fascinating Story of the Organisation of the Funeral Industry' (1955) *FSJ*, May, pp. 230–233.

professional furtherance.[57] This became the thrust of a draft registration bill published in May 1922, but never progressed.[58] Two years later a more detailed document appeared, but was soon withdrawn.[59] In 1928–1929 the BUA formed a registration committee, while conferences on registration were held in February and April 1929.[60] At this stage it was estimated that there were 10,000 undertakers in Britain with 4,000 being members of the BUA.

The most important attempt at registration was in the 1930s under the aegis of the president of the Cremation Society of Great Britain, Lord Horder. He urged a link between doctors, undertakers and other disposal-related stakeholders through the National Council for the Disposition of the Dead.[61] Lord Horder presented his Funeral Directors (Registration) Bill to the House of Lords on 2 June 1938.[62] He said that funeral directors who could conform to examination requirements would be registered under a statutory board, the chairman of which should be appointed by the Minister of Health. Lord Strabolgi countered this by arguing that registration would lead to a monopoly situation ('a closed corporation') and increase the cost of funerals. The bill was defeated. The NAFD said they would welcome a governmental inquiry as a result of the introduction of the Funeral Directors (Registration) Bill.[63] Wilson and Levy simply believed that the NCDD would create a 'trade cartel'.[64]

With the intervention of World War II, it was not until the 1950s that the issue re-emerged, with NAFD exploring the registration of

---

[57]'Editorial: Registration' (1898) *TUJ*, May, p. 76.
[58]'Registration' (1922) *BUA Monthly*, May, pp. 250–251.
[59]*Hansard*, 14 May 1924, col. 2200. See also 'Thoughts on the Registration Bill' (1925) *TUJ*, May, pp. 169–170 and Nodes H.K. (1925) 'State Registration', *BUA Monthly*, August, pp. 36–39.
[60]'State Registration Conference. Joint Meeting in London' (1930) *BUA Monthly*, March, pp. 200–211 and 'State Registration Conference. Report of Proceedings of Second Meeting' (1929) *BUA Monthly*, May, pp. 259–263.
[61]'Important Medical Support of the Undertaker. Lord Horder's Statement' (1933) *BUA Monthly*, August, p. 41. See also Jupp P.C. (2008a) 'The Council for the Disposition of the Dead 1931–1939', *FSJ*, July, pp. 103–106.
[62]'Funeral Directors (Registration) Bill' (1938) House of Lords, Debates, 2 June, cols 853–866 and 'Registration of Undertakers' (1938) *TUFDJ*, June, pp. 213–214. See also 'Registration Bill Prospects' (1938) *TUFDJ*, May, p. 179 and Jupp, P.C. (2006) *From Dust to Ashes: Cremation and the British Way of Death,* Basingstoke: Palgrave Macmillan, pp. 114–119.
[63]'Funeral Directors (Registration) Bill' (1939) *TNFD*, May, p. 432.
[64]Wilson A. and Levy H. (1938) *Burial Reform and Funeral Costs,* Oxford: Oxford University Press, p. 176.

embalmers.[65] One critic suggested that it would lead to the state control of funerals and the prohibition of embalming at home. The matter progressed no further.[66] As indicated in Chapter 7, by this time other aspects of control were affecting the funeral industry. While municipalisation and nationalisation had been dropped, the voluntary agreement to supply a basic funeral for £20 had taken effect in 1949. It was clear that while the industry was interested in registration to elevate its status, the external objective was to control funeral costs.

Despite these attempts the issue of registration has been discussed on a number of occasions since the failed NCDD Bill, for example, by the National Union of Funeral and Cemetery Workers in 1968,[67] at the NAFD Conference in 1969,[68] exploration of Royal Charter status in 1980[69] and for embalmers,[70] while individual registration was suggested by the BIFD.[71] Soon after their arrival in the United Kingdom in the 1990s SCI produced a document promoting the registration of all funeral businesses; SCI would have been familiar with such control as they operated in parts of the world where registration was mandatory.[72] When the Office of Fair Trading investigated the funeral industry in 2001, 81 per cent of those completing a survey recommended the statutory licensing of all funeral directors' premises, while 68 per cent said that this should only apply to individuals.[73]

Following publication of the *Report of the Infant Cremation Commission* (2014), the Burial and Cremation (Scotland) Act 2016 contained a paragraph giving authority for the licensing of funeral directors. At this

---

[65]'Embalmers Joint Committee' (1953) *FSJ*, November, p. 516; 'Registration – A Step Forward' (1954) *FSJ*, May, pp. 203–204; and 'BES Digest' (1953) *TFD*, December, p. 240.

[66]Swainson E. (1955) 'Save Us From Registration! "The Spider's Webb"', *FSJ*, March, pp. 108–109. The National Union of Funeral and Cemetery Workers appeared to support registration. See 'Include Us in Registration Negotiations' (1955) *FSJ*, September, pp. 430–434 and 'NAFD Delegates Vote against Registration' (1954) *FSJ*, June, pp. 255–257.

[67]'On the State Registration of Funeral Directors' (1968) *FSJ*, March, pp. 125–126. See also 'FTATU Seeks Registration and Plans 'Fair List'' (1980) *FSJ*, September, pp. 377–378.

[68]Buckland M. (1969) 'Registration for Funeral Directors', *TFD*, pp. 366–386.

[69]'Preparing Ground for Royal Charter Application' (1980) *FSJ*, May, pp. 203–204.

[70]'Report from the Sub-Committee on Official Registration and Recognition', *The Embalmer*, Vol. 29, No. 3, pp. 13–14.

[71]Moar D. (1997) 'Registration of Funeral Directors', *FSJ*, June, p. 40.

[72]'A Glimpse into the Future' (1997) *FSJ*, December, pp. 48–54.

[73]*Funerals* (2001) London: Office of Fair Trading, p. 5.

stage it is unclear what form this will take, but the legislation refers to the holding of personal license, presumably based on qualification.[74]

Around this time the NAFD/Cruse Bereavement Care YouGov survey indicated that the regulation of the funeral sector was preferred by 42 per cent of UK adults.[75] However, at the NAFD conference in 2016, members voted for self-regulation in contrast to external regulation.[76] At the time of writing (May 2017), many funeral directors believe that the regulation of colleagues in Scotland will be adopted in the remainder of the United Kingdom.

Education

Although training for embalmers has existed since the early years of the twentieth century, failure to secure registration presented the NAFD with the opportunity to refocus its aspirations by improving status through education. As the previous section highlighted, it was the absence of structured training and a qualification that was a stumbling block to achieving professional status through registration. However, as this analysis reveals, the industry was hindered by slow progress and it was not until 1959 that a qualification for funeral directors became available. In this respect the UK differs from America, where state licensing requires practitioners to possess sanitary and funeral-related training before interaction with clients.[77]

Education does provide an important opportunity in the professionalisation process through the display of post-nominal letters such as Dip FD or MBIE. In respect of funeral directors in Belfast, Prior notes their keenness to 'be perceived as professionals' and that in doing so they 'often pin certificates of competence and qualification on the walls of their offices, much as an optician, a dental surgeon or a pharmacist might do'.[78]

---

[74] Burial and Cremation (Scotland) Act 2016, Part 5, Section 94, Clauses 1–3. http://www.legislation.gov.uk/asp/2016/20/pdfs/asp_20160020_en.pdf. (Accessed 5 September 2016).
[75] 'Funerals Matter. How the British Public Views the Funeral Profession in 2016' (2016) NAFD/Cruse Bereavement Care, p. 11.
[76] 'NAFD Conference 2016' (2016) *FDM*, June, p. 18.
[77] For a contemporary assessment of funeral service education in the US see Flory D. (2008) 'Education and the Business of Funeral Service', *The Director*, Vol. 80, No. 4, pp. 46–51.
[78] Prior L. (1989) *The Social Organization of Death: Medical Discourse and Social Practices in Belfast,* Basingstoke: Macmillan, p. 160.

Recognition of the importance of education for the funeral sector became increasingly important following the founding of the BIE in 1927 and the promotion of its membership diploma. Support came from surprising sources. In 1929, the *BUA Monthly* reproduced a letter published in *Town and Country News*:

> How many people recognise to-day that by engaging unqualified undertakers they open up possibilities of serious risk?... Were State Registration introduced, the public would be able to enjoy the confidence that only the expert and qualified men could be engaged in the work; there would be closer co-operation between the medical profession and the undertakers, with the result that the latter would know what precautions were necessary with regard to the living and the dead.[79]

However, despite the registration attempts, there was still no consensus on education. In 1937, the BUA started an educational campaign to encourage funeral directors to enrol on their courses in sanitation.[80] Just before World War II the suggestion of a national college of embalming was tabled.[81] Little activity took place during World War II with the exception of a conference paper given in 1943 by Florence Hurry entitled 'A Wider Outlook' in which she said that funeral service education must not be exclusive to embalmers.[82] In January 1946, the NAFD announced the launch of a college with an educational programme consisting of book-keeping, business organisations, burial law, coroner's law, registration, workmen's compensation, public liability, life assurance, transport management, public relations and then embalming.[83] The college did not open, but these subjects formed the basis of the *Study Notes* published in 1948. The London association made possession of the qualification as a

---

[79]'State Registration of Undertakers. Facts the Public Must Face' (1929) *BUA Monthly*, April, p. 240.
[80]Advertisement 'Educational Campaign' (1937) *TNFD*, January, p. 149. See also 'Examination Results' (1938) *TNFD*, July, p. 13.
[81]'What about a Real National C of E?' (1939) *TNFD*, January, pp. 269–270.
[82]Hurry F.D. (1943) 'A Wider Outlook', *TNFD*, August, pp. 74–75. This paper parallels with the one from twelve years earlier by W. Swainson. See Swainson W.E. (1931) 'Review of the British Undertakers' Association Activities with Special Reference to Education', *TUJ*, December, pp. 397–399.
[83]Dodgson W. (1946) 'New Education Programme Outlined', *TNFD*, May, p. 439.

condition of membership.[84] The capital's activity stimulated the NAFD to instigate a national qualification taught through study groups and the Diploma in Funeral Directing (Dip FD) was first examined in 1959.[85] Possession of the Diploma then became a criterion of NAFD membership until 1983.[86]

The Diploma in Funeral Directing together with membership by examination of the BIE gave the industry two distinct qualifications. Both schemes of study centred around possession of technical knowledge and in respect of embalming, its practical application. However, they lacked theoretical content; Bernard Smale comments somewhat antagonistically: 'No matter how prestigious their Diploma appears to be to the uninitiated, it is in fact lacking any high degree of technical, theoretical or specialized contents.'[87] To a limited extent, this was addressed in the 1990s when a higher diploma was introduced containing basic managerial content, although this only ran for a short period.

In line with wider changes in training qualifications to embrace different learning styles, NVQ and BTEC were introduced in the 1990s, but with limited uptake.[88] Some firms have acquired 'Investors in Industry' awards while a few firms have acquired a British Standards Institution number in recognition of their standard of service to the public.[89] The latter demonstrate a keenness to be perceived alongside other organisations with this accreditation in addition to utilisation of a mainstream business device that is gaining in recognition.

An important development occurred when two foundation degrees were launched in 2008: 'mortuary science' by the University of Chester

---

[84]'London' (1947) *TNFD*, April, p. 285. See also 'London Examinations' (1948) *TNFD*, January, p. 265.
[85]'Looking to the Future' (1956) *TFD*, June, pp. 120–121 and 'NAFD Notes: The First Examination' (1959) *FSJ*, January, pp. 14–15.
[86]'Diploma No Longer to be NAFD Membership Requirement' (1983) *FSJ*, June, p. 257.
[87]Smale B. (1985) *Deathwork: A Sociological Analysis of Funeral Directing*, Unpublished PhD thesis, University of Sussex, p. 189.
[88]Hutsby B. (1992) 'The NAFD Diploma in Funeral Directing – Its Future', *TFD*, August, pp. 14–15; May G.C. (1992) 'Education and Training in the Funeral Industry', *TFD*, November, pp. 20–21; Elliott A. (1994) 'Westminster Seminar Outlines National Vocational Qualifications', *FSJ*, August, pp. 67–71; Maddaford A. (1995) 'Education – Into the Next Millennium', *TFD*, November, pp. 21–29; and Holland R. (1995) 'NVQ/SVQs in Funeral Service', *TFD*, November, pp. 30–31.
[89]Pattison A. (1995) 'Quality Systems for Funeral Services – The Reality', *FSJ*, February, pp. 54–61.

and 'funeral service' by the University of Bath.[90] Evidence that the industry was heading towards a degree can be traced back to 1982.[91] However, as with the suggestion of a university chair for embalming, the idea made little headway.[92] The availability of such courses has placed the industry on a new level for the following reasons. First, prior to these being offered, preparation for industry qualifications was provided by funeral directors and embalmers who possessed industry-awarded teaching certificates. Few had external qualifications or teaching experience. The foundation degrees have removed assessment away from the industry and place it within established examination frameworks, enabling the degrees to be benchmarked against other national awards. Secondly, university-run courses have not replaced existing technical courses but supplemented learning by broadening the range of subjects to which students are exposed. For example, the social context of death was included in Bath's course. Thirdly, that universities are willing to embrace such courses indicates that death studies are becoming mainstream. Fourthly, although differing in content and duration, the courses can be paralleled with American funeral service educational programmes. In this respect the United Kingdom can be seen to be mirroring the pattern of progress in a country that has been influential on funeral directing in respect of introducing embalming and the funeral home in addition to the 'service culture'. Both foundation degree programmes were closed in 2012.

As the above indicates, while training in embalming has existed since 1900, it was not until the 1950s that any education for funeral directors became available. This latter development recognised the increasing complexity of funerals. However, possession of qualifications is voluntary and enquiries indicate that they are not held by the vast majority of funeral arrangers/directors.[93] This reflects not only how some funeral directors view the necessity of education, but also the unwillingness of the industry to consult or recruit external education specialists to assist them in the task. The complexity and cost of the existing qualifications may also be

---

[90]'Country's First-Ever Mortuary Science Degree Begins' (2008) *The Embalmer*, Vol. 51, No. 1, p. 15 and 'Foundation Degree Underway at the University of Bath' (2008) *TFD*, October, pp. 10–11.
[91]'Degree Course within 3 Years?' (1982) *FSJ*, June, pp. 245–246. This was probably at an unidentified Yorkshire polytechnic referred to by G.F. Rose in his report to the BIE Conference See. 'Education' (1982) *The Embalmer*, Vol. 25, No. 1, p. 9.
[92]'University Chair' (2001) *The Embalmer*, Vol. 44, No. 3, pp. 18–19.
[93]For a general survey of this matter see Parsons B. (2002) 'Funeral Service Education in England', *The Director*, Vol. 74, No. 4, pp. 34–38.

an issue in addition to the fact that large organisations have their own in-house training programmes.

Code of Ethics/Code of Practice

Adherence to a code is the benchmark of any profession. Although a code of ethics has existed for over 100 years, it was not until 1979 that the NAFD's Code of Practice came to prominence. The 1907 code contained clauses such as dealing with infectious cases, the etiquette when two undertakers were called to a house, confidentiality and newspaper advertising; it was heavily influenced by an American document devised in 1889.[94] Touting was expressly prohibited.[95] However, the code was given little promotion and there are few references to its existence over the next 25 years. The BUA Code was relaunched in 1928 and condensed 'ideals of service' into nine points, but again it received little publicity.[96] It was, however, not until 1969, when professional standards were discussed at the NAFD conference, that the matter gathered ground.[97] The following year a 'Code of Conduct' was approved that covered confidentiality; advertising; conduct; solicitation; exploitation; minimum-price funerals; relations with other funeral directors; discipline and a complaints procedure.[98] These components formed the basis of the Code of Practice formulated in conjunction with the Office of Fair Trading, which was launched in March 1979.[99] The code has been amended since this time, with the most fundamental change occurring in 2014 when members of the NAFD voted to remove the basic simple funeral specification.

As indicated in Chapter 7, there have been criticisms that members do not always adhere to the code. Although the OFT no longer endorses the code, it continues to be widely promoted by the NAFD as a benchmark

---

[94]'Code of Ethics' (1907) *TUJ*, July, p. 168 and 'Code of Ethics' (1908) *TUJ*, July, p. 154. For the American code see 'A Code of Ethics for Undertakers' (1905) *TUJ*, July, p. 168.
[95]'Notes' (1905) *TUJ*, January, p. 1.
[96]'National Introductory Address' (1928) *BUA Monthly*, March, p. 198. This first appeared the previous year, 'Suggested National Address' (1927) *BUA Monthly*, January, p. 136.
[97]Robinson R. (1969) 'Professional Conduct', *FSJ*, July, pp. 354–360.
[98]'Code of Conduct' (1970) *FSJ*, June, pp. 306–311. See also 'Letter: How Lambeth Contract Operates (from E.E. Field)' (1986) *FSJ*, April, p. 129.
[99]'Funeral Code Will Help Those Under Stress' (1979) *FSJ*, April, pp. 153–154 and 'NAFD Code of Practice on Funerals' (1979) *FSJ*, May, pp. 211–217.

for standards.[100] With the fragmentation of the industry in the 1990s, other codes emerged such as those of the FSC (which no longer operates) and SAIF.[101] The former Funeral Ombudsman, along with others, have called for a single code of practice, but the industry continues to be served by the NAFD and SAIF codes, being similar in scope.[102] It is possible, however, that one code will emerge as a result of the Burial and Cremation (Scotland) Act.

Presentational Changes

Stimulated by the quest for professional status has been the change in language, dress, conduct and premises. It is the 'competence of actions and believability in performance' achieved by the use of appropriate vocabulary that is necessary for an aspiring profession.[103] Thompson notes, 'A rose by any other name may smell as sweet, but death work by almost any other name does not sound quite as harsh'.[104] Terms that primarily contain body-related words are dealt with through symbolically negating the language.[105] Avoidance of death-related phrases or words is a hallmark.[106] It is in interaction with clients that the noticeable adjustments to

---

[100] 'OFT's Report on the Funeral Business' (1989) *FSJ*, February, pp. 20–21; 'John Lodge hits out at OFT' (1989) *FSJ*, June, p. 11; and 'Funeral Costs', *Hansard*, 6 February 1989, cols 776–782.
[101] 'The FSC is very much here to stay' (1993) *FSJ*, December, pp. 29–33.
[102] 'Redress and the Funeral Profession' (2000) *FSJ*, January, pp. 67–70.
[103] Unruh D.R. (1979) 'Doing Funeral Directing: Managing Sources of Risk in Funeralization', *Urban Life*, Vol. 8, No. 2, pp. 247–263. See also Unruh D.R. (1976) 'The Funeralization Process: Towards a Model of Social Time', *Mid-American Review of Sociology*, Vol. 1, No. 1, pp. 9–25; Barley S.R. (1980) 'Taking the Burdens: The Strategic Role of the Funeral Director', Working Paper, Alfred P. Sloan School of Management; and Barley S.R. (1983) The Codes of the Dead. The Semiotics of Funeral Work', *Urban Life*, Vol. 12, No. 1, pp. 3–31.
[104] Thompson W.E. (1991) 'Handling the Stigma of Handling the Dead: Morticians and Funeral Directors', *Deviant Behaviour: An Interdisciplinary Journal*, Vol. 12, p. 412.
[105] *Ibid.* See 'Watch your Language' (1953) *FSJ*, June, p. 273. For an early American example see 'Modern Funeral Language' (1925) *BUA Monthly*, April, p. 271. See also 'Ante-Funeral Management. Some more "Observation by Observer"' (1923) *BUA Monthly*, March, p. 252.
[106] Thompson W.E. (1991) 'Handling the Stigma of Handling the Dead: Morticians and Funeral Directors', *Deviant Behaviour: An Interdisciplinary Journal*, Vol. 12, p. 412.

terminology can be detected. Metcalf and Huntington quote Kaut's findings of the use of death-related euphemisms when they state:

> these... may have less to do with the insecurities of the public over mortality than with the insecurities of the specialists over their professional status. These titles represent a desire to shake off their pallid public image and acquire more of the *éclat* of the medical profession.[107]

Although specifically referring to the American industry, Habenstein finds changes such as 'undertaker's parlour' to 'funeral home' and 'embalming' becoming 'preparation'.[108] Although both have been adopted in this country, others, such as 'vital statistics form' in place of 'death certificate', have so far escaped the vocabulary of British funeral directors.[109] Howarth believes that the language funeral directors speak 'is the language of altruism which constantly refers to public protection; willingness to serve; and the need for consumer trust.'[110] Certainly the objectives advanced for the application of embalming – presentation, preservation and sanitation – confirm the use of protectional terminology through emphasising the benefits.

Of an allied nature to the above in terms of presentation is the dress and appearance of the funeral director. Habenstein recognises the importance of image as created by clothing when he states: 'A "professional" funeral director simply should not, in common sense terms, look like the stereotypical truck driver, lawyer, or graduate student.'[111]

The increasing disinclination by society to wear black at funerals has been noted by Taylor and correspondingly this has been reflected in the apparel of some funeral personnel.[112] Many, however, continue to be

---

[107] Metcalf P. and Huntington R. (1991) *Celebrations of Death: The Anthropology of Mortuary Ritual,* second edition, Cambridge: Cambridge University Press, p. 201.
[108] Habenstein R.W. (1962) 'Sociology of Occupations: The Case of the American Funeral Director', in A.M. Rose ed., *Human Behaviour and Social Processes,* London: Routledge & Kegan Paul, p. 234.
[109] Bailey W. (1983) *Euphemisms and Other Double-Talk,* New York: Doubleday, p. 274.
[110] Howarth G. (1992) *The Funeral Industry in the East End of London: An Ethnographic Study,* Unpublished PhD thesis, University of London, p. 236.
[111] Habenstein R.W. (1962) 'Sociology of Occupations: The Case of the American Funeral Director', in A.M. Rose ed., *Human Behaviour and Social Processes,* London: Routledge & Kegan Paul, p. 234.
[112] Taylor L. (1983) *Mourning Dress: A Costume and Social History,* London: George Allen & Unwin.

adorned by a garment such as a mourning coat and also wear a top hat. Accessories such as flowing weepers [black fabric attached to top hats], associated with the nineteenth century, have attracted ridicule from some commentators.[113] For non-funeral attire the *Manual of Funeral Directing* encourages funeral directors to discard black as it represents 'the intrusion of death into a household' and to adopt 'A plain dark suit, clean and well pressed, such as many doctors and solicitors choose...'.[114] The latter indicates the industry's anxiety to be paralleled with the established professions. In confirmation of such change, all chauffeur bearers employed by Howard Hodgson in the 1990s were supplied with light grey suits along with silver and blue striped ties.

While conduct relating to business practices has been discussed above, it is in the area of personal behaviour where there has been increasing attention. Many of the articles that were published around the time the BUA was founded discuss essential attributes of a professional person. Writing in 1903, Albert Fay identified the qualities required when dealing with a family and also clergy.[115] Another talked of the funeral director behaving in a 'gentlemanly' manner, while warning against repeating 'any of those little confidings'.[116] Some years later George Ball included in his list of qualities that should be possessed by a funeral director as a personality quietness and confidence; clarity; observation; tact; reverence; watchfulness and service, while 'The Man in Charge' by G.O. Thompson, published in 1932, warned of criticising other funeral directors, and the need for 'worthiness' and 'integrity'.[117]

As outlined in Chapter 2, attempts at addressing the presentational image can be seen to have occurred through the reordering of funeral premises to create a comfortable, non-clinical and neutral atmosphere

---

[113]Cowling C. (2010a) *The Good Funeral Guide,* London: Continuum, p. 131 and Cowling C. (2010b) 'The Long Decline of the Victorian Funeral. Has It Had Its Day?' *FSJ*, March, pp. 84–87.
[114]*Manual of Funeral Directing* (2009) Solihull: NAFD, Ch. 18, p. 3.
[115]Fay A.W. (1903) 'Funeral Etiquette', *TUJ*, February, pp. 34–35.
[116]'Undertaking as a Profession' (1904) *TUJ*, August, p. 165. See also Broome J.C. (1904) 'The Modern Undertaker', *TUJ*, November, pp. 233–234. See also Richmond E.A. (1925) 'How the Undertaker Can Help the Clergy', *BUA Monthly*, April, pp. 256–257.
[117]Ball G. (1925) 'The Special Qualities Demanded for Undertaking', *BUA Monthly*, December, pp. 126–127 and Thompson G.O. (1932) 'The Man in Charge', *BUA Monthly*, January, pp. 154–155. See also 'The Importance and Privilege of Real Funeral Directing' (1942) *TNFD*, January, p. 234 and 'The Key to Funeral Directing' (1943) *TNFD*, June, pp. 460–461.

away from the perceived gloomy ambience of the nineteenth-century undertaking establishment. The policies of acquisition and subsequent rationalisation by the large organisations have contributed to this process as premises are often scaled-down and also modernised. The newly created branches have office and reception accommodation decorated in soft colour schemes, often pastel shades with floral motifs. The formal office composition comprising the desk separating the funeral director from the clients has been increasingly replaced by a boardroom table 'conference' style approach. Alternatively, a couch and easy chairs are provided. The term 'office' is often replaced with 'arrangement room', while 'funeral home' has become substituted by 'branch'. Worthy of note is the absence of religious symbolism in the public reception and window display areas, thus creating a neutral atmosphere in denominational terms, and stressing that funeral directors are anxious to serve all sections of the community irrespective of religious persuasion.

Change in Occupational Title and Role Redefinition

Although attempts to replace 'undertaker' with 'funeral director' can be traced to the early part of the twentieth century, it is the action of the occupational association to adopt this new identity that can be seen as a turning point in reinforcing this new identity. The purpose was to reflect the change from a craft-based trade to the management of a complex event.

Different titles to describe the undertaker were explored when the BUA was founded in 1905 (including a suggestion that the BUA be called the National Association of Funeral Directors, which it adopted 30 years later). While there is evidence to show that the term 'funeral director' was used extensively in the United States and to a lesser extent in Britain, it was not until 1921 that the matter was raised during a BUA conference. The speaker considered 'funeral director' not only more modern, but also more applicable; 'undertaker' was dated.[118] As noted above, those promoting the sanitary agenda in the 1920s and 1930s believed that the BUA was about organisation, education and legislation rather than trade union issues.[119] However, it would be 1932 before consideration was given by the BUA to renouncing its trade union status to become an incorporated

---

[118]'Undertaker or Funeral Directors?' (1921) *TUJ*, July, pp. 226–227.
[119]Cottridge A.J.E. (1926) 'The BUA Watchwords: Organisation, Education; Legislation', *BUA Monthly*, September, pp. 60–61.

institution, giving it the status of a professional association.[120] This change occurred in 1935 when the name National Association of Funeral Directors was adopted. The *NFD* noted in 1942 that the term 'undertaker' was increasingly obsolete and gave the example of telephone directories amending their classification to 'funeral directors'.[121]

Turner and Edgley view this change in occupational title as 'perhaps the largest single clue to the dramaturgical functions the industry now sees itself as performing'.[122] Adoption of 'funeral director' implies overseeing an event in which others participate, in contrast to 'undertaker', which sounds more task-orientated. Thus the change of description is significant in terms of date for two reasons. First, the 1930s witnessed increasing centralisation of funerals by some organisations (such as the larger Co-operative societies) and a restructuring of roles and secondly, the same period witnessed the acquisition of responsibility in terms of caring for the body. As Chapter 6 indicated, the large organisations utilise task fragmentation where staff function in predetermined spheres of competence. Funeral directors in centralised organisations literally represent what the new title implies: directing or overseeing the operation in contrast to physically 'undertaking' individual tasks. Thus the task of body-handling falls within the job description of the operational (chauffeur bearer/coffin fitter), while preservation and presentation is assigned to the embalmer. In pragmatic terms, the funeral director has become distanced from the dead body, the source of stigmatisation.[123]

Howarth suggests that funeral directors base their claim for professional status on the practice of embalming: 'It is the pseudo-scientific nature of the work such as embalming that forms the basis for the industry's claim to professional respectability…'.[124] This was recognised as early as 1911 by

---

[120]'The Question of Status' (1932) *BUA Monthly*, June, p. 279. See also Fletcher T. (1932) 'The Trade Union Status', *TUJ*, January, pp. 5–8 and 'Trade Union Status' (1931) *BUA Monthly*, December, pp. 127–129.

[121]'Let's Bury "Undertaker"' (1942) *TNFD*, January, p. 220.

[122]Turner R.E. and Edgley C. (1976) 'Death as Theatre: A Dramaturgical Analysis of the American Funeral', *Sociology and Social Research*, Vol. 60, No. 4, p. 384. See also Pine V.R. (1995) 'Public Behaviour in the Funeral Home', in J.B. Williamson and E.S. Schneidman eds, *Death: Current Perspectives*, fourth edition, Mountain View: Mayfield.

[123]Saunders K. (1988) 'The Profession of Embalmer – An Outsider's View'. *The Embalmer*, Vol. 31, No. 5, pp. 3–4. See also Saunders K. (1993) 'What are Embalmers Like? An Outsider's Attempt at Scientific Definition', *The Embalmer*, Vol. 36, No. 2, pp. 30–31.

[124]Howarth G. (1993a) 'Investigating Deathwork: A Personal Account', in D. Clark ed., *The Sociology of Death: Theory, Culture, Practice*, Oxford: Blackwell, p. 234.

H.K. Nodes, while in the post-war years when the number of embalmments were increasing George Lear commented that, 'It is through embalming and through embalming alone that the funeral director can develop…'.[125]

The relationship between embalming and professionalisation can be viewed from two perspectives. First, embalming transfers the source of stigmatisation away from the funeral director. By 'passing' the body to operational workers for handling, then to the embalmer for preservation, the funeral director is 'clean'.[126] This is particularly so in large organisations where contact is usually minimal, often confined to escorting clients into the chapel of rest. This not only emphasises task fragmentation as employees work in specific spheres, but also emphasises that they are becoming specialists. Conversely, it can be argued that in organisations where a few staff perform all funerary tasks, which may include embalming, they have a broader level of knowledge and skills.

Secondly, responsibility for preservation of the dead being with this specialist gives the embalmer scope for professionalising. Embalming is seen not in parallel to routine body-handling, but as a craft in which an object of contamination is humanised through arresting the natural process of decomposition and by beautification to create a 'sleeping-death' appearance[127] It is a relatively simple craft to acquire, although those preparing for examinations must be familiar with considerable knowledge embracing anatomy and chemistry.[128] Embalmers are keen to point to the technical nature of their task, and most importantly to the sanitary effect of embalming, through adopting a vocabulary that includes words such as protection, presentation and psychological benefits. In addition, qualification brings with it a degree of recognition by others in funeral-related occupations.

Adoption of a new title has also presented the opportunity to emphasise the caregiving role rather than the body-handling function of the funeral director.[129] Writing about funeral directors in Belfast, Lindsay Prior notes

---

[125]Nodes H.K. (1911) 'Professional Progress in England', *TUJ*, January, p. 5 and Lear G. (1953) 'The Key to Progress', *TNFD*, January, pp. 14–16.
[126]Goffman E. (1963) *Stigma: Notes on the Management of Spoilt Identity,* Englewood Cliffs: Prentice-Hall.
[127]I am indebted to Phil Gore for this phrase.
[128]Thompson W.E. (1991) 'Handling the Stigma of Handling the Dead: Morticians and Funeral Directors', *Deviant Behaviour: An Interdisciplinary Journal,* Vol. 12, p. 421 & 419.
[129]For an assessment of this change in the work of the funeral director in New Zealand see Schäfer C. (2007) 'Post-Mortem Personalisation: Pastoral Power and the New Zealand Funeral Directors', *Mortality* Vol. 12, No. 1, pp. 4–21.

that 'Some undertakers go so far as to reinterpret their role so as to play down their involvement with corpses and emphasise their role as ministers to the bereaved.'[130] Although the industry in the United States was quick to identify this dimension, it was not until the late 1930s that the subjects of bereavement or the psychology of loss were first mentioned in British trade periodicals. Some were contributed by American authors, who had become acquainted with the importance of aftercare for the bereaved following research into the survivors of the fire at Boston's Cocoanut Grove that claimed 490 casualties.[131] It would, however, be the late 1960s before lectures on grief and bereavement would become a feature at NAFD conferences, and the 1980s before a basic awareness of bereavement issues was incorporated into the NAFD Diploma's syllabus.[132] Funeral directors in the United States use such terms such as 'grief counsellor' and 'grief facilitator' or are said to work in the 'business of grief management', but these have not been adopted in Britain.[133]

While the change of name reflects developments in the tasks undertaken it also focuses on the new image as a service provider; staff speak of being employed 'in funeral service'. This new avenue of emphasis highlights the increased responsibility the funeral director has acquired. The role has changed from supplying the coffin and transport to providing a complex set of individually negotiated services; strategies that provide

---

[130] Prior L. (1989) *The Social Organization of Death: Medical Discourse and Social Practices in Belfast*, Basingstoke: Macmillan, p. 160.

[131] Quist W.P. (1938) 'Psychology of Grief', *TUFDJ*, June, pp. 215–217; Martin E.A. (1940) 'How to Handle the Grief-Stricken', *TUFDJ*, May, pp. 129–130; and Madsen I.B. (1940) 'A Women's Viewpoint on How to Handle the Grief Stricken', *TUFDJ*, November, pp. 271–272. For Cocoanut Grove fire see Lindemann E. (1944) 'Symptomatology and Management of Acute Grief', *American Journal of Psychiatry*, Vol. 101, pp. 141–148; Benzaquin P. (1959) *Holocaust*, New York: Henry Holt; Esposito J.C. (2005) *Fire in the Grove: The Cocoanut Grove Tragedy and its Aftermath*, Cambridge: Da Capo Press; and Schorow S. (2005) *The Cocoanut Grove Fire*, Beverly: Commonwealth Editions.

[132] 'The Psychology of Emotional Complexities' (1941) *TNFD*, November, pp. 161–162; 'Really Practical Professional Psychology' (1943) *TNFD*, January, pp. 252–253; 'The Application of Psychology in the Handling of the Funeral Service' (1943) *TNFD*, September, pp. 106–107; and 'Psychology of Bereavement' (1967) *FSJ*, June, pp. 304–305. See also Jackson E.N. (1974) 'Helping People Manage Crises', *TFD*, July, pp. 327–331.

[133] Porter W.H. Jr (1968) 'Some Sociological Notes on a Century of Change in the Funeral Business', *Sociological Symposium*, Vol. 1, p. 43 and Paul R.J. (1997) 'Funerals and Funeral Directors: Rituals and Resources for Grief Management', in J.D. Morgan ed., *Readings in Thanatology*, Amityville: Baywood.

mechanised comfort, personal comfort and technical comfort are offered by the funeral director.[134] This vocational characteristic of the industry was recognised as early as 1906 by John Hussey. Describing himself as an 'Ecclesiastical Furnisher' rather than funeral director, he drew parallels between those identified in the Bible who prepared the bodies of the dead with the contemporary function, while also noting the 'calling' of the work.[135] Funeral directing is sometimes defined as a 'sacred calling' and it is clear that it involves personal sacrifices of time and energy. This device enables funeral directors to parallel themselves with allied professions such as clergy. However, unless there has been prior exposure to the work of funeral directors, it is hard to claim that it is a vocation in the same way as a priest will have been 'called' to minister.

Task specialisation has also resulted in the greater involvement of women in funeral service. Through laying-out the dead women historically made an important contribution to the funeral process, but in an informal capacity.[136] From around the 1920s onwards, however, body preparation tasks have shifted to the largely male-dominated function of the funeral director. More recently women have begun to broaden their position in all aspects of funeral directing along with cemetery and crematoria management. There are a number of features of this heightened profile that are worthy of mention. It may be that the part-time or flexible working patterns offered by some organisations have appealed to women. This may be the case in respect of funeral arranging where the skills required for working with the bereaved necessitate tact, sympathy and the performance of 'emotional labour'.[137]

An obvious extension of this has been the proliferation of women in bereavement counselling and a number of funeral companies now offer these services. (It should be noted that some of the first articles in the British funeral journals about bereavement were written by women.[138])

---

[134]Hyland L. and Morse J.M. (1995) 'Orchestrating Comfort', *Death Studies*, Vol. 19, No. 5, pp. 453–474.
[135]Hussey J. (1906) 'The Sacredness of Our Calling', *TUJ*, January, p. 22. For an American article published around the same time see Pike G.R. (1909) 'The Undertaker's Higher Ministry', *TUJ*, January, pp. 17–18.
[136]In the 1911 Census only a small number of women are identified as working in funeral service. Battersea: 33 men, 1 woman; Camberwell: 40 men, 2 women; Deptford: 12 men, 3 women; and Lambeth: 39 men, 2 women.
[137]Hochschild A.R. (1983) *The Managed Heart,* Berkeley and Los Angeles: University of California Press.
[138]Eddy A. (1946) 'Women's Place in Modern Funeral Directing', *FSJ*, February, pp. 63–65; Ashton E. (1946) 'An Appeal to the Ladies', *FSJ*, May, p. 156;

Finally, it may be that their proximity to death work as funeral arrangers has led some women to explore the operational or frontline aspects of funeral work such as directing funerals or embalming. An analysis of the 2009 membership list of the BIE revealed one-quarter were female.[139] Certainly, equal opportunity legislation has assisted women's position in what has been a heavily male-dominated industry.[140]

Challenging the Stereotypical Image

Funeral directors have always experienced an image problem. Stemming from allegations of manipulation, the Dickensian characterisation of a mercenary figure provided much material for ridicule in *Punch* and other publications in addition to the music hall.[141] As highlighted in Chapter 7, practices such as touting fuelled the portrayal of the funeral director as either comical or corrupt. Contemporary popular culture only reinforces

---

'A Woman Speaks Out...Embalming: How Soon?' (1942) *TNFD*, October, pp. 130–131; 'The Position of Woman Power' (1942) *TNFD*, April, p. 324; 'Elaine on Ideal Service. Lady's Assistant's Important Place in Funeral Directing' (1944) *TNFD*, January, pp. 13–14; 'Elaine on Ideal Service. War Gives Women Their Big Chance' (1944) *TNFD*, April, pp. 115–117; and 'Elaine on Ideal Service. Advice on Training and Practical Experience' (1944) *TNFD*, July, pp. 195–196. For a very early contribution see Docking Mrs (1915) 'Some Impressions I Have Received as an Undertaker's Wife', *TUJ*, July, pp. 186–187.

[139] For the first female embalmer see 'Interview with Mrs Morrison. The First English Lady Embalmer' (1909) *TUJ*, March, pp. 63–64 and 'Notes' (1909) *TUJ*, April, p. 75. Gender analysis of members of the British Institute of Embalmers membership directory (2009).

[140] Cline S. (1995) *Lifting the Taboo: Women, Death and Dying*, London: Abacus; Field D., Hockey J. and Small N. eds (1997) *Death, Gender and Ethnicity*; and Strugnell C. and Silverman P.R. (1971) 'The Funeral Director's Wife as Caregiver', *Omega*, Vol. 2, No. 3, pp. 174–178. For the US see Mellskog P. (2005) 'The Feminine Face of the Funeral Business', *The Director*, Vol. 77, No. 4, pp. 32–38; Cathles A., Harrington D.E. and Krynski K. (2010) 'The Gender Gap in Funeral Directors: Burying Women with Ready-to-Embalm Laws?' *British Journal of Industrial Relations*, Vol. 48, No. 4, pp. 688–705; and Rundblad G. (1995) 'Exhuming Women's Premarket Duties in the Care of the Dead', *Gender & Society*, Vol. 9, No. 2, pp. 173–192. One commentator believed that registration of funeral directors would lead to more women. See 'The Woman's Page' (1925) *BUA Monthly*, May, p. 300.

[141] Parsons B. (2013) 'Mr Punch and the Undertakers', *FDM*, February, pp. 48–51; Parsons B. (2012b) 'Dickens, the Undertakers and Burial', *ICCM Journal*, Vol. 80, No. 4, pp. 22–33.

the stereotype. Keith Waterhouse was at one time employed as a funeral director in Leeds, and his film *Billy Liar* (1959) mocked the generation gap between partners in a funeral business who wanted to maintain traditions while also being anxious to embrace modern ideas.[142] Funereal comedy featured in *Loot* by Joe Orton (1967) and *Harold and Maude* (1971), while television series such as *That's Your Funeral, In Loving Memory, William and Mary* and *The Sins* have just ridiculed funeral directors.[143] Through setting each episode in the context of a death and funeral, the hugely popular US series *Six Feet Under* (2001–2005) was partly successful in conveying the complexities, expectations and tensions apparent in funeral service.[144] The American industry, however, regarded the TV series as 'comic, satiric or [having a] discomforting effect'.[145]

Although the British funeral industry escaped Jessica Mitford's vitriol when *The American Way of Death* appeared in 1963, the presence of SCI during the 1990s gave the media the opportunity to create sensational headlines reinforcing the unscrupulous image of an industry focused on exploiting the vulnerable. Accusations of 'Americanising' funerals in the style of Evelyn Waugh's 60-year-old novel *The Loved One* (1948), and of a predatory organisation acquiring all family businesses, was a perception fuelled by the media, but without foundation.[146] Much inaccurate information was based on agenda-driven motives, inadequate research and anecdote but formed the basis of comment and generalisations. In hurrying to complete *The American Way of Death Revisited* before she died (in the event it was released two years after her death in 1996), Mitford produced a very inadequate and skewed commentary

---

[142]For further literature with a funeral directing theme see Allingham M. (1948) *More Work for the Undertaker,* London: William Heinemann.

[143]The film *Bernie* (2013) recounts with black humour the true story of a Texan assistant funeral director (Bernie Tiede) who befriended a wealthy widow only to commit murder and place her body in a deep freezer.

[144]See Zaleski J.S. (2005) '"Last Writes" for *Six Feet Under*', *The Director,* Vol. 77, No. 11, pp. 34–40. See also Harper S. (2009) 'Advertising *Six Feet Under*', *Mortality,* Vol. 14, No. 3, pp. 203–225.

[145]Cahill S.E. (1999) 'The Boundaries of Professionalization: The Case of North American Funeral Direction', *Symbolic Interaction,* Vol. 22, No. 2, p. 117.

[146]Waugh E. (1948) *The Loved One,* London: Chapman Hall. Seldom mentioned is a further satirical and more detailed American funeral service novel: Belfrage C. (1950) *Abide With Me,* New York: Guardian Books. Equally, Harmer R.M. (1963) *The High Cost of Dying,* New York: Collier Books published in the same year as Mitford's work (1963) is often overlooked.

on the landscape of British funeral service of the 1990s.[147] Other articles (such as one by Plimmer that describes funeral directors as 'professional hand-wringers in decorous suits'[148]) and publications simply patronise the funeral director.[149]

For its part the industry is largely resigned to accepting this somewhat inevitable situation of a hostile media and commentators unable to discuss funeral service in a sophisticated manner. However, in an attempt to counterbalance this image, a number of fly-on-the-wall type documentaries about both funeral directors and embalmers have been produced. Dating from 1965, *Walk Down Any Street* featuring F.A. Albin was the first of a modest number of observational and balanced programmes. Others followed in the 1980s and 1990s.[150] The series *Don't Drop the Coffin* (2003) starring Barry Albin-Dyer is probably the most well-known of this genre. Biographies of funeral directors (and others working in death-related occupations) have also attempted to show the complex yet human dimension to the work.[151]

---

[147]Mitford J. (1998) *The American Way of Death Revisited,* London: Virago. See also 'Funerals in England' (1963) *FSJ,* November, p. 592; Mitford J. (1997) 'Death, Incorporated', *Vanity Fair,* March, pp. 54–61; Hast R. (1985) 'An Interview with Jessica Mitford', *TFD,* February, pp. 17–20; and Mitford J. (1980) *The Making of a Muckraker,* London: Quartet. See also Lynch T. (1998) 'A Deathly Silence', *The Sunday Telegraph Magazine,* 11 October, pp. 28–31.

[148]Plimmer M. 'How I Let My Father Leave by the Backdoor', *The Daily Telegraph,* 24 May 1997.

[149]West K. (2013) *RIP Off! Or the British Way of Death,* Kibworth Beauchamp: Matador.

[150]For example, *The Apprentice* (BBC2, 7 March 1982), *Inside Story: Undertakers* (BBC2, 13 October 1992); *Everyman* (BBC1, 9 April 1995), *Great Undertakings* (Channel 4, February 2000), *Dead Good Job* (BBC2, 12 September 2012) and *Grave Trade* (History Channel, 2013).

[151]Albin-Dyer B. [with Williams G.] (2002) *Don't Drop the Coffin,* London: Hodder & Stoughton; Barkell C. (2004) *Your Death is My Life,* Plymouth: Headstone Publications; Rymer D. (1998) *A Reluctant Funeral Director,* London: Minerva; West, J. (1988) *Jack West Funeral Director: Forty Years with Funerals,* Ilfracombe: Stockwell; Tury I. (2011) *Who Put the 'Fun' in Funeral? Diary of a Funeral Director,* Authorhouse; Baker J. (2012) *A Life in Death: Memoirs of a Cotswold Funeral Director,* Mill Place Publishing. For the US see Lynch T. (1997) *The Undertaking: Life Studies from the Dismal Trade,* London: Jonathan Cape; Lynch T. (2001) *Bodies in Motion and at Rest,* London: Vintage; and Mayfield K. (2014) *The Undertaker's Daughter,* London: Simon and Schuster. A number of interviews with employees in death-related occupations can also be located, for example a mortuary technician in *Working Lives Volume Two 1945–1977* (1977) Hackney Centerprise Trust Ltd, a cemetery worker and undertaker in Terkel S. (2002) *Will the Circle be Broken? Reflections on Death and Dignity,* London: Granta;

Most attempts by the industry to cultivate a professional image take place at a local and personal level. Employee involvement in community-based activities, links with charities, sponsorship and engagement with the public during open days, remembrance services and premises dedication ceremonies give individuals and organisations the opportunity to reveal a long-term commitment to the bereaved. The same can be said for membership of 'worthy' associations such as churches, Rotary, Round Table or the chamber of commerce.

The extent to which the image portrayed by Mitford and the media has had an effect on clients using the services of a funeral director is uncertain. Perceptions would appear to be on two levels. While the media portray the funeral director as comic or corrupt, personal encounters suggest that most clients find funeral directors supportive and also offering good value for money. As per evidence contained in reports from the 1980s and 1990s mentioned in Chapter 7, many clients are grateful for supportive gestures, professionalism and level of service, a position confirmed by the 2016 NAFD/Cruse Bereavement Care report. Similarly, research by Bailey suggests that the assumption of funeral directors being motivated by financial objectives is largely without basis and that while funeral arrangements take place within a commercial framework, mourners' experience shows staff to be personally not manipulative, but caring.[152]

Williams M. (2010) *Down Among the Dead Men,* London: Constable & Robinson; and various occupations in Morrision B. and Grant L. (1999) *A Way of Life: Portraits from the Funeral Trade*. Manchester: Len Grant Photography. See also Kirk L. and Start H. (1999) 'Death at the Undertakers', in J. Downes and T. Pollard eds, *The Loved Body's Corruption: Archaeological Contributions to the Study of Human Mortality,* Glasgow: Cruithne Press and Ramsland K. (2002) *Cemetery Stories,* London: Fusion Press.
[152]Bailey T. (2010) 'When Commerce Meets Care: Emotion Management in ' Funeral Directing', *Mortality,* Vol. 15, No. 3, pp. 205–222.

Bibliography

Abbott P. and Wallace C. eds (1990) *The Sociology of The Caring Professions*, Hampshire: Falmer Press.
Adams C. (1989) 'Funerals – A Report by the OFT', *Pharos International*, Vol. 55, No. 4, pp. 133–143.
Adams, S. (1993) 'A Gendered History of the Social Management of Death in Foleshill, Coventry, During the Interwar Years', in Clark D. ed., *The Sociology of Death: Theory, Culture, Practice*, Oxford: Blackwell, pp. 149–168.
Adamson S. and Holloway M. (2012) "A Sound-Track of Your Life" – Music in Contemporary UK Funerals', *Omega*, Vol. 65, No. 1, pp. 33–54.
Albin-Dyer B. (2002) *Don't Drop the Coffin*, London: Hodder & Stoughton.
Albin-Dyer B. and Parsons B. (2011) *Up and Down Like Tower Bridge*, London: Strong Shoulders Press.
Allighan G. (1947) 'Burial and the State', *Report of the Conference of the Institute of Burial and Cremation Administration*, pp. 33–42.
Allingham M. (1948) *More Work for the Undertaker*, London: William Heinemann.
Ariès P. (1974) *Western Attitudes Towards Death from the Middle Ages to the Present*, London: Marion Boyars.
Ashton E. (1946) 'An Appeal to the Ladies', *FSJ*, May, p. 156.
Ashton L.C. (1952) 'The Place of Embalming in Funeral Directing',*TNFD*, August, pp. 68–71.
Baer B.A. (1971) 'The World's First Flying Hearse', *Casket & Sunnyside*, Centennial Issue, Vol. 101, pp. 44 & 46.
Bailey C. (1997) 'A View from the Front', *FSJ*, April, pp. 35 & 39.
Bailey T. (2010) 'When Commerce Meets Care: Emotion Management in UK Funeral Directing', *Mortality*, Vol. 15, No. 3, pp. 205–222.
Bailey W. (1983) *Euphemisms and Other Double-Talk*, New York, NY: Doubleday.
Baker, J. (2012) *A Life in Death: Memoirs of a Cotswold Funeral Director*. Mill Place Publishing.
Ball G. (1925) 'The Special Qualities Demanded for Undertaking', *BUA Monthly*, December, pp. 126–127.
Ball P. (1995) 'Ill Informed on Subject of Embalming', *FSJ*, January, p. 33.
Banks C. (1924) 'What Every Undertaker Should Know About Microbes'. *BUA Monthly*, December, pp. 152–153.
Banting D. (1998) 'The Life of William Westbrook Banting – Undertaker to the Crown', *FSJ*, May, pp. 78–85.
Barkell C. (2004) *Your Death is My Life*, Plymouth: Headstone Publications.
Barley S.R. (1980) 'Taking the Burdens: The Strategic Role of the Funeral Director', Working Paper. Alfred P Sloan School of Management.

Barley S.R. (1983) 'The Codes of the Dead. The Semiotics of Funeral Work', *Urban Life*, Vol. 12, No. 1, pp. 3–31.
Barnes G.C. (1916) 'The Disposal of the Dead from the Public Health Standpoint', *TUJ*, September, pp. 242–246.
Basnett I. (1914) 'Municipal Funerals', *The Englishwoman*, Vol XXIII, No 67, pp. 23–28.
Belfrage C. (1950) *Abide with Me*, New York, NY: Guardian Books.
Benson P. (1937) 'What We Would Like', *TUFDJ*, December, pp. 427–432.
Benzaquin P. (1959) *Holocaust*, New York, NY: Henry Holt.
Berridge K. (2001) *Vigor Mortis*, London: Profile.
Berridge K. (2002) 'Coffin Fits', *The Spectator*, 9 November, pp. 72–73.
Blair A.O.H. (1977) 'The Price Commission's Inquiry into Funeral Charges', *Cremation Society Conference Report*, pp. 63–69.
Bland O. (1986) *The Royal Way of Death*, London: Constable.
Blauner R. (1964) *Alienation and Freedom*, Chicago, IL: University of Chicago Press.
Blauner R. (1966) 'Death and Social Structure', *Psychiatry*, Vol. 29, 378–394.
Blood R.O. and Wolfe D.M. (1960) *Husbands and Wives*, Glencoe: Free Press.
Bondeson J. (2001) *Buried Alive: The Terrifying History of Our Most Primal Fear*, New York, NY: W.W. Norton.
Bourke J. (2005) *Fear: A Cultural History*, London: Virago.
Bowman L. (1959) *The American Funeral: A Study in Guilt, Extravagance and Sublimity*, Washington, DC: Public Affairs Press.
Bradbury M. (1999) *Representations of Death: A Social Psychological Perspective*, London: Routledge.
Bradfield C.D. and Myers R.A. (1980) 'Clergy and Funeral Directors: An Exploration in Role Conflict', *Review of Religious Research*, Vol. 21, No. 3, pp. 343–350.
Bradfield J. (1997) 'DIY and Green Funerals – ABN Welfare & Wildlife Trust', *TFD*, August, pp. 7–12.
Brennan M. (2008) 'Mourning and Loss: Finding Meaning in the Mourning for Hillsborough', *Mortality*, Vol. 13, No. 1, pp. 1–23.
Bridgeman J.S. (2000) 'The Way Forward for the Funeral Profession', *FSJ*, February, pp. 57–70.
Broome J. (1908) 'Relationship of Undertakers, their Clients, and Burial Authorities', *TUJ*, March, pp. 63–64.
Broome J. (1934) 'Reminiscences of Undertaking 50–60 Years Ago', *TUJ*, February, pp. 67–68.
Broome J.C. (1904) 'The Modern Undertaker', *TUJ*, November, pp. 233–234.
Brown C. (1995) 'Funerals – The Consumers' Perspective', *Pharos International*, Vol. 61, No. 4, pp. 162–167.
Brown, E. W. (1917) 'Hull on the Upgrade', *TUJ*, October, pp. 273–274.
Buckland M. (1969) 'Registration for Funeral Directors', *TFD*, pp. 366–386.
Cahill S.E. (1995) 'Some Rhetorical Directions of Funeral Direction: Historical Entanglements and Contemporary Dilemmas', *Work and Occupations*, Vol. 22, No. 115, pp. 115–136.

Cahill S.E. (1999) 'The Boundaries of Professionalization: The Case of North American Funeral Direction', *Symbolic Interaction*, Vol. 22, No. 2, pp. 105–119.
Callender R. (2012a) 'Dancing Around the Bonfire', in R. Callender ed., *Writing on Death*, Winchester: Natural Death Centre/Strange Attractor Press, pp. 132–143.
Callender R. et al. (2012b) *The Natural Death Handbook*, fifth edition, London: Natural Death Centre/Strange Attractor Press.
Canine J. D. (1996) *The Psychosocial Aspects of Death and Dying*, Stamford, CT: Appleton & Lange.
Cannadine D. (1981) 'War and Death, Grief and Mourning in Modern Britain', in J. Whaley ed., *Mirrors of Mortality*, London: Europa.
Carr-Saunders A.M., Sargant Florence P., and Peers R. (1938) *Consumers' Co-operation in Great Britain: An Examination of the British Co-operative Movement*, London: George Allen & Unwin.
Carter H.D.E. (1968) 'Does Embalming Affect Cremation?' *FSJ*, April, pp. 183–190.
Cathles A., Harrington D.E., and Krynski K. (2010) 'The Gender Gap in Funeral Directors: Burying Women with Ready-to-Embalm Laws?' *British Journal of Industrial Relations*, Vol. 48, No. 4, pp. 688–705.
Cave D. (2002) 'Gay and Lesbian Bereavement', in D. Dickenson, M. Johnson and J.S. Katz eds., *Death, Dying and Bereavement*, second edition, London: Sage, pp. 363–366.
Chadwick E. (1843) *A Supplementary Report on the Results of a Special Inquiry into the Practice of Interment in Towns*, London: W Clowes.
Chamberlain A.T. and Pearson M.P. (2001) *Earthly Remains: The History and Science of Preserved Bodies*, London: British Museum Press.
Chamberlain M. and Richardson R. (1983) 'Life and Death', *Oral History*, Vol. 11, No. 1, pp. 31–43.
Chambers D. (1985) 'The St Pancras Coroner's Court', *Camden History Review*, Vol. 13, pp. 22–25.
Chambers D. (1990) *No Funerals on Picnic Day! Victorian Funeral Industry Associations 1890–1990*, Melbourne: Australian Funeral Directors Association.
Chapple A. and Ziebland S. (2010) 'Viewing the Body after Bereavement Due to a Traumatic Death: Qualitative Study in the UK', *British Medical Journal*, Vol. 340, p. c2032. doi:10.1136/bmj.c2032
Charmaz K., Howarth G. and Kellehear A. eds (1997) *The Unknown Country: Death in Australia, Britain and the USA*, Basingstoke: Macmillan.
Chiappelli J. and Chiappelli T. (2008) 'Drinking Grandma: The Problem of Embalming', *Journal of Environmental Health*, Vol. 71, No. 5, pp. 24–28.
Church R.A. and Smith B.M.D. (1966) 'Competition and Monopoly in the Coffin Furniture Industry, 1870–1915', *The Economic History Review* (New Series), Vol. 19, No. 3, pp. 621–641.
Clark H. and Carnegie E. (2010) *She Was Aye Workin': Memories of Tenement Women in Edinburgh and Glasgow*, Dorchester: White Cockade Publishing.
Clarke A. (1996) 'Where, Oh Death, is Now Thy Sting?' *The Friend*, 13 September, pp. 13–14.

Clarke D. (2002) 'Death in Staithes', in D. Dickenson, M. Johnson and J.S. Katz eds, *Death, Dying and Bereavement*, second edition, London: The Open University/Sage, pp. 4–9.
Clarke J.S. (1944a) *Funeral Reform*, London: Social Security League.
Clarke J.S. (1944b) 'Funeral Reform', *TUFDJ*, August, pp. 229–230.
Clarke J.S. (1946) 'Funeral Ethics in a Modern State', *Report of the Conference of the National Association of Cemetery and Crematorium Superintendents*, June, pp. 18–23.
Clarke J.M. (2006) *The Brookwood Necropolis Railway*, fourth edition. Usk: Oakwood Press.
Clayden A., Green T., Hockey J. and Powell M. (2014) *Natural Burial: Landscape, Practice and Experience*, London: Routledge.
Cline S. (1995) *Lifting the Taboo: Women, Death and Dying*, London: Abacus.
Coates D.R. (1973) 'The Price of Dying', *FSJ*, February, pp. 66–67.
Cole P. (1921) 'Incorporation and Registration', *BUA Monthly*, June, pp. 338–340.
Connett D. (1985) 'Fight to the Death on Council Funerals', *The Embalmer*, Vol. 28, No. 3, p. 48.
Coope R. (1928) 'The Troubles of Ye Olde English Coffin Maker', *TUJ*, October, pp. 247–248 and 351.
Cooper J. (1979) *Class*, London: Eyre Methuen.
Corden A. and Hirst A. (2015) 'The Meaning of Funeral Poverty: An Exploratory Study', Working Paper WP 2668, York: University of York.
Coriolis. (1967) *Death Here is Thy Sting*, Toronto: McClelland and Stewart.
Cork N. (1930) 'The Practice of Embalming', *TUJ*, November, pp. 387–289.
Cottridge A.J.E. (1918) 'What is an Undertaker? Who Shall be Admitted as Association Members?' *TUJ*, July, p. 186.
Cottridge A.J.E. (1924a) 'Preservative Disinfectant', *BUA Monthly*, September, pp. 69–71.
Cottridge A.J.E. (1924b) 'Signs of Death. Simple Tests Which Every Undertaker Should Know and Practice', *BUA Monthly*, December, pp. 159–160.
Cottridge A.J.E. (1924c) 'The Urgent Need of Post Graduate Tuition in Modern Embalming', *BUA Monthly*, June, pp. 697–698.
Cottridge A.J.E. (1925a) 'Anatomy and Post-Mortem Sanitation', *BUA Monthly*, June, pp. 311–312.
Cottridge A.J.E. (1925b) 'A New Campaign', *BUA Monthly*, April, p. 257.
Cottridge A.J.E. (1926) 'The BUA Watchwords: Organisation, Education; Legislation', *BUA Monthly*, September, pp. 60–61.
Cottridge A.J.E. (1931) 'Signs of Death', *BUA Monthly*, pp. 82–83.
Cottridge A.J.E. (1932) 'Medical Officers of Health', *BUA Monthly*, May, p. 252.
Cottridge A.J.E. (1933a) 'The Professional Undertaker and the Public Health', *Public Health*, January, pp. 132–134.
Cottridge A.J.E. (1933b) 'The Professional Undertaker and the Public Health', *TUJ*, February, pp. 57–58.
Cottridge A.J.E. (1943) 'Mr James Goulborn', *TNFD*, May, p. 416.

Cowling C. (2010a) *The Good Funeral Guide*, London: Continuum.
Cowling C. (2010b) 'The Long Decline of the Victorian Funeral. Has It Had Its Day?' *FSJ*, March, pp. 84–87.
Cowling, C. (2012) 'The New Priests: Secular Celebrants and Ceremonies', in R. Callender ed., *Writing on Death*, Winchester: Natural Death Centre/Strange Attractor Press, pp. 84–90.
Craughwell, T.J. (2007) *Stealing Lincoln's Body*, Cambridge, MA: Belhnap/Harvard.
Crazy Coffins: Verrückte Särge aus England (2005) Nottingham: Vic Fern. Exhibition catalogue to accompany exhibition of the Museum für Sepulkralkultur, Kassel.
Cribb P.W. (1980) 'Some Observations on the Funeral Customs of Immigrant Communities at the Crematorium', *Resurgam*, Vol. 23, No. 1, pp. 5–7.
Crichton, I. (1976) *The Art of Dying*, London: Peter Owen.
Cromer M. (2006) *Exit Strategy: Thinking Outside the Box*, New York, NY: Jeremy P Tarcher/Penguin.
Curl J.S. (1986) 'Architecture for a Novel Purpose: Death and the Railway Age' *Country Life*, June 12, pp. 1716–1717.
Curl J.S. (2002) *Death and Architecture*, Stroud: Sutton Publishing.
Davies C. (1996) 'Dirt, Death, Decay and Dissolution', in G. Howarth and P.C. Jupp eds, *Contemporary Issues in the Sociology of Death, Dying and Disposal*, Basingstoke: Macmillan, pp. 60–71.
Davies D. (1995) *British Crematoria in Public Profile*, Maidstone: The Cremation Society of Great Britain.
Davies D. (1997) *Death, Ritual and Belief*, London: Cassell.
Davies D. (2012) 'Revisiting British Crematoria in Public Profile', *Pharos International*, Vol. 78, No. 3, pp. 4–7.
Davies D. and Rumble H. (2012) *Natural Burial: Traditional – Secular Spiritualties and Funeral Innovation*, London: Continuum.
Davies D. and Shaw A. (1995) *Reusing Old Graves: A Report on Popular British Attitudes*, Crayford: Shaw and Sons.
Davies T.A. (1959) 'The Centre of Funeral Service is Embalming', *TFD*, October, pp. 217–218.
Dawes M.C. (1999) 'The Great Northern London Cemetery and its Railway Service', *The London Railway Record*, No. 21, October, pp. 256–260.
Dawes M.C. (2003) *The End of the Line: The Story of the Railway Service to the Great Northern London*, Cemetery Barnet: Barnet & District Local History Society.
Day J.C. (1986) 'Lambeth's Municipal Funeral Service', *FSJ*, August, p. 311.
Day R.E. (1939) 'Letters to the Editor: Burial Reform and Funeral Costs', *TUFDJ*, June, p. 207.
Denison K.M. (2000) 'The Implications of Events Surrounding the Death and Funeral of Diana, Princess of Wales', *Pharos International*, Vol. 66, No. 2, pp. 5–8.

Denyer, P. (1997) 'Singing the Lord's Song in a Strange Land', in P.C. Jupp and T. Rogers eds, *Interpreting Death: Christian Theology and Pastoral Practice*, London: Cassell, pp. 197–202.

Dickens C. (1850) 'From the Raven in the Happy Family', *Household Words*, 8 June, pp. 241–242.

Dickens C. (1852) 'Trading in Death', *Household Words*, 27 November, pp. 140–245.

Dittrick H. (1948) 'Notes and Queries: Devices to Prevent Premature Burial', *Journal of the History of Medicine and Allied Sciences*, Vol. 3, pp. 161–171.

Dobson J. (1953) 'Some Eighteenth Century Experiments in Embalming', *Journal of the History of Medicine and Allied Sciences*, Vol. 7, pp. 431–441.

Docking Mrs. (1915) 'Some Impressions I Have Received as an Undertakers' Wife', *TUJ*, July, pp. 186–187.

Dodge G.B. (1909) 'Modern Embalming', *TUJ*, December, pp. 285–286.

Dodgson M.J. (1977) *Embalming – Is it Necessary?* Institute of Burial and Cremation Administration Conference Report, pp. 14–18.

Dodgson W. (1946) 'New Education Programme Outlined', *TNFD*, May, p. 439.

Donnelley R.G. (1964) 'The Family Business', *Harvard Business Review*, July–August, pp. 93–105.

Doyle C.G. (1974a) 'Death in Modern Society', *TFD*, July, p. 335 & pp. 341–343.

Doyle C.G. (1974b) 'Undertakers and Undertaking', *TFD*, May, pp. 239–242 and July, pp. 335–343.

Drakeford M. (1998) 'Last Rights? Funerals, Poverty and Social Exclusion', *Journal of Social Policy*, Vol. 27, No. 4, pp. 507–524.

Dunk J. and Rugg J. (1994) *The Management of Old Cemetery Land*, Crayford: Shaw and Sons.

Dunn M. (2000) *The Good Death Guide*, Oxford: Pathways Books.

Dunstan R.E. (1967) *Government: Wise Parent or Tycoon* (an Aim of Industry Publication) pp. 9–10.

Dyer A. (1913a) 'American Methods and Some Suggestions for Adoption in the British Isles', *TUJ*, July, pp. 199–202.

Dyer A. (1913b) 'Interview with Mr A. Dyer of Walthamstow', *TUJ*, April, pp. 109–110.

Dyer A. (1914) 'Modern Embalming and the Undertaker', *TUJ*, February, p. 37.

Dyer A. (1949) 'On Ideals', *FSJ*, January, pp. 21–22.

Dyer W.G. (1956) 'The Interlocking of Work and Family in Social Systems among Lower Occupational Families', *Social Forces*, Vol. 34, No. 3, pp. 230–233.

Ebbutt T.H. (1969) 'Planning a Generation Ahead for Funeral Requirements', *FSJ*, January, pp. 17–22.

Eddy A. (1946) 'Women's Place in Modern Funeral Directing', *FSJ*, February, pp. 63–65.

Elliott A. (1994) 'Westminster Seminar Outlines National Vocational Qualifications', *FSJ*, August, pp. 67–71.

Ellis C. (1948) 'The Age-Long Profession of Funeral Directing', *TNFD*, March, pp. 235–237.

Elliston G.S. (1936) 'The Disposal of the Dead from the Health and Economic Standpoints', *TUFDJ*, October, pp. 337–342.

Esposito J.C. (2005) *Fire in the Grove: The Cocoanut Grove Tragedy and its Aftermath*, Cambridge: Da Capo Press.

Etzioni A. (1964) *Modern Organisations*, London: Prentice Hall.

Evans B. and Lawson A. (1981) *A Nation of Shopkeepers*, London: Plexus.

Farrell J.J. (1980) *Inventing the American Way of Death 1830–1920*, Philadelphia, PA: Temple University Press.

Farrin J. (1999) 'A British Way of Death?' *FSJ*, October, pp. 77–92.

Farthing D.S. (1978) 'The Organisation of Funerals in Great Britain', *FSJ*, September, pp. 367–370.

Faust, C.D.G. (2008) *This Republic of Suffering: Death and the American Civil War*, New York, NY: Knopf.

Fay A.W. (1903) 'Funeral Etiquette', *TUJ*, February, pp. 34–35.

Fellows A. (1910) 'Death Certificates: The Weaknesses of the Present Law', *TUJ*, November, p. 266.

Fellows A. (1911) 'Death Certificates: Urgent Need of Reform of the Law', *TUJ*, November, p. 296.

Fellows A. (1952) *The Law of Burial and Generally of the Disposal of the Dead*, second edition, London: Haddon, Best & Co.

Ferran W.H. (1984) 'The Death Grant', *Pharos*, Vol. 50, No. 2, pp. 55–65.

Field D., Hockey J. and Small N. eds (1997) *Death, Gender and Ethnicity*, London: Routledge.

Field C.P.J. (1989) 'Funeral Directing – The Next Decade', *Pharos International*, Vol. 55, No. 3, pp. 98–107.

Firth S. (1996) 'The Good Death: Attitudes of British Hindus', in G. Howarth and P.C. Jupp eds, *Contemporary Issues in the Sociology of Death, Dying and Disposal*, Hampshire: Macmillian Press, pp. 96–107.

Firth S. (2002) 'Changing Hindu Attitudes to Cremation in the UK', *Pharos International*, Vol. 68, No. 1, pp. 35–40.

Fisher P. (2009a) 'Houses for the Dead: The Provision of Mortuaries in London 1866–1889', *The London Journal*, Vol. 34, No. 1, pp. 1–15.

Fisher P. (2009b) 'Death, Decomposition and the Dead-House: The English Public Mortuary', *FSJ*, May, pp. 90–95.

Fletcher G. (1962) *The London Nobody Knows*, London: Penguin.

Fletcher T. (1932) 'The Trade Union Status', *TUJ*, January, pp. 5–8.

Flory D. (2008) 'Education and the Business of Funeral Service', *The Director*, Vol. 80, No. 4, pp. 46–51.

Flynn D. (1993) *The Truth About Funerals*, Burlington: Funeral Consultants International Inc.

Foggart J. (1904) 'Embalming and Sanitation: Their Value to an Up-to-Date Undertaker', *TUJ*, October, pp. 205–206.

Forbes D. (1917) 'Public Health and the Disposal of the Dead', *TUJ*, July, pp. 182–184. (see also 'Disposal of the Dead' (1917) *The Medical Officer*, 1 September, pp. 66–67.)

Francis D., Kellaher L. and Neophytou G. (2005) *The Secret Cemetery*, Oxford: Berg.
Francis J. (2004) *Time to Go: Alternative Funerals. The Importance of Saying Goodbye*, Lincoln: Iuniverse
Freeman A.C. (1906a) *The Planning of Poor Law Buildings and Mortuaries*, London: St Bride's Press.
Freeman A.C. (1906b) 'Waiting Mortuary for the Prevention of Premature Burial', *Burial Reformer*, Vol. 1, No. 5, April–June, pp. 37–39.
Fric L. (1997) 'The Economics of Death', in J.D. Morgan ed., *Readings in Thanatology*, Amityville, NY: Baywood, pp. 77–115.
Fritz P.S. (1994) 'The Undertaking Trade in England: Its Origins and Early Development, 1660–1830', *Eighteenth-Century Studies*, Vol. 28, No. 2, pp. 241–253.
Fulton R. (1961) 'The Clergyman and the Funeral Director: A Study in Role Conflict', *Social Forces*, Vol. 39, pp. 317–323.
Garbett C.F. (1933) *The Challenge of the Slums*, London: Society for Promoting Christian Knowledge.
Garces-Foley K. and Holcomb J. S. (2006) 'Contemporary American Funerals: Personalizing Tradition', in K. Garces-Foley ed. *Death and Religion in a Changing World*, New York, NY: ME Sharpe, pp. 207–227.
Garson J.G. (1902) 'Embalming the Dead', *The Lancet*, Vol. 10, No. May, pp. 1301–1305.
Garson J. (1909) 'Principles and Practices of Embalming', *TUJ*, April, pp. 80–81 and May, pp. 106–110.
Gaunt P. (1977) 'The British Institute of Embalmers', *The Embalmer*, Vol. 20, No. 1, pp. 7–12.
Gill S. and Fox J. (2004) *The Dead Good Funerals Book*, Ulverston: Engineers of the Imagination.
Gittings C. (2007) 'Eccentric or Enlightened? Unusual Burial and Commemoration in England, 1689–1823', *Mortality*, Vol. 12, No. 4, pp. 321–349.
Glasser B. and Strauss, A. (1968) *Time for Dying*, Chicago, IL: Aldine.
Goffman E. (1959) *The Presentation of Self in Everyday Life*, Harmondsworth: Penguin.
Goffman E. (1963) *Stigma: Notes on the Management of Spoilt Identity*, Englewood Cliffs, NJ: Prentice-Hall.
Goodman E. (1969) *The Impact of Size*, London: The Acton Society Trust.
Gore C.G. F. (1846) 'The Mute', in *Sketches of English Character*, Vol. 2, London: Richard Bentley.
Gore P. (1991) 'Progress of Embalming Practice', *The Embalmer*, Vol. 34, No. 4, pp. 10–11.
Gore P. (1993) *From Undertaking to Funeral Directing – The Development of Funeral Firms in East Kent*, Unpublished MPhil dissertation, University of Kent, Kent.
Gore P. (2001) 'Funeral Ritual Past and Present', in J. Hockey, J.S. Katz & N. Small eds, *Grief, Mourning and Death Ritual*, Buckingham: Open University Press, pp. 212–217.
Gorer G. (1955) 'The Pornography of Death', *Encounter*, October, pp. 49–52.

Gorer G. (1965) *Death, Grief, and Mourning in Contemporary Britain*, London: The Cresset Press.
Gormley R. (1995) 'Social Funds and Unreal Expenses', *Pharos International*, Vol. 60, No. 2, pp. 103–104.
Gornall L. (1993) 'The Departure of the Co-operatives', *TFD*, August, p. 27.
Goss D. (1991) *Small Business and Society*, London: Routledge.
Goulborn J. (1904) 'Anastomosis, Osmosis, and the Circulation of Fluid in Arterial Embalming', *TUJ*, February, pp. 32–33.
Gould G. (1996) 'Letter from America: Local Ownership as a Competitive Advantage', *Insight Special Edition*, May, Issue 13.
Graham L.T. (1984) 'Funeral on the Rates – No Answer to the Problem of Increasing Funeral Costs', *TFD*, December, pp. 22–23.
Grainger R. (1988) *The Unburied*, Worthing: Churchman Publishing, p. 142.
Griffiths J. (1924) 'A Model Funeral Directing Establishment: The Derby & District Funeral Company Limited's Efficient Organisation', *BUA Monthly*, January, pp. 546–549.
Habenstein, R.W. (1962) 'Sociology of Occupations: The Case of the American Funeral Director', in A.M. Rose ed., *Human Behaviour and Social Processes*, London: Routledge & Kegan Paul, pp. 225–246.
Habenstein R.W. and Lamers W.M. (1963) *Funeral Customs the World Over* (Review edition), Milwaukee, WI: Bulfin.
Habenstein R.W. and Lamers W.M. (1981) *The History of American Funeral Directing*, second edition, Milwaukee, WI: National Funeral Directors Association.
Habenstein R.W. and Lamers W.M. (1995) *The History of American Funeral Directing*, third edition, Milwaukee, WI: National Funeral Directors Association.
Hailes J. (2007) *The New Green Consumer Guide*, London: Simon and Schuster.
Haler A. (2009) 'The Biocides Directive', *Pharos International*, Vol. 75, No. 1, pp. 10–12.
Haler D.C. (1969) 'The Pathologist's Objections to Embalming', *TFD*, February, pp. 90–91.
Hall A.C.A. (1949) 'When the Funeral Director Provides a Chapel', *FSJ*, June, pp. 352–353.
Hallam E., Hockey J. and Howarth G. (1999) *Beyond the Body: Death and Social Identity*, London: Routledge.
Hammerton H.J. (1952) *This Turbulent Priest: The Story of Charles Jenkinson, Parish Priest and Housing Reformer*, London: Lutterworth Press.
Harmer R.M. (1963) *The High Cost of Dying*, New York, NY: Collier Books.
Harper S. (2009) 'Advertising *Six Feet Under*', *Mortality*, Vol. 14, No. 3, pp. 203–225.
Harper S. (2010a) 'The Social Agency of Dead Bodies', *Mortality*, Vol. 15, No. 4, pp. 308–322.
Harper S. (2010b) 'Behind Closed Doors? Corpses and Mourners in English and American Funeral Premises', in J. Hockey, C. Komaromy and K. Woodthorpe

eds, *The Matter of Death: Space, Place and Materiality*, Basingstoke: Palgrave Macmillan, pp. 100–116.

Harr J. (2001) *Funeral Wars*, London: Short Books.

Harrah B.K. and Harrah D.F. (1976) *Funeral Service: A Bibliography*, Metuchen: The Scarecrow Press.

Harrington D.L. (2007) 'Markets. Preserving Funeral Market with Ready-to-Embalm Laws', *Journal of Economic Perspectives*, Vol. 21, No. 4, pp. 201–216.

Harrington I. (1972) 'Solemn Undertaking', *New Statesman*, 22 December, Vol. 84, No. 2179, pp. 940–941.

Harrington I. (1973) 'Solemn Undertaking', *FSJ*, February, pp. 65–66.

Harrison A. (1914) 'The State and the Family', *English Review*, January, pp. 278–284.

Hasluck, P.N. (1905) *Coffin-Making and Undertaking*, London: Cassell & Co.

Hast R. (1985) 'An Interview with Jessica Mitford', *TFD*, February, pp. 17–20.

Hathaway W.S. (1970) 'When to Use an Air Hearse', *Casket & Sunnyside*, Vol. 100, No. 3, pp. 18–19 & 24.

Hay A. (1985) 'Cremation and the Environment', *Pharos International*, Vol. 52, No. 1, pp. 16–25.

Herbert F.G. (1947) 'Post-War Reform', *Journal of the National Association of Cemetery and Crematorium Superintendents*, Vol. 13, No. 2, May, pp. 9–10.

Hertz R. (1960) *Death and the Right Hand: A Contribution to the Study of the Collective Representations of Death*, trans R. Needham and C. Needham, London: Cohen and West.

Hilton D.D. and Okubadejo O.A. (2010) 'Where Do People Die?' *Resurgam*, Vol. 53, No. 3, pp. 148–149.

Hindley P. (1998) 'A Vision for the Funeral Industry', *FSJ*, December, pp. 88–96.

Hindley P. (1999) 'Is the Price Right?' *FSJ*, February, p. 42.

Hitchcock B. (1924) 'The Upholders' Company', *BUA Monthly*, December, pp. 161–162.

Hochschild A.R. (1983) *The Managed Heart*, Berkeley and Los Angeles, CA: University of California Press.

Hockey J. (2003) 'Purchasing at Need Funerals: The Changing Context', *Pharos International*, Vol. 69, No. 2, pp. 8–11.

Hodgson H.O.P. (1992) *How to Become Dead Rich*, London: Pavilion.

Hoey B. (2011) *The Royal Train: The Inside Story*, Sparkford: JH Haynes.

Hohenschuh W.P. (1905) 'How to Conduct a Funeral', *TUJ*, September, p. 219.

Holland R. (1995) 'NVQ/SVQ's in Funeral Service', *TFD*, November, pp. 30–31.

Holloway M. et al. (2010) *Spirituality in Contemporary Funerals: Final Report*, Hull: Arts and Humanities Research Council/University of Hull.

Holloway M., Adamson S., Argyrou V., Draper P. and Marlau D. (2013) 'Funerals Aren't Nice But It Couldn't Have Been Nicer. The Makings of a Good Funeral', *Mortality*, Vol. 18, No. 1, pp. 30–53.

Hopwood D. (1996) 'Funeral Marketing in the 1990s', *Pharos International*, Vol. 62, No. 1, pp. 14–17.

Horbury J. (1987) 'A Personal Profile of Howard Hodgson', *FSJ*, August, pp. 312–316.
Horbury J. (1995) 'How are Things Settling Down at SCI?' *FSJ*, February, pp. 33–40.
Horder L.M. (1936) 'The Public Health Aspect of the Disposition of the Dead', *TNFD*, September, pp. 67–68.
Horridge W. (1943) 'Municipal Funeral Homes?' {letter}, *Journal of the Institute of Burial and Cremation Administration*, Vol. 19, No. 2, May, pp. 12–13.
Horridge W. (1948) 'Mortuaries, Chapels of Rest or Funeral Homes', *Journal of the Institute of Burial and Cremation Administration*, Vol. 24, No. 3, August, pp. 26–29.
Howarth G. (1992) *The Funeral Industry in the East End of London: An Ethnographic Study*, Unpublished PhD thesis, University of London, London.
Howarth G. (1993a) 'Investigating Deathwork: A Personal Account', in D. Clark ed., *The Sociology of Death: Theory, Culture, Practice*. Oxford: Blackwell, pp. 221–237.
Howarth G. (1993b) 'AIDS and Undertakers: The Business of Risk Management', *Critical Public Health*, Vol. 4, No. 3, pp. 47–53.
Howarth G. (1996) *Last Rites: The Work of the Modern Funeral Director*, Amityville, NY: Baywood.
Howarth G. (2007) 'Whatever Happened to Social Class? An Examination of the Neglect of Working Class Cultures in the Sociology of Death', *Healthcare Sociology Review*, Vol. 16, No. 5, pp. 425–435.
Howell D.V.P. (1949) 'National Health Insurance', *TNFD*, April, pp. 450–452.
Hoy W.G. (2013) *Do Funerals Matter? The Purposes and Practices of Death Rituals in Global Perspective*, New York, NY: Routledge.
Hughes E.C. (1958) *Men and Their Work*, Glencoe: Free Press.
Humphrey C. (1948) 'Disposal of the Dead by the State', *Journal of the Institute of Burial and Cremation Administration*, Vol. 15, No. 2, May, pp. 9–10.
Humphreys J. (1995) 'Pre-Paid Funeral Plans', *Pharos International*, Vol. 60, No. 3, pp. 127–136.
Hurren E.T. (2012) *Dying for Victorian Medicine. English Anatomy and its Trade in the Dead Poor, c.1834–1929*, Basingstoke: Palgrave Macmillan.
Hurry F.D. (1943) 'A Wider Outlook', *TNFD*, August, pp. 74–75.
Hussein I. (1997) 'The PFI from a Public Sector Manager's Perspective', *Pharos International*, Vol. 63, No. 1, pp. 19–21.
Hussey J. (1906) 'The Sacredness of Our Calling', *TUJ*, January, p. 22.
Hutsby B. (1992) 'The NAFD Diploma in Funeral Directing – Its Future', *TFD*, August, pp. 14–21.
Hutsby B. (2013) 'Dispatches: The Outcome', *FDM*, September, pp. 12–13.
Hyland L. and Morse J.M. (1995) 'Orchestrating Comfort', *Death Studies*, Vol. 19, No. 5, pp. 453–474.
Illich I., Zola I.K., McKnight J., Caplan J. and Shaiken H. (1977) *Disabling Professions*, London: Marion Boyars.
Inman, R.J. (1988) 'Guidelines for Embalming an AIDS Body', *The Embalmer*, Vol. 31, No. 1, pp. 4–5.

Inman-Cook R. (2011) 'The Funeral Industry Interview', *TFD*, May, pp. 34–36.
Innes J. (1934) 'Public Health Services', *BUA Monthly*, January, pp. 148–150.
Ironside V. (1996) *You'll Get Over It: The Rage of Bereavement*, London: Hamish Hamilton, pp. 14–29.
Irwin M. (2008) 'The Bright Side of Death: Dickens and Black Humour', *The Dickensian*, Spring, No. 272, Part 1, pp. 17–31.
Jackson E.N. (1974) 'Helping People Manage Crises', *TFD*, July, pp. 327–331.
Jalland P. (1996) *Death in the Victorian Family*, Oxford: Oxford University Press.
Jalland P. (1999) Victorian Death and Its Decline 1850–1918', in P.C. Jupp and C. Gittings eds., *Death in England*, Manchester: Manchester University Press, pp. 230–255.
Jalland P. (2010) *Death in War and Peace: A History of Loss & Grief in England, 1914–1970*, Oxford: Oxford University Press.
Jeffreys S. (1987) 'Queuing Up at Death's Door', *TFD*, January, pp. 10–11.
Johnson A. (1944) 'Professional Standards and How They Are Obtained', *Journal of American Dental Association*, September, No. 3, pp. 1181–1189.
Johnson E.C. (1967) 'The Lives of the Teachers. Pioneer Embalming Educators of America. Prof Felix A Sullivan', *The De-Ce-Co Magazine*, February, Vol. 59, No. 1, pp. 14 & 22.
Johnson E.C. (1974) 'Life and Times of Felix Sullivan, Noted Embalmer', *Casket and Sunnyside*, Vol. 104, No. 7, pp. 18, 20–21, 23, & 49.
Johnson E.C. (1975) 'Cattell's Skill with Lincoln's Remains Publicized Embalming,' *Casket and Sunnyside*, September, Vol. 105, No. 9, pp. 16, 18, 20, & 53–54.
Johnson E.C. (1983) 'Civil War Embalming', *The Embalmer*, July, Vol. 26, No. 4, p. 25.
Johnson E.C., Johnson G.R. and Williams M.J. (1988) 'The Introduction of Embalming to England', *The Embalmer*, Vol. 21, No. 4, p. 16.
Johnson E.C., Johnson G.R., and Williams M.J. (1990) 'The Origin and History of Embalming and History of Modern Restorative Art', in R.G. Mayer ed., *Embalming: History, Theory and Practice*, Stamford, CT: Appleton & Lange, pp. 419–428.
Johnson M., Cullen L., Heatley R. and Hockey J. (2001) *The Psychology of Death: An Exploration of the Impact of Bereavement on the Purchasers of 'At Need' Funerals*, Bristol: International Institute on Health and Ageing.
Johnson M.E.C. and Johnson, G. (1987) 'The Man Who Embalmed Evita: Dr Pedro Ara', *The Embalmer*, Vol. 30, No. 1, pp. 14–26.
Johnstone J.J. (1924) 'The Disposal of the Dead', *BUA Monthly*, February, pp. 567–570.
Jupp P.C. (1990) *From Dust to Ashes: The Replacement of Burial by Cremation in England 1840–1967*, The Congregational Lecture 1990, London: The Congregational Memorial Hall Trust.
Jupp P.C. (1995) 'The Work of Funerals and the National Funerals College', *Pharos International*, Vol. 61, No. 2, pp. 48–54.

Jupp P.C. (1997a) 'Unsatisfactory Services for the Dead', *Church Times*, 23 May.
Jupp P.C. (1997b) 'The Dead Citizens Charter', *Pharos International*, Vol. 63, No. 4, pp. 18–28.
Jupp P.C. (1997c) 'The Context of Funeral Ministry Today', in P.C. Jupp and T. Rogers eds., *Interpreting Death: Christian Theology and Pastoral Practice*, London: Cassell. pp. 3–16.
Jupp P.C. (2006) *From Dust to Ashes: Cremation and the British Way of Death*, Basingstoke: Palgrave Macmillan.
Jupp P.C. (2008a) *The Council for the Disposition of the Dead 1931–1939*, FSJ, July, pp. 103–106.
Jupp P.C. ed. (2008b) *Death Our Future: Christian Theology and Funeral Practice*, London: Epworth.
Jupp P.C. (2009) 'The Aberdeen Coffins Case and the Future of British Cremation', *Pharos International*, Vol. 75, No. 3, pp. 28–30.
Jupp P.C. et al. (2017) *Cremation in Modern Scotland: History, Architecture and the Law*, Edinburgh: Birlinn.
Jupp P.C. and Walter T. (1999) 'The Healthy Society: 1918–98', in P.C. Jupp and C. Gittings eds, *Death in England*, Manchester: Manchester University Press. pp. 256–282.
Kalkofen R.W. (1989) 'After a Child Dies: A Funeral Director's Perspective', *Issues in Comprehensive Paediatric Nursing*, Vol. 12, No. 4, pp. 285–297.
Kastenbaum R.J. (1981) *Death, Society and Human Experience*, second edition, St Louis, MO: Mosby.
Kastenbaum R.J. and Aisenberg R. (1976) *The Psychology of Death*, New York, NY: Springer.
Kay, P. (2009) 'The Great Northern Main Line in London: Cemetery', *The London Railway Record*, April, No. 59, pp. 182–193.
Kear A. and Steinberg D.L. eds (1999) *Mourning Diana: Nation, Culture and the Performance of Grief*, London: Routledge.
Kearl M.C. (1989) *Endings: A Sociology of Death and Dying*, Oxford: Oxford University Press.
Keat P.J. (2001) *Goodbye to Victoria: The Last Queen Empress. The Story of Queen Victoria's Funeral Train*, Usk: The Oakwood Press.
Kellaher L.A. (2000) 'Ashes as a Focus for Memorialisation?' *Pharos International*, Vol. 66, No. 2, pp. 9–16.
Kellaher L.A. and Hockey J.L. (2002) 'Where Have All the Ashes Gone?' *Pharos International*, Vol. 68, No. 4, pp. 14–19.
Kellaher L. A. and Prendergast D. (2004) Resistance, Renewal or Reinvention: The Removal of Ashes from Crematoria', *Pharos International*, Vol. 70, No. 4, pp. 10–13.
Kellaway H.A. (1946) 'Mutes, Feathermen, Pages and Trappings', *FSJ*, December, pp. 463–464.
Kellehear A. (1984) 'Are We a "Death-Denying" Society? A Sociological Review', *Social Science and Medicine*, Vol. 18, No. 9, pp. 713–723.

Kenny C. (1998) *A Northern Thanatology: A Comprehensive Review of Illness, Death and Dying in the North West of England from the 1500s to the Present Time*, Dinton: Quay Books.

Kerr C. et al. (1974) *Industrialism and Industrial Man*, Harmondsworth: Penguin.

Kiernan J. (2008) 'The Casket Story: History of the Modern Burial Box', *American Funeral Director*, Vol. 131, No. 6, pp. 18–20.

King J.S. (2006) 'P45 and a Wooden Shovel', *Pharos International*, Vol. 72, No. 3, pp. 6–7.

Kingston T.W. (1906) 'Funeral Reform', *TUJ*, May, pp. 127–128.

Kirk L. and Start H. (1999) 'Death at the Undertakers', in J. Downes and T. Pollard eds. *The Loved Body's Corruption: Archaeological Contributions to the Study of Human Mortality*, Glasgow: Cruithne Press, pp. 200–208.

Kitching W.C. (1935) 'The Observations of an Embalmer in the PM Room', *BUA Monthly*, May, pp. 238–239.

Kohner N. (2000) 'Pregnancy, Loss and the Death of a Baby: Parent's Choices', in D. Dickenson, M. Johnson and J.S Katz eds, *Death, Dying and Bereavement*, second edition, London: Sage, pp. 355–359.

Korczynski R.E. (1996) 'Formaldehyde Exposure in the Funeral Industry', *Journal of Safety Research*, Vol. 27, No. 3, p. 198.

Kübler-Ross R.E. (1974) *Questions and Answers on Death and Dying*, New York, NY: Collier Books.

Laderman G. (2003) *Rest in Peace: A Cultural History of Death and the Funeral Home in Twentieth-Century America*, Oxford: Oxford University Press.

Lady W.W. (1926) 'Our Mission as Funeral Directors', *BUA Monthly*, July, pp. 4–5.

Lamers W.M. Jr quoted in Raether H.C. and Slater R.C. (1975) *The Funeral Director and His Role as Counselor*, Milwaukee, WI: National Funeral Directors Association.

Laqueur T.W. (1983) 'Bodies, Death, and Pauper Funerals', *Representations*, Vol. 1, No. 1, February, pp. 109–131.

Larner A. (1992) 'The Role of Women in the Funeral Profession', *Pharos International*, Vol. 58, No. 2, pp. 48–50.

Laungani P. (1998) 'The Changing Patterns of Hindu Funerals in Britain', *Pharos International*, Vol. 64, No. 4, pp. 4–10.

Lear G. (1932a) What My Experiences in America Taught me', *TUJ*, November, pp. 351–358.

Lear G. (1932b) 'American Funeral Directing and Embalming', *TUJ*, December, pp. 387–388.

Lear G. (1933a) 'The Fundamental of Modern Embalming', *TUJ*, April, pp. 109–112 & 132.

Lear G. (1933b) 'Raising the Standard', *TUJ*, May, pp. 147–149 & 164–165.

Lear G. (1935a) 'A Go-Ahead and Practical Service', *BUA Monthly*, September, p. 77.

Lear G. (1935b) 'Post Mortem Sanitation: A Sheer Necessity', *BUA Monthly*, pp. 99–100.
Lear G. (1937a) 'Some Difficult Cases', *TUFDJ*, April, pp. 113–115, 122.
Lear G. (1937b) 'Stock-Taking', *TUFDJ*, November, pp. 367–370.
Lear G. (1948) 'Embalming and Cremation', *The Practitioner*, Vol. 161, pp. 94–100.
Lear G. (1952) 'Embalming – Here, There – But Not Everywhere', *TNFD*, September, pp. 115–117.
Lear G. (1953) 'The Key to Progress', *TNFD*, January, pp. 14–16.
Leavitt B. (1915) 'Lifting a Business into a Profession', *TUJ*, December, pp. 329–332.
Leigh P. (1850) 'Address from an Undertaker to the Trade', *Household Words*, No. 13, 22 June, pp. 301–304.
Lello S.B. (1902) 'Embalming', *TUJ*, October, pp. 96–98.
Leming M.R. and Dickinson G.E. (1994) *Understanding Dying, Death and Bereavement*, third edition, Fort Worth, TX: Harcourt Brace.
Leverton B. (1982) 'A Family Undertaking: Memoirs of a St Pancras Funeral Furnisher', *Camden History Review*, Vol. 10, pp. 10–12.
Levy H. (1942) 'Funeral Waste', *The Spectator*, 4 December, No. 5971, p. 525 and *Journal of the National Association of Cemetery and Crematorium Superintendents*, Vol. 19, No. 1, February 1943, pp. 5–7.
Liddell C. (2007) '25 Years with the BIFD', *The BIFD Journal*, Vol. 21, No. 1, pp. 22–25.
Lindemann E. (1944) 'Symptomatology and Management of Acute Grief', *American Journal of Psychiatry*, Vol. 101, pp. 141–148.
Litten J. W. S. (2002) *The English Way of Death: The Common Funeral Since 1450*, London: Robert Hale.
Litten J.W.S. (2004) *A Brief History of Hardwick Road Cemetery, King's Lynn, Norfolk*, King's Lynn: The Friends of Hardwick Road Cemetery.
Littlewood J. (1992) *Aspects of Grief: Bereavement in Adult Life*, London: Routledge.
Lloyd Hughes, D. (2007) 'Eva in the Shadows: The Partial Revenge of Dr Pedro Ara', *Hispanic Research Journal*, Vol. 8(2), pp. 123–140.
Lymn Rose N. (1997) 'Legislation', *FDM*, October, pp. 8–12.
Lynch T. (1997) *The Undertaking: Life Studies from the Dismal Trade*, London: Jonathan Cape.
Lynch T. (1998) 'A Deathly Silence', *The Sunday Telegraph Magazine*, 11 October, pp. 28–31.
Lynch T. (2001) *Bodies in Motion and at Rest*, London: Vintage.
Maddaford A. (1995) 'Education – Into the Next Millennium', *TFD*, November, pp. 21–29.
Madsen I.B. (1940) 'A Women's Viewpoint on How to Handle the Grief Stricken', *TUFDJ*, November, pp. 271–272.

Maguire D. (1996) 'The Role of the Modern Funeral Director', *Pharos International*, Vol. 62, No. 3, pp. 142–145.
Mallalieu A. (2009) 'Up in Smoke or Six Feet Under', *Pharos International*, Vol. 75, No. 2, pp. 4–9.
Mancroft L. (1950) 'Funerals are Private Affairs: Intrusion Cannot be Tolerated', *FSJ*, July, pp. 395–296.
Martin E.A. (1940) 'How to Handle the Grief-Stricken', *TUFDJ*, May, pp. 129–130.
Mauksch H.O. (1975) 'The Organizational Context of Dying', in E. Kübler-Ross ed., *Death: The Final Stage of Growth*, New York, NY: Touchstone/Simon & Schuster, pp. 6–24.
May G.C. (1992) 'Education and Training in the Funeral Industry', *TFD*, November, pp. 20–21.
Mayfield K. (2014) *The Undertaker's Daughter*, London: Simon and Schuster.
McFarland E. (2008) 'Working with Death: An Oral History of Funeral Directing in late Twentieth-Century Scotland', *Oral History*, Vol. 36, No. 1, pp. 69–80.
McGill A. (1990) 'A Black Plume for Duchess', *FDM*, November, pp. 20–21.
McHale B. in Fox J. (1994) 'The Future of Funerals: Options for Change. Dead Citizens Charter', *FSJ*, August, pp. 61–63.
McHale B. (2002) 'Cremation Lore and Law', in P.C. Jupp and H.J. Grainger eds, *Golders Green Crematorium 1902–2002: A London Centenary in Context*, London: London Cremation Company.
McWalter J.C. (1907) 'The Prevention of Post-Mortem Putrefaction', *BMJ*, 14 September, pp. 673–674.
Meek H. (1995) 'The Funeral Services Market: Strategies for the 1990s', *FSJ*, January, pp. 62–69.
Mellskog P. (2005) 'The Feminine Face of the Funeral Business', *The Director*, Vol. 77, No. 4, pp. 32–38
Metcalf P. and Huntington, R. (1991) *Celebrations of Death: The Anthropology of Mortuary Ritual*, second edition, Cambridge, MA: Cambridge University Press.
Miller S. (1932) 'The Physiological Aspects of Death', *BUA Monthly*, February, pp. 176–177.
Mitchell S. (2011) *British Hearses*, Leeds: Zeteo Publishing.
Mitchell S. and Reader D. (2008) 'Transport to Paradise – Part 2: The Motor Hearse', *FSJ*, October pp. 97–110
Mitchell, S. and Reader, D. (2012) *The British Hearse Vol. 1: 1800–1920*, Dean Reader (Private publication).
Mitchell, S. and Reader, D. (2014) *The British Hearse Vol. 2: The 1920's*. Dean Reader (Private publication).
Mitford J. (1963) *The American Way of Death*, London: Quartet.
Mitford J. (1980) *The Making of a Muckraker*, London: Quartet.
Mitford J. (1997) 'Death, Incorporated', *Vanity Fair*, March, pp. 54–61.
Mitford J. (1998) *The American Way of Death Revisited*, London: Virago.
Moar D. (1997) 'Registration of Funeral Directors', *FSJ*, June, p. 40.

Moar D. (2000) 'How Green is Green? The Argument for Deep Research', *FSJ*, April, pp. 60–63.
Moody J.B. and Fleming G. (2006) *The Great Salisbury Train Disaster Centenary 1906–2006: Voices from the Boat Train*, Salisbury: Timezone Publishing.
Morgan M.R. (1914) 'Undertaking and Co-Partnership', *TUJ*, August, pp. 218–219.
Morgan M.R. (1916) 'Registration and the Needs of the Moment', *TUJ*, December, p. 326.
Morgan M.R. (1917) 'Lectures on Temporary Preservation', *TUJ*, November, p. 287, and continued in December pp. 314–315.
Morgan M.R. (1919) 'American Impressions', *TUJ*, November, pp. 336–337, then continued in December, p. 370 and (1920) January, pp. 25–26.
Morley J. (1971) *Death, Heaven and the Victorians*, London: Studio Vista.
Morrell J. and Smith S. (2006) *We Need to Talk About the Funeral*, Totnes: Alphabet and Image Publishers.
Morrision B. and Grant L. (1999) *A Way of Life: Portraits from the Funeral Trade*, Manchester: Len Grant Photography.
Mortimer J.G.M. (2004) *The History of the Funeral Bier: Exemplified by the Various Biers in Churches in North Herefordshire*, Leominster: JGM Mortimer (Private publication).
Mulkay M. (1993) 'Social Death in Britain', in D. Clark ed., *The Sociology of Death: Theory, Culture, Practice*, Oxford: Blackwell, pp. 31–49.
National Association of Funeral Directors (2009), *Manual of Funeral Directing*, Solihull.
Naylor M.J.A. (1989) *Funeral Rituals in a Northern City*, Unpublished PhD thesis, University of Leeds, Leeds.
Naylor M. (2004) 'Opening Geoffrey Gorer's Door: A Personal Overview of Funerals 1983–2003', *Pharos International*, Vol. 70, No. 3, pp. 17–23.
Neal W.E. (1953) 'State Funerals? The Dead End', *TFD*, August, p. 163.
Nesfield M. (1952) 'Does it Cost Too Much to Die?' *TNFD*, September, p. 112.
Newall V. (1985) 'Folklore and Cremation', *Folklore*, Vol. 96, No. 2, pp. 139–155.
Newcomb, W. D. (1931) 'Sanitary Preservation – Its Advantages and Disadvantages', *BUA Monthly*, January, pp. 150–153.
Nicholson, P. (1974) 'The British Way of Death', *The Illustrated London News*, Vol. 262, No. 6912, pp. 64–66.
Noble G.A. (1924) 'Undertaking as a Profession: Its Problems and Responsibilities', *BUA Monthly*, September, pp. 67–68.
Nodes H.K. (1911) 'Professional Progress in England', *TUJ*, January, p. 5.
Nodes H.K. (1925) 'State Registration', *BUA Monthly*, August, pp. 36–39.
Nodes W.O. (1948) '*Period between Death and Disposal*', Report of the Conference of the Institute of Burial and Cremation Administration, pp. 29–31.
Packard J.M. (1995) *Farewell in Splendour: The Death of Queen Victoria and Her Age*, Stroud: Sutton Publishing.
Painter A. (1962) 'Many Problems', *FSJ*, July, pp. 343–344.

Palgi P. and Abramovitch H. (1984) 'Death: A Cross-Cultural Perspective', *American Review of Anthropology*, Vol. 13, pp. 385–417.

Palmer G. (1993) *Death: The Trip of a Lifetime*, New York, NY: Harper Collins.

Parkes C.M. (1996) *Bereavement: Studies of Grief in Adult Life*, third edition, London: Routledge.

Parsons, B. (1997) *Change and Development of the British Funeral Industry in the Twentieth Century, with Special Reference to the Period 1960–1994*, Unpublished PhD thesis, University of Westminster, London.

Parsons B. (2001) *The London Way of Death*, Stroud: Sutton Publishing.

Parsons B. (2002) 'Funeral Service Education in England', *The Director*, Vol. 74, No. 4, pp. 34–38.

Parsons B. (2003) 'Conflict in the Context of Care: An Examination of Role Conflict between the Bereaved and the Funeral Director in the UK', *Mortality*, Vol. 8, No. 1, pp. 67–87.

Parsons B. (2004) 'Farewell to the Appendages of Sorrow: The End of the Funereal Plume', *BIFD Journal*, Vol. 18, No. 3, pp. 13–15.

Parsons B. (2005a) *Committed to the Cleansing Flame: The Development of Cremation in Nineteenth Century England*. Reading: Spire Books.

Parsons B (2005b) 'Where Did the Ashes Go? The Development of Cremation and Disposal of Ashes 1885–1950. Part 1: Burying the Cremated', *ICCM Journal*, Vol. 73, No. 1, pp. 6–12.

Parsons B. (2005c) 'Where Did the Ashes Go? The Development of Cremation and Disposal of Ashes 1885–1950 Part 2 – From Grave to Gardens: Scattering and Gardens of Remembrance', *ICCM Journal*, Vol. 73, No. 2, pp. 28–42.

Parsons B. (2005d) 'T.H. Sanders: A History', *BIFD Journal*, Vol. 19, No. 1, pp. 28–31.

Parsons B. (2005e) 'Benjamin Ward Richardson: A Forgotten Pioneer of Embalming', *The Embalmer*, Vol. 48, No. 4, pp. 16–20.

Parsons B. (2006a) 'Halford Lupton Mills', *The Embalmer*, Vol. 48, No. 3, pp. 15–18.

Parsons B. (2006b) 'The Bier in Action', *FSJ*, June, pp. 101–105.

Parsons B. (2008a) 'Music at Funerals: The Challenge of Keeping in Tune with the Needs of the Bereaved', in P.C. Jupp ed., *Death Our Future: Christian Theology and Funeral Practice*, London: Epworth, pp. 202–211.

Parsons B. (2008b) 'Transport to Paradise – Part 3: Unusual and Novel Funeral Transport', *FSJ*, November, pp. 80–99.

Parsons B. (2009a) 'Unknown Undertaking: The History of Dottridge Bros Wholesale Manufacturers to the Funeral Trade', *Archive: The Quarterly Journal for British Industrial and Transport History*, No. 63, pp. 41–53.

Parsons B. (2009b) 'Embalming in the First Half of the Twentieth Century: A Few Notable Embalmments', *The Embalmer*, Vol. 52, No. 1, pp. 11–18.

Parsons B. (2010) 'New or Rediscovered', *ICCM Journal*, Vol. 78, No. 3, pp. 47–53.

Parsons B. (2011a) 'A Dying Business? Mortality and Funeral Directing in West London', Paper presented at the Tenth International Conference of the Social Context of Death, Dying and Disposal, Nijmegen, 9–12 September.
Parsons B. (2011b) 'The Funeral of Queen Victoria', *FSJ*, February, pp. 83–90.
Parsons B. (2012a) 'George Lear Revisited', *The Embalmer*, Vol. 55, No. 4, pp. 19–25.
Parsons B. (2012b) 'Dickens, the Undertakers and Burial', *ICCM Journal*, Vol. 80, No. 4, pp. 22–44.
Parsons B. (2012c) 'A Nineteenth Century Initiative Continued: London Proprietary Cemeteries in the Twentieth Century,' *ICCM Journal*, Vol. 80, No. 2, pp. 62–81.
Parsons B. (2012d) 'Identifying Key Changes. The Progress of Cremation and its Influence of Music at Funerals in England, 1874–2010', *Mortality*, Vol. 17, No. 2, pp. 2–15.
Parsons B. (2013) 'Mr Punch and the Undertakers', *FDM*, February, pp. 48–51.
Parsons B. (2014a) *Bunny France: Memoir of a Holborn Funeral Director*, London: A France & Son.
Parsons B. (2014b). *J.H. Kenyon: A Short History*, London: J.H. Kenyon.
Parsons B. (2014c) *From Brook Street to Brookwood: Nineteenth Century Funeral Reform and St Alban the Martyr Holborn Burial Society*, London: Anglo-Catholic History Society.
Parsons B. (2014d) 'W.S. Bond: A Short History', London: W.S. Bond.
Parsons B. (2014e) *The Undertaker at Work: 1900–1950*, London: Strange Attractor Press.
Parsons B. (2014f) 'Abandoning Burial. Explaining a Regional Shift towards Cremation', Paper presented at the Fifteenth Cemeteries Colloquium, University of York, York, 16 May.
Parsons B. (2015) 'Coffin Making in the 1930s: A Unique Insight', *Archive: The Quarterly Journal for British Industrial and Transport History*, No. 87, pp. 57–63.
Parsons B. (2017a) 'Funeral Directors and Distance Transportation of the Dead', *The Embalmer*, Vol. 55, No. 4, pp. 31–39.
Parsons B. (2017b) 'Ninety Years On: The Registration of Births and Deaths Act 1926', *ICCM Journal*, Vol. 85, No. 2, pp. 56–59.
Parsons B. (2017c) *Frederick W. Paine Funeral Directors: A History*, London: F.W. Paine.
Parsons, B. (2017d) 'Premature Burial and the Undertakers', in S. McCorristine, ed., *When is Death?* London: Palgrave Macmillan, pp. 69–85.
Parsons B. (2017e) 'Funeral Directors and the Promotion of Cremation: A Regional Perspective', *Pharos International*, Vol. 83, No. 3, pp. 32–41.
Parsons, B. (Forthcoming-a) 'Placed on Rail: Transportation of the Dead by Train in the UK'.
Parsons, B. (Forthcoming-b) 'Portrait of Mortality: Croydon 1937. Death and Disposal in a London suburb'.

Passmore Bishop B. (1945a) 'Response. A Reply to the Pamphlet Entitled 'Funeral Reform' Issued by the Social Security League', *TNFD*, February, p. 2.
Passmore Bishop B. (1945b) 'Getting in Front of Our Shadows', *TNFD*, August, pp. 70–73.
Pattenden N. (2015) *Salisbury 1906: An Answer to the Enigma*, third edition, Swindon: The South Western Circle.
Pattison A. (1995) 'Quality Systems for Funeral Services – The Reality', *FSJ*, February, pp. 54–61.
Paul R.J. (1997) 'Funerals and Funeral Directors: Rituals and Resources for Grief Management', in J.D. Morgan, ed., *Readings in Thanatology*, Amityville, NY: Baywood, pp. 255–273.
Pearce J. (1996) 'Non-Religious Funerals in the 90's', *FSJ*, April, pp. 48–55.
Pearson F. (2007) 'Flameless Combustion', *Pharos International*, Vol. 73, No. 3, pp. 26–29.
Pember Reeves M. (1913) *Round About a Pound a Week* (1979 edition), London: Virago.
Perritt J.D. (1935) 'The National Association of Funeral Directors. The National President on the New Constitution', *TUJ*, November, p. 371.
Pike G.R. (1909) 'The Undertaker's Higher Ministry', *TUJ*, January, pp. 17–18.
Pine V.R. (1969) 'Comparative Funeral Practices', *Practical Anthropology*, No. 16, pp. 49–62
Pine V.R. (1975) *Caretaker of the Dead: The American Funeral Director*, New York, NY: Irvington.
Pine V.R. (1995) 'Public Behaviour in the Funeral Home,' in J.B. Williamson and E.S. Schneidman, eds, *Death: Current Perspectives*, fourth edition, Mountain View, CA: Mayfield, pp. 168–182.
Pine V.R. and Phillips D.L. (1970) 'The Cost of Dying: A Sociological Analysis of Funeral Expenditures,' *Social Problems*, Winter, Vol. 17, No. 3, pp. 405–417.
Plimmer M. (1997) 'How I Let My Father Leave by the Backdoor,' *The Daily Telegraph*, 24 May.
Polson C.J., Brittain R.P. and Marshall T.K. (1953) *The Disposal of the Dead*, London: English Universities Press.
Polson C.J. and Marshall T.K. (1975) *The Disposal of the Dead*, third edition, London: English Universities Press, p. 375.
Porter C. (1906) 'Parliament and the Undertaking Trade', *TUJ*, April, p. 110.
Porter C. (1906) 'Past, Present and Future', *TUJ*, pp. 190–194.
Porter W.H. Jr (1968) 'Some Sociological Notes on a Century of Change in the Funeral Business', *Sociological Symposium*, Vol. 1, pp. 36–46.
Potter G. (1955) *Father Potter of Peckham*, London: Hodder and Stoughton.
Potts C.R. (1993) *Windsor to Slough: A Royal Branch Line*, Headington: Oakwood Press.
Prior L. (1989) *The Social Organization of Death: Medical Discourse and Social Practices in Belfast*, Basingstoke: The Macmillan Press.
Puckle B.S. (1926) *Funeral Customs: Their Origin and Development*, London: Werner Laurie.

Pym D. (1990) 'Letters to the Editor', *FSJ*, January, p. 49.
Quigley C. (1998) *Modern Mummies: The Preservation of the Human Body in the Twentieth Century*, Jefferson: McFarland & Co.
Quist W.P. (1938) 'Psychology of Grief', *TUFDJ*, June, pp. 215–217.
Raether H.C. (1990) *Funeral Service: A Historical Perspective*, Milwaukee, WI: National Funeral Directors Association.
Ramsland K. (2002) *Cemetery Stories*, London: Fusion Press.
Rando T.A. (1989) 'The Funeral Director as a Grief Facilitator', in H.C. Raether, ed., *The Funeral Director's Practice Management Handbook*, Englewood Cliffs, NJ: Prentice Hall, pp. 14–52.
Reader, D. (2008a) *A Pictorial History of the British Hearse 1800–2008*, Dean Reader (Private publication)
Reader D. (2008b) 'Coachbuilders', *The Mourning News*, Issue 32.
Reader D. and Mitchell S. (2015) *The British Hearse Vol. 3: The 1930s*, Dean Reader (Private publication).
Richardson, R. (1989) 'Why was Death So Big in Victorian Britain?' in R. Houlbrook ed., *Death, Ritual and Bereavement*, London: Routledge, pp. 105–117.
Richmond E.A. (1925) 'How the Undertaker Can Help the Clergy', *BUA Monthly*, April, pp. 256–257.
Rickman C. (2007) 'Improving the Crematorium Experience for…Mourners: A Funeral Director's View 1', *Pharos International*, Vol. 73, No. 1, pp. 3–5.
Roberts E. (1989). 'The Lancashire Way of Death', in R. Houlbrooke ed., *Death, Ritual and Bereavement*, London: Routledge, pp. 188–287.
Roberts R. (1971) *The Classic Slum: Salford Life in the First Quarter of the Century*, Harmondsworth: Penguin Books
Robinson R. (1969) 'Professional Conduct', *FSJ*, July, pp. 354–360.
Rolph C.H. (1949) 'The High Cost of Dying', *The New Statesmen and Nation*, 2 April, p. 319.
Rose G.C.F. (1930) 'Forensic Medicine', *BUA Monthly*, December, pp. 135–136.
Rose W. (1973) *The Village Carpenter*, Wakefield: EP Publishing.
Routley A. (1993) 'Fashions in Coffins', *FSJ*, May, pp. 33–37.
Rowell G. (1977) *The Liturgy of Christian Burial*, London: Society for Promoting Christian Knowledge.
Rowell G. (2000) 'Tucked Up for Eternity', *Church Times*, 2 June.
Rudinger E. (1967) *What To Do When Someone Dies*, London: Consumers' Association.
Rugg J. and Hussein I. (2003) 'Burying London's Dead: A Strategic Failure', *Mortality*, Vol. 8, No. 2, pp. 209–221.
Rundblad G. (1995) 'Exhuming Women's Premarket Duties in the Care of the Dead', *Gender & Society*, Vol. 9, No. 2, pp. 173–192.
Rymer D. (1998) *A Reluctant Funeral Director*, London: Minerva.
Salomone J.J. (2003) 'The Evolution of the Funeral Home and the Occupation of the Funeral Directors', in C.D. Bryant ed., *Handbook of Death and Dying. Volume Two: The Responses to Death*, Thousand Oaks, CA: Sage Publishing, pp. 575–586.

Saunders C.M. ed. (1990) *Hospice and Palliative Care: An Interdisciplinary Approach*, London: Edward Arnold.

Saunders K. (1988) 'The Profession of Embalmer – An Outsider's View', *The Embalmer*, Vol. 31, No. 5, pp. 3–4.

Saunders K. (1991) 'Service Without a Smile: The Changing Structure of the Death Industry', *The Service Industries Journal*, Vol. 11, No. 2, pp. 202–218.

Saunders K. (1993) 'What are Embalmers Like? An Outsider's Attempt at Scientific Definition', *The Embalmer*, Vol. 36, No. 2, pp. 30–31.

Saunders K.C. (1995) 'The Occupational Role of Gravediggers: A Service Occupation in Acute Decline', *The Service Industries Journal*, Vol. 15, No. 1, pp. 1–13.

Scales W. (1949a) 'The Layout of Funeral Premises', *TNFD*, May, pp. 507–509 and June, pp. 571–573.

Scales W. (1949b) 'When You Build a New Funeral Home', *TNFD*, August, pp. 66–68.

Schäfer C. (2007) 'Post-Mortem Personalisation: Pastoral Power and the New Zealand Funeral Directors', *Mortality*, Vol. 12, No. 1, pp. 4–21.

Schorow, S. (2005) *The Cocoanut Grove Fire*, Beverly, CA: Commonwealth Editions.

Scott, D. (1952) 'Funeral Directing is a Family Business. Unsuited to State Control', *TNFD*, September, p. 125.

Scott N.M. (2011) *The British Hearse and the British Funeral*, Brighton: Book Guild Publishing.

Scudamore E.F. (1935) 'Disinfectants', *TUJ*, August, pp. 261–262.

Seabrook J. (1967) *The Unprivileged*, Harmondsworth: Penguin.

Searle C. and Chew S. eds (1990) *Remember Hillsborough*, Runcorn: Archive/Sheffield City Council/Sheffield Star.

Searle R. and Webb K. (1953) *Looking at London and People Worth Meeting*, London: News Chronicle.

Sherry H.A. (1905) 'The Sanitary Advantages of Modern Embalming', *TUJ*, August, pp. 188–190.

Singh G. (2007) 'Sikhs Say 'No' to Funeral Pyres', *Pharos International*, Vol. 73, No. 3, pp. 32–36.

Singh H. (2008) 'Sikhs Say 'No' to Funeral Pyres', *Pharos International*, Vol. 74, No. 1, pp. 44–55.

Smale B. (1985) *Deathwork: A Sociological Analysis of Funeral Directing*, Unpublished PhD thesis, University of Sussex, Sussex.

Smale B. (1997) 'The Social Construction of Funerals in Britain,' in K. Charmaz, G. Howarth and A. Kellehear eds, *The Unknown Country: Death in Australia, Britain and the USA*, Basingstoke: Macmillan, pp. 113–126.

Smith G. (1840) *The Gannal Process By Which the Progress of Decay is Arrested: The Cases of Contagion or Infection Prevented, and the Necessity of Embalming Superseded*.

Smith, R.G.E. (1996) *Death Care Industries in the United States*, Jefferson: McFarland & Co.

Speyer J. (2006) 'An Argument for Environmentally Friendly Natural Burial', *Pharos International*, Vol. 72, No. 2, pp. 6–8.
Spilsbury B. (1929) 'Identification of a Dead Body', *TUJ*, December, pp. 399–400.
Spilsbury B. (1930) 'The Sanitary Care of the Dead', *TUJ*, July, pp. 237–238.
Spongbery A.L. and Becks, P.M. (2000) 'Inorganic Soil Contamination from Cemetery Leachate', *Water, Air and Soil Pollution*, Vol. 117, pp. 313–327.
Spottiswood J. (1987) 'A Matter of Love and Death', *Evening Standard*, 30 November, pp. 26–27.
Spottiswood J. (1991) *Undertaken with Love*, London: Robert Hale.
Squires D. (2007) 'Improving the Crematorium Experience for…Mourners: The Local Authority Perspective', *Pharos International*, Vol. 73, No. 3, pp. 6–9.
Stewart M. (2010) 'Are there Regional Variations in Woodland Burials? Does it Appeal to a Specifically English, rather than British, Culture of Tree and Countryside?' Paper presented at the University of Bath's Conference 'A Good Send Off', 19 June.
Strange J.-M. (2005) *Death, Grief and Poverty in Britain, 1870–1914*, Cambridge: Cambridge University Press.
Strugnell C. and Silverman P.R. (1971) 'The Funeral Director's Wife as Caregiver', *Omega*, Vol. 2, No. 3, pp. 174–178.
Struthers J. (1890) 'On the Preservation of Bodies for Dissection,' *Edinburgh Medical Journal*, Vol. 36, pp. 297–303.
Sudnow D. (1967) *Passing On: The Social Organization of Dying*, Englewood Cliffs, NJ: Prentice-Hall.
Sullivan J.V. (1936) 'Cemetery Ethics', *Fifth Joint Conference of Cemetery and Crematorium Authorities: A Report of Proceedings with Addresses and Papers Read NACCS/FBCA*, p. 68.
Sullivan S. and Fisher D. (2008) 'Resomation User', *Pharos International*, Vol. 74, No. 1, pp. 3–18.
Sullivan S. (2006) 'Water Resolution', *Pharos International*, Vol. 72, No. 4, pp. 14–18.
Sullivan S. (2007) 'Water Resomation – A Mercury Free Alternative to Cremation', *Resurgam*, Vol. 50, No. 1, pp. 14–18.
Sullivan S. (2009) 'Resomation Update', *Pharos International*, Vol. 75, No. 3, pp. 4–8.
Summers J. (1940) 'Lessons from an American Tour. Mr John Summers of Cardiff Sees Ideal Funeral Home', *TUFDJ*, February, pp. 87–89.
Swainson E. (1955) 'Save Us From Registration! "The Spider's Webb"', *FSJ*, March, pp. 108–109.
Swainson W.E. (1931) 'Review of the British Undertakers' Association Activities with Special Reference to Education', *TUJ*, December, pp. 397–399.
Swainson E. (1950) 'Embalming: The Scientific Approach', *TNFD*, July, pp. 671–672, August, pp. 713 & 716–717, and September, pp. 761–763.
Taylor A. (1987) 'Report from Mersey District PRO', *TFD*, November, p. 13.

Taylor C. (1979) 'The Funeral Industry', in H. Wass ed., *Dying: Facing the Facts*, Washington, DC: Hemisphere.

Taylor J.S. (1930) 'Ancient and Modern Methods of Disposing of the Dead', *BUA Monthly*, April, pp. 210–212.

Taylor L. (1983) *Mourning Dress: A Social and Costume History*, London: George Allen & Unwin.

Terkel S. (1974) *Working*, Harmondsworth: Penguin.

Terkel S. (2002) *Will the Circle be Broken? Reflections on Death and Dignity*, London: Granta.

The New Survey of London Life and Labour Vol II *London Industries I* (1931) London: P.S. King.

Thomas G. (1959) 'Parliament and the Disposal of the Dead', *Report of the Institute of Burial and Cremation Administration/Federation of British Cremation Authorities Conference Report*, pp. 11–15.

Thompson G.O. (1932) 'The Man in Charge', *BUA Monthly*, January, pp. 154–155.

Thompson W. (1902) 'Funeral Management: The Coffin or Shell', *The British Embalmer and Funeral Trades Monthly*, No. 2, April, p. 15.

Thompson W.E. (1991) 'Handling the Stigma of Handling the Dead: Morticians and Funeral Directors', *Deviant Behaviour: An Interdisciplinary Journal*, Vol. 12, pp. 403–429.

Townroe B.S. (1934) 'Westminster', *TUJ*, May, pp. 159–160.

Townsend E. (1987) 'Hodgson Expands Funeral Empire', *The Embalmer*, Vol. 30, No. 3, p. 27.

Tozer B. (1906) 'Premature Burial and the Only True Sign of Death', *The Nineteenth Century*, October, pp. 544–559.

Trompette P. and Lemmonier M. (2009) 'Funeral Embalming: The Transformation of a Medical Innovation', *Science Studies*, Vol. 22, No. 2, pp. 9–30.

Troyer J.E. (2010) 'Technologies of the HIV/AIDS Corpse', *Medical Anthropology*, Vol. 29, No. 2, pp. 129–149.

Turner E. (1977) 'The British Way of Death', *Resurgam*, Vol. 20, No. 1, pp. 4–5.

Turner R.E. and Edgley C. (1976) 'Death as Theatre: A Dramaturgical Analysis of the American Funeral', *Sociology and Social Research*, Vol. 60, No. 4, pp. 377–392.

Tury I. (2011) *Who Put the 'Fun' in Funeral? Diary of a Funeral Director*, Authorhouse.

Tylee F. (1929) 'Black Bands and Orange Blossom', *The Dickensian*, Vol. 25, pp. 277–280.

Unruh D.R. (1976) 'The Funeralization Process: Towards a Model of Social Time', *Mid-American Review of Sociology*, Vol. 1, No. 1, pp. 9–25.

Unruh D.R. (1979) 'Doing Funeral Directing: Managing Sources of Risk in Funeralization', *Urban Life*, Vol. 8, No. 2, pp. 247–263.

Valentine C. and Woodthorpe K. (2014) 'From Cradle to the Grave: Funeral Welfare from an International Perspective', *Social Policy and Administration*, Vol. 48, No. 5, pp. 515–536.

Van Beck T. (2006) 'Legacy of a Fat Undertaker', *TFD*, February, pp. 30–33.

Van Gennep A. (1960) *The Rites of Passage*, trans M.B. Vizedom and G.L. Caffee, London: Routledge and Kegan Paul.
Venables Y. (2015) *Stan Cribb: An East End Farewell*, London: Simon & Schuster.
Voytal J. (1996) Cremation and the Private Sector Finance Initiative, *Pharos International*, Vol. 62, No. 3, pp. 133–139.
Wadey A. (2010) *What To Do When Someone Dies*, London: Which? Books.
Walter T. (1987) 'Emotional Reserve and the English Way of Death', in K. Charmaz, G. Howarth and A. Kellehear eds, *The Unknown Country: Death in Australia, Britain and the USA*, Basingstoke: Macmillan, pp. 127–140.
Walter T. (1990) *Funerals And How To Improve them*, London: Hodder and Stoughton.
Walter T. (1991) 'The Mourning after Hillsborough', *Sociological Review*, Vol. 39, No. 3, pp. 599–625.
Walter T. (1994) *The Revival of Death*, London: Routledge.
Walter, T. (1996) 'Ritualising Death in a Consumer Society', *Royal Society of Arts Journal*, April, Vol. 144, pp. 32–40.
Walter T. (1998) 'A Sociology of Grief?' *Mortality*, Vol. 3, No. 1, pp. 83–87.
Walter T. (1999) *The Mourning for Diana*, Oxford: Berg.
Walter T. (2017) 'Bodies and Ceremonies: Is the UK Funeral Industry Still Fit for Purpose?' *Mortality*, Vol. 22, No. 3, pp. 194–208.
Warwick T. (1994) 'The Funeral: Meaning, Value and Function', *Australian Funeral Director*, March, pp. 25–28.
Waugh E. (1948) *The Loved One*, London: Chapman Hall.
Webb T.G. (1935) 'The Drikold Method for Pre-Burial Sanitation', *TUJ*, October, pp. 325–326.
West J. (1988) *Jack West Funeral Director: Forty Years with Funerals*, Ilfracombe: Stockwell.
West J. (1997) 'Campaign for Fair Funeral Practices', *FSJ*, November, pp. 53–56.
West K. (1994) 'Seeing Ourselves as Others See Us', *FSJ*, November, pp. 56–63.
West K. (2007) How Green is My Funeral?' *ICCM Journal*, Vol. 75, No. 4, pp. 13–15.
West K. (2010) *A Guide to Natural Burial*, London: Shaw & Sons, p. 153.
West K. (2013) *RIP Off! Or the British Way of Death*, Kibworth Beauchamp: Matador.
Whiston R.W. (1976) 'Coffin Manufacture and the Use of Synthetic Materials', *Institute of Burial and Cremation Administration Conference Report*, pp. 40–44.
White S. (2006) 'Funeral Pyres and the Law in England and Wales', *Pharos International*, Vol. 72, No. 1, pp. 19–23.
White S. (2009a) 'Open Air Funeral Pyres', *Pharos International*, Vol. 76, No. 2, pp. 4–5.
White S. (2009b) 'Religion – Human Rights – Open Air Funerals', *Pharos International*, Vol. 75, No. 4, pp. 10–11.
White S. (2010) 'Funeral Pyres in a Legal Limbo', *Pharos International*, Vol. 76, No. 3, pp. 30–35.

Whorton J.C. (2010) *The Arsenic Century: How Victorian Britain was Poisoned at Home, Work and Play*, Revised edition, Oxford: Oxford University Press.

Wiigh-Mäsak S. (2006) 'Promession', *Pharos International*, Vol. 72, No. 1, pp. 3–4.

Wilde B. (1991) 'Materials Used in Coffin and Furnishing Manufacture', *TFD*, June, pp. 17–18.

Wilde B. (1992a) 'The Role of the Manufacturers of Coffins and Furnishings in Responding to the EPA', *Pharos International*, Vol. 58, No. 4, pp. 132–141.

Wilde B. (1992b) 'The History of Coffin and its Fittings', *FDM*, November, pp. 39–41.

Wilensky H. (1964) 'The Professionalization of Everyone?' *American Journal of Sociology*, Vol. 70, pp. 137–158.

Williams M. (2010) *Down Among the Dead Men*, London: Constable & Robinson.

Williamson A.B. (1937) 'What is the Place of the Funeral Director in the Health Services?' *TNFD*, August, pp. 45–47.

Willis A.G. (1940) 'Modern Rules and Regulations for Cemeteries', *TUFDJ*, May, pp. 139–145.

Willis S.P. (1907) 'Burial by the State', *The Lancet*, 16 February, Vol. 169, No. 4355, p. 463.

Wills S.P. (1910) 'Burial by the State', *Perils of Premature Burial*, January–March, p. 64.

Wilson A. (1939) *More Thoughts and Talks*, London: The Right Book Club.

Wilson A.T (1933) 'Public Cemeteries and Cremation. A Layman's View', *TUJ*, February, pp. 61–63.

Wilson A. and Levy H. (1938) *Burial Reform and Funeral Costs*, Oxford: Oxford University Press.

Wilson G. (1938) 'Public Health Act and Embalmers', *TUFDJ*, June, pp. 203–206.

Wilson H.M. (1925) 'The Horse – His Home and Management 1', *BUA Monthly*, April, pp. 265–266.

Wilson P. (1991) 'The Impact of the Environmental Protection Act on the Funeral Service', *TFD*, Vol. 71, No. 7, pp. 12–13.

Winter W.G. (1927) 'Early Days in Funeral Directing in England', *TUJ*, August, p. 281.

Woodall R. D. (1993) 'The Undertaker Who Taught Slimming', *FSJ*, September, pp. 60–61.

Woodthorpe K. (2010) 'Private Grief in Public Spaces: Interpreting Memorialisation in the Contemporary Cemetery', in J. Hockey, C. Komaromy and K. Woodthorpe eds, *The Matter of Death: Space, Place and Materiality*, Basingstoke: Palgrave Macmillan, pp. 117–132.

Woodthorpe K., Rumble H. and Valentine C. (2013) 'Putting 'the Grave' into Social Policy: State Support for Funerals in Contemporary UK Society', *Journal of Social Policy*, Vol. 42, No. 3, pp. 605–622.

Worpole K. (2006) *Modern Hospice Design*, London: Routledge.

Wray G.G. (1930) 'Smallpox', *BUA Monthly*, July, pp. 6–7.

Wyatt K. (2003) *A Yorkshire Undertaking*, Yorkshire: CT Butterfield.
Wynter Blyth, A. (1905) 'The Hygiene of the Death Chamber', *TUJ*, July, pp. 156–161.
Yardley J. (2007) 'Improving the Crematorium Experience for...Mourners: The Private Company Crematorium Manager's Perspective', *Pharos International*, Vol. 73, No. 3, pp. 3–5.
Youngson R.M. (1989) *Grief: Rebuilding Your Life After Bereavement*, Newton Abbot: David & Charles.
Zaleski J.S. (2005) '"Last Writes" for *Six Feet Under*', *The Director*, Vol. 77, No. 11, pp. 34–40.
Zbarsky I. & Hutchinson S. (1997) *Lenin's Embalmers*, London: Harvillss.

Monopolies and Mergers Commission Reports

Monopolies and Mergers Commission *Co-operative Wholesale Society Limited and House of Fraser PLC: A Report on the Acquisition by the Co-operative Wholesale Society Limited of the Scottish Funerals Business of House of Fraser PLC* (1987) Cm229, London: HMSO.
Monopolies and Mergers Commission *Service Corporation International and Plantsbrook Group PLC – A Report on the Merger Situation* (1995) Cm2880, London: HMSO.

Office of Fair Trading Reports

Funerals: A Report (1989)
Pre-Paid Funeral Plans (1995)
Funerals (2001)
Survey of Funeral Directors. A Report of the Results (2001)
Consumers Experiences of Arranging Funerals. A Report (2001)
Competition Acquisition by the Cooperative Group (CWS) Limited of Fairways Group UK Limited (2006)

Other Reports

Charter for the Bereaved (1996) London: Institute of Burial and Cremation Administration.
Dead Citizens Charter: The Complete Edition (1996) Stamford, CT: The National Funerals College.
Funeral Cost Comparison Research. Report Prepared for SAIF. (2010) Ipsos MORI.
Funerals Matter. How the British Public Views the Funeral Profession in 2016, Solihull: NAFD.
Summary of the UK Funeral Profession (1997) Edinburgh: Golden Charter.

Parliamentary Publications & Legislation

Beveridge W. (1942) *Social Insurance and Allied Services*, London: HMSO. Cmd: 6404.

Burial Law and Policy in the 21st Century: The Need for a Sensitive and Sustainable Approach (2004) London: HMSO.

Committee of the Work of the Committee on Death Certification and Coroners (1971) Cmnd 4810.

Cemeteries Report and Proceedings of the Committee together with the Minutes of Evidence taken before the Environment Sub-committee (2000) London: The Stationery Office.

Cemeteries (2001) Environment, Transport and Regional Affairs Committee HC91-1.

Cremation Committee Report of the Interdepartmental Committee appointed by the Secretary of State for the Home Department (1950) Cm 8009.

Foster K. (1987) *A Survey of Funeral Arrangements*, London: HMSO.

Funeral Charges (1977) Price Commission Report No. 22.

Hansard's Parliamentary Debates (various dates).

Hennessy P.J. (1980) *Families, Funerals and Finances – A Study of Funeral Expenses and How They Are Paid*, London: HMSO.

Huddersfield Corporation Act 1956 4 & 5 Eliz Ch. lxxiii.

Smith J. (2003a). *The Shipman Inquiry: Death Certification and the Investigation of Deaths by Coroners*. Second Report Cm 5853.

Smith J. (2003b). *The Shipman Inquiry: Death Certification and the Investigation of Deaths by Coroners*. Third Report Cm 5854.

Support for the Bereaved. (2016). House of Commons Work and Pensions Committee. Ninth Report of Session 2015–2016.

Web resources

Dignity PLC Annual Report and Accounts 2015. www.dignityfunerals.co.uk

'Funeral Poverty: A Plan for Managing the Impact of Funeral Costs'. (2013). Citizens Advice. Centre Wiltshire http://cabwiltshire.org.uk/phocadownload/funeralpoverty_feb2013.pdf

Gregory (undated) Future Consideration in Paying for Funerals. Briefing Paper' Centre on Household Assets and Savings Management. http://www.birmingham.ac.uk/Documents/college-social-sciences/social-policy/CHASM/briefing-papers/2014/Future-Considerations-in-Paying-for-Funerals—LG.pdf

Public Health Funerals (2010) Local Government Association. https://inews.co.uk/essentials/news/uk/worrying-picture-isolation-numbers-paupers-funerals-soar/

'Cost of Dying 2014. The Eighth Annual Report' (2014). file:///C:/Users/sutherland/Downloads/SunLife-Cost-Of-Dying-Report-2014.pdf

'Funeral Poverty in the UK: Issues for Policy' (2014). http://www.bath.ac.uk/ipr/pdf/policy-briefs/affording-a-funeral.pdf

'Are We Losing the Plot?' (2014) Royal London/ICCM. http://www.iccmk.com/iccm/library/2758%20Royal%20London%20Funeral%20poverty%20report%20V3%2001.12.14.pdf

'NAFD Pricing Survey 2014'. https://gallery.mailchimp.com/91a20d214f6f0a4fb90c5b3ee/files/NAFD_Pricing_Survey_2014_FINAL.pdf?utm_source=NAFD+e-newsletter+MEMBER+listing&utm_campaign=f0658c7341-NAFD_April_Newsletter4_17_2013+2&utm_medium=email&utm_term=0_e7810c9bed-f0658c7341-92620425

'Hounslow Community Funeral Service' http://www.hounslow.gov.uk/community_funerals_may14.pdf (Accessed 5 January 2015) and 'The Nottingham Funeral' http://www.nottinghamcity.gov.uk/article/22195/The-Nottingham-Funeral.

'10 Things You Should Know About Funerals'. http://www.which.co.uk/news/2012/01/10-things-you-should-know-about–funerals-277448. https://www.quakersocialaction.org.uk/taking-social-action/our-practical-work/funeral-poverty/down-earth

'Is the Prepaid Funeral Planning Market Working Well for Consumers?' (2017) Fairer Finance/Dignity PLC.https://www.fairerfinance.com/assets/uploads/documents/Funeral-plan-report-FINAL-6-July-2017.pdf (Accessed on 25 July 2017) http://www.dignityfunerals.co.uk/media/2366/dignity_annual_report_and_accounts.pdf p16

Burial and Cremation (Scotland) Act 2016 Part 5 Section 94 Clause 1, 2, & 3. http://www.legislation.gov.uk/asp/2016/20/pdfs/asp_20160020_en.pdf www.quakersocialaction.org.uk

'Hounslow Community Funeral Service'. http://www.hounslow.gov.uk/community_funerals_may14.pdf. (Accessed 5 January 2015) and 'The Nottingham Funeral'. http://www.nottinghamcity.gov.uk/article/22195/The-Nottingham-Funeral. (Accessed 5 January 2015). See also '10 Things You Should Know About Funerals'. http://www.which.co.uk/news/2012/01/10-things-you-should-know-about–funerals-277448. (Accessed 4 January 2015).

Funerals Matter. How the British Public Views the Funeral Profession in 2016, Solihull: NAFD.

https://www.quakersocialaction.org.uk/taking-social-action/our-practical-work/funeral-poverty/down-earth. (Accessed 7 May 2017).

Archival and Unpublished material

Metropolitan Borough of Paddington, *Report of the Public Health Committee*
Bermondsey Borough Council minutes
Kensington Borough Council minutes

British Undertakers' Association, *Year Book and Diary* 1919
DC Henley (1997) 'Within my Preserve: An autobiography'. Unpublished data.
T.H. Ebbutt funeral records
J.H. Kenyon funeral records
F.W. Paine funeral records

Periodicals

The American Funeral Director
American Journal of Psychiatry
American Journal of Sociology
The Animal World
Archive: The Quarterly Journal for British Industrial and Transport History
Australian Funeral Director
BIFD (British Institute of Funeral Directors) Journal
British Medical Journal
BUA Monthly
The British Embalmer and Funeral Trades Monthly
The British Journal of Industrial Relations
The Builder
The Burial Reformer
Camden History Review
Casket and Sunnyside
Church Times
Critical Public Health
The Daily Chronicle
The Daily Graphic
The Daily Mirror
The Daily News and Leader
The Daily Telegraph/The Sunday Telegraph/Sunday Telegraphy Magazine
The De-Co-Co Magazine
Death Studies
Deviant Behaviour: An Interdisciplinary Journal
The Dickensian
The Director
The Economist
Economic History Review (New Series)
Edinburgh Medical Journal
Eighteenth-Century studies
The Embalmer
Encounter
English Review

Evening Standard
Fabian Quarterly
Fifeshire Advertiser
Financial Times
FOKGC (Friends of Kensal Green Cemetery) Newsletter
Folklore
Foreshore Advertiser
The Friend
The Funeral Director
Funeral Service Journal
Gender and Society
The Guardian
Harvard Business Review
Hearse & Rider: The Official Publication of Motorcycle Funerals Limited
Healthcare Sociology Review
The Hospital
Household Words
The Huddersfield Daily Examiner
The Illustrated Carpenter and Builder
The Illustrated London News
ICCM (Institute of Cemetery and Crematorium Management) Journal
Insight Special Edition
Issues in Comprehensive Paediatric Nursing
Journal of Economic Perspectives
Journal of Environmental Health
Journal of the History of Medicine and Allied Science
Journal of the Institute of Burial and Cremation Administration
Journal of the National Association of Cemetery and Crematorium Superintendents
Journal of Safety Research
Journal of Social Policy
Justice of the Peace and Local Government Review
Kensington News & West London Times
Labour Research
The Lancet
Literary Gazette
London Journal
London Railway Record
Manchester Evening News
The Medical Officer
Medical Anthropology
Mid-American Review of Sociology
Mortality
Motor Car Journal
The Mourning News

The National Funeral Director
The New Statesman
The New Statesman and Nation
The Nineteenth Century
Omega
Oral History
The People
Perils of Premature Burial
Pharos
Pharos International
Picture Post
Practical Anthropology
The Practitioner
The Producer
Psychiatry
Public Health
Punch
Representations
Resurgam
Review of Religious Research
Royal Society of Arts Journal
Science Studies
The Service Industries Journal
Social Forces
Social Policy and Administration
Sociology and Social Research
Sociological Problems
Sociological Review
Sociological Symposium
South London Press
The Spectator
The Sun
Symbolic Interaction
The Times/The Sunday Times
Town and Country News
Urban Life
The Undertakers' Journal
The Undertakers' and Funeral Directors' Journal
The Undertakers' and Funeral Directors' Journal and Monumental Masons' Review
Vanity Fair
Yorkshire Evening Post
Water, Air and Soil Pollution
The Weston Mercury and Somersetshire Herald
Which?
Work and Occupations

Index

American funeral, 36, 37, 42, 185, 222
Anatomical specimens, 53–54
Ashes, 12, 18n, 54, 35, 83, 97, 110, 123, 157

Bereavement, 43, 153, 158, 170, 210, 219, 230–231
British Embalmers' Society (BES), 56
British Funeral Workers' Association (BFWA), 173
British Institute of Embalmers (BIE)
 founding, 62
 membership, 215–216
British Institute of Funeral Directors (BIFD), 215
British Undertakers' Association (BUA), 38, 52, 60–93, 100, 113, 131, 167, 169, 173–174, 183, 214–217, 220, 223, 226, 227
 founding, 126
 and Miller *v* Hurry, 173–174
Brookwood Cemetery, 27
Burial, woodland, 7, 75

Carriage master, 5, 103, 107, 112, 113, 118, 126, 127, 131, 132, 134, 141, 142, 157, 173, 204
Caskets,
 for ashes, 97
 metal, 91, 92
 open, 72
Cemeteries, woodland, 19, 20, 96
Centralisation, funerals managed by, 132, 134–135, 142–144, 153, 228

Chappell, Francis, 132, 133, 139, 140
Chapels of rest,
 in crematoria, 35
 dedication, 31
 design, 30
 use of, 34, 39–40, 46–47
Cocoanut Grove Fire, 230n, 131
Co-operatives societies,
 Birmingham, 39
 insurance society, 129
 retail, 150
 royal arsenal, 30, 133, 186
 scotmid, 150, 159
 wholesale, 157
Co-operative Funeralcare, 26, 48, 135, 145, 150, 154, 158, 162, 164, 166, 191, 213
Co-operative Group Ltd, 150
Coffins
 alternative, 90–92
 children's, 78
 construction, 35, 129, 130
 cremation, 11, 82, 87–89, 93
 furniture, 93–98
 labour-saving, 87
 lead, 88, 79, 116
 linings, 93–94, 98
 mass-produced, 85, 132
 metal, 87, 88, 117
 Medium-density fibreboard (MDF), 81, 91, 93, 94, 96,
 nameplates, 93–94
 suppliers, 83–84
College of Arms, 4, 26
Consumers' Association, 189, 191–194

Cremation
  ashes caskets, 96, 97
  certification, 74
  coffins, 11, 82, 87–89, 93
  development of, 82, 87, 97, 119–120
  during twentieth century, 11
  early, 10, 11
  transport and, 119–123
  open air, 20

Death
  at home, 8, 10, 23–26
  benefit, 129, 130, 171
  certificates, 21, 205, 225
  grant, 171, 178, 180, 183–189
  in hospital, 9
  in twentieth century, 6–8
  'sleeping', 72, 229
Death Café Movement, 21
Decomposition, 23, 51, 67, 70, 83, 229
Dickens, Charles, 5, 167, 181
Dignity Plc., 135, 149, 210
Dry ice, 67
Dottridge Bros, 28, 55, 58, 61, 67, 83, 84, 88–91, 97, 101
DWP Funeral Expenses Payment, 189

Education
  embalmers, 219
  funeral directors, 214–215, 219–222
Embalmers
  full-time, 64, 68, 70
  number of, 68, 229
Embalming
  ancient, 46, 53
  cost of, 59, 68–69
  environmental issues and, 75–76
  fluids, 57n39
  history, 53–64
  introduction into UK, 54–56
  in US, 53–64
  modern arterial, 53–64
  permanent, 59
  progress of, 64–71
  theatres, 40, 46–47, 74

Family firms, 125, 132, 137, 145, 151, 159, 160, 163
Federation of British Crematorium Authorities (FBCA), 89
Field, J.D. 140n41
Funeral accounts 78, 178, 195, 206
Funeral advisers, 157
Funeral arrangements, 12, 27, 122, 129, 183, 191, 194, 235
Funeral ceremonies
  contemporary, 17–19
  'green', 12, 19, 20
  historic, 11–22
Funeral costs
  consumer interest, 189–197
  reports, 189, 191, 193, 194
Funeral directors
  and allegations of corruption and overcharging, 6, 195, 202
  as crematoria owners, 164–166
  and professionalisation, 200–202, 213–235
  code of practice, 152, 191, 193–4, 215, 217
  dual-activity, 134
  female, 136
  internet-based, 157
  language, 224–225
  municipalisation, 174–181
  nationalisation, 181–182, 218
  qualification, 219–223, 214–216
  registration, 56, 167, 179–180, 186, 192, 203, 214, 216–219
  regulation, 46, 177, 214–216, 165
  and retention of trading names, 160–164
Funeral homes, 36, 38, 39, 41–45, 47, 60, 181
Funeral Ombudsman Scheme (FOS), 152, 224

Funeral Partners, 135, 150, 151, 154
Funeral Planning Council, 152
Funeral reform, of ceremonies, 11–22
Funeral Standards Council (FSC), 193

Great Southern Group, 133, 139, 140, 146, 147, 155, 156, 165, 190

Hearse
  horse-drawn, 99, 100, 102–108, 112
  motor, 16, 105–109, 115, 118, 121, 130, 172
Hodgson, Howard, 137–142, 146–148, 161, 187, 211, 226

Kenyon J.H., 52, 57, 59, 80, 102, 105, 112, 116, 126, 133, 139, 141, 142

Laying-out, 34, 36, 49–52, 207, 231
Local authority funerals, 176, 177, 179–181, 195
London Funeral Carriage Proprietor's Association (LFCPA), 172

Mergers and acquisitions, 139–148
Monopolies and Mergers Commission (MMC), 134, 148
Motor hearse
  introduction, 110–111
  models, 111–112
  wartime restrictions, 113–115, 192, 195
Mortuaries
  private, 27, 28, 30, 39, 42, 47
  public, 24, 25, 29, 33
Municipal funerals, 174–179, 183–189

National Association of Cemetery and Crematorium Superintendents (NACCS), 176, 179, 180
National Association of Funeral Directors (NAFD), 190–194, 205, 210–211, 214–215, 220, 223–224, 230, 235
National Society of Allied and Independent Funeral Directors (SAIF), 151–154, 160, 164, 194, 215–216, 224
Nationalisation, 181–182
Natural Death Centre, 15, 157

Organisation, types of funeral
  co-operative, 129–133, 140, 150, 158–159, 162, 164, 166, 213, 228
  department stores, 126
  family/independent, 127–129, 134–135, 136–139, 145, 154–164
  large firms, 47, 48, 135, 140–147, 149, 159–160

Paine, F.W., 10, 26, 30, 44, 47, 100, 105, 109, 116, 117, 119–123, 132, 133, 140, 160, 177
  and cremation, 119–123
  and transport, 117–119
Plantsbrook Group, 147, 148
Pre-paid funeral plans, 139, 159, 189–197
Professionalisation
  and code of ethics/practice, 223–224
  and the desire to professionalise, 200–202
  and education, 219–223
  and language, 224–227
  and occupational associations, 214–216
  and occupational title, 227–232
  presentational changes, 224–227

and registration, 216–219
and stereotypical images, 225, 232–235
and stigmatisation, 206–213

SAIF (See National Society of Allied and Independent Funeral Directors)
Service Corporation International (SCI), 73, 134, 147–149, 150, 152–154, 161–162, 164–165

Transport, funerary
and cremation, 117–119
bearing, 99
farm carts, 107, 115
gun carriage, 107
horse-drawn hearses, 99, 100, 102–108, 112
international, 116–117
motor hearses, 16, 105–109, 115, 118, 121, 130, 172
rail, 108–110, 114
shouldering the coffin, 99–100
wheel bier, 100–102, 172
walking funerals, 99–100, 114

Undertakers (see funeral directors)
Urns and caskets, 96, 97, 98

World War I, 104, 107, 113, 130–131
World War II, 44, 51, 84, 89–90, 110, 113, 172, 177, 217

Yew Holdings, 135, 150